D1556369

FIGHTING
SHIPS
OF THE WORLD

£2·99
8/44
ωR

FIGHTING SHIPS
OF THE WORLD

OVER 600 CARRIERS, SUBMARINES & DESTROYERS

ROBERT JACKSON & STEVE CRAWFORD

First published in 2004 for Grange Books
An imprint of Grange Books plc
The Grange
Kingsnorth Industrial Estate
Hoo, Nr Rochester
Kent ME3 9ND
www.grangebooks.co.uk

Copyright © 2004 Amber Books Ltd

All rights reserved. No part of this work may be reproduced, stored in a
retrieval system, or transmitted in any form, by any means, electronic,
mechanical, photocopying, recording or otherwise, without prior
permission of the copyright holder.

A catalogue record for this book is available from the British Library.

ISBN 1-84013-647-2

Produced by
Amber Books Ltd
Bradley's Close
74–77 White Lion Street
London N1 9PF
www.amberbooks.co.uk

Printed in Singapore

Picture credits
Pages 7 and 8 courtesy of TRH Pictures Ltd.
All artworks courtesy of Art-Tech Ltd.

Contents

Introduction

Any country's navy is a symbol of that nation's maritime strength, its ambition, and its wealth. The ships described and illustrated in this book cover a huge variety of types and sizes of vessel, from the early ironclads of the nineteenth century such as HMS *Warrior* of the Royal Navy, to the vast nuclear-powered aircraft carriers like USS *George Washington* and secretive submarines like USS *Ohio* of today's US Navy.

All the ships illustrated in this book were all built to fight. That is their ultimate purpose, and the technical innovations which have attempted to give one ship a fighting edge over another has always been the driving force behind their design and construction. What began in the 1850s with steam engines in the iron-clad hulls of wooden proto-battleships, such as the French *Gloire*, created within 40 years the big-gun battleship, epitomised by Japan's armoured giant *Yamato* of World War II. Ships such as the *Yamato* were the archetypal 'big' warship, but smaller vessels were and are as important to a navy as its capital ships.

It was clear that the advantages of a fighting ship with steam power, armour plate and big guns were too great to be ignored for the sake of the practical problems involved in getting the right balance of all three. A ship needed enough armour to defend itself against the guns of an enemy vessel, a hull big enough to house the engines necessary to propel that weight at sufficient speed, and guns big enough to

USS *George Washington* is one of the Nimitz-class nuclear-powered aircraft carriers which patrol the world's oceans.

Introduction

Seen on patrol, HMS *Boxer* was a Batch II Broadsword-class frigate that has now been decommissioned and will be used as a practice target by the Royal Navy.

match, if not outrange, any others. It was a technical conundrum which many tried to solve, and which resulted in a huge variety of ship designs.

In 1889, the British Admiralty ordered an entirely new fleet of 70 ships, including eight standard first-class battleships. The lead vessel of this fleet was the *Royal Sovereign* of 1892. Her hull and guns were steel, she was protected by armour plate up to 450mm (17.7in) thick and carried guns of 343mm (13.5in) calibre. Even though she displaced nearly 16,000 tonnes (15,744 tons), she could make 16 knots.

The era of the big-gun battleship had arrived. But the cost was enormous. Naval expenditure in Britain rose by 290 per cent during the 1890s, and by the end of the decade the cost of each new Royal Navy battleship was approaching £1.5 million. The world had embarked on its first great arms race, and every industrialised country saw the possession of a navy as a mark of their power and self-esteem. Imperial Germany and the United States both spent twice as much as the British on their navies in an effort to catch up.

But in 1906 the British launched HMS *Dreadnought*, a ship which combined every single technical advance to date, from new steam turbine engines to electrically controlled gun turrets. *Dreadnought* made every other battleship obsolete, including those in her own navy, and gave her name to an entirely new class of warship.

However, *Dreadnought*'s time as the world's number one did not last very long. By 1908 the Royal Navy was building so-called 'Super-Dreadnoughts', ships such as *Iron*

Duke, which were over 8128 tonnes (8000 tons) heavier. The future of the capital ship seemed to lay in bigger and bigger battleships carrying guns of ever-increasing size. But questions were now being asked as to the battleship's future. Many were wondering exactly how useful in battle these huge floating gun batteries would be.

Countries such as Germany were ceding the battleship contest and were beginning to develop other warship types like the battle cruiser, vessels designed for fast commerce raiding rather than naval battles. More ominously, Germany was also investing in a fleet of torpedo-carrying submarines. The U-boat war in the battle of the Atlantic would devastate the Allied convoys until 1943, when submarine detection equipment became sufficiently developed.

AIRCRAFT CARRIERS

It was to be the aircraft, though, which would ultimately make the battleship redundant . Pioneers such as Brigadier-General 'Billy' Mitchell in the United States proved that ships could be destroyed by bombardment from the air. The United States Navy launched its first aircraft carrier, USS *Langley*, in 1922. There was a new offensive weapon in the naval arsenal, but throughout the 1920s and 1930s traditionalists held firm that any future naval warfare would be decided by battleships.

At the beginning of World War II, battleships such as *Haruna* of Japan and the Royal Navy's HMS *Nelson* still represented the most powerful war machines made by man. But by 1942 the type had been completely eclipsed by a new kind of warfare. Air raids by torpedo planes on Taranto and Pearl Harbor and the sinking of *Repulse* and *Prince of Wales* off Malaya proved that a battleship could not exist without control of the air space above it. The age of the aircraft carrier had arrived.

In the Cold War the threat to land-based bombers forced both sides to develop nuclear-powered ballistic missile submarines capable of long patrols and virtually indetectable. However it is the US Navy's carrier battle group that now represents the apogee of modern naval power. A carrier battle group consists of one or two carriers, each capable of deploying an air wing (which on average contains nine squadrons of aircraft, ranging from F/A-18 and F-14 fighters to SH-60 helicopters). This represents a massive capability for force projection. And yet the carriers require substantial naval assets to protect them from both air and submarine attack: guided-missile cruisers, guided-missile destroyers, anti-submarine warfare destroyers, anti-submarine warfare frigates and even one or two nuclear submarines – proof that a capital ship, no matter how powerful, is always vulnerable, and that all ships are dependent on each other.

A1

The A-class vessels were the first submarines designed in Britain, although they were originally based on the earlier US Holland type which had entered Royal Navy service in 1901. *A1* was basically a slightly lengthened *Holland*, but from *A2* onwards they were much larger. They were also the first submarines to be made with a proper conning tower to allow surface running in heavy seas. Originally fitted with a single bow-mounted torpedo tube, the class was equipped with a second one from *A5* onwards. Built by Vickers, the class helped the Royal Navy to develop and refine its submarine doctrine and operating skills. Thirteen boats were built between 1902 and 1905, and some served in a training capacity during World War I. One of the class, *A7*, was lost with all hands when she dived into the sands at Whitesand Bay.

Country:	Great Britain
Type:	Attack submarine
Launch date:	July 1902
Crew:	11
Displacement:	Surfaced: 194 tonnes (191 tons) Submerged: 274.5 tonnes (270 tons)
Dimensions:	30.5m x 3.5m (100ft x 10ft 2in)
Surface range:	593km (320nm) at 10 knots
Armament:	Two 460mm (18in) torpedo tubes
Powerplant:	One 160hp petrol engine, one 126hp electric motor
Performance:	Surfaced: 9.5 knots, submerged: 6 knots

Abukuma

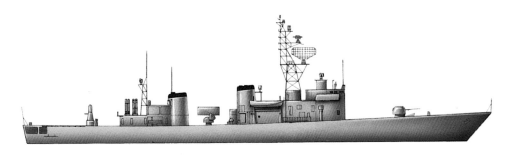

The original *Abukuma* of this class was a World War II Japanese cruiser which was sunk during the Battle of Leyte Gulf in October 1944. Her namesake is classed as a destroyer escort (DE) by the Japanese Maritime Self-Defence Force, but is more properly classed as a frigate. There are five other vessels in the class: the *Jintsu*, *Ohyodo*, *Sendai*, *Chikuma* and *Tone*. The first pair of the class was approved in the 1986 defence estimates whereas the last couple were approved in the 1989 estimates. Their main gun has an elevation of 85 degrees and can fire a 6kg (13.2lb) projectile over a distance of 16km (8.6nm) in the surface engagement role, or 12km (6.5nm) in the anti-aircraft role. The torpedoes used are the Honeywell Mk46 Mod 5 Neartip anti-submarine type, which have a range of 11km (5.9nm) at 40 knots.

Country:	Japan
Type:	Frigate (destroyer escort)
Launch date:	21 December 1988
Crew:	120
Displacement:	2591 tonnes (2550 tons)
Dimensions:	109m x 13.4m x 4m (357ft 4in x 44ft x 13ft)
Range:	6485km (3500nm)
Main armament:	One 76mm (3in) gun; Phalanx CIWS; ASROC A/S system; six 324mm (12.75in) torpedo tubes
Powerplant:	Two shafts, two gas turbines, two diesels
Performance:	27 knots

Adelaide

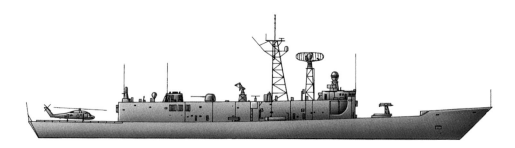

HMAS *Adelaide* and her sisters (*Canberra, Sydney, Darwin, Melbourne* and *Newcastle*) are the Royal Australian Navy's variants of the Oliver Hazard Perry class of guided-missile frigate. All six ships have been modernized and are equipped to carry the Sikorsky Seahawk ASW helicopter. The weapons system is being upgraded, with various options being considered. These include the installation of a short-range missile system – probably Evolved Sea Sparrow – as well as the fitting of enhanced electronic, mine avoidance and torpedo countermeasures. HMAS *Adelaide, Darwin* and *Canberra* are at Fleet Base West, with the remainder at Fleet Base East. For operational tasks, the vessels are fitted with enhanced communications and other equipment such as electro-optical sights. All the ships can operate in the fighter direction role.

Country:	Australia
Type:	Guided missile frigate
Launch date:	21 June 1978
Crew:	184
Displacement:	4165 tonnes (4100 tons)
Dimensions:	138.1m x 13.7m x 7.5m (453ft x 45ft x 24ft 6in)
Range:	7783km (4200nm)
Main armament:	One 76mm (3in) gun; Phalanx CIWS; Harpoon SSMs and Standard SAMs; six 324mm (12.75in) torpedo tubes
Powerplant:	Single shaft, two gas turbines
Performance:	29 knots

Admiral Graf Spee

Limited by the 1919 Treaty of Versailles to a maximum displacement of 10,200 tonnes (10,039 tons), Germany produced the cleverly designed 'pocket' battleship. Great savings were achieved by using electric welding and light alloys in the hull. *Admiral Graf Spee*, with her two sister ships, *Deutschland* and *Admiral Scheer*, were intended primarily as commerce-raiders. The ship was scuttled off Montevideo, Uruguay, after engaging three British cruisers, *Exeter*, *Ajax* and *Achilles*, in the Battle of the River Plate in December 1939. This ship was officially classified as being an 'armoured ship' by the Germans, though it was popularly referred to as being a 'pocket' battleship, a title which stuck. In actual fact neither term is strictly correct, for she was in reality an armoured cruiser of an exceptionally powerful type.

Country:	Germany
Type:	Battleship
Launch date:	30 June 1934
Crew:	926
Displacement:	10,160 tonnes (10,000 tons)
Dimensions:	186m x 20.6m x 7.2m (610ft 3in x 67ft 7in x 23ft 7in)
Range:	37,040km (20,000nm) at 15 knots
Armament:	Six 279mm (11in), eight 150mm (6in) guns
Powerplant:	Eight sets of MAN diesels, two shafts
Performance:	26 knots

Agamemnon

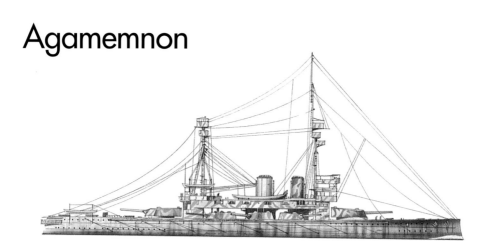

A *gamemnon* was one of the Lord Nelson class and the last of Britain's
pre-dreadnoughts. Laid down in 1904, her construction coincided with that of
HMS *Dreadnought*. As a result *Agamemnon's* completion was delayed until 1908,
by which time *Dreadnought* had made history and the Lord Nelson class was
launched into virtual obsolescence. Characterised by their large secondary
armament, which differed of course from the all big-gun dreadnoughts, the class
was known at the time for having a rather French look to its design, with a high
superstructure and low unequal-sized funnels. *Agamemnon* served in the eastern
Mediterranean during World War I, and saw action in the Dardenelles. During
these operations she was hit over 60 times, and on 15 May 1916 her gunners shot
down Zeppelin L85 at Salonika.

Country:	Great Britain
Type:	Battleship
Launch date:	23 June 1906
Crew:	810
Displacement:	16,347 tonnes (16,090 tons)
Dimensions:	124m x 135m x 24m (410ft x 44ft 6in x 79ft 6in)
Range:	17,000km (9180nm) at 10 knots
Armament:	Four 304mm (12in), ten 234mm (9.2in), 24 12-pounder guns, five torpedo tubes
Powerplant:	Twin shaft four cylinder engine
Performance:	18 knots

Agincourt

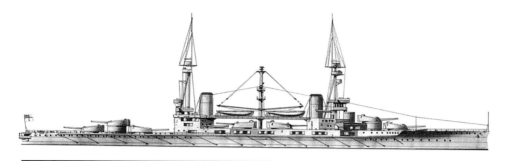

Originally ordered in Britain by the Brazilian Government and named
Rio de Janiero when she launched in 1913, the Brazilians found they could
not afford her. She was sold on to Turkey as *Sultan Osman I,* but never delivered.
Completed in August 1914, she was appropriated by the Royal Navy for war
service and renamed *Agincourt*. In design she had many unusual features, not
least her length and big main armament of 14 304mm (12in) guns on seven twin
turrets. However, this huge amount of weight weakened her hull which was in any
case woefully underprotected. She was nevertheless known in her time as a good
sea boat. Her tripod main mast was reduced to a pole in 1917 and later removed.
After World War I, *Agincourt* was unsuccessfully offered for sale back to Brazil,
and sold for scrap in the 1920s.

Country:	Great Britain
Type:	Battleship
Launch date:	22 January 1913
Crew:	1270
Displacement:	27,940 tonnes (27,500 tons)
Dimensions:	204.7m x 27.1m x 8.2m (671ft 6in x 89ft x 27ft)
Range:	8100km (4500nm) at 12 knots
Armament:	14 304mm (12in), 20 152mm (6in), 10 76mm (3in) guns
Powerplant:	Four shaft geared turbines
Performance:	22 knots

Akagi

A kagi was designed as a 41,820 tonne (41,161 ton) battlecruiser but, while still on the stocks, the Washington Naval Treaty of 1922 (whereby Japan was forced to restrict her naval programme) caused the design to be altered. Built to dispatch up to 60 aircraft, she was modified to carry heavier aircraft and more light guns. As converted, she had three flight decks forward, no island and two funnels on the starboard side, one pointing up, the other out and down. During reconstruction (1935–38) the two lower flight decks forward were removed and the top flight deck extended forward to the bow. An island was added on the port side. *Akagi* led the Japanese carrier assault on Pearl Harbor on 7 December 1941, but was destroyed seven months later by bombs dropped by US Navy divebombers at the decisive Battle of Midway.

Country:	Japan
Type:	Aircraft carrier
Launch date:	22 April 1925
Crew:	2000
Displacement :	29,580 tonnes (29,114 tons)
Dimensions:	249m x 30.5m x 8.1m (816ft 11in x 100ft x 26ft 7in)
Range:	14,800km (8000nm) at 14 knots
Armament:	10 203mm (8in), 12 119mm (4.7in) guns, 91 aircraft
Powerplant:	Four shaft turbines
Performance:	32.5 knots

Akitsuki

By far the largest destroyers built in series by the Japanese, the Akitsuki-class ships were originally conceived as anti-aircraft escorts. They were the only eight-gun destroyers in the Japanese fleet, and it would seem that the quadruple torpedo tube mounting was a later addition. Anti-aircraft armament was progressively strengthened during the war. The most distinctive feature of the class was the complex casing of the single stack. Extensive trunking enabled the funnel to be sited far enough abaft the bridge both to reduce the smoke problem and aid visibility, while placing it sufficiently far back to permit extra anti-aircraft platforms to be installed where the afterstack would normally have been. Twelve ships of this class were built, of which six were sunk. The *Akitsuki* herself was lost on 25 October 1944.

Country:	Japan
Type:	Destroyer
Launch date:	2 July 1941
Crew:	285
Displacement:	2743 tonnes (2700 tons)
Dimensions:	134.1m x 11.6m x 4.11m (440ft x 38ft 1in x 13ft 6in)
Range:	14,797km (7990nm)
Main armament:	Four twin 100mm (3.94in) and two twin 25mm AA guns; one quadruple 610mm (24in) torpedo tube mounting
Powerplant:	Two sets of geared steam turbines
Performance:	33 knots

Alberto da Giussano

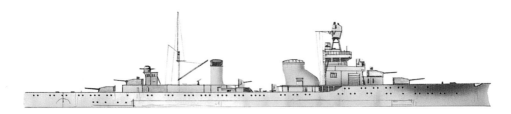

One of a class of four units built to counter the powerful French Lion class destroyers, *Alberto da Giussano* represented an extremely efficient class of ship. Lightly armoured, she was one of the fastest destroyers in the world at the time of her launch; one of her class achieved a speed of 42 knots during trials and maintained a steady 40 knots for eight hours. Classified as a light cruiser before the outbreak of World War II, the *da Giussano* became part of the Italian Navy's 4th Division at Italy's entry into the war in June 1940, and undertook many minelaying operations. Together with another light cruiser, she was sunk by the British destroyers *Legion* and *Maori* in December 1941. Together with a sister ship, *Alberico da Barbiano*, she was sunk by the British destroyers *Legion* and *Maori* on 13 December 1941, 900 lives being lost in the two ships.

Country:	Italy
Type:	Destroyer
Launch date:	27 April 1930
Crew:	220
Displacement:	5170 tonnes (5089 tons)
Dimensions:	169.4m x 15.2m x 4.3m (555ft 9in x 49ft 10in x 14ft 1in)
Range:	7037km (3800nm)
Main armament:	Eight 152mm (6in) guns
Powerplant:	Two sets of geared steam turbines
Performance:	40 knots

Alfa

The second Soviet titanium-hulled submarine design, the Project 705 Lira, known in the West as the Alfa class, came to light in December 1971, when the first unit was commissioned. Five more followed in 1972–82. A single reactor and turbine plant drive the boat at a phenomenal 42 knots under water. When British and American submariners first encountered the Alfa they were astounded, but what was not realised at the time was that there was a serious flaw in the lead-bismuth system of the Alfa's 40,000hp reactor cooling system. The plant was very unreliable, and the cost led to the Lira/Alfa being nicknamed the 'Golden Fish'. In addition, the design was not stressed for deep diving, as was assumed in the West – with the result that NATO navies allocated massive R&D funding to the development of deep-running torpedoes.

Country:	Soviet Union
Type:	Attack submarine
Launch date:	1970
Crew:	31
Displacement:	Surfaced: 2845 tonnes (2800 tons), submerged: 3739 tonnes (3680t)
Dimensions:	81m x 9.5m x 8m (265ft 9in x 31ft 2in x 26ft 3in)
Armament:	Six 533mm (21in) torpedo tubes; conventional or nuclear torpedoes; 36 mines
Powerplant:	Liquid-metal reactor, two steam turbines
Range:	Unlimited
Performance:	Surfaced: 20 knots, submerged: 42 knots

Almirante class

The Chilean Navy has traditionally operated a mixture of British and American warships since its inception. The Chilean Navy's two Almirante-class destroyers – *Riveros* and *Williams* – were ordered from Vickers-Armstrong Ltd of Barrow in 1958 and completed in 1960. The vessels were fitted with twin rudders, affording exceptional manoeuvrability, and the ventilation and heating systems were designed to suit the Chilean climate, which varies greatly along the country's lengthy coastline, which extends from the tropics to Cape Horn. Each ship was armed with four Exocet SSM launchers and with Seacat quadruple SAM launchers. The main armament was disposed in four single mountings, two superimposed forward and two aft. The guns were entirely automatic, with a range of 11,430m (12,500yds) and an elevation of 75 degrees. Both ships were sunk as targets in 1998.

Country:	Chile
Type:	Destroyer
Launch date:	12 December 1958 (*Riveros*, first unit)
Crew:	266
Displacement:	3353 tonnes (3300 tons)
Dimensions:	122.5m x 13.1m x 4.0m (402ft x 43ft x 13ft 4in)
Range:	9650km (5208nm)
Main armament:	Four 102mm (4in) guns; four 40mm(1.5in); six 324mm (12.75in) torpedo tubes; Squid A/S mortars
Powerplant:	Two shafts, geared turbines
Performance:	34.5 knots

Almirante Brown

Originally to have been a class of six, with four to have been built in Argentina, the Meko 360H2 Almirante Brown-class design is based on the modularised systems concept, whereby each of the weapons and sensor systems carried form a separate modular unit and can be interchanged with a replacement or newer system without the usual reconstruction that otherwise accompanies the modernisation of a ship. The four ships (*Almirante Brown*, *La Argentina*, *Heroina* and *Sarandi*) were all built by the German firms of Thyssen Rheinstahl and Blohm und Voss, and were commissioned between 1983 and 1984. *Almirante Brown* took part in the allied Gulf operations in 1990. Fennec helicopters were delivered in 1996 to improve ASW capability and provide over-the-horizon targeting for SSMs. All four units are based at Puerto Belgrano.

Country:	Argentina
Type:	Destroyer
Launch date:	28 March 1981
Crew:	200
Displacement:	3414 tonnes (3360 tons)
Dimensions:	125.9m x 14m x 5.8m (413ft 1in x 46ft x 19ft)
Range:	7783km (4200nm)
Main armament:	Four twin Exocet launchers; one octuple SAM launcher; one 127mm (5in) DP gun; two triple 324mm (12.75in) torpedo tubes
Powerplant:	Twin shafts, four gas turbines
Performance:	30.5 knots

Almirante Cochrane

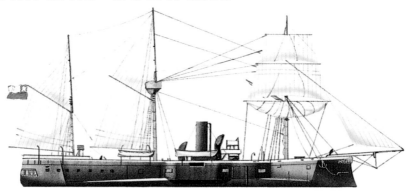

A lmirante Cochrane and her sister ship, *Blanco Encalada*, both combined good protection with a powerful armament on a small displacement. *Almirante Cochrane*'s guns were in an armoured box. Both of these battleships took part in the war with Peru when Chile seized large parts of the Peruvian coastline. *Blanco Encalada* was the first battleship to have the dubious honour of being sunk by a modern torpedo. Launched in 1874, *Almirante Cochrane* was named in honour of Thomas, Lord Cochrane (1775–1860), Earl of Dundonald, the British naval officer who commanded the Chilean Navy in the war of independence. *Almirante Cochrane* fought on the Congressional side during the civil war of 1891; she was subsequently used as a torpedo and gunnery school ship, and was broken up in 1934.

Country:	Chile
Type:	Battleship
Launch date:	25 January 1874
Crew:	300
Displacement:	3631 tonnes (3574 tons)
Dimensions:	64m x 13.9m x 6.7m (210ft x 45ft 7in x 22ft)
Range:	2223km (1200nm) at 10 knots
Armament:	Six 209mm (8.2in) guns
Powerplant:	Twin shaft horizontal compound engine
Performance:	12.75 knots

Almirante Padilla

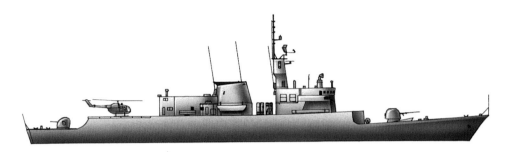

Prior to the *Padilla* entering service, the most powerful unit in the Colombian Navy was a Halland-type destroyer, also German-built. Commissioned in 1983, the *Almirante Padilla* and her three sister ships, commissioned a year later, gives the Colombian Navy a considerable surface attack capability, although the ships of this class are now overdue for modernization. A refit programme, which would include the fitting of surface-to-air missiles and new engines, remains top priority, but the required funding is not available. The ships were built by Howaldtswerke, Kiel. Each carries an MBB 105 helicopter for anti-submarine warfare, and is fitted with a Thomson-CSF Sea Tiger search radar with a range of 110km (60nm). The ships carry the Atlas Elektronik ASO 4-2 hull-mounted active attack sonar. A similar class of vessel was built for the Malaysian Navy.

Country:	Colombia
Type:	Corvette
Launch date:	6 January 1982
Crew:	94
Displacement:	2134 tonnes (2100 tons)
Dimensions:	99m x 11.3m x 3.7m (325ft 1in x 37ft 1in x 12ft 1in)
Range:	11,112km (6000nm)
Main armament:	One 76mm (3in) gun; one Oerlikon 30mm (1.1in); eight Exocet SSMs; six 324mm (12.75in) torpedo tubes
Powerplant:	Two shafts, four diesels
Performance:	27 knots

Alvand

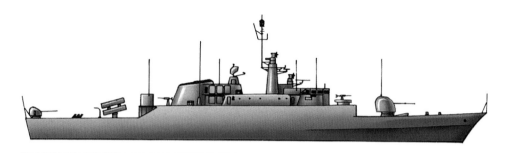

On 25 August 1966, it was announced that Vosper Ltd of Portsmouth had received an order for four 'destroyers' for the Iranian Navy. They were in fact of the small *Vosper* Mk5 frigate type, with one main gun forward, two secondary guns aft, anti-aircraft and anti-submarine weapons. Each vessel was fitted with gas turbines for high speed and diesels for long-range cruising. Originally known as the Saam class, the vessels all received new identities after the Iranian revolution and became the Alvand class. One of the boats, the *Sahand*, was sunk by the US Navy during a confrontation in the Persian Gulf on 18 April 1988. Another vessel, the *Sabalan*, had her back broken by a laser-guided bomb in the same skirmish, but was repaired and was operational again by the end of 1991. The other two vessels are the *Alvand* and *Alborz*.

Country:	Iran
Type:	Frigate
Launch date:	25 July 1968
Crew:	125
Displacement:	1372 tonnes (1350 tons)
Dimensions:	94.5m x 11.1m x 4.3m (310ft x 36ft 5in x 14ft 1in)
Range:	6485km (3500nm)
Main armament:	One 114mm (4.5in) and two 35mm guns; 5 SSMs; AS mortars
Powerplant:	Two shafts, two gas turbines, two diesels
Performance:	39 knots

Amazon

The Type 21 Amazon-class general purpose frigate was a private shipbuilder's design to replace the obsolete Type 41 Leopard- and Type 61 Salisbury-class frigates. Because of numerous beaurocratic problems, private and official ship designers were not brought together on the project, resulting in a class which handled well and was well liked by its crews, but lacked sufficient growth potential to take the new generation of sensor and weapon fits. Completed in May 1974, HMS *Amazon* was the only Type 21 not to see action in the 1982 South Atlantic campaign. A serious fire aboard the vessel in 1977 brought to light the dangers of an aluminium superstructure. However, it was not until after the Falklands conflict (in which the Type 21s *Ardent* and *Antelope* were lost) that the Royal Navy reverted to using steel. The surviving Type 21s were sold to Pakistan in 1993/4.

Country:	Great Britain
Type:	Frigate
Launch date:	26 April 1971
Crew:	177
Displacement:	3404 tonnes (3350 tons)
Dimensions:	117m x 12.7m x 5.9m (384ft x 41ft 8in x 19ft 6in)
Range:	9265km (5000nm)
Main armament:	One single 14mm (4.5in) DP gun; four single 20mm AA guns; two triple 324mm (12.75in) ASW torpedo tubes
Powerplant:	Twin shafts, four gas turbines
Performance:	32 knots

America

The *Kitty Hawk* class were the first aircraft carriers not to carry conventional guns. Intended to be larger, improved versions of the earlier Forrestal class, *Kitty Hawk* (CV 63) and *Constellation* (CV 64) were the first two built. The third, *America* (CV 66), was launched in 1964, and incorporated further improvements based on operational experience. Her dimensions were slightly different to those of her sisters, with a narrower smokestack. She was the first carrier to be equipped with an integrated Combat Information Centre (CIC) and is also fitted with a bow-mounted sonar. A fourth ship, *John F. Kennedy* (CV 67), was built after the US Congress refused to sanction a nuclear-powered vessel in 1964. Policy has since changed, and all large US carriers since then have used nuclear propulsion. *America* was decommissioned in 1996.

Country:	USA
Type:	Aircraft carrier
Launch date:	1 February 1964
Crew:	3306, 1379 with air group
Displacement:	81,090 tonnes (79,813 tons) fully loaded
Dimensions:	324m x 77m x 10.7m (1063ft x 252ft 7in x 35ft)
Range:	21,600km (12,000nm) at 12 knots
Armament:	Three Mark 29 launchers for NATO Sea Sparrow SAMs, three 20mm (0.79in) Phalanx CIWS (Close-in Weapons System), 90 aircraft
Powerplant:	Four shaft geared turbines
Performance:	33 knots

Ammiraglio di Saint Bon

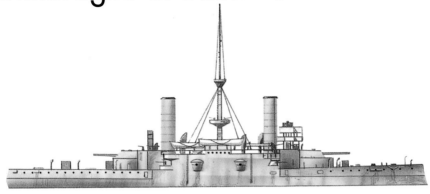

Launched in 1897, *Ammiraglio di Saint Bon* was a compact, heavily protected vessel. A flagship of the Italian Navy, *Ammiraglio di Saint Bon* was a fine example of the emphasis that Italian naval planners of the time were putting on armour. For example, her 152mm (6in) guns were housed in an armoured central battery. Improvements in metallurgical technology in the late 1800s meant that the ship's speed would not be impaired by her solid build. *Ammiraglio di Saint Bon* took part in the Italo-Turkish War; in 1912 she supported Italian forces occupying Tripoli, and in the same year she operated in the Aegean Sea in support of Italian forces occupying the island of Rhodes during the Balkan War. During World War I she was based on Venice for operations in the Adriatic. She was decommissioned in June 1920.

Country:	Italy
Type:	Battleship
Launch date:	29 April 1897
Crew:	450
Displacement:	10,156 tonnes (9996 tons)
Dimensions:	105m x 21m x 7.6m (344ft 6in x 69ft x 25ft)
Range:	3200km (2000 miles) at 10 knots
Armament:	Four 254mm (10in), eight 152mm (6in) guns
Powerplant:	Two vertical triple expansion engines developing 14,000hp; 12 cylindrical boilers
Performance:	18 knots

Andrea Doria

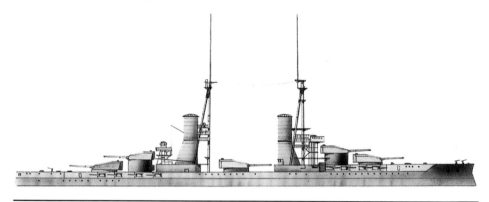

L aid down in 1912, and completed four years later in 1916, *Andrea Doria*, and her sister ship *Caio Duilio*, both underwent a very rigorous reconstruction programme from 1937 to 1940. *Andrea Doria*'s top speed was increased from 21.5 to 27 knots and in addition she was given improved armour on her turrets and engine rooms. During World War I she operated in the southern Adriatic, and subsequently in 1919 she operated in the Black Sea, supporting the Allied Intervention Force operating in South Russia on the loyalist side during the civil war. During World War II *Andrea Doria* took part in convoy battles and in some notable actions, including the First Battle of Sirte. She was placed on the Reserve in 1942, and in the following year she surrendered to the British at Malta. Both ships remained in service until 1958.

Country:	Italy
Type:	Battleship
Launch date:	30 March 1913
Crew:	1198
Displacement:	26,115 tonnes (25,704 tons)
Dimensions:	176m x 28m x 8.8m (577ft 5in x 91ft 10in x 28ft 10in)
Range:	8784km (4800nm) at 10 knots (before reconstruction)
Armament:	13 304mm (12in), 16 152mm (6in) guns
Powerplant:	Twin shaft geared turbines
Performance:	26 knots

Andromeda

HMS *Andromeda* was a Batch 3 ship of the 26-strong Leander class of frigate. From the 17th Leander, the design was amended by increasing the beam. HMS *Andromeda* was the first of five broadbeamed Leanders to be fitted with Sea Wolf short-range surface-to-air missiles and with the sea-skimming Exocet anti-ship missile, recommissioning in 1980. After refitting, HMS *Andromeda* and the other four Batch 3 vessels were the most powerful of their class. A successful design, the Leander class sold well to overseas navies, the ships in foreign service being generally better armed than those serving in the Royal Navy. India's Leanders, known as the Godavari class, were fitted with a mixture of Western and Russian systems. Leander-class vessels were also sold to Australia and the Netherlands. The last Royal Navy Leander, HMS *Scylla*, was retired in 1992.

Country:	Great Britain
Type:	Frigate
Launch date:	24 May 1967
Crew:	260
Displacement:	3009 tonnes (2962 tons)
Dimensions:	113.4m x 13.1m x 4.5m (372ft x 43ft x 14ft 10in)
Range:	8894km (4800nm)
Main armament:	Twin 114mm (4.5in) guns; two single 20mm (0.7in) AA guns; two triple 324mm (12.75in) ASW torpedo tubes; Exocet, Sea Wolf
Powerplant:	Two shaft geared steam turbines
Performance:	27 knots

Annapolis

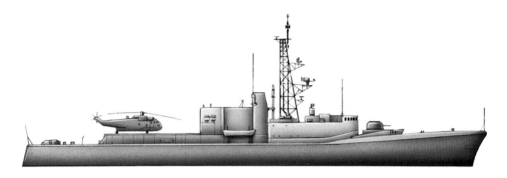

Completed in 1964, the *Annapolis* and her sister ship, *Nipigon*, were developed from the original St Laurent class and served in the destroyer escort role alongside two other groups, the Mackenzie and Restigouche classes. As originally built, the ship's armament included a Mk10 Limbo three-barrelled ASW mortar. As they were fitted with a hangar and armed with a Sea King ASW helicopter each, the *Annapolis* and *Nipigon* were designated DDH. The two ships underwent a full Destroyer Life Extension (Delex) programme between 1982 and 1985, being fitted with new air radar, sonar, communications and electronic warfare equipment. *Annapolis* has now been placed in reserve; *Nipigon*'s main armament and radars were removed in 1994 but replaced in 1995, and she is now being used as a sonar test vessel.

Country:	Canada
Type:	Frigate
Launch date:	27 April 1963
Crew:	246
Displacement:	2946 tonnes (2900 tons)
Dimensions:	111.5m x 12.8m x 4.1m (366ft x 42ft x 13ft 6in)
Range:	7970km (4300nm)
Main armament:	Two 76mm (3in) guns; six 324mm (12.75in) torpedo tubes
Powerplant:	Two shafts, turbines
Performance:	28 knots

Appalachian

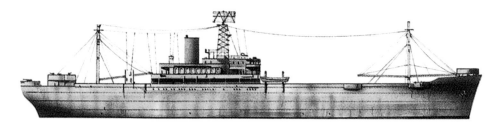

*A*ppalachian was one of an important group of ships that acted both as the headquarters ship and as air control for the amphibious assaults on Japanese-held islands during World War II. In January 1945 she was headquarters ship for Amphibious Group 3, which operated in support of the large-scale US landings at Lingayen Gulf in the Philippines. The landings were heavily contested by Japanese Kamikaze suicide pilots, who managed to sink a US carrier and damage several more, but *Appalachian* escaped unharmed. *Appalachian*, which was designated *AGC.1*, was the first of seventeen US amphibious force flagships, which served in all theatres of war. She later served briefly as Pacific Fleet flagship in 1947, before being removed from the active list that same year. She was broken up in 1960.

Country:	USA
Type:	Command ship
Launch date:	1943
Crew:	507 and 368 HQ personnel
Weight:	14,133 tonnes (13,910 tons)
Dimensions:	132.6m x 19.2m x 7.3m (435ft x 63ft x 24ft)
Range:	5560km (3000nm) at 16 knots
Armour:	Varied, depending on protection of key points
Armament:	Two 127mm (5in), eight 40mm (1.6in) guns
Powerplant:	Single shaft turbine
Performance:	17 knots

Aquila

A quila began her life as the 33,764-tonne (33,232 ton) cruise ship *Roma*. She was requisitioned by the Italian Navy in 1941 for conversion into the first Italian aircraft carrier. Several improvements were undertaken during World War II. For example, more powerful engines were installed as well as an enormous second underwater keel, into which cement was poured to increase stability. In September 1943, when almost completed at Genoa, *Aquila* was seized by the Germans following Italy's surrender, and on 19 April 1945 she was severely damaged by Italian human torpedoes to prevent her being used by the Germans as a blockship. She was intended to carry an air group of 51 aircraft, and her turbines were taken from the uncompleted cruisers *Silla* and *Emilio*. *Aquila* never saw service and was broken up in 1951.

Country:	Italy
Type:	Aircraft carrier
Launch date:	1943
Crew:	1165 and 24 air personnel
Displacement:	28,810 tonnes (28,356 tons)
Dimensions:	231.5m x 29.4m x 7.3m (759ft 6in x 96ft 5in x 24ft)
Range:	5400km (4150nm) at 18 knots
Armament:	Eight 135mm (5.3in) guns, 36 aircraft
Powerplant:	Four shaft geared turbines
Performance:	32 knots

Araguaya

A raguaya and her five sisters were built to replace six British H-class destroyers which, under construction for Brazil, were taken over by the Royal Navy at the outbreak of World War II. They followed the same design but used American equipment. All were built between 1943 and 1946 at the Ilha des Cobras Navy Yard. *Araguaya* was launched in 1946 and discarded in 1974. All the ships of this class were named after rivers, the others being the *Acre, Amazonas, Araguari, Apa* and *Ajuricaba*. The original H-class destroyers destined for Brazil were to have been named *Jurua, Javary, Jutahy, Juruena, Jaguaribe* and *Japarua*. They saw war service with the Royal Navy as *Handy, Havant, Havelock, Hearty, Highlander* and *Hurricane*. The H class destroyers were efficient, capable ships. Two of those taken over by the RN, *Handy* and *Hurricane,* were lost in action.

Country:	Brazil
Type:	Destroyer
Launch date:	20 November 1943
Crew:	190
Displacement:	1829 tonnes (1800 tons)
Dimensions:	98.5m x 10.7m x 2.6m (323ft x 35ft x 8ft 6in)
Range:	9265km (5000nm)
Main armament:	Four 127mm (5in); two 40mm (1.6in) guns
Powerplant:	Two shaft geared turbines
Performance:	35.5 knots

Ardent

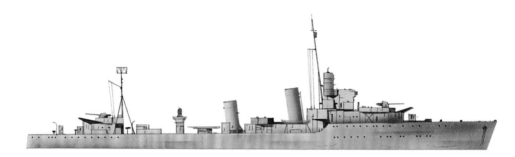

A *rdent* was one of a class of eight units with which the Royal Navy began a new era of destroyer construction, after a lapse of eight years from the end of World War I. The class introduced quadruple torpedo tubes and had full shields for their 11.9cm (4.7in) guns. *Ardent* and her sister ship *Acasta* were sunk in June 1940 by the German battlecruisers *Scharnhorst* and *Gneisenau* while escorting the aircraft carrier *Glorious*, which also fell victim to the German guns. Apart from the above-named, the ships of this class were the *Achates* (lost 31 December 1942), *Acheron* (lost 17 December 1940), *Active*, *Antelope*, *Anthony* and *Arrow*. Two more ships of this design served with the Royal Canadian Navy as the *Saguenay* and *Skeena*. The former was damaged in a collision off Newfoundland in November 1942 and the latter ran aground on the coast of Iceland in 1944.

Country:	Great Britain
Type:	Destroyer
Launch date:	1929
Crew:	138
Displacement:	2022 tonnes (1990 tons)
Dimensions:	95.1m x 9.8m x 3.7m (312ft x 32ft 3in x 12ft 3in)
Range:	4630km (2500nm)
Main armament:	Four 120mm (4.7in) guns; eight 533mm (21in) torpedo tubes
Powerplant:	Twin shaft geared turbines
Performance:	35 knots

Ariete

The Ariete-class ships were improved versions of the Spica class of 1936–8. The vessels of this class were not laid down until 1942 and 1943, by which time the Italians had the benefit of much combat experience. Over 40 units were planned in an extended programme but, although construction was spread over three yards, only 16 were laid down. These were the *Alabarda*, *Ariete*, *Arturo*, *Auriga*, *Balestra*, *Daga*, *Dragone*, *Eridano*, *Fionda*, *Gladio*, *Lancia*, *Pugnale*, *Rigel*, *Spada*, *Spica* and *Stella Polare*. Only the *Ariete* served with the Italian navy, a month before the armistice. The remainder, in various stages of construction, fell into German hands, and 13 saw sea service. Only two, the *Ariete* and *Balustra*, survived the war. The reason so many Italian warships were captured by the Germans was that they were being built in northern Italy, and were readily accessible.

Country:	Italy
Type:	Torpedo boat
Launch date:	6 March 1943
Crew:	155
Displacement:	813 tonnes (800 tons)
Dimensions:	82.85m x 8.6m x 2.8m (269ft 9in x 28ft 2in x 9ft 2in)
Range:	1852km (1000nm)
Main armament:	Two single 100mm (3.94in) and two single 37mm (1.45in) AA guns; two triple 540mm (17.72in) torpedo tubes; up to 28 mines
Powerplant:	Two sets of geared steam turbines
Performance:	31 knots

Arizona

A	*rizona*, like her sister ship *Pennsylvania*, was an improved and enlarged version of the Nevada class, her main armament being housed in four triple turrets. Launched in 1915, and completed the following year, *Arizona* did not see any action during World War I. In 1941 she sailed to the Pacific to join the US fleet based at Pearl Harbor. On the morning of 7 December the Japanese launched an air attack without warning. One of the first ships hit was *Arizona*. A bomb is believed to have struck one of her forward turrets which detonated the magazine beneath. The ship blew up taking over a thousand of her crew with her. *Arizona* was one of four US battleships sunk at Pearl Harbor; a fifth was beached and three more damaged. Today her remains still lie in the shallow waters of the harbour where she is preserved as a war grave.

Country:	USA
Type:	Battleship
Launch date:	19 June 1915
Crew:	1117
Displacement:	32,045 tonnes (32,567 tons)
Dimensions:	185.4m x 29.6m x 8.8m (608ft x 97ft 1in x 28ft 10in)
Range:	14,400km (8000nm) at 10 knots
Armament:	12 356mm (14in), 22 127mm (5in) guns
Powerplant:	Four shaft geared turbines
Performance:	21 knots

Ark Royal

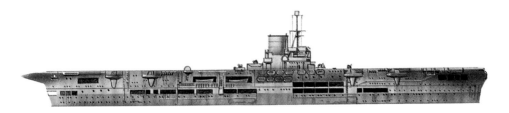

*A*rk Royal was the first large purpose-built aircraft carrier to be constructed for the Royal Navy, with a long flight deck some 18m (60ft) above the deep water load line. The aircraft carrier's full complement was 60 aircraft, although she never actually carried this many as such a load would have reduced her fighting capability. During her war operations, she took part in the Norwegian campaign of 1940 and was subsequently transferred to the Mediterranean Theatre, where she joined 'Force H' at Gibraltar. In May 1941 one of her Swordfish aircraft torpedoed the German battleship *Bismarck*, destroying the warship's steering gear – an act that led to *Bismarck* being sunk some hours later by the British Fleet. In November 1941 *Ark Royal* was torpedoed by the German submarine *U81* and capsized after 14 hours.

Country:	Great Britain
Type:	Aircraft carrier
Launch date:	13 April 1937
Crew:	1580
Displacement:	28,164 tonnes (27,720 tons)
Dimensions:	243.8m x 28.9m x 8.5m (800ft x 94ft 9in x 27ft 9in)
Range:	14,119km (7620nm) at 20 knots
Armament:	16 114mm (4.5in) guns, 60 aircraft
Powerplant:	Triple shaft geared turbines
Performance:	31 knots

Arleigh Burke

This large class of guided-missile destroyer was designed to replace the ageing Adams- and Coontz-class destroyers which entered service in the early 1960s. The principal mission of the Arleigh Burke class is to provide effective anti-aircraft cover, for which they have the SPY 1D version of the Aegis area defence system. The Arleigh Burkes are the first US warships to be fully equipped for warfare in a nuclear, chemical or biological environment, the crew being confined in a citadel located within the hull and superstructure. The ships are heavily protected; plastic Kevlar armour is fitted over all vital machinery and operations room spaces for this purpose. Armament includes one 127mm (5in) DP gun and two 20mm Phalanx CIWS mountings, and the ships are fitted with a platform for an ASW helicopter. There is also a laser designator for the guidance of the DP gun's Deadeye shells.

Country:	USA
Type:	Guided missile destroyer
Launch date:	16 September 1989
Crew:	303
Displacement:	8534 tonnes (8400 tons)
Dimensions:	81m x 18.3m x 9.1m (266ft 3in x 60ft x 30ft)
Range:	11,118km (6000nm)
Main armament:	Harpoon and Tomahawk anti-ship and land attack cruise missiles; one 127mm (5in) gun.
Powerplant:	Twin shaft gas turbine
Performance:	32 knots

Armando Diaz

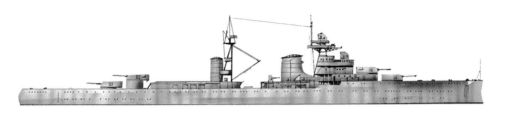

*A*rmando Diaz and her sister ship *Luigi Cadorna* were part of the Italian Navy's building programme of between 1929 and 1930, and were originally classified as light cruisers. They bore a strong resemblance to the previous group of fast cruisers, but they had more internal space, which in turn permitted reduced upperworks and a smaller bridge. These improvements helped to enhance the vessels' stability in heavy seas. Both ships had a seaplane catapult on the rear superstructure. They could carry up to 138 mines, depending on the type. Both ships, reclassified as destroyers, operated extensively in the Mediterranean during World War II, but *Armando Diaz* was sunk in February 1941 when the British submarine HMS *Upright* torpedoed her while she was in the process of escorting a convoy.

Country:	Italy
Type:	Destroyer
Launch date:	10 October 1932
Crew:	220
Displacement:	5406 tonnes (5321 tons)
Dimensions:	169.3m x 15.5m x 5.5m (555ft 6in x 50ft 10in x 18ft)
Range:	5185km (2800nm)
Main armament:	Eight 152mm (6in) guns
Powerplant:	Twin shaft geared turbines
Performance:	36.5 knots

Arpad

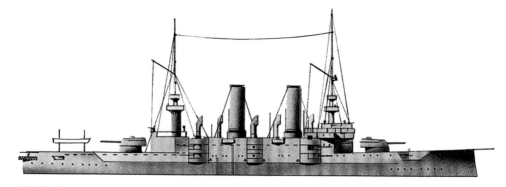

*A*rpad was developed as a small battleship type which was intended for
service in the Adriatic. Although the vessel was fairly well protected, her
main armament was weak. Nevertheless, her secondary battery was certainly as
powerful as that of any battleship in service at the time. *Arpad* was one of the
first warships to rely heavily on electricity in order to work the main guns,
hoists and ventilators. *Arpad* was one of the Hapsburg class of pre-Dreadnought
battleships. She took her name from the 10th-century chief of the Magyars, who
was also the national hero of Hungary. Launched in 1901 and completed in 1903,
Arpad then underwent a substantial refit in 1911–12. At the end of World War I
she was put to use as a training ship; she was interned at Pola in 1918 and broken
up in Italy in 1920.

Country:	Austria
Type:	Battleship
Launch date:	11 September 1901
Crew:	638
Displacement:	8965 tonnes (8823 tons)
Dimensions:	114.8m x 19.9m x 7.5m (376ft 6in x 65ft 2in x 24ft 6in)
Range:	6670km (3600nm) at 10 knots
Armament:	Three 240mm (9.5in), 12 152mm (6in) guns
Powerplant:	Twin screw triple expansion engines
Performance:	19.6 knots

Artigliere

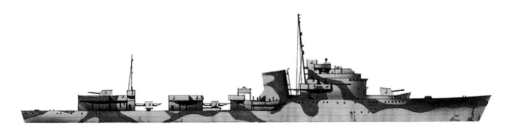

By 1936, Italy had developed a successful destroyer design, and in 1937 was ready to lay down the first batch of what eventually formed the largest single class of destroyer built for the Italian Navy. Twenty-one units were built, all of which saw extensive war service as effective escorts. They were capable of taking a great deal of punishment, although as with all pre-war destroyers, the anti-aircraft armament proved ineffective and was soon improved. During the night of 11–12 October 1940, the *Artigliere*, serving with the 12th DD Flotilla, was engaged in a night action with the British cruiser HMS *Ajax* and received heavy hits. She was taken under tow, but the next day, following reports that the British cruiser HMS *York* was approaching, her crew were taken off and the vessel herself was cast adrift and sunk.

Country:	Italy
Type:	Destroyer
Launch date:	12 December 1937
Crew:	230
Displacement:	2540 tonnes (2500 tons)
Dimensions:	106.7m x 10.2m x 3.5m (350ft x 33ft 4in x 11ft 6in)
Range:	4447km (2400nm)
Main armament:	Four 120mm (4.7in) guns
Powerplant:	Twin screw geared turbines
Performance:	38 knots

Asagiri

The fast guided-missile destroyer *Asagiri* and her seven sister ships (*Yamagiri, Yuugiri, Amagiri, Hamagiri, Setogiri, Sawagiri* and *Umigiri*) were all laid down between 1985 and 1988 and commissioned between 1989 and 1991. The last four named above were fitted during building with an improved air search radar, undated fire control radars, and a helicopter datalink. All eight vessels are now equipped with a towed sonar array. In service, the first ships were found to have a high infrared signature, and modifications were subsequently carried out to the mainmast and forward funnel to reduce the problem. The funnel is slightly offset to port and the after funnel to the starboard side of the fuselage. The large hangar structure is asymmetrical, extending to the after funnel on the starboard side but only as far as the mainmast on the port.

Country:	Japan
Type:	Destroyer
Launch date:	19 September 1966
Crew:	220
Displacement:	3556 tonnes (3500 tons)
Dimensions:	137m x 14.6m x 4.5m (449ft 4in x 48ft x 14ft 6in)
Range:	8153 km (4400nm)
Main armament:	One 76mm (3in) gun; Harpoon SSMs; Sea Sparrow SAMs; six 324mm (12.75in) torpedo tubes
Powerplant:	Two shafts, four gas turbines
Performance:	30+ knots

Asagumo

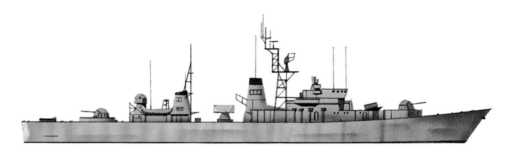

The *Asagumo* and her six sister ships – *Makigumo, Minegumo, Murakumo, Natsugumo, Yamagumo* and *Aokumo* – were part of a Japanese Navy modernization programme initiated in the early 1960s. *Yamagumo* was ordered under the 1962 fiscal year new construction programme, *Makigumo* under the 1963 programme, and *Asagumo* under the 1964 programme. The ships all have the word 'cloud' in their names: *Makigumo*, for example, means 'Rolling Cloud', while *Yamagumo* means 'Mountain Cloud'. *Asagumo* was the second Japanese destroyer to bear the name; the first was sunk by the American cruiser *Denver* in Surigao Strait during the Battle of Leyte on 25 October 1944. The Japanese tend to name their warships after natural features and the elements; for example, there were the Moon, Rain and Cloud classes in service alongside the Asagumos.

Country:	Japan
Type:	Destroyer
Launch date:	25 November 1966
Crew:	210
Displacement:	2083 tonnes (2050 tons)
Dimensions:	114m x 11.8m x 4m (374ft x 38ft 9in x 13ft)
Range:	11,380km (6145nm)
Main armament:	Four 76mm (3in) guns; six torpedo tubes
Powerplant:	Twin shaft diesel engines
Performance:	28 knots

Asahi

In 1896 Japan began a naval expansion programme. Because her own shipyards were not yet ready to accommodate such a programme, *Asahi* and her three sister ships were ordered from British yards. All four vessels were designed by G.C. Macrow along the lines of the Royal Navy's Canopus class. *Asahi* saw extensive operational service in the 1904–05 war with Russia serving as Admiral Togo's flagship. She took part in the blockade of Port Arthur, where she was moderately damaged by a mine, and on 27 May 1905 she sustained nine shell hits in the decisive Battle of Tsushima. She was later preserved as a memorial. In 1923 *Asahi* was converted to a submarine depot ship. Finally, on 25 May 1942 she was torpedoed and sunk by the US submarine *Salmon* in the South China Sea.

Country:	Japan
Type:	Battleship
Launch date:	13 March 1899
Crew:	836
Displacement:	15,443 tonnes (15,2000 tons)
Dimensions:	133.5m x 23m x 8.4m (438ft x 75ft 6in x 27ft 6in)
Range:	16,677km (9000nm) at 10 knots
Armament:	Four 304mm (12in), 14 152mm (6in) guns
Powerplant:	Twin screw, vertical triple expansion engines
Performance:	18 knots

Asashio

The Asashio class of 10 units were larger versions of the two preceding classes of destroyer. Their arrival marked Japan's abandonment of any restrictions imposed by pre-World War II treaties. The new steam turbines proved unreliable at first, and problems with the steering gear were not corrected until December 1941. In due course, however, this design overcame most of the faults inherent in previous classes, and became the basic plan for the next two classes of destroyer, Kagero and Yugumo. During the war, the Asashi class was used extensively in the protection of the Japanese Combined Fleet. *Asashio* and *Arashio* were sunk in 1943, when a transport force they were escorting was annihilated by air attack in the Bismarck Sea. Three more vessels – *Michishio*, *Asagumo* and *Yamagumo* – were sunk in the Battle of Leyte.

Country:	Japan
Type:	Destroyer
Launch date:	16 December 1936
Crew:	200
Displacement:	2367 tonnes (2330 tons)
Dimensions:	118.2m x 10.4m x 3.7m (388ft x 34ft x 12ft)
Range:	7408km (4000nm)
Main armament:	Six 127 mm (5in) guns
Powerplant:	Twin shaft geared turbines
Performance:	35 knots

Assar-i-Tewfik

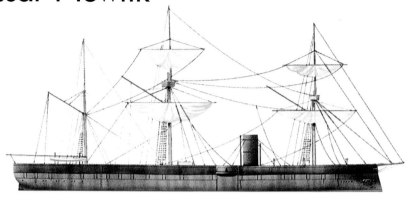

Formerly known as the Egyptian ironclad *Ibrahmieh,* which had been launched in 1868, the ship was renamed *Assar-i-Tewfik.* She had six of her heavy guns concentrated in an armoured battery, which also protected the funnel base. As a further improvement, two more guns were mounted directly above the battery. This new arrangement helped reduce the average size of battleships, and resulted in greater manoeuvrability. In December 1916 *Assar-i-Tewfik* went into action off the Dardanelles in the Balkan war against Bulgaria, receiving some damage. Then, on 11 February 1912, she ran aground near Podima in the Bosphorus while supporting troops in action and had to be abandoned. Defined as a coastal battery ship, *Assar-i-Tewfik* was similar to the French Trident class of vessel.

Country of origin:	Turkey
Type:	Ironclad
Launch date:	30 November 1868
Crew:	320
Displacement:	4762 tonnes (4687 tons)
Dimensions:	83m x 16m x 6.5m (272ft 4in x 52ft 6in x 21ft 4in)
Range:	2965km (1600nm) at 10 knots
Armament:	Eight 228mm (9in) muzzle-loading guns
Powerplant:	Single shaft compound engines
Performance:	13 knots

Astore

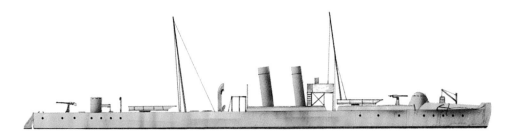

L aunched in June 1907, *Astore* was one of a group of six torpedo boats completed between 1907 and 1909 as a follow-on design to the eight-strong Cigno class. She was classified as a high seas torpedo boat, and was intended for service in the Atlantic. Apart from her three torpedo tubes, she was lightly armed, and her radius of action was reduced to 590km (318nm) at full speed. The Italian Navy had 19 such vessels in service, all laid down from 1905 onwards. They all had distinguished active careers during World War I. *Astore* and her five sister ships served mostly in the Atlantic, where their main task was convoy escort. Two of the ships were later converted into fast minesweepers, but the remainder stayed substantially in the same configuration throughout. All ships in the class survived the war and were discarded in 1923.

Country of origin:	Italy
Type:	Torpedo boat
Launch date:	22 June 1907
Crew:	150
Displacement:	220 tonnes (216 tons)
Dimensions:	50.3m x 5.3m x 1.75m (160ft 2in x 17ft 5in x 5ft 9in)
Range:	3335km (1800nm)
Main armament:	Three 47mm (1.8in) guns; three 450mm (17.7in) torpedo tubes
Powerplant:	Twin screw triple expansion engines
Performance:	25.8 knots

Athabaskan

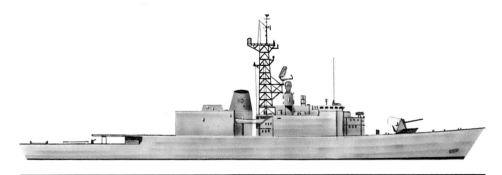

Launched between 1970 and 1971, *Athabaskan* and her three sisters (*Algonquin*, *Huron* and *Iroquois*) were designed specifically for anti-submarine warfare operations. They have the same hull design, dimensions and basic characteristics as an earlier class of large, general-purpose frigates, cancelled in the early 1960s. Properly designated Destroyer Helicopter Escorts (DDH), they carry two Sea King ASW helicopters. They are equipped with anti-rolling tanks to stabilise them at low speed, a pre-wetting system to counter radioactive fallout, and an enclosed citadel from which control of all machinery is exercised. A comprehensive electronics system includes an effective long-range radar warning device. The Athabaskan class ships formed a valuable contribution to NATO's ASW forces during the Cold War. They were upgraded in the early 1990s.

Country:	Canada
Type:	Destroyer
Launch date:	27 November 1970
Crew:	246
Displacement:	4267 tonnes (4200 tons)
Dimensions:	129.8m x 15.5m x 4.5m (426ft x 51ft x 15ft)
Range:	8334km (4500nm)
Main Armament:	One 127mm (5in) gun; one triple A/S mortar
Powerplant:	Twin screw, gas turbines
Performance:	30 knots

Attu

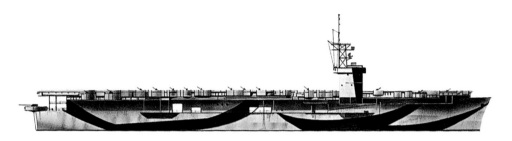

In 1942, shipbuilder Henry J. Kaiser was employed in the mass production of cargo vessels to replace those that had been lost in action. It was decided at that time to complete 50 of the unfinished hulls as escort carriers. The resultant vessel was named *Attu* (*CVE 102*). Her 49 sister ships of the Casablanca class, were all completed within a single year. The Casablanca class carried an air group of nine bombers, nine torpedo bombers and nine fighters. They were the first vessels of their kind to be built as escort carriers from the keel up. All of the Casablanca class went on to serve in the Pacific, with the exception of *Guadalcanal* and *Kasaan Bay*, both of which saw service in the Atlantic. In 1947, *Attu* was converted for mercantile use and renamed *Gay*. She was subsequently scrapped at Baltimore in 1949.

Country:	USA
Type:	Aircraft carrier
Launch date:	27 May 1944
Crew:	860
Displacement:	11,076 tonnes (10,902 tons)
Dimensions:	156.1m x 32.9m x 6.3m (512ft 3in x 108ft x 20ft 9in)
Range:	18,360km (10,200nm) at 10 knots
Armament:	One 127mm (5in), 38 40mm (1.5in) guns, 27 aircraft
Powerplant:	Twin screw reciprocating engines
Performance:	15 knots

Audace

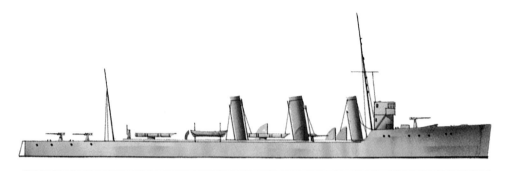

Ordered from Yarrow shipbuilders by the Imperial Japanese Navy as the destroyer *Kawakaze*, and laid down in 1913, this vessel was transferred from Japan to Italy while still under construction and initially named *Intrepido*. Launched in 1916 and completed the following year, in 1929 she was reclassed from destroyer to torpedo boat. During World War II she was used for minelaying duties, mostly in the Adriatic. On 9 September 1943, following Italy's armistice with the Allies, she was seized by the Germans in Venice and designated TA20. She continued with minelaying operations, narrowly escaping attack by the large Free French destroyers *Le Terrible* and *Le Fantasque* on 18 March 1944. Her luck finally ran out on 1 November 1944, when she was sunk in action with the corvettes *UJ202* and *UJ208* by the British escort destroyers *Avon Vale* and *Wheatland*.

Country:	Italy
Type:	Torpedo boat
Launch date:	4 May 1913
Crew:	120
Displacement:	1016 tonnes (1000 tons)
Dimensions:	86m x 8.3m x 2.8m (283ft x 27ft 6in x 9ft 6in)
Range:	2779km (1500nm)
Main armament:	Seven 102mm (4in) guns
Powerplant:	Twin screw geared turbines
Performance:	27 knots

Audace

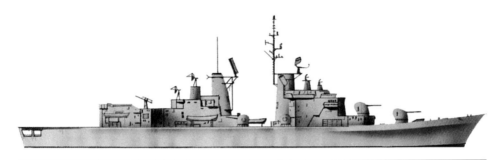

Essentially enlarged versions of the earlier Impavido class, *Audace* and her sister *Ardito* are good examples of multi-function fleet escorts with the primary role of destroying enemy submarines. Two helicopters with a comprehensive weapons kit and sensors are carried by each vessel. *Audace* has a flush-decked hull of high freeboard and an uncluttered superstructure, but some of her weapons have a poor arc of fire due to the height of the superstructure. The double hangar is housed aft, while the fore bridge houses the communications and sensor equipment. The embarked helicopters (two AB212s or one Sea King) carry both Mk44 and Mk46 torpedoes, Mk54 depth bombs and anti-ship missiles. The two Audace-class ships proved to be such excellent vessels that two units of an improved Audace design were ordered to replace the Impavido-class destroyers.

Country:	Italy
Type:	Destroyer
Launch date:	2 October 1971
Crew:	381
Displacement:	4470 tonnes (4400 tons)
Dimensions:	135.9m x 14.6m x 4.5m (446ft x 48ft x 15ft)
Range:	6482km (3500nm)
Main Armament:	Two 127mm (5in) guns; one SAM launcher
Powerplant:	Two shaft geared turbines
Performance:	33 knots

Audacious

Built in answer to the growing strength and ambition of the German Navy, *Audacious*, one of the King George V class, was part of the 1911 British battleship expansion programme. She carried the foremast before the funnels, giving better vision to fire control when underway, a standard arrangement on all subsequent dreadnoughts. While on patrol in October 1914, *Audacious* struck a mine off Ireland and all attempts to tow her to safety failed. She was the first major British warship lost in World War I. Of the other two vessels in her class, *King George V* served as a gunnery training ship after World War I, and was broken up in 1926, and *Centurion* went on to see service in World War II as a floating AA battery in the Mediterranean. She was sunk off Normandy in June 1944 to form part of an artificial harbour.

Country:	Great Britain
Type:	Battleship
Launch date:	14 September 1912
Crew:	782
Displacement:	26,111 tonnes (25,700 tons)
Dimensions:	182.1m x 27.1m x 8.7m (597ft 6in x 89ft x 28ft 6in)
Range:	12,114km (6730nm) at 10 knots
Armament:	10 342mm (13.5in), 16 102mm (4in) guns
Powerplant:	Four shaft geared turbines
Performance:	21 knots

Augusto Riboty

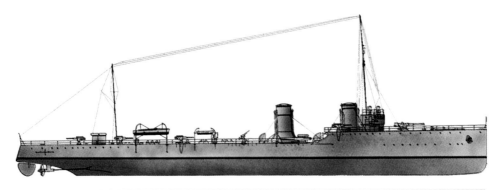

A *ugusto Riboty* and her two sister ships were originally planned to be lightly
armoured light cruisers to be laid down in 1913. However, they emerged as
flotilla leaders with heavy armament. *Carlo Alberto Racchia* and *Carlo Mirabello*
were both sunk by mines, but *Augusto Riboty* survived World War II. She was
allocated to the Soviet Union under the terms of the peace treaty, but remained in
Italy and was scrapped in 1951. Minelaying was Riboty's principal occupation during
the conflict, although in October 1940 she was engaged in transporting Italian troops
to Albania as part of the invasion support force. Early in 1943 she was also involved
in transporting troops and supplies to the Axis forces fighting in Tunisia. As their
surface vessels and aircraft had suffered unacceptable losses by 1943, the Axis were
forced to rely more on submarines for supplying their forces.

Country:	Italy
Type:	Flotilla Leader
Launch date:	24 September 1916
Crew:	150
Displacement:	2003 tonnes (1972 tons)
Dimensions:	103.7m x 9.7m x 3.6m (340ft x 32ft x 12ft)
Range:	4259km (2300nm)
Main Armament:	Eight 102mm (4in) guns
Powerplant:	Twin shaft turbines
Performance:	22 knots

Australia

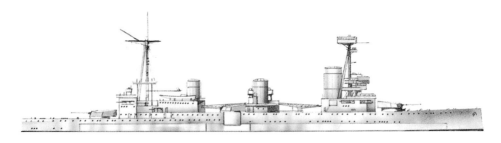

*A*ustralia was a new type of cruiser. Improvements in speed had been achieved by reducing armour protection, and by reducing the main guns by two. In addition, the middle group of turrets, placed in échelon, had a greater field of fire. *Australia* was built on the Clyde in 1913, and after completion she sailed to the Pacific to become the flagship of the Royal Australian Navy. She returned to Britain mid-way through World War I, but was unable to take part in the Battle of Jutland as the result of a collision with the battlecruiser *New Zealand* in fog. In December 1916 *Australia* was damaged in another collision, this time with the battlecruiser *Repulse*. *Australia* was decommissioned in December 1921, and was subsequently used as a target ship, until she was sunk off Sydney in April 1924.

Country:	Australia
Type:	Cruiser
Launch date:	25 October 1911
Crew:	800
Displacement:	21,640 tonnes (21,300 tons)
Dimensions:	180m x 24.3m x 9m (590ft x 80ft x 30ft)
Range:	11,394km (6330nm) at 10 knots
Armament:	Eight 304mm (12in) guns
Powerplant:	Four screw geared turbines
Performance:	26.9 knots

Avon

Before World War II, measures had been put in hand by the Royal Navy to build vessels – frigates – that were suitable for escorting Britain's vital ocean convoys. *Avon* was one of over 90 ships of the River class laid down between 1941 and 1943 and completed between 1942 and 1944. They were ocean-going anti-submarine escorts and proved better adapted to that role than the smaller Flower-class corvettes. Two sets of engines were installed and in later vessels the fuel capacity was increased from 447 to 656 tonnes (440 to 646 tonnes). The original light armament was also increased. After World War II many ships of this class were passed to other navies, where they continued to give good service until the 1960s. *Avon*, which was launched in June 1943, went to the Portuguese Navy in 1949 as the *Nuno Tristao*. HMS *Awe* was also transferred to Portugal at the same time.

Country:	Great Britain
Type:	Frigate
Launch date:	19 June 1943
Crew:	140
Displacement:	2133 tonnes (2100 tons)
Dimensions:	91.8m x 11m x 3.8m (301ft 4in x 36ft 8in x 12ft 9in)
Range:	5556kn (3000nm)
Main Armament:	Two 102mm (4in) guns
Powerplant:	Twin screw vertical triple expansion engines
Performance:	20 knots

Avvoltoio

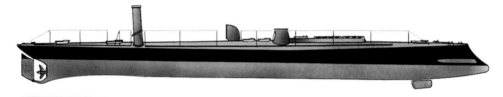

A *vvoltoio* was rated as a second-class torpedo boat; commissioned in 1881, she was designated 2Y from 1886, the 'Y' signifying that she had been built in Yarrow. Launched in 1879, *Avvoltoio* was typical of the torpedo boats of her day. Since surprise was the principal weapon of such craft, early types were fast and small, lightly built, and unprotected, their sole purpose being to get close enough to enemy capital ships to use their torpedoes effectively. *Avvoltoio* was the second such type adopted by the Italians; she was discarded in 1904. During the period when *Avvoltoio* came into service, Italy was still smarting over the war with Austria which ended with the disastrous battle of Lissa just over a decade earlier, when two Italian ironclads were sunk and another damaged. Italian naval leaders were determined to build a maritime force that would dominate the Adriatic.

Country:	Italy
Type:	Torpedo boat
Launch date:	1879
Crew:	20
Displacement:	25 tonnes (25 tons)
Dimensions:	26m x 3.3m x 1.3m (86 ft x 11ft x 4ft 6in)
Range:	Not known
Main armament:	Two 356mm (14in) torpedo tubes; one 1-pounder revolving cannon
Powerplant:	Single screw vertical triple expansion engine
Performance:	21.3 knots

B1

Construction of the improved B-class submarines was under way before the A-class boats were completed. An extended superstructure on top of the hull gave improved surface performance, while small hydroplanes on the conning tower improved underwater handling. By 1910 the Royal Navy had 11 B-class boats. They were not comfortable craft in which to serve; their interior stank of raw fuel, bilge-water and dampness, all pervaded by a stench of oil, and when submerged there was a constant risk of explosion from violent sparks produced by unshieded electrical components in an atmosphere saturated with petrol vapour. Six B-class submarines were sent to Gibraltar and Malta. *B1* was broken up in 1921. The first RN VC of World War I was awarded to a B-class boat commander.

Country:	Great Britain
Type:	Attack submarine
Launch date:	October 1904
Crew:	16
Displacement:	Surfaced: 284 tonnes (280 tons), submerged: 319 tonnes (314 tons)
Dimensions:	41m x 4.1m x 3m (135ft x 13ft 6in x 9ft 10in)
Surface range:	2779km (1500nm) at 8 knots
Armament:	Two 475mm (18in) torpedo tubes
Powerplant:	Single screw petrol engine, electric motor
Performance:	Surfaced: 13 knots, submerged: 7 knots

Baden

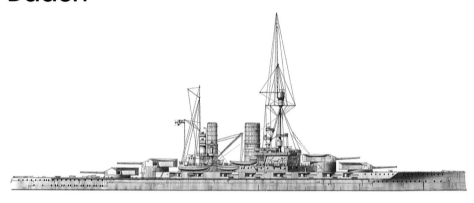

Baden and her sister *Bayern* were completed in 1916. In contrast to earlier classes in the Imperial German Navy, such as the König, their main armament was increased from 304mm (12in) to 380mm (15in). This was to match the guns rumoured to be carried on the new British Queen Elizabeth class. Unusually for a battleship of the period *Baden* was coal-fired, since wartime fuel oil supplies in Germany were too unpredictable. Commissioned too late to have much impact on World War I, *Baden* was Fleet Flagship from October 1916, replacing *Friedrich der Grosse*, and surrendered in 1918. She was not scheduled to be surrendered, but was substituted for the incomplete *Mackensen*. She was unsuccessfully scuttled at Scapa Flow in 1919, and after being salvaged by the Royal Navy was used as a gunnery target, then sunk.

Country:	Germany
Type:	Battleship
Launch date:	30 October 1915
Crew:	1271
Displacement:	32,197 tonnes (31,690 tons) deep load
Dimensions:	179.8m x 30m x 8.43m (589ft 10in x 98ft 5in x 27ft 8in)
Range:	9000km (5000nm) at 10 knots
Armament:	Eight 380mm (15in), 16 150mm (5.9in) guns
Powerplant:	Three shaft turbines
Performance:	22 knots

Badr

Although better described as a Fast Attack Craft (Missile), *Badr* is really a small frigate, carrying much the same armament as larger vessels; the intention is to double the SSM capability in due course with the installation of eight lightweight Otomat or Harpon. She is one of six Ramadan-class boats in service with the Egyptian Navy, all commissioned between 1981 and 1982. The craft were built at the Portchester yard of Vosper Thorneycroft Ltd, some of the hulls being manufactured at Portsmouth Old Yard and towed to Portchester for fitting out. The boats underwent an electronic warfare systems upgrade between 1995 and 1996. They are fitted with the Marconi Sapphire Weapons Control System, with two radar/TV and two optical directors. *Badr*'s British origins keep with a tradition that has seen the Egyptian Navy equipped mostly with British warships since its earliest days.

Country:	Egypt
Type:	Frigate
Launch date:	25 November 1980
Crew:	30
Displacement:	312 tonnes (307 tons)
Dimensions:	52m x 7.6m x 2.3m (170ft 7in x 25ft x 7ft 6in
Range:	2570km (1388nm)
Main armament:	One 76mm (3in) gun; two 40mm (1.5in) gun; OTO Melara SSM; portable SA-N-5 SAM
Powerplant:	Four shafts, four diesel engines
Performance:	40 knots

Baleno

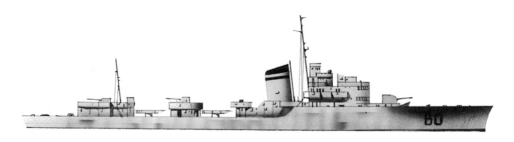

B *aleno* was one of a class of four fast destroyers – the Folgore class – built for the Italian Navy in the early 1930s. They saw hard service in the Mediterranean, being progressively fitted with heavier anti-aircraft armament, and none survived the war, all being sunk in action. On 16 April 1941, *Baleno* and another destroyer, *Luca Tarigo*, were escorting five merchant ships from Sicily to Tripoli. The convoy was sighted by four British destroyers, which attacked immediately. In spite of a gallant fight, the *Luca Tarigo* and the merchantmen were sunk with heavy loss of life. *Baleno* managed to limp away with a severe list, heavily damaged and taking on water. Her crew were unable to carry out enough repairs to keep her afloat, and she capsized and sank the next day. The other vessels in the class – *Folgore, Fulmine* and *Lampo* – were all sunk in action with British surface ships.

Country:	Italy
Type:	Destroyer
Launch date:	22 March 1931
Crew:	450
Displacement:	10,156 tonnes (9996 tons)
Dimensions:	105m x 21m x 7.6m (344ft 6in x 69ft x 25ft)
Range:	3200km (2000 miles)
Armament:	Four 254mm (10in) guns; eight 152mm (6in) guns
Powerplant:	One Ford GAA V-8 petrol engine developing 335.6 or 373 kW (450 0r 500 hp)
Performance:	18 knots

Balilla

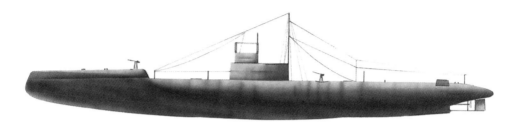

Balilla was originally ordered by the Germany Navy from an Italian yard and was allocated the number *U42*, but the boat never saw German service. Taken over by the Italian Navy in 1915 and named *Balilla,* she saw some service in the Adriatic, but while on patrol on 14 July 1916 she was sunk by Austrian torpedo boats with the loss of all 38 crew members. The principal task of the Italian submarines operating in the Adriatic in World War I was to patrol the coastline of Dalmatia, which had many harbours and inlets that were used by the Austro-Hungarian fleet. Operating conditions were difficult, as the waters were fairly shallow and it was not easy to take evasive action if attacked. Both Austrians and Italians made extensive use of seaplanes once it was found that submerged submarines could often be seen from them.

Country:	Italy
Type:	Attack submarine
Launch date:	August 1913
Crew:	38
Displacement:	Surfaced: 740 tonnes (728 tons), submerged: 890 tonnes (876 tons)
Dimensions:	65m x 6m x 4m (213ft 3in x 19ft 8in x 13ft 1in)
Surface range:	7041km (3800nm) at 10 knots
Armament:	Four 450mm (17.7in) torpedo tubes, two 76mm (3in) guns
Powerplant:	Two-shaft diesel/electric motors
Performance:	Surfaced: 14 knots, submerged: 9 knots

Balny

B*alny*, launched in 1886, was one of a group of 10 ocean-going torpedo boats designed by Normand as a development of existing launches; in particular *Balny* was based upon the design of Poti, which that shipyard had built for the Imperial Russian Navy. However, the ships were not really big enough for their task and rolled badly in heavy seas. This meant that they were clearly not suited to working in their main operational area, which was the Bay of Biscay. All French torpedo craft at this time were designed with offensive operations against Italian naval bases in mind, and possibly against British bases too, as relations between France and Britain in the latter years of the nineteenth century were often tense. All that was to change in just a few more years, when Germany emerged as the principal threat.

Country:	France
Type:	Torpedo boat
Launch date:	January 1886
Displacement:	66 tonnes (65 tons)
Dimensions:	40.8m x 3.4m x 1m (134ft x 11ft x 3ft 3in)
Range:	Not known
Main armament:	Two 355mm (14in) torpedo tubes in the bow
Powerplant:	Single screw compound engine
Performance:	19 knots

Baptista de Andrade

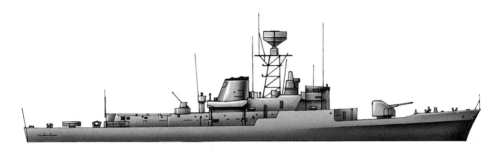

The *Baptista de Andrade* and her three sister ships (*Joao Roby, Afonso Cerquiera* and *Oliveiro E Carmo*) entered service with the Portuguese Navy in the mid-1970s, and a planned modernization programme, which was to include surface-to-surface missiles and SAMs, has been postponed several times. Originally intended for South Africa, the ships were all built by Empresa Nacional Bazan at Cartagena. Their main Creusot-Loire 100mm (3.9in) gun has a rate of fire of 80 rounds per minute and has a range of 17km (9nm) in the surface engagement role or 8km (4.4nm) in the anti-aircraft role, for which it can be elevated to an angle of 80 degrees. The torpedoes carried are the Honeywell Mk46 lightweight anti-submarine variety, which have a speed of 40 knots and are effective up to 11km (5.9nm). Only the *Joao Roby* and *Oliveiro E Carmo* remain in service.

Country:	Portugal
Type:	Frigate
Launch date:	March 1973
Crew:	122
Displacement:	1402 tonnes (1380 tons)
Dimensions:	84.6m x 10.3m x 3.1m (277ft 6in x 33ft 9in x 10ft 2in)
Range:	1019km (5500nm)
Main armament:	One 100mm (3.9in) gun; two Bofors 40mm(1.5in); six 324mm (12.75in torpedoes
Powerplant:	Two shafts, two diesels
Performance:	22 knots

Barham

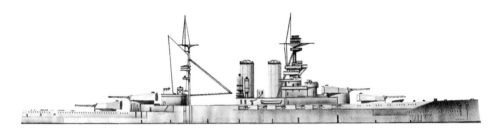

*B**arham** and her three sisters were designed to compete with new battleships (with 355mm [14in] guns) being designed by Germany, Japan and the USA. The class was equipped with newly designed 380mm (15in) guns, which proved more accurate than the previous 343mm (13.5in) guns, and also carried a much bigger bursting charge. Barham was badly damaged at Jutland in 1916. All ships in the class underwent modernisation in the early 1930s. Barham was sunk with heavy loss of life off Sollum in the Mediterranean by U331 on 25 November 1941. The other ships in Barham's class were Malaya, Queen Elizabeth, Valiant and Warspite. After extensive war service, they were broken up in 1947–48. Valiant and Queen Elizabeth were badly damaged in a daring attack by Italian frogmen in Alexandria harbour in 1941.*

Country:	Great Britain
Type:	Battleship
Launch date:	31 October 1914
Crew:	951
Displacement:	32,004 tonnes (31,500 tons)
Dimensions:	196m x 27.6m x 8.8m (643ft x 90ft 6in x 29ft)
Range:	26,100km (14,500nm) at 10 knots
Armament:	Eight 381mm (15in), 14 152mm (6in) guns
Powerplant:	Four shaft turbines
Performance:	24 knots

Barrozo

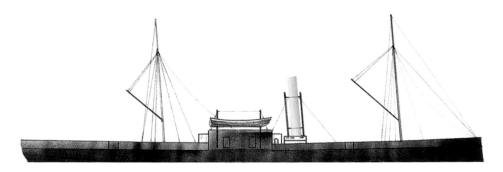

As a country with a long coastline, Brazil always maintained a substantial navy, almost from the moment the country gained its independence from Portugal in 1822. During the conflict with Paraguay it acquired a fleet of small armoured monitors which, like *Barrozo*, waged a river campaign in the interior of the South American continent. *Barrozo* was an armoured central battery ship with a wooden hull, which served extensively in the 1865–70 war with Paraguay. Towards the end of the war in July 1870, the Paraguayans tried to capture *Barrozo* and *Rio Grande* by drifting down river in canoes and then boarding the ships. *Rio Grande* was boarded first, and most of her crew were killed. Meanwhile, *Barrozo* had steamed alongside and was able to kill all the boarders on *Rio Grande*'s deck with grape shot. *Barrozo* was discarded in 1885.

Country:	Brazil
Type:	Monitor
Launch date:	1864
Crew:	70
Displacement:	1375 tonnes (1354 tons)
Dimensions:	57m x 11.2m x 2.4m (186ft x 37ft x 8ft)
Range:	1853km (1000nm) at 8 knots
Armament:	Two 178mm (7in), three 120mm (4.7in) guns
Powerplant:	Single screw single expansion engine
Performance:	9 knots

Basileus Georgios

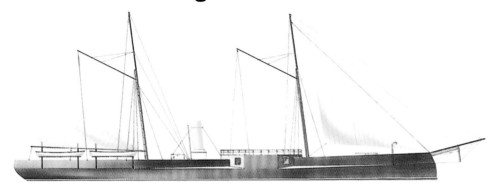

Basileus Georgios was a small central battery ship with a full length armour belt. The armour made up 340 tonnes (335 tons) of the displacement, giving the diminutive battleship greater offensive and defensive capabilities on a small displacement than any other battleship of her time. The battery was placed forward of centre and ahead of the funnel, with end ports in the corners to enable firing ahead or astern. *Basileus Georgios*, named after George I, King of Greece (1845–1913) was one of two small ironclads which had been acquired in the mid-19th century. These remained the principal vessels in service with the Greek Navy until the advent of the three small battleships of the Hydra class (*Hydra*, *Psara* and *Spetsai*) in 1887. No further measures were taken to enhance Greek sea power until 1900.

Country:	Greece
Type:	Battery ship
Launch date:	1867
Crew:	152
Displacement:	1802 tonnes (1774 tons)
Dimensions:	61m x 10m x 4.8m (200ft x 33ft x 16ft)
Range:	2409km (1300nm) at 12 knots
Armament:	Two 229mm (9in) guns
Powerplant:	Twin screw compound engines
Performance:	12.2 knots

Battle class

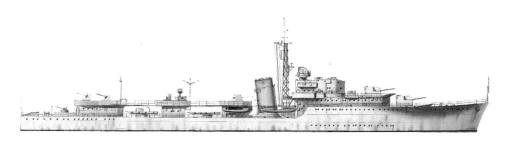

The Battle-class destroyers had their genesis about the time of Matapan, when the Royal Navy was still desperately seeking ways of countering the aerial threat that had been so badly underestimated in the 1930s. Bitter experience had shown that the dive-bomber needed to be countered by plenty of metal, but although the 'pom-pom' was an excellent weapon, main battery guns were capable of only 40 degrees or 55 degrees maximum elevation. The specification for the new destroyer called for 85 degrees and a high rate of fire. The overall result was a very large ship with considerable endurance and twinned gun houses, both sited forward. Only five units were completed before the end of hostilities in Europe, and were deployed to the Pacific in 1945. In that theatre they served in the British Task Force 57, which formed part of the US Fifth Fleet and was based on Ulithi Atoll.

Country:	Great Britain
Type:	Destroyer
Launch date:	December 1943 (first unit)
Crew:	232
Displacement:	2418 tonnes (2380 tons)
Dimensions:	115.52m x 12.26m x 3.28m (379ft x 40ft 3in x 10ft 9in)
Range:	8032km (4337nm)
Main armament:	Two twin and one single 114mm (4.5in) DP plus two twin and two single 40mm (1.5in) AA guns; two quintuple 533mm (21in) torpedo tubes
Powerplant:	Two sets of geared steam turbines
Performance:	35.5 knots

Béarn

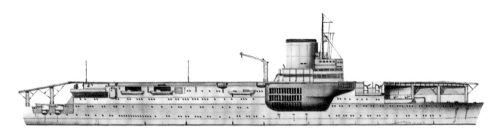

The aircraft carrier *Béarn* was converted from the incomplete hull of a Normandie class battleship, and her original turbine propulsion was replaced by the combined system which was designed for that vessel. In October 1939 she formed a key element of a hunting group (Force L) based on Brest, which, together with other British and French naval forces, was engaged in the search for the German pocket battleship *Admiral Graf Spee*. Apart from that, *Béarn* was not used as a frontline carrier in World War II because of her low speed, but she gave valuable service as an aircraft ferry. After the fall of France in 1940, *Béarn* was captured and held at Martinique to prevent her return to France. After the war she served off Indo-China (Vietnam) during France's conflict there. She was scrapped in 1949.

Country:	France
Type:	Aircraft carrier
Launch date:	April 1920
Crew:	875
Displacement:	28,854 tonnes (28,400 tons)
Dimensions:	182.5m x 27m x 9m (599ft x 88ft 11in x 30ft 6in)
Range:	14,824km (6000nm) at 10 knots
Armament:	Eight 152mm (6in) guns, 40 aircraft
Powerplant:	Four screw geared turbines, triple expansion engines
Performance:	21.5 knots

Bellerophon

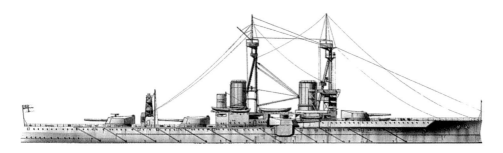

Launched in 1907, *Bellerophon* and her sisters *Temeraire* and *Superb* closely followed the dimensions of HMS *Dreadnought*, though their torpedo defences were increased with improvements to bulkhead armour and secondary armament. When completed in 1909 the Bellerophon class also had masts in front of funnels. This avoided the smoke problems to the command top encountered on *Dreadnought*, which had a single mast behind its forward funnel. *Bellerophon* had an unlucky early career, being damaged in a collision with the battlecruiser *Inflexible* in 1911 and subsequently with the merchant vessel *St Clair* in 1914. She served with the Home Fleet and fought at Jutland in 1916. After World War I she was converted to a gunnery training ship and scrapped under the terms of the Washington Treaty of the 1920s.

Country:	Great Britain
Type:	Battleship
Launch date:	27 July 1907
Crew:	735
Displacement:	22,245 tonnes (22,102 tons)
Dimensions:	160.3m x 25.2m x 8.3m (526ft 6in x 82ft 6in x 278ft 3in)
Range:	10,296km (5720nm) at 12 knots
Armament:	10 305mm (12in), 16 102mm (4in) guns, three torpedo tubes
Powerplant:	Four shaft, geared steam turbines
Performance:	21 knots

Benbow

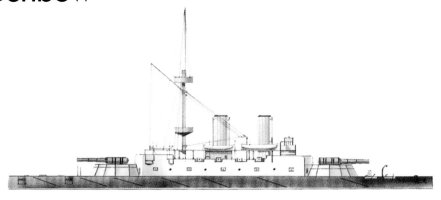

*B*enbow was one of the Rodney class of battleship built in answer to the French Formidable class then under construction. Original armament was to have been four 343mm (13.5in) and eight 152mm (6in) guns, but the Woolwich Arsenal was unable to deliver these and so two 112-tonne (111-ton) guns were mounted instead, in large open barbettes, one fore and one aft. The weight saved was used to install an extra pair of 152mm (6in) guns. There were many problems with the main armament, and the entire battleship class was delayed, *Benbow* herself taking six years to complete. *Benbow* was named after Admiral John Benbow (1653–1702) who was killed in action in the West Indies. The warship spent most of her active service life in the Mediterranean before being paid off in 1904. She was scrapped in 1909.

Country:	Great Britain
Type:	Battleship
Launch date:	15 June 1885
Crew:	523
Displacement:	10,770 tonnes (10,600 tons)
Dimensions:	99m x 21m x 8.2m (325ft x 68ft x 27ft 10in)
Range:	9265km (5000nm) at 8 knots
Armament:	Two 412mm (16.25in), 10 152mm (6in) guns
Powerplant:	Twin screw inverted compound engines
Performance:	17.5 knots

Ben-my-Chree

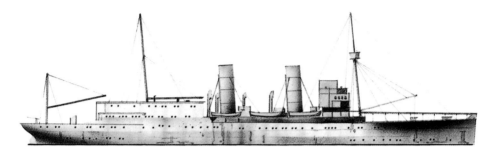

*B*en-my-Chree, a former passenger vessel on the Isle of Man route, was converted into a seaplane carrier in 1915. She was fitted with a large hangar aft, plus a flying-off ramp on the fore deck. She was equipped with the new Sopwith Schneider seaplane fighters. This aircraft had a 100hp rotary engine, an upward-firing Lewis gun and the ability to climb to 3048m (10,000ft) in a little over 30 minutes. With such improvements as these, the Sopwith Schneider presented the first serious threat to the Zeppelin airships which were attacking targets in Great Britain. Later, armed with two torpedo-carrying Short seaplanes, *Ben-my-Chree* served in the Dardanelles campaign, her aircraft sinking two Turkish vessels. While anchored in Kastelorgio harbour in 1917, *Ben-my-Chree* was attacked by Turkish shore batteries and sunk.

Country:	Great Britain
Type:	Seaplane carrier
Launch date:	23 March 1908
Crew:	250
Displacement:	3942 tonnes (3880 tons)
Dimensions:	114m x 14m x 5.3m (375ft x 46ft x 17ft 6in)
Range:	2223km (1200nm) at 10 knots
Armament:	Four, Short 184 seaplanes
Powerplant:	Twin screw turbines
Performance:	24.5 knots

Benedetto Brin

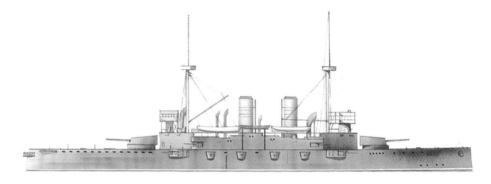

Benedetto Brin was designed by one of the world's leading naval architects at the time and on completion was named after him. The warship's design was a compromise, with her protection being reduced in favour of both speed and firepower. *Benedetto Brin* and her sister *Regina Margherita* were unique ships and had good sea-keeping capabilities. Launched in 1901 and completed in 1905, the warship *Benedetto Brin* was involved in naval operations off Tripoli in 1911 and subsequently in the Aegean Sea in the following year. On 27 September 1915, *Benedetto Brin* was destroyed by a magazine explosion in Brindisi harbour, either as a result of Austrian sabotage or of an accident involving unstable cordite. About half her crew – 421 men – perished in the dramatic incident.

Country :	Italy
Type:	Battleship
Launch date:	7 November 1901
Crew:	812 – 900
Displacement:	13,426 tonnes (13,215 tons)
Dimensions:	138.6m x 23.8m x 8.8m (449ft 6in x 78ft 3in x 29ft)
Range:	18,000km (10,000nm) at 12 knots
Armament:	Four 304mm (12in), four 203mm (8in), 12 152mm (6in) guns
Powerplant:	Twin screw, triple expansion engines
Performance:	20.3 knots

Benson

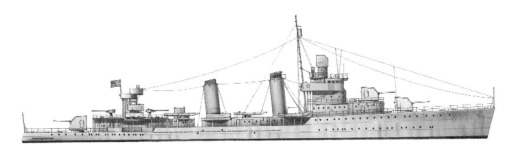

The Benson-Livermore class of destroyers used the same hull and machinery as the earlier Sims class, but had the boiler spaces divided for improved damage control, necessitating a return to two funnels. Only the first 24 hulls were completed with the full designed armament. Ninety-six Bensons were built between 1939 and 1943, and though the last 64 were officially the separate Livermore class, there were only marginal differences, leading to the latter type having a slightly greater displacement. On 10 April 1941, one of the Benson class, the USS *Niblack*, became the first US destroyer in World War II to carry out a depth charge attack on a suspected submarine contact off Iceland. This occurred while she and others of her class were operating the 'Neutrality Patrol', with orders to attack any U-boat that threatened American shipping.

Country:	USA
Type:	Destroyer
Launch date:	15 November 1939
Crew:	250
Displacement:	1646 tonnes (1620 tons)
Dimensions:	106m x 11m x 3m (347ft 9in x 36ft 4in x 10ft 4in)
Range:	9265km (5000nm)
Main armament:	Five single 127mm (5in) DP guns; two quintuple 533mm (21in) torpedo tubes
Powerplant:	Two sets of geared steam turbines
Performance:	37 knots

Berlin

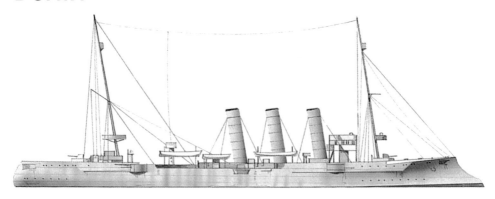

Berlin was a Brandenburg frigate of medium size developed from the larger and slower ships of the line. They were built as a consequence of the growing need for a special vessel to carry out fast scouting work, with sufficient speed to outrun the sloops that were usually deployed as lookouts for a main battle fleet. Frigates were never intended to fight the standard ships of the line, but were employed in cruising the world's oceans, protecting the commercial trade of their own country and attacking that of the enemy. *Berlin* was a good sea boat, and the experience gained from her performance led other countries to develop their own frigates along similar lines. These vessels grew from ships carrying around 20 cannon to larger types mounting over 40 guns on a single deck. The term 'frigate' lapsed from naval terminology in the 19th century, and did not reappear until World War II.

Country:	Germany
Type:	Frigate
Launch date:	22 September 1903
Crew:	375
Displacement:	1016 tonnes (1000 tons)
Dimensions:	48.7m x 11.5m (160ft x 38ft)
Range:	Unlimited, depending on provisions
Main Armament:	Twenty 24-pounder guns
Powerplant:	Sail
Performance:	4 knots

Beskytteren

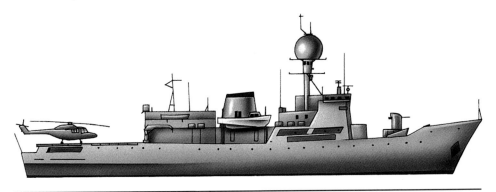

The Royal Danish Navy, though small, has always prided itself on maintaining an effective force of warships, and is very experienced at operating in northern waters. The navy has several frigates, but is equipped mainly with fast attack craft armed with either missiles or torpedoes, and small patrol boats. *Beskytteren* was built in Denmark by the Aalborg Vaerft; she was laid down in December 1974 and commissioned in February 1976. The *Beskytteren* was a modified Hvidbjornen-class frigate with a strengthened structure for ice operations. Used by the Royal Danish Navy for fishery protection duties, in 2000 she was handed over to the Estonian Navy and rechristened *Admiral Pitka*. The vessel carries a Westland Lynx Mk 91 helicopter for reconnaissance and is fitted with two Thorn-EMI Sea Gnat six-barrelled chaff launchers.

Country:	Denmark
Type:	Frigate
Launch date:	27 May 1975
Crew:	56
Displacement:	2002 tonnes (1970 tons)
Dimensions:	74.7m x 12.2m x 5.3m (245ft x 40ft x 17ft 5in)
Range:	7222km (3900nm)
Main armament:	One 76mm (3in) DP gun
Powerplant:	Single shaft, 3 diesels
Performance:	18 knots

Bettino Ricasoli

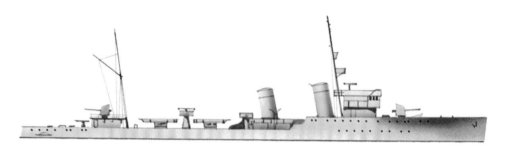

The *Bettino Ricasoli* was one of a group of four vessels built to update the World War I Palestro class. The armament was unusual in that there were two guns mounted aft on a platform with the third on the forecastle. The normal crew of 120 could be increased to 152 in time of war. *Bettino Ricasoli*'s machinery proved unreliable in service, and even at her best she could barely reach 33 knots. She was sold to Sweden and renamed *Puke* (*Pike*), but her engines continued to give trouble and she was stricken in 1947. The sale to Sweden was unusual in that the majority of Sweden's warships were Swedish-built, and probably came about as a result of the need to strengthen the neutral country's coastal defences with the onset of World War II. Sweden, however, was never under threat of invasion by Germany; for commercial and political reasons she was far more useful as a neutral.

Country:	Italy
Type:	Destroyer
Launch date:	29 January 1926
Crew:	120
Displacement:	1480 tonnes (1457 tons)
Dimensions:	85m x 8.5m x 2.8m (278ft 6in x 28ft 2in x 8ft 10in)
Range:	3704km (2000nm)
Main Armament:	Three 120mm (4.7in) guns
Powerplant:	Twin screw geared turbines
Performance:	33 knots

Bismarck

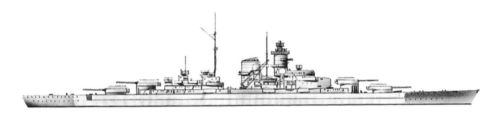

The 1919 Treaty of Versailles imposed tight restrictions on German naval developments. In spite of this, the Germans managed to carry out secret design studies, and when the Anglo–German Naval Treaty of 1935 came into force, were able to respond quickly. They began the construction of two battleships, *Bismarck* and *Tirpitz*. As they had been unable to properly test new hull forms, they used the World War I *Baden* design. While they were equipped with powerful modern engines and were fine, well-armed warships, the dated armour configuration meant that the steering gear and much of the communications and control systems were poorly protected. In May 1941, *Bismarck* was sent on a raiding mission into the Atlantic, but the Royal Navy caught up with her. In the ensuing battles she sunk *Hood*, before suffering so much damage that her crew scuttled her.

Country:	Germany
Type:	Battleship
Launch date:	14 February 1939
Crew:	2039
Displacement:	50,955 tonnes (50,153 tons)
Dimensions:	250m x 36m x 9m (823ft 6in x 118ft x 29ft 6in)
Range:	15,000km (8100nm) at 18 knots
Armament:	Eight 380mm (15in), 12 152mm (6in) guns, six aircraft
Powerplant:	Three shaft geared turbines
Performance:	29 knots

Blaison

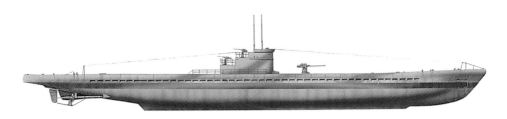

Blaison was formerly the German Type IXB submarine *U-123*. She was operational from May 1940 until August 1944, when, unable for technical reasons to comply with orders to break out of Lorient and sail for Norway, she was scuttled. She was raised and commissioned into the French Navy as *Blaison* in 1947, serving until 1951. She was then placed in reserve and eventually scrapped in August 1958. Several other ex-German submarines also served with the French Navy post-war; they were the Type IXC *U510*, which surrendered at St Nazaire and became the *Bouan;* the Type VIIC *U471*, which was repared after being damaged by air attack at Toulon and commissioned as *Mille;* and the Type VIIC *U766*, which surrendered at La Pallice and became the *Laubie.* The most sought-after prize, though, was the new Type XXI.

Country:	France
Type:	Attack submarine
Launch date:	1940
Crew:	48
Displacement:	Surfaced: 1050 tonnes (1034 tons), submerged: 1178 tonnes (1159 tons)
Dimensions:	76.5m x 6.8m x 4.7m (251ft x 22ft 4in x 15ft 5in)
Surface range:	4632km (2500nm) at 16 knots
Armament:	Six 533mm (21in) torpedo tubes; one 105mm (4.1in) gun
Powerplant:	Two twin-shaft diesel engines, two electric motors
Performance:	Surfaced: 18 knots, submerged: 7.3 knots

Blitz

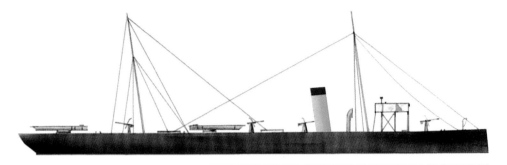

B*litz* and her sister ship *Komet* were designed to combat the much-improved type of torpedo boats that were then entering service with the world's navies. Normal gunboats were too slow to keep up with the fleet, so the torpedo gunboat, with its high speed and large number of light guns, seemed to be the answer. The ships were, in effect, prototype destroyers. Torpedo tubes were positioned with one in the bow, one firing aft and two on a turntable amidships. Apart from *Komet*, the other ships in the Blitz class were *Meteor*, *Planet*, *Trabant*, *Satellit*, *Magnet* and *Huszar*. The latter sank in December 1908 and the rest were ceded to Italy after World War I with the exception of *Satellit*, which went to France. They were broken up in 1920. All the destroyers except *Blitz* and *Komet* were built to different designs for evaluation purposes, so that one could be selected for standardization.

Country:	Austria
Type:	Destroyer
Launch date:	7 July 1888
Crew:	56
Displacement:	433 tonnes (426 tons)
Dimensions:	59m x 7m x 2m (193ft 6in x 22ft 11in x 6ft 6in)
Range:	Not known
Main armament:	Nine 3-pounder guns; four 355mm (14in) torpedo tubes
Powerplant:	Single screw, triple expansion engines
Performance:	26 knots

Bodryi

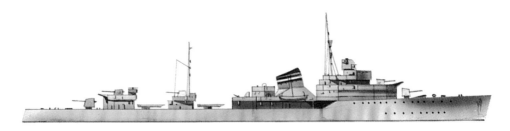

In the early 1930s the weakness of the Russian destroyer force was obvious and, as a result, in 1932 a new type of destroyer was designed with the help of Italy. However, it was not until 1935 that the first vessel of the new class, known as the Type 7, was laid down. *Bodryi* was among the first group of 28 ships, which were found to lack seaworthiness under the often severe conditions of the Arctic and northern Pacific areas in which they were intended to serve. In fact, *Bodryi*'s area of operations was the Black Sea where she served in the Soviet Navy's 2nd Destroyer Division. In the winter of 1941–42 she was heavily involved in transporting troops and supplies to the besieged fortress of Sevastopol. Damaged beyond repair in an air attack in July 1942, she was eventually broken up in 1958. In all, 20 ships of this class were lost in World War II.

Country:	Soviet Union
Type:	Destroyer
Launch date:	1936
Crew:	180
Displacement:	2072 tonnes (2039 tons)
Dimensions:	113m x 10m x 4m (370ft 3in x 33ft 6in x 12ft 6in)
Range:	4630km (2500nm)
Main Armament:	Four 127mm (5.1in) guns
Powerplant:	Twin screw geared engines
Performance:	32 knots

Bombarda

B *ombarda* was one of 59 Gabbiano-class escorts built under a wartime
specification that called for a cheap, quick-to-build anti-submarine vessel for
service in the Mediterranean. Two auxiliary electric motors of 150hp each were
fitted to allow silent AS search at 6 knots, although these were not incorporated in
Bombarda. Most of the class were seized by the Germans shortly after Italy's
armistice with the Allies; *Bombarda* was captured on the slip on 11 September
1943 and numbered *UJ206*. She was severely damaged in an air attack at Venice on
25 April 1944 and scuttled there by the Germans a year afterwards. Later refloated
and rebuilt for post-war service with the Italian Navy, she was not withdrawn from
use until 1975. Other long-serving ships of the class were *Baionetta, Chimera,
Cormorano, Crisalide, Farfalla, Gabbiano, Ibis, Scimitarra, Sibilla* and *Urania*.

Country:	Italy
Type:	Corvette
Launch date:	31 August 1942
Crew:	109
Displacement:	740 tonnes (728 tons)
Dimensions:	64.3m x 8.7m x 2.5m (211ft x 28ft 7in x 8ft 4in)
Range:	5556km (3000nm)
Main armament:	One 102mm (4in) gun; depth charges
Powerplant:	Twin screw diesel engines
Performance:	18 knots

Bombardiere

Launched in March 1942, *Bombardiere* was one of the second group of Soldati-class destroyers that eventually formed the largest class of destroyer built for the Italian Navy. Their anti-aircraft armament, inadequate at first, was progressively improved. On 21 November 1942, she was in company with the destroyers *Legionario* and *Velite*, escorting a small convoy in the Bay of Naples, when she was attacked by the British submarine HMS *Splendid*; she evaded the torpedoes, which destroyed the *Velite*. On 17 January 1943, while engaged in a reinforcement operation to Tunisia, she was sunk by the submarine HMS *United* (Lt Roxburgh) off Marettimo. Three vessels of this class, *Legionario, Mitragliere* and *Velite*, were transferred to France under the terms of the Peace Treaty and renamed *Duchaffault, Jurien de la Graviäre* and *Duperre*.

Country:	Italy
Type:	Destroyer
Launch date:	23 March 1942
Crew:	250
Displacement:	2540 tonnes (2500 tons)
Dimensions:	107m x 10m x 3.5m (350ft x 33ft 7in x 11ft 6in)
Range:	6300km (3400nm)
Main Armament:	Five 120mm (4.7in) guns
Powerplant:	Twin screw turbines
Performance:	38 knots

Bombe

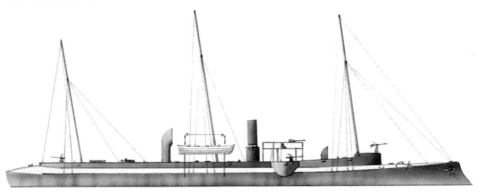

Bombe and her seven sister vessels of this class were distinguished by their three light raking masts, originally with a fore and aft rig, and a single raking funnel abaft the foremast. The boilers fitted in this class gave a great deal of trouble, and completion was delayed as a result. The bow was slightly ram-shaped; the stern had an overhang and the sides curved in to a narrow upper deck. The ships had 12.7mm (0.5in) of armour plate to protect their conning towers, and the main guns were mounted forward and aft and in sponsons on either beam, wuith the torpedo tubes further aft. One ship in the class, *Dragonne*, was fitted for experimental trials with howitzers in 1896. All eight vessels – *Bombe, Couleuvrine, Dague, Dragonne, Fleche, Lance, Sainte-Barbe* and *Salve* – were completed between 1887 and 1890, and were stricken between 1906 and 1914.

Country:	France
Type:	Torpedo gunboat
Launch date:	April 1885
Crew:	70
Displacement:	375 tonnes (369 tons)
Dimensions:	59.2m x 6m x 3.1m (194ft 3in x 19ft 7in x 10ft 5in)
Range:	Not known
Main armament:	Two 355mm (14in) torpedo tubes; four 3-pounder guns; three 1-pounder revolvers
Powerplant:	Twin screw vertical compound engines
Performance:	18–19 knots

Borea

***B**orea* and her five sisters formed the first major class of torpedo craft to be built in Italy. All ships were later reboilered, and their armament was modified. In 1915, minelaying equipment was added. *Nembo* was sunk in 1916 by the Austrian submarine *U16* which, in turn, was sunk by the exploding depth charges on the sinking ship. *Borea* was sunk by the Austrian destroyers *Csepel* and *Balaton* on 14 May 1917. Much of the Italian Navy's destroyer activity in World War I was centred in the Adriatic, where priority was given by both sides to mining the approaches to one another's harbours. The Italians had the more difficult task, for the Dalmatian coastline was riddled with natural harbours and inlets that gave shelter to Austrian shipping. Two more vessels of the Nembo class, to which *Borea* belonged, were lost in action with Austro–Hungarian naval forces.

Country:	Italy
Type:	Destroyer
Launch date:	12 December 1902
Crew:	90
Displacement:	386 tonnes (380 tons)
Dimensions:	64m x 6m x 2.3m (210ft x 19ft 6in x 7ft 6in)
Range:	1850km (1000nm)
Main Armament:	Five 76mm (3in) guns; four 355mm (14in) torpedo tubes
Powerplant:	Twin screw triple expansion engine
Performance:	26 knots

Borea

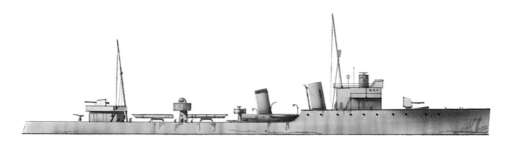

This class of eight fast destroyers were improved versions of the earlier Sauro class, being slightly longer and having more powerful machinery. In sea trials, the design speed of 36 knots was often exceeded. One of the class, *Turbine*, managed to maintain 40 knots for over four hours, although 33 knots was an average figure under operational conditions. Afer a few years of operational use, *Borea* was modified to carry anti-shipping mines; she could hold up to 52 of these weapons depending on type and size. All these ships served in the Italian Navy in World War II, although none survived the conflict. The *Borea* was sunk by Swordfish aircraft from the carrier HMS *Illustrious* off Benghazi on 17 September 1940. One of the class, *Euro*, was sunk by German bombers on 1 October 1943, a few weeks after Italy surrendered to the Allies.

Country:	Italy
Type:	Destroyer
Launch date:	28 January 1927
Crew:	105
Displacement:	1697 tonnes (1670 tons)
Dimensions:	93m x 9m x 4m (305ft 9in x 30ft x 9ft 10in)
Range:	2224 km (1200nm)
Main Armament:	Four 120mm (4.7in) guns
Powerplant:	Twin screw geared turbines
Performance:	36 knots

Bourrasque

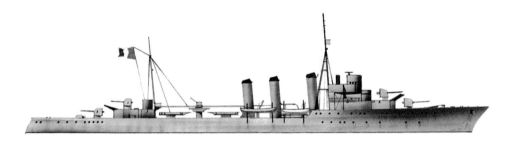

The 12 vessels of the Bourrasque class formed part of the 1922 programme by which France planned to upgrade her navy. *Bourrasque* was well armed and compared favourably with her contemporaries. However, any advantage that might have been gained from using a large-calibre gun was lost because the rate of fire was only four to five rounds per minute. All ships in the class underwent armament modifications, and some were stripped of the aft 127mm (6in) gun to improve stability. *Bourrasque* was lost while evacuating troops from Dunkirk on 30 May 1940, being shelled and mined off Nieuport. Two ships of this class, *Mistral* and *Ouragan*, were in British ports at the time of the armistice in June 1940, and were taken over. *Mistral* was manned by a Royal Navy crew until 1944 and *Ouragan* served with the Polish Navy for a time before being turned over to the Free French.

Country:	France
Type:	Destroyer
Launch date:	5 August 1925
Crew:	104
Displacement:	1930 tonnes (1900 tons)
Dimensions:	105.7m x 10m x 4.2m (347ft x 31ft 9in x 14ft)
Range:	4630km (2500nm)
Main Armament:	Four 127mm (5in) guns
Powerplant:	Twin screw geared turbines
Performance:	26 knots

Bouvet

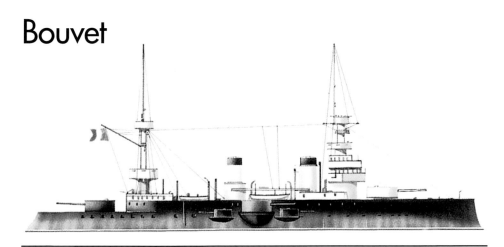

Named after Admiral Pierre François Henri Bouvet (1775–1860), commander of the French naval forces during the Napoleonic Wars, *Bouvet* was the last of the basic Charles Martel design and was thought to be the best of the group. She lacked the massive superstructure of the preceding group, and had a built-up stern which improved seaworthiness. In January 1903, she was damaged in a collision with the battleship *Gaulois* in the Mediterranean. After a substantial refit in 1913 she escorted Mediterranean convoys after the outbreak of World War I. In March 1915, *Bouvet* took part in an attack in the Dardanelles, during which she was seriously damaged by Turkish guns before running onto a mine. She rapidly filled with water, and her bulkheads collapsed. She sank in two minutes with the loss of 660 lives.

Country:	France
Type:	Destroyer
Launch date:	24 April 1896
Crew:	710
Displacement:	12,200 tonnes (12,007 tons)
Dimensions:	118m x 21m x 8.3m (386ft 6in x 70ft 2in x 27ft 6in)
Range:	7412km (4000nm) at 10 knots
Armament:	Two 305mm (12in), two 275mm (10.8in) guns
Powerplant:	Triple screw, vertical expansion engines
Performance:	18 knots

Boykiy

Boykiy was one of six Krupny-class destroyers built during the 1960s. They were originally completed as missile ships. Initial construction started in 1958 at Leningrad. Original armament was the SS-N-1 anti-ship missile, but when this became obsolete, the whole group was converted to the anti-submarine warfare role. Other ships in the class were the *Gnevnyi, Gordyi, Plamyonny* and *Zorkyi*. They were the first Soviet destroyers to have a helicopter platform fitted as standard, probably because a helicopter was necessary to provide mid-course corrections to the anti-ship missiles. They were also the last developments of the original *Kotlin* destroyer concept to be built, later designs making use of gas turbine propulsion or new high-pressure steam plant. Three ships of the class were converted to the SAM role.

Country:	Soviet Union
Type:	Destroyer
Launch date:	15 December 1960
Crew:	360
Displacement:	4826 tonnes (4750 tons)
Dimensions:	140m x 15m x 5m (458ft 9in x 45ft 9in x 16ft 6in)
Range:	11,112km (6000nm)
Main Armament:	Eight 57mm (2.25in) guns, plus missiles
Powerplant:	Twin screw geared steam turbines
Performance:	34 knots

Brandenburg

The four Type 123 Brandenburg-class frigates (the others are *Schleswig-Holstein*, *Bayern* and *Mecklenburg-Vorpommern*) were all commissioned between 1994 and 1996 and are based with the 6th Frigate Squadron of the German Navy at Wilhelmshaven. They were formerly known as the Deutschland class, and were ordered in 1989 to replace the deleted Hamburg class. They are extremely well armed and carry a formidable array of electronic equipment, including air search D-band and air/sea search F-band radars. They are fitted with the Atlas Elektronik/Paramax SATIR combat data system and their design, developed by Blohm und Voss, incorporates stealth technology. On-board space is allocated for a Task Group Commander and his battle staff. The ships of this class are optimized for combat in the relatively confined waters of the Baltic.

Country:	Germany
Type:	Frigate
Launch date:	28 August 1992
Crew:	199 plus 19 aircrew
Displacement:	4775 tonnes (4700 tons)
Dimensions:	138.9m x 16.7m x 6.8m (455ft 8in x 54ft 9in x 22ft 3in)
Range:	6430km (3472nm)
Main armament:	One 76mm (3in) DP gun; four Exocet; 16 Sea Sparrow SAMs; four 324mm (12.75in) anti-submarine torpedo tubes
Powerplant:	Two shafts, two gas turbines, two diesels
Performance:	29 knots

Bremen

A Germanised modification of the gas turbine-powered Dutch Kortenaer design, the eight-ship Bremen class of Type 122 frigates replaced the German Navy's elderly Fletcher-class destroyers and Köln-class frigates. The first order was placed in 1977, and the first ship was commissioned in May 1982. The ships are fitted with fin stabilisers; a complete NBC defence citadel system is also fitted. The eight ships in service are the *Bremen* (F207), *Niedersachsen* (F208), *Rheinland-Pfalz* (F209), *Emden* (F210), *Köln* (F211), *Karlsruhe* (F212), *Augsburg* (F213) and *Lübeck* (F214). Like the Brandenburgs, the Bremen class were intended for operations in the Baltic, but some units have been deployed farther afield in recent years. All have received an updated EW fit since 1994, and current plans call for them to remain in first-line service well into the twenty-first century.

Country:	Germany
Type:	Frigate
Launch date:	27 September 1979
Crew:	204
Displacement:	2977 tonnes (2930 tons)
Dimensions:	130.5m x 14.4m x 6m (428ft 1in x 47ft 3in x 19ft 7in)
Range:	12,970km (7000nm)
Main Armament:	Two quadruple Harpoon missile launchers; one octuple NATO Sea Sparrow SAM launcher; two RAM close-range SAM launchers; one 76mm (3in) gun; four 324mm (12.75in) torpedo tubes
Powerplant:	Two gas turbines, two diesels
Performance:	32 knots

Bretagne

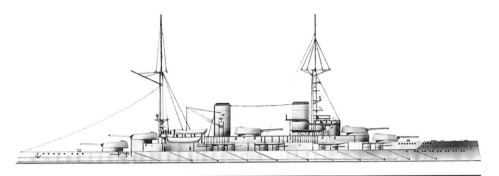

Because France found herself falling behind in the dreadnought naval race, *Bretagne* and her sisters *Provence* and *Lorraine* were based on the design of the preceding Courbet class to cut down construction time. *Bretagne* served in the Mediterranean from 1916–18, then underwent a series of extensive modernisations in 1921–23, 1927–30 and 1932–35. With the surrender of France in 1940, *Bretagne* and other French naval warships were called upon to join a British alliance, but the French admiral Gensoul refused. British warships, their gunfire directed by Swordfish spotter aircraft from the carrier *Ark Royal*, opened fire on the French vessels in their anchorage at Oran in Algeria. Heavy shells tore into the magazine of *Bretagne*, which blew up and capsized with the loss of 1012 lives.

Country:	France
Type:	Battleship
Launch date:	21 April 1913
Crew:	1133
Displacement:	29,420 tonnes (28,956 tons)
Dimensions:	166m x 27m x 10m (544ft 8in x 88ft 3in x 32ft 2in)
Range:	8460km (4700nm) at 10 knots
Armament:	10 340mm (13.4in) guns
Powerplant:	Quadruple screw geared turbines
Performance:	20 knots

Brin

B*rin* (named after the celebrated Italian naval engineer Benedetto Brin) was one of a class of long-range submarines with a partial double hull developed from the Archimede class. A distinguishing feature of the Brin class was their tall conning tower. She was active from the beginning of Italy's involvement in World War II, initially forming part of a submarine squadron covering the approaches to the Aegean Sea. In 1941, as part of an Italian submarine group based on French Atlantic ports, she operated against Allied convoys in the sea area west of Gibraltar. Following the Italian armistice in September 1943, *Brin,* under Allied command, transferred to Ceylon and was used to train Allied anti-submarine warfare forces in the Indian Ocean, a role in which she became quite famous. She was discarded in 1948.

Country:	Italy
Type:	Attack submarine
Launch date:	3 April 1938
Crew:	58
Displacement:	Surfaced: 1032 tonnes (1016 tons), submerged: 1286 tonnes (1266 tons)
Dimensions:	70m x 7m x 4.2m (231ft 4in x 22ft 6in x 13ft 6in)
Surface range:	18,530km (10,000nm) at 10 knots
Armament:	Eight 533mm (21in) torpedo tubes, one 100mm (3.9in) gun
Powerplant:	Twin screw diesel engines, two electric motors
Performance:	Surfaced: 17 knots, submerged: 8 knots

Broadsword

The British Leander class of general-purpose frigate, which entered service in the 1960s, served the Royal Navy well for many years; 26 were built. The Leaders were to have been succeeded by 26 examples of the Type 22 Broadsword class, conceived as ASW ships for use in the Greenland–Iceland–UK gap against Soviet high-performance nuclear submarines, but in the event only 14 were produced. *Brilliant* and *Broadsword* distinguished themselves in action during the 1982 Falklands war. All the Batch 1 vessels were sold to Brazil: *Broadsword* on 30 June 1995, *Brilliant* and *Brazen* on 30 August 1996, and *Battleaxe* on 30 April 1997. The Batch 2 Broadswords, *Boxer, Beaver, Brave, London, Sheffield* and *Coventry*, have now all been decommissioned. *Boxer* and *Brave* are to be used as targets, while the others may be sold.

Country:	Great Britain
Type:	Frigate
Launch date:	12 May 1976
Crew:	286
Displacement:	4470 tonnes (4400 tons)
Dimensions:	131m x 14.8m x 4.2m (430ft 5in x 48ft 8in x 14ft)
Range:	7408km (4000nm)
Main Armament:	Four M38 Exocet launchers; two 30mm (1.6in) guns; two sextuple Sea Wolf SAM; Sting Ray torpedoes
Powerplant:	Twin screw gas turbine engines
Performance:	30 knots

Broadsword III

The Broadswords were built in three batches, of which Batch 3 was a general purpose variant. The four Batch 3 units are HMS *Cornwall*, *Cumberland*, *Campbeltown* and *Chatham*. All the Batch 3 vessels have enlarged flight decks for the operation of Sea King or EH101 Merlin helicopters, although a single Westland Lynx is usually embarked for peacetime operations. The Batch 3 ships are fitted with two Rolls-Royce Spey SM1A and two Rolls-Royce Tyne gas turbines; the more powerful Spey SM1C engines might be retrofitted in due course. The Seawolf GWS25 short-range SAM system is being progressively upgraded, as is the electronic warfare fit. The Batch 3 Broadswords are deployed with the 2nd Frigate Squadron. They are highly capable ships, and the appelation 'frigate' seems rather inappropriate when applied to vessels displacing some 5000 tonnes.

Country:	Great Britain
Type:	Frigate
Launch date:	14 October 1985 (HMS Cornwall)
Crew:	273
Displacement:	4877 tonnes (4800 tons)
Dimensions:	148.1m x 14.8m x 6.4m (458ft 10in x 48ft 6in x 21ft)
Range:	7238km (3906nm)
Main armament:	Four 30mm (1.1in); two 20mm (0.7in) guns; Exocet SSMs; Seawolf SAMs; six 324mm (12.75in) Stingray torpedo tubes
Powerplant:	Two shafts, four gas turbines
Performance:	30 knots

Bullfinch

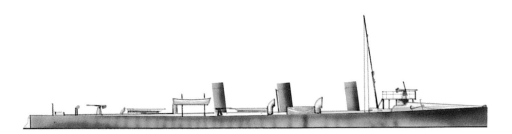

By the late nineteenth century, the combination of torpedo and torpedo boat represented a real threat to the Royal Navy's capital ships. The solution was to counter the torpedo boats with gun-armed 'catchers' that could be deployed from capital ships, and by the 1890s these had evolved into larger, independent vessels called 'torpedo boat destroyers' designed to accompany larger units. Between 1892 and 1893, the first six ships, now called simply 'destroyers', were ordered for service with the Royal Navy. By 1895, 36 destroyers, led by HMS *Gossamer* and HMS *Rattlesnake*, had been launched and were succeeded by an improved class, the first of which were HMS *Havoc* and HMS *Hornet*, which could make 30 knots and were armed with two torpedo tubes mounted on the centreline, one 12-pounder and five six-pounder guns. HMS *Bullfinch* was one of 68 built over these two classes.

Country:	Great Britain
Type:	Destroyer
Launch date:	10 February 1898
Crew:	63
Displacement:	396 tonnes (390 tons)
Dimensions:	65m x 6m x 2.5m (214ft 6in x 20ft 6in x 7ft 10in)
Range:	2778km (1500nm)
Main Armament:	One 12-pounder; five six-pounders; two 457mm (18in) torpedo tubes
Powerplant:	Twin screw triple expansion engines
Performance:	30 knots

Byedovi

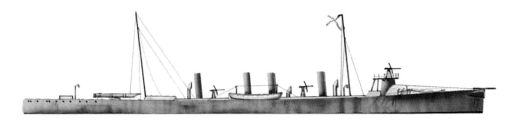

Byedovi was one of a group of 22 destroyers of this class laid down in Russian yards between 1900 and 1903 that followed the successful British-built *Sokol* of 1895 in general design. Many of the class saw service in the Russo-Japanese war of 1904–5, and gave good service. After the Battle of Tsushima in May 1905, *Byedovi* – one of the few Russian warships that was still undamaged – attempted to escape to Vladivostok with the wounded Russian commander, Admiral Rozhestvensky, on board. However, she was intercepted by Japanese destroyers and compelled to surrender. Impressed into service with the Imperial Japanese Navy, she was scrapped in 1922. Some of these vessels took part in the final evacuation of White Russian refugees from the Black Sea ports in 1920 and ferried them to North Africa, mostly to Bizerta. Their eventual fate is unknown.

Country:	Russia
Type:	Destroyer
Launch date:	1902
Crew:	80
Displacement:	355 tonnes (349 tons)
Dimensions:	56.6m x 6m x 3m (185ft 6in x 19ft 6in x 9ft 8in)
Range:	2778km (1500nm)
Main Armament:	One 12-pounder and five three-pounder guns; three 380mm (15in) torpedo tubes
Powerplant:	Twin screw vertical triple expansion engines
Performance:	26.5 knots

C1 class

The C1 class of submarine, designated I-16 in Japanese Navy service, was the product of a massive naval building programme initiated by the Japanese government after the expiry of the London Naval Treaty. There were five boats in the class (*I-16, I-18, I-20, I-22* and *I-24*) and they had an extremely long radius of action, being able to remain at sea for 90 days without replenishment. At the beginning of 1943 *I-16* had her 140mm (5.5in) gun removed and the number of torpedoes reduced. With special fittings she could carry a 14m (46ft) landing craft, or equipment and stores for Japanese troops on islands isolated by the Allied advance. The *I-16* was sunk off the Solomon Islands by a 'hedgehog' ASW mortar salvo from a US destroyer escort group on 19 May 1944. The USS *England* of this group sank six Japanese submarines in 12 days.

Country:	Japan
Type:	Attack submarine
Launch date:	28 July 1938
Crew:	100
Displacement:	Surfaced: 2605 tonnes (2564 tons), submerged: 3761 tonnes (3701 tons)
Dimensions:	108.6m x 9m x 5m (256ft 3in x 29ft 5in x 16ft 4in)
Surface range:	25,928km (14,000nm)
Armament:	Eight 533mm (21in) torpedo tubes; one 140mm (5.5in) gun
Powerplant:	Two-shaft diesel/electric motors
Performance:	Surfaced: 23.5 knots, submerged: 8 knots

C3

All the C-class boats gave good service to the Royal Navy, and were well liked by their crews. In 1910, by which time 37 were in service, three of them, escorted by the sloop *Rosario*, were towed to the Far East to join the China Squadron at Hong Kong, a truly epic voyage for submarines in those early pioneer days, and three more went to Gibraltar. During World War I four C-class boats were sent to Russia, but were scuttled to prevent them falling into German hands in the Baltic. *C3* herself had a dramatic exit; on 23 April 1918 she was filled with high explosive and, commanded by Lt Richard D. Sandford, crept into Zeebrugge harbour and was exploded under a steel viaduct as part of the British blocking operation there. The two officers and four men aboard were picked up, although wounded; Sandford was awarded the Victoria Cross.

Country:	Great Britain
Type:	Attack submarine
Launch date:	1906
Crew:	16
Displacement:	Surfaced: 295 tonnes (290 tons), submerged: 325 tonnes (320 tons)
Dimensions:	43m x 4m x 3.5m (141ft x 13ft 1in x 11ft 4in)
Surface range:	2414km (1431nm) at 8 knots
Armament:	Two 457mm (18in) torpedo tubes
Powerplant:	Single screw petrol engine, one electric motor
Performance:	Surfaced: 12 knots, submerged: 7.5 knots

Caiman

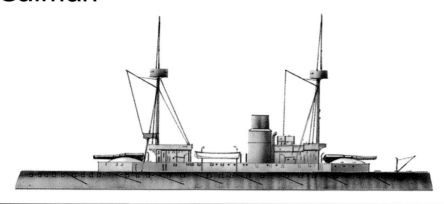

At the end of the 1870s, France abandoned the broadside ironclad battleships in her use, and instead adopted the barbette system of mounting the heavy guns high above the waterline away from any damage that could be caused by rough seas. *Caiman* was laid down in 1878. She was one of four large coastal defence vessels which were noted for their heavy armour and ordnance, with two heavy guns placed in barbettes. The other vessels in this class were *Indomptable*, *Requin* and *Terrible*. All of the vessels except *Terrible* were rebuilt between 1895 and 1901 to include both new boilers and new armament. *Requin*, rebuilt with two funnels on the centreline and military masts, survived to serve in World War I. *Caiman* ended her days as a discarded hulk at Rochefort in 1910; she was broken up in 1927.

Country:	France
Type:	Battleship
Launch date:	21 May 1885
Crew:	373
Displacement:	7650 tonnes (7259 tons)
Dimensions:	82.6m x 18m x 8m (271ft x 59ft x 26ft 2in)
Range:	3243km (1750nm) at 10 knots
Armament:	Two 420mm (16.5in) guns
Powerplant:	Twin screw, vertical compound engines
Performance:	15 knots

Cairo

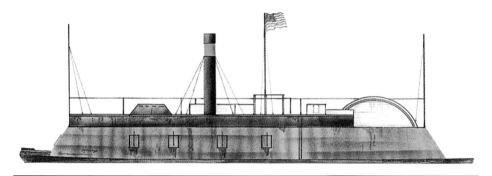

The Union ship *Cairo* was a converted low-draught paddle steamer. Typical of the type of craft which fought along the rivers during the American Civil War, *Cairo* and hundreds like her were instrumental in denying the rebels use of the continent's waterways, which effectively split up the Confederacy. These craft served with the Western Flotilla and took part in a number of notable actions; on 6 February 1862, for example, they bombarded the rebel-held Fort Henry, commanding the Tennessee River, into submission. *Cairo* had a low wooden hull surmounted by a large armoured casement with sloping sides. Muzzle-loading guns were stationed broadside and forward. Additional armour was constructed round the engines and rear paddle. *Cairo* was sunk by a Confederate mine in the Mississippi on 2 December 1862.

Country:	USA
Type:	Armoured steamer
Launch date:	Not known
Crew:	50
Displacement:	902 tonnes (887 tons)
Dimensions:	53m x 16m x 2m (173ft 9in x 4ft 9in x 6ft 6in)
Range:	Not known
Armament:	Three 203mm (8in), three 178mm (7in) guns
Powerplant:	Single stern wheel driven by two non-condensing reciprocating engines
Performance:	8 knots

Calatafimi

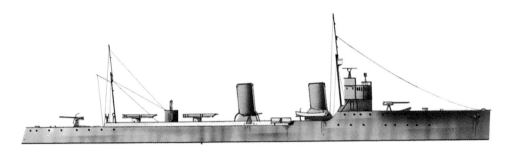

Originally ordered in 1915, *Calatafimi* and her three sisters were delayed due to a shortage of materials created by the demands of the army; *Calatafimi* herself was not launched until March 1923. In 1938 the vessels were reclassified as torpedo boats and their armament was altered, a single 102mm (4in) gun replacing the twin mount aft. After the Italian surrender in September 1943, *Calatafimi*, together with several other boats of her class, was impressed into service by the Germans for service in the Aegean. Renamed *TA19*, she took part in many escort operations with the 9th Torpedo Boat Flotilla before being torpedoed and sunk by the Greek submarine *Pipinos* on 9 August 1944. As the war in Europe approached its end this type of vessel was hounded to destruction not only by surface forces, but by rocket-armed aircraft like the Beaufighter and Hurricane.

Country:	Italy
Type:	Destroyer
Launch date:	17 March 1923
Crew:	105
Displacement:	894 tonnes (880 tons)
Dimensions:	85m x 8m x 3m (278ft 9in x 26ft 3 in x 9ft 9in)
Range:	3333km (1800nm)
Main Armament:	Four 102mm (4in) guns; six 444mm (17.5in) torpedo tubes
Powerplant:	Two shaft geared turbines
Performance:	30 knots

Calliope

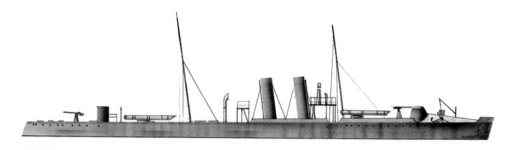

Launched in August 1906, *Calliope* was one of a group of eight torpedo boats based upon the design of Thorneycroft, who were among the world's leading builders of torpedo craft. Built by Pattison of Naples, the last of the class were launched in 1909 and were intended for service in the Adriatic. They were good, stoutly-built seagoing vessels, their hull plates thicker than those of the previous Perseo class. Two of the class were fitted with oil-burning boilers which slightly reduced the displacement and gave greater endurance. *Calliope*'s armament was later changed to two 76mm (3in) guns and one machine gun. All ships in the class gave good service during World War I. *Calliope* was stricken in 1924. *Calliope* was the second Italian torpedo boat to bear the name; the first was a member of the Euterpe class of 1883.

Country:	Italy
Type:	Torpedo boat
Launch date:	27 August 1906
Crew:	65
Displacement:	220 tonnes (216 tons)
Dimensions:	53m x 5m x 2m (173ft 11in x 17ft 5in x 5ft 10in)
Range:	1482km (800nm)
Main armament:	Three 47mm (1.85in) guns; three 450mm (17.7in) torpedo tubes
Powerplant:	Twin screw vertical triple expansion engines
Performance:	26.5 knots

Canada

In 1911 Chile had two new battleships under construction, but all work on these vessels ceased in 1914 and *Almirante Latorre*, the most advanced of the two, was subsequently bought by the Royal Navy and renamed *Canada*. Her sister ship, the *Almirante Cochrane*, was also taken over by the British and converted into a carrier named *Eagle*. *Canada* was a lengthened 'Iron Duke' type battleship. She had two large unequal funnels and a high tripod foremast and pole mainmast. Completed in 1915, *Canada* spent her entire war service with the Grand Fleet at Scapa Flow. She was one of the most effective battleships in the fleet; she saw action at the Battle of Jutland in 1916, and took part in the blockade of Germany. *Canada* was returned to Chile in 1920 and continued to see service as one of that country's capital ships.

Country:	Chile
Type:	Battleship
Launch date:	27 November 1913
Crew:	1176
Displacement:	32,634 tonnes (32,120 tons)
Dimensions:	202m x 28m x 9m (660ft 9in x 92ft x 29ft)
Range:	8153km (4400nm) at 10 knots
Armament:	10 355mm (14in) guns
Powerplant:	Quadruple screw geared turbines
Performance:	22.8 knots

Canberra

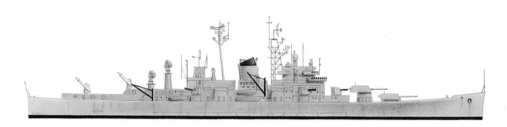

Originally commissioned in 1941 as a Baltimore class cruiser, *Canberra* saw much war service in the central Pacific from 1944, in the battle for Truk and in heavy raids on Japanese-held islands as part of the US Task Group 58. In October 1944, she was badly damaged by a torpedo off Okinawa. She was rebuilt and recommissioned in 1955 as one of two Boston-class missile cruisers. *Canberra* and her sister *Boston* were the first US Navy vessels specifically designed as anti-aircraft missile ships and were rushed into service during the Cold War. Armed with Terrier missiles in place of their aft turrets, their forward turrets were also to be replaced with missiles, though this never occurred. Instead, other ships were converted to increase the US Navy's anti-aircraft missile capability. *Canberra* was stricken in 1978.

Country:	USA
Type:	Cruiser
Launch date:	19 April 1943
Crew:	1544
Displacement:	18,234 tonnes (17,947 tons)
Dimensions:	205.4m x 21.25m x 7.6m (673ft 5in x 69ft 8in x 24ft 11in)
Range:	13,140km (7300nm) at 12 knots
Armament:	Two Terrier surface-to-air missiles (72 missiles per launcher), six 203mm (8in), 10 127mm (5in) guns
Powerplant:	Four shaft geared turbines
Performance:	33 knots

Canopus

Canopus-class battleships were intended for service on the Pacific station where the growing power of Japan and Russia was causing concern. The Canopus class were the first British battleships to have water tube boilers, which provided higher power and greater economy. They were also some of the last predreadnoughts. At full speed *Canopus* used 10 tonnes (9 tons) of coal per hour. Launched in 1897, she was stationed at the Falkland Islands during World War I, and was briefly in action against von Spee's cruiser squadron in December 1914, though she did not engage. She later took part in the Dardanelles operation in 1915, before returning to home waters. The only damage *Canopus* sustained during her career was in August 1904, when she was in collision with the battleship *Barfleur* in Mounts Bay. She was sold in 1920.

Country:	Great Britain
Type:	Battleship
Launch date:	12 October 1897
Crew:	750
Displacement:	14,520 tonnes (14,300 tons)
Dimensions:	118m x 23m x 8m (390ft x 74ft x 26ft)
Range:	14,824km (8000nm) at 10 knots
Armament:	Four 304mm (12in), 12 152mm (6in) guns
Powerplant:	Twin screw, triple expansion engines
Performance:	18.5 knots

Capitan Prat

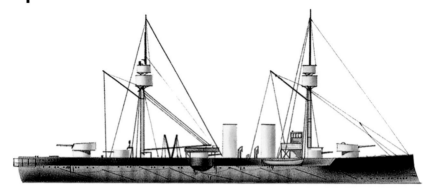

During 1887 the Chilean government decided to modernise its navy by
purchasing the latest type of warships from Europe. A 6096-tonne (6000-ton)
battleship was part of the programme. The French firm of Forges et Chantiers
de la Méditerranée won the contract, and *Capitan Prat* was laid down in 1888.
Her 239mm (9.4in) guns were mounted singly in turrets, one at each end of the
vessel and one on each side of the hull. A secondary battery of eight 120mm
(4.7in) guns was mounted in twin turrets on the upper deck. Armour alone took
up one third of her displacement. Until World War I, *Capitan Prat* was Chile's
most powerful warship. After reconstruction in 1909–10 she served as a
submarine depot ship. The vessel, named after a naval officer killed in action
when his ship was sunk by a Peruvian ironclad, was stricken in 1935.

Country:	Chile
Type:	Battleship
Launch date:	12 December 1890
Crew:	480
Displacement:	7011 tonnes (6910 tons)
Dimensions:	100m x 18.5m x 7m (328ft x 60ft 8in x 22ft 10in)
Range:	8616km (4650nm) at 10 knots
Armament:	Four 239mm (9.4in) guns
Powerplant:	Twin screw, horizontal triple expansion engines
Performance:	18.3 knots

Carabiniere

The Italian frigates *Alpino* and *Carabiniere*, originally named *Circe* and *Climene*, were provided for under the 1959–60 programme. The original Circe-class project was modified in 1962. The new design was an improved version of the Centauro class, combined with the Bergamini class. They had similar basic characteristics, but a heavier displacement and increased engine power. Two other ships of the same type, to have been named *Perseo* and *Polluce*, were provided for under the 1960–61 programme, but were suspended for reasons of economy. The Alpino-class frigates were the first Italian warships to be powered by gas turbines, but they were capable of making a steady 22 knots on diesels alone. Part of their task was to provide an ASW screen for the US Sixth Fleet. *Alpino* is now a mine-countermeasures ship and *Carabiniere* is a weapons trial vessel.

Country:	Italy
Type:	Frigate
Launch date:	30 September 1967
Crew:	254
Displacement:	2743 tonnes (2700 tons)
Dimensions:	113m x 13m x 4m (371ft x 43ft 6in x 12ft 7in)
Range:	7408km (4000nm)
Main Armament:	Six 76mm guns; six 305mm (12in) torpedo tubes; one A/S mortar
Powerplant:	Twin screw, diesels, gas turbines
Performance:	28 knots (all engines)

Carlo Bergamini

The four frigates of this class – the others being the *Carlo Margottini*, *Luigi Rizzo* and *Virginio Fasan* – were all laid down in 1957 with the exception of the last-named, which was laid down in 1960. They were novel for their type in that they had diesel- instead of steam propulsion. Later, the vessels were given an enhanced anti-submarine capability, being allocated an AB204 A/S helicopter each. The flight deck was enlarged, and this made it necessary to remove the single gun and mountings astern. The single-barrelled automatic depth charge mortars fitted to these frigates have a range of 915m (1000yds) and a rate of fire of 15 depth charges per minute. The Bergamini class were designed to be the smallest type of warship capable of operating an anti-submarine helicopter, but this was over-ambitious, and as originally built they were disappointing.

Country:	Italy
Type:	Frigate
Launch date:	16 June 1960
Crew:	160
Displacement:	1676 tonnes (1650 tons)
Dimensions:	94m x 11m x 3m (308ft 3in x 37ft 3in x 10ft 6in)
Range:	7412km (4000nm)
Main Armament:	Three 76mm (3in) guns; six 305mm (12in) torpedo tubes; one A/S depth charge mortar
Powerplant:	Twin screw diesel
Performance:	26 knots

Cassard

Four destroyers of the Cassard class were originally laid down, but two were subsequently cancelled. The *Cassard* and her sister ship, *Jean Bart*, were laid down in September 1982 and March 1986 respectively at the Lorient Naval Dockyard, and commissioned in July 1988 and September 1991. The building programme was subjected to serious delays because of financial constraints and doubts about the effectiveness of the increasingly obsolescent Standard SM-1 surface-to-air missile system; there are plans to replace this with the Aster 30 system as the ships are refitted. The radar and countermeasures equipment carried by the two ships is of French design. The ships have a helicopter platform at the stern for use by a single Aerospatiale Panther, now replacing the Lynx which was carried earlier. Both ships are based at Toulon.

Country:	France
Type:	Destroyer
Launch date:	6 February 1985
Crew:	225
Displacement:	4806 tonnes (4730 tons)
Dimensions:	139m x 14m x 6.5m (455ft 11in x 45ft 9in x 21ft 3in)
Range:	13,182km (7118nm)
Main armament:	One 100mm (3.9in) gun; Exocet; Mistral anti-sea-smimming missiles; standard SAMs; ASW torpedoes
Powerplant:	Two shafts, four diesel engines
Performance:	29.5 knots

Castle class

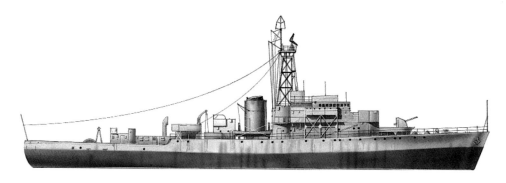

In terms of size, the Castle class of anti-submarine corvette was somewhat larger than the earlier Flower class, which it closely resembled. The Castles were elegant ships, and incorporated all the lessons learned from their forebears. They also incorporated the new Squid anti-submarine mortar, a weapon too heavy to be retrofitted into the Flower-class corvettes or River-class frigates. The Squid's big advantage was that it could lay a pattern of three heavy bombs around a submerged target up to 502m (550yd) ahead while the contact was still in the ship's sonar beam. The performance of the Castle-class vessels did not match that of the frigates, so they were not used as close convoy escorts; instead, they were formed into homogenous escort groups, which were later being deployed in large numbers towards the end of World War II.

Country:	Great Britain
Type:	Corvette
Launch date:	June 1943 (first units)
Crew:	120
Displacement:	1070 tonnes (1060 tons)
Dimensions:	76.8m x 11.2m x 3.05m (252ft x 36ft 9in x 10ft)
Range:	6910km (3725nm)
Main armament:	One 102mm (4in) gun; 10 20mm (0.7in) AA; AS mortar and depth charges
Powerplant:	Single shaft, triple expansion steam engine
Performance:	16.5 knots

Centauro

L aunched in April 1954, *Centauro* was one of a class of four vessels built to
Italian plans and specifications and funded under the US off-shore programme
of the 1950s which aimed to increase the military power of friendly nations. All
units had automatic anti-submarine and medium anti-aircraft armament, plus US
sonar equipment. The guns were mounted one above the other in twin gun houses
and could fire 60 rounds per minute. All four ships underwent armament
modification between 1966 and 1967, the changes including the mounting of three
76mm (3in) guns, replacing the two 2-barrelled 76mm (3in) and the four 40mm
(1.5in) AA guns. The other vessels in the class were the *Canopo*, *Cigno* and
Castore. In 1960 the four ships, originally classified as destroyers with 'D' pennant
numbers, were reclassified as frigates and allocated 'F' pennant numbers.

Country:	Italy
Type:	Destroyer
Launch date:	4 April 1954
Crew:	255
Displacement:	2255 tonnes (2220 tons)
Dimensions:	103.3m x 11.5m x 3.5m (339ft x 38ft x 11ft 6in)
Range:	4630 km (2500nm)
Main Armament:	Four 76mm (3in) guns
Powerplant:	Twin screw geared turbines
Performance:	26 knots

Centurion

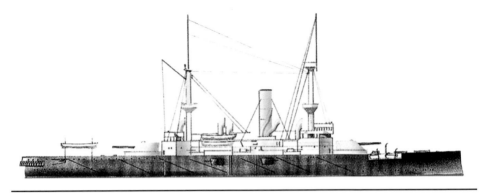

*C*enturion and her sister vessel *Barfleur* were second-class battleships that formed part of the large expansion programme for the Royal Navy begun in 1889. They were intended to counteract the powerful armoured cruisers of the Russian Navy in the Pacific. The relatively light draught of the vessels enabled them to navigate China's rivers with ease. From 1894 to 1901, *Centurion* saw action on the China Station, helping to protect British and Allied interests in the various Boxer uprisings. After reconstruction work in 1901–03, in which she was rearmed and had her foremast removed, *Centurion* returned to China, where in 1904 she was badly damaged in a collision with the battleship *Glory*. In 1910 *Centurion* was sold for scrap and subsequently broken up at Morecambe, Cumbria.

Country:	Great Britain
Type:	Battleship
Launch date:	3 August 1892
Crew:	620
Displacement:	10,668 tonnes (10,500 tons)
Dimensions:	110m x 21m x 7.7m (360ft x 70ft x 25ft 6in)
Range:	11,118km (6000nm) at 10 knots
Armament:	Four 254mm (10in) guns
Powerplant:	Twin screw, triple expansion engines
Performance:	18.5 knots

Chao Phraya

The four ships of the Chao Phraya class are basically Jianghu-class vessels, two of them Type IIIs. These vessels were built for the Thai Navy by the China State Shipbuilding Corporation under a contract signed in July 1988. Although plans were made to build two more in Thailand, they were subsequently shelved. The Thai Navy originally wanted only the hulls built in China, as it was planned to install equipment purchased in the USA, but as a condition for the deal, China insisted on fitting out the ships completely and on installing Chinese armament simultaneously. When the ships arrived in Thailand between 1991 and 1992, the shipbuilding standards were found to be so poor that they had to be docked for extensive repair, and also to improve damage control facilities. The poor workmanship in Chinese yards is due almost entirely to an over-emphasis on strict regimentation.

Country:	Thailand
Type:	Frigate
Launch date:	24 June 1990
Crew:	168
Displacement:	1955 tonnes (1924 tons)
Dimensions:	103.2m x 11.3m x 10.2m (338ft 6in x 37ft 1in x 10ft 2in)
Range:	5626km (3038nm)
Main armament:	Two or four 100mm (3.9in) guns; eight 37mm (1.4in) guns; A/S mortars and depth charges
Powerplant:	Two shafts, four diesel engines
Performance:	30 knots

Charlemagne

With *Charlemagne* and her two sister ships, France followed the design trend of other great powers at the time and adopted twin mountings for the main armament. Completed in 1899, her design tried to achieve too much on a small displacement, but even so she was a good economical steamer. She burnt less than 10 tonnes (9 tons) of coal per hour at full speed. In March 1903, she was in collision with one of her sister vessels, the *Gaulois* (the other was the *Saint Louis*) but she escaped damage. In World War I *Charlemagne*'s role was to escort Mediterranean convoys. The steamer also took part in operations at Salonika and in the Dardanelles, where she was damaged by shore batteries. Returning to service after repair and refit, *Charlemagne* was stricken in 1918 and broken up in 1920.

Country:	France
Type:	Battleship
Launch date:	17 October 1895
Crew:	694
Displacement:	11,277 tonnes (11,100 tons)
Dimensions:	114m x 20m x 8m (374ft x 66ft 5in x 27ft 6in)
Range:	7783km (4200nm) at 10 knots
Armament:	Four 304mm (12in) guns
Powerplant:	Triple screw, triple expansion engines
Performance:	18 knots

Charles Martel

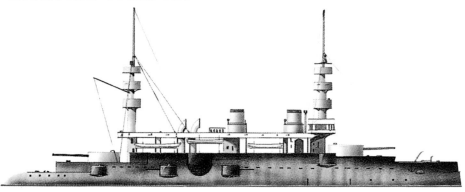

Laid down in 1891, *Charles Martel* was part of the French naval programme intended to replace all their wooden-hulled ironclads by 1900. In the usual French practice she had her main armament laid out in lozenge or diamond fashion. The two 304mm (12in) guns were mounted fore and aft in armoured turrets, while the two 274mm (10.8in) weapons were in smaller turrets, on sponsons which protruded from each side of the hull. Her secondary armament was eight 140mm (5.5in) guns in electrically driven turrets on the main and upper deck. She had a distinctive appearance, with a high forecastle, and a covered flying bridge linking both masts. Her interior was also broken up into dozens of separate watertight compartments, which helped reduce the chance of catastrophic damage from a penetrating hit. She saw service throughout World War I and was stricken and scrapped in 1922.

Country:	France
Type:	Battleship
Launch date:	20 August 1893
Crew:	644
Displacement:	11,880 tonnes (11,693 tons)
Dimensions:	115m x 22m x 8m (378ft 11in x 71ft 2in x 27ft 6in)
Range:	6022km (3520nm) at 10 knots
Armament:	Two 304mm (12in), two 274mm (10.8in) guns
Powerplant:	Twin screw, triple expansion engines
Performance:	18 knots

Charlie I class

The Charlie I class were the first Soviet nuclear-powered guided-missile submarines capable of launching surface-to-surface cruise missiles without having to surface first. They were similar in some respects to the Victor class, although there are visible differences that include a bulge at the bow, the almost vertical drop of the forward end of the fin, and a slightly lower after casing. The Charlie I carried the SS-N-15 nuclear-tipped anti-submarine missile, which has a range of 37km (20nm) and also the SS-N-7 submerged-launch anti-ship missile for pop-up surprise attacks. The Charlie Is were all built at Gorky between 1967 and 1972. One was leased to India in January 1988, and another sank off Petropavlovsk in June 1983; it was later salvaged, only to sink again by its jetty in 1985. The remaining ten, all based in the Pacific, were decommissioned in the 1990s.

Country:	Soviet Union
Type:	Attack submarine
Launch date:	1967
Crew:	100
Displacement:	Surfaced: 4064 tonnes (4000 tons), submerged: 4877 tonnes (4800t)
Dimensions:	94m x 10m x 7.6m (308ft x 32ft 9in x 25ft)
Range:	Unlimited
Armament:	Eight SS-N-7 cruise missiles, six 533mm (21in) torpedo tubes
Powerplant:	Nuclear, one pressurized water reactor, one steam turbine
Performance:	Surfaced: 20 knots, submerged: 27 knots

Charlie II class

The Charlie II class, built between 1972 and 1980 at Gorki, was an improved Charlie I with a 9m (29ft 6in) insertion in the hull forward of the fin to house the electronics and launch systems necessary for targeting and firing the SS-N-15 and SS-N-16 weapons. In both Charlie classes, once the missiles were expended the submarine had to return to base to be reloaded. The six Charlie II boats were also armed with the SSN-9 Siren anti-ship missile, which cruises at 0.9 Mach and has a range of 110km (60nm) and can be fitted with either a nuclear (250kT) or conventional warhead. The Charlie II-class vessels were all based with the Northern Fleet, and made occasional deployments to the Mediterranean before decommissioning in the mid-1990s. One boat of this class sank off the Kamchatka peninsula in June 1983; it was raised in August, but did not re-enter service.

Country:	Soviet Union
Type:	Attack submarine
Launch date:	1973
Crew:	110
Displacement:	Surfaced: 4572 tonnes (4500 tons), submerged: 5588 tonnes (5500t)
Dimensions:	102.9m x 10m x 7.8m (337ft 7in x 32ft 10in x 25ft 7in)
Range:	Unlimited
Armament:	Six 533mm (21in) and two 650mm (25.6in) torpedo tubes; eight cruise missiles
Powerplant:	Nuclear, one pressurized water reactor
Performance:	Surfaced: 20 knots, submerged: 26 knots

Chen Yuan

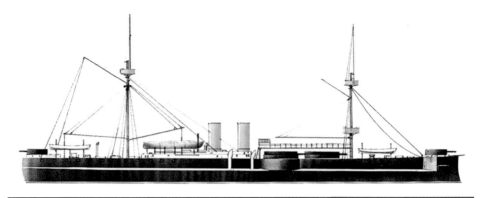

By the end of the 1870s the Chinese had decided to modernise their navy along the lines of powers in the West. As a consequence, a major programme was begun in the 1880s, and *Chen Yuan* and her sister *Ting Yuen* became China's only battleships. Both were steel-hulled, and featured a strongly armoured central citadel which covered the engines, boilers and magazines. Both were German-built by the Vulcan shipyards at Stettin, and sailed to China under the German mercantile flag. In September 1894, *Chen Yuan* was severely damaged in the Battle of the Yalu during the Sino-Japanese War and later went aground at Wei Hai Wei, where she was damaged again by Japanese batteries and foundered. In 1895, she was captured by the Japanese, refloated and commissioned in the Imperial Japanese Navy. She was scrapped in 1914.

Country:	China
Type:	Battleship
Launch date:	28 November 1882
Crew:	350
Displacement:	7792 tonnes (7670 tons)
Dimensions:	94m x 18m x 6m (307ft 9in x 59ft x 20ft)
Range:	8338km (4500nm) at 10 knots
Armament:	Four 304mm (12in), two 152mm (6in) guns
Powerplant:	Twin screw, horizontal compound engines
Performance:	15.7 knots

Chidori

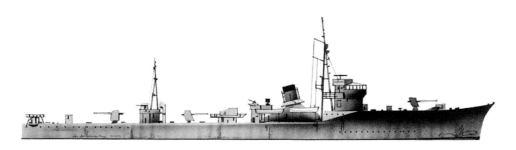

*C*hidori was one of the Tomozuru class of four vessels laid down between 1931 and 1933. With their armament of three 127mm (5in) guns and two 533mm (21in) torpedo tubes, they were virtually small destroyers, but they turned out to be dangerously unstable because of excessive topweight. *Tomozuru* capsized in heavy weather while running trials in March 1934, but was brought into port and righted. All ships in the class were rebuilt to correct the defect, and had a lighter armament mounted, plus the additions of 61 tonnes (60 tons) of permanent ballast to increase displacement. Once modified, the Tomozurus were amongst the most efficient and dangerous of Japanese anti-submarine vessels. *Chidori* was sunk by the US submarine *Tilefish* (Lt-Cdr Kaithley) on 22 December 1944. The *Hatsukari* alone survived the war, being surrendered at Hong Kong.

Country:	Japan
Type:	Torpedo boat
Launch date:	1 April 1933
Crew:	100
Displacement:	749 tonnes (737 tons)
Dimensions:	82m x 7.4m x 2.5m (269ft x 24ft 3in x 8ft 2in)
Range:	2779km (1500nm)
Main armament:	Three 127mm (5in) guns; two 533mm (21in) torpedo tubes
Powerplant:	Twin screw turbines
Performance:	28 knots

Chikugo

Chikugo was built by the Mitsui Zozen Company, Tamano, as part of the 1967 new construction programme and was launched on 13 January 1970. Designed and built with structural features to reduce noise and vibration, the Chikugo class ships – 11 of which were laid down in 1968 – were used primarily for coastal ASW missions around the Japanese home islands. To facilitate their use in this role, they were equipped to carry and operate the SQS35(J) variable-depth sonar from an open well which was located offset to starboard at the stern. They were also the smallest warships in the world designed to carry the ASROC ASW missile launcher system; the midships launcher was trained to the bearing and then elevated to fire a two-round salvo of the solid-fuel RUR-5A rockets with their torpedo payloads out to a range of 9.2km (5.7 miles). All 11 ships have now been stricken.

Country:	Japan
Type:	Frigate
Launch date:	13 January 1970
Crew:	165
Displacement:	1493 tonnes (1470 tons)
Dimensions:	93m x 11m x 4m (305ft 5in x 35ft 5in x 11ft 6in)
Range:	6482km (3500nm)
Main Armament:	Two 76mm (3in) guns
Powerplant:	Twin screw diesels
Performance:	25 knots

Cigno

Launched in 1956, the *Cigno* and her three sister ships (see entry for *Centauro*) were built for the Italian Navy to Italian designs, but were financed by the US offshore programme. All had US sonar equipment and carried automatic anti-submarine and medium anti-aircraft armament. The Italian-made 76mm (3in) guns were mounted in twin turrets and could fire 60 rounds per minute. In the 1960s, the gun turrets were replaced by three single 76mm (3in) mounts. The main ASW weapon was the new Italian Menon mortar. The ships were in fact designed as escort destroyers rather than frigates, and their hull was a scaled-down version of the Impetuoso-class design. The ships were decommissioned in rotation as each vessel was replaced by one of the Maestrale class. All four vessels in the class had retired from service by the late 1980s.

Country:	Italy
Type:	Frigate
Launch date:	20 March 1955
Crew:	255
Displacement:	2455 tonnes (2220 tons)
Dimensions:	103.3m x 11.5m x 4m (339ft x 38ft x 11ft 6 in)
Range:	4630km (2500nm)
Main Armament:	Four 76mm (3in) guns
Powerplant:	Twin screw geared turbines
Performance:	28 knots

Clémenceau

Clémenceau was one of three French battleships laid down between 1935 and 1939. The others were *Richelieu* and *Jean Bart*; a fourth – *Gascoigne* – was ordered but later cancelled. When France fell in 1940, the Germans found *Clémenceau*'s incomplete hull in dock at Brest. When the Allies invaded France, the Germans considered using it to block the harbour entrance, but she was sunk during a bombing raid in August 1944. The illustration shows her as she would have looked if completed according to the 1940 plans. Her two sister ships both saw service; *Richelieu* was taken over by the Allies and served in the Indian Ocean in 1944–45, and *Jean Bart*, having been damaged by gunfire during the Allied landings in North Africa in 1942, was completed after the war and took part in the Anglo-French Suez operations in 1956.

Country:	France
Type:	Battleship
Launch date:	1943
Crew:	1550
Displacement:	48,260 tonnes (47,500 tons)
Dimensions:	247.9m x 33m x 9.6m (813ft 2in x 108ft 3in x 31ft 7in)
Range:	(est): 15,750km (8500nm) at 14 knots
Armament:	Eight 381mm (15in) guns
Powerplant:	Quadruple screw, geared turbines
Performance:	(est): 25 knots

Clémenceau

*C*lémenceau *(R98)* and her sister *Foch (R99)* were originally intended as part of class of six fleet carriers, but only two were built. *Clémenceau* was ordered from Brest dockyard in May 1954, while *Foch* began construction at St Nazaire and was completed at Brest. They were the first French purpose-built carriers, and *Clémenceau* underwent constant modification during design and construction. She served the French Navy well, operating in the Pacific, off the coast of Lebanon, and taking part in the 1991 Gulf War. During her career she was extensively modernised, with new defensive weapons and command systems added. Her air wing normally comprised 16 Super Étendards, 3 Étendard IVP, 10 F-8 Crusaders, 7 Alizé, plus helicopters. In later years she operated more helicopters than fixed-wing aircraft. She was replaced by the nuclear-powered *Charles de Gaulle.*

Country:	France
Type:	Aircraft carrier
Launch date:	21 December 1957
Crew:	1338, or 984 (as a helicopter carrier)
Displacement:	33,304 tonnes (32,780 tons)
Dimensions:	257m x 46m x 9m (843ft 2in x 150ft x 28ft 3in)
Range:	13,500km (7500nm) at 12 knots
Armament:	Eight 100mm (3.9in) guns, 40 aircraft
Powerplant:	Twin screw geared turbines
Performance:	32 knots

Cleveland

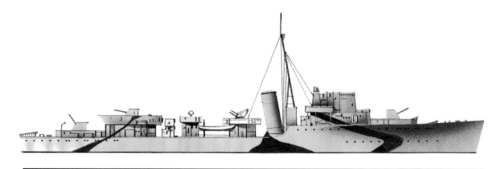

In 1938, the worsening situation on the world stage caused great alarm in Britain, and efforts were made to increase the strength of the Royal Navy. However, when World War II broke out, Britain was still short of destroyers to escort her vital Atlantic convoys. By 1940 the Royal Navy decided to put in hand a programme of small destroyers that could be quickly and easily constructed. *Cleveland* was one of the first group of Hunt-class destroyers subsequently built. Originally they were designed to carry six 102mm (4in) guns, but this armament proved too top-heavy, and the number of guns was reduced to four. Although ballast and stabilisers were added to reduce roll in a seaway, movement was jerky. Launched in April 1940, *Cleveland* survived World War II, only to be wrecked in June 1957, on her final voyage to the shipbreakers.

Country:	Great Britain
Type:	Destroyer
Launch date:	1 November 1941
Crew:	146
Displacement:	922 tonnes (907 tons)
Dimensions:	85.3m x 8.8m x 3.8m (280ft x 29ft x 12ft 6in)
Range:	3704km (2000nm)
Main Armament:	Four 102mm (4in) guns
Powerplant:	Twin screw geared turbines
Performance:	26 knots

Collingwood

Collingwood was the prototype of the new British Admiral battleship class laid down in the summer of 1880. Later units varied, especially in the fitting of heavier guns, but she was to set the overall design for British battleships for the next 20 years. A transverse water chamber was fitted at each end of the vessel to steady her when rolling. The main deck ran from end to end of the hull, upon which were carried the four heavy guns mounted in pairs in two barbettes on the centreline. Because of her low freeboard, *Collingwood* was very wet in a seaway. In 1886 she was damaged when a faulty 12in gun burst on trials. In 1887 she joined the Mediterranean Fleet and served with it for 10 years before returning home for a refit as a coastguard ship. She was placed on the reserve in 1903 and scrapped in 1909.

Country:	Great Britain
Type:	Battleship
Launch date:	22 November 1882
Crew:	498
Displacement:	9652 tonnes (9500 tons)
Dimensions:	99m x 21m x 8m (324ft 10in x 68ft x 26ft 3in)
Range:	12,917km (7000nm) at 10 knots
Armament:	Four 304mm (12in), six 152mm (6in) guns
Powerplant:	Twin screw, inverted compound engines
Performance:	17 knots

Collins

The contract for the licence production of six Swedish-designed Kockums Type 471 SSKs by the Australian Submarine Corporation, Adelaide, was signed on 3 June 1987. Fabrication work began in June 1989, the bow and midships sections of the first submarines being built in Sweden. Diving depth of the boats is 300m (984ft). The submarines are named *Collins, Farncomb, Waller, Dechaineux, Sheean* and *Rankin*. The boats can carry 44 mines in lieu of torpedoes if required. The Collins-class submarines are very quiet, and their long range makes them very suited to operations in the southern Pacific. All are based at Fleet Base West, with east coast deployments. There have been a number of problems with the Collins class, with *Dechaineux* narrowly avoiding sinking after a hose broke underwater. *Collins* has spent long periods in dock under repair and upgrade.

Country:	Australia
Type:	Attack submarine
Launch date:	28 August 1993
Crew:	42
Displacement:	Surfaced: 3100 tonnes (3051 tons), submerged: 3407 tonnes (3353 tons)
Dimensions:	77.8m x 7.8m x 7m (255ft 2in x 25ft 7in x 23ft)
Surface range:	18,496km (9982nm) at 10 knots
Armament:	Six 533mm (21in) torpedo tubes; Sub Harpoon SSM
Powerplant:	Single shaft, diesel/electric motors
Performance:	Surfaced: 10 knots, submerged: 20 knots

Colossus

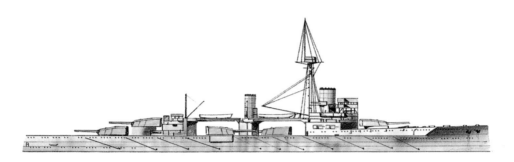

Colossus and her sister ship *Hercules* formed part of the rapid British naval expansion programme of 1909. *Colossus* had an improvement over previous dreadnoughts in that she was built with stronger armour protection. To save weight the aftermast was omitted, but the foremast, with its vital fire control centre, was placed behind the first funnel, although this meant that she suffered severely from smoke interference. *Colossus* was one of the last British battleships to mount 305mm (12in) guns; the next major group would carry the new 343mm (13.5in) weapons. During the Battle of Jutland in 1916, where she was flagship of the Battle Fleet's 5th Division, she was hit by two shells. She subsequently served as a cadet training ship before being sold for scrap and broken up at Alloa, Scotland, in 1922.

Country:	Great Britain
Type:	Battleship
Launch date:	9 April 1910
Crew:	755
Displacement:	23,419 tonnes (23,050 tons)
Dimensions:	166m x 26m x 9m (546ft x 85ft x 28ft 9in)
Range:	12,024km (6680nm) at 12 knots
Armament:	10 305mm (12in) guns
Powerplant:	Four shaft turbines
Performance:	21 knots

Comet

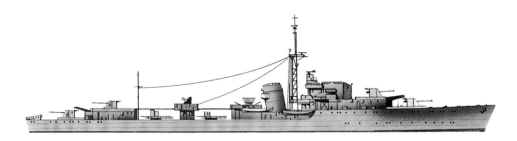

HMS *Comet*, launched in June 1944, was one of 31 C-class destroyers built in the last two years of World War II. They all followed the same basic pattern, with two guns firing ahead and two aft. There was a single sloping funnel behind the bridge. Additional anti-aircraft guns were added as the vessels entered service, and one of the class, HMS *Contest*, was the first British destroyer with an all-welded hull. All vessels in the class survived the war. Four went to Norway in 1946, and four were handed over to Pakistan in the 1950s. Two more saw service with the Royal Canadian Navy. HMS *Comet* was scrapped at Troon, Scotland, in November 1962. Together with the Battle class, the C class were among the last true destroyers built for the Royal Navy, for with the disappearance of the line of battle there was no further need for conventional destroyers.

Country:	Great Britain
Type:	Destroyer
Launch date:	22 June 1944
Crew:	186
Displacement:	1737 tonnes (1710 tons)
Dimensions:	111m x 11m x 4m (362ft 9in x 35ft 8in x 14ft 5in)
Range:	4074km (2200nm)
Main Armament:	Four 114mm (4.5in) guns
Powerplant:	Twin screw turbines
Performance:	36.7 knots

Commandant Teste

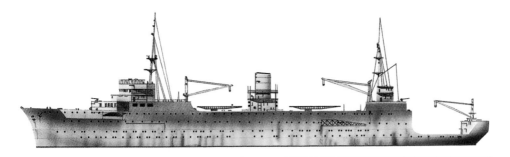

C *ommandant Teste* served in the Mediterranean until World War II. She was
scuttled at Toulon when France surrendered, and was not raised again until
the end of the war. The scuttling was somewhat premature; although a large part
of the French fleet was disarmed under the terms of the armistice, it was agreed
that no vessels were to be handed over to the Germans. At that time there were
two battleships, two large destroyers, eight smaller destroyers, seven submarines
and 200 small craft in British harbours, with the rest of the French fleet at Oran.
After refitting, she served as a store ship. In the late 1940s there were plans to
convert her to a flush-decked aircraft carrier, but the plans were never effected.
She was scrapped in 1950, after serving for nearly 30 years in one role or
another, albeit with a short stay under the waves!

Country:	France
Type:	Seaplane carrier
Launch date:	12 April 1929
Crew:	400
Displacement:	11,684 tonnes (11,500 tons)
Dimensions:	167m x 27m x 7m (548ft x 88ft 7in x 22ft 9in)
Range:	7412km (4000nm) at 15 knots
Armament:	13mm (3.9in) guns
Powerplant:	Twin screw turbines
Performance:	21.4 knots

Comte de Grasse

Built as replacements for the many Gearing-class destroyers, the Spruance class, to which *Comte de Grasse* belonged, remain extremely capable anti-submarine warfare vessels. Constructed by the modular assembly technique – whereby large sections of the hull are constructed in various parts of the shipyard and then welded together on the slipway – these were the first large US warships to employ all gas turbine propulsion. The successful hull design of the Spruance-class destroyers was used, with modifications, on two other classes of US warship, and has reduced rolling and pitching tendencies, so providing a better weapons platform. All vessels in the Spruance class have undergone major weapons changes over the years. Targets at long range are engaged by on-board ASW helicopters. Although some remain in service, *Comte de Grasse* is no longer on the active list.

Country:	USA
Type:	Destroyer
Launch date:	26 March 1976
Crew:	296
Displacement:	7925 tonnes (7800 tons)
Dimensions:	171.7m x 16.8m x 8.8m (563ft 3in x 55ft 2in x 29ft)
Range:	20,383km (11,000nm)
Main armament:	Two 127mm (5in) DP guns; Tomahawk and Harpoon SSM; Sea Sparrow SAM; Phalanx CIWS; ASROC
Powerplant:	Two shafts, four gas turbines
Performance:	32.5 knots

Confienza

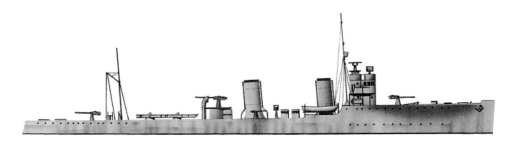

Launched in December 1920, *Confienza* was one of a class of four vessels that were an improved version of the *Audace*, launched in 1913. In 1938 all vessels in *Confienza*'s class were reclassified as torpedo boats, but plans to revise the armament were never followed through. The smaller weapons carried included two 76mm (3in) anti-aircraft guns plus two machine guns and four 450mm (17.7in) torpedo tubes. Three of the group were war losses. These were the *Palestro*, sunk by HM submarine *Osiris*, *San Martino*, taken over by the Germans and sunk in an air raid, and *Solferino*, also taken over and sunk by British destroyers. On 18 December 1940, *Confienza* sank the British submarine *Triton* (Lt Cdr Watkins) in the Strait of Otranto. She herself was sunk in a collision with the naval auxiliary vessel *Capitano Cecchi* off Brindisi.

Country:	Italy
Type:	Destroyer
Launch date:	18 December 1920
Crew:	190
Displacement:	1093 tonnes (1076 tons)
Dimensions:	82m x 8m x 3m (268ft 8in x 26ft 3in x 9ft 2in)
Range:	2778km (1500nm)
Main Armament:	Four 102mm (4in) guns
Powerplant:	Twin screw vertical triple expansion engines
Performance:	28 knots

Connecticut

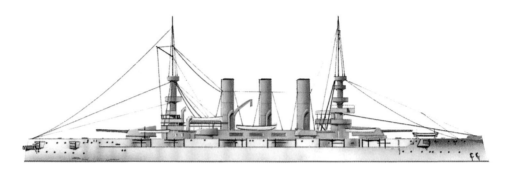

Part of a six-strong class, *Connecticut* was an enlarged version of the previous Virginia class and repeated the use of three different calibres for the main armament, except that the 152mm (6in) weapons were updated to 178mm (7in). Both the 304mm (12in) and 203mm (8in) gun turrets were electrically powered. The main armour belt ran from 1.2m (4ft) above to 1.5m (5ft) below the waterline. *Connecticut* compared very favourably with British and Japanese capital ships of the same period. She was flagship of the US Atlantic Fleet in 1906–07, and saw service with the Atlantic fleet during World War I. She was fitted with AA guns in 1916, and at the end of World War I she made four voyages as a troop transport. She saw service with the Pacific Fleet in 1921–22, and was decommissioned in 1923.

Country:	USA
Type:	Battleship
Launch date:	29 September 1904
Crew:	881
Displacement:	17,948 tonnes (17,666 tons)
Dimensions:	140m x 23m x 7m (456ft 4in x 76ft 10in x 24ft 6in)
Range:	9265km (5000nm) at 10 knots
Armament:	Four 305mm (12in), eight 203mm (8in) and 12 178mm (7in) guns
Powerplant:	Twin screw, vertical triple expansion engines
Performance:	18 knots

Conqueror

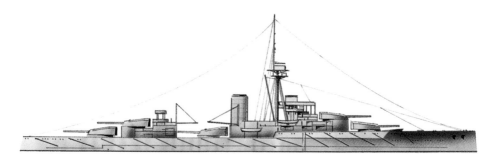

An increase in displacement over the previous class enabled *Conqueror* and her three sisters to mount the new 343mm (13.5 in) guns, making these vessels the first of the so-called 'super dreadnoughts'. *Conqueror* also carried the 533mm (21in) torpedo instead of the 450mm (18in) version. While she featured a more sleek design than the early dreadnoughts, there was one major weakness in *Conqueror*'s layout. The vitally important fire control mast was positioned between the funnels, resulting in severe smoke interference at high speeds. In December 1914 she was damaged in collision with the battleship *Monarch*; after repair she rejoined the Grand Fleet and fought in the Battle of Jutland in 1916. She was sold and broken up in 1922. Her sister ships were *Monarch*, *Orion* and *Thunderer*.

Country:	Great Britain
Type:	Battleship
Launch date:	1 May 1911
Crew:	752
Displacement:	26,284 tonnes (25,870 tons)
Dimensions:	177m x 27m x 9m (581ft x 88ft 7in x 28ft)
Range:	12,470km (6730nm) at 10 knots
Armament:	10 343mm (13.5in) guns
Powerplant:	Quadruple shaft turbines
Performance:	21 knots

Conqueror

O ne of three Churchill-class nuclear-powered attack submarines (SSNs), HMS *Conqueror* was the boat that sank the Argentinian cruiser *General Belgrano* on 2 May 1982, at the start of the Falklands War. The Churchills were modified Valiant-class SSNs and were somewhat quieter in service, having benefited from the experience gained in operating the earlier boats. When the Churchills were first built their main armament was the Mk 8 anti-ship torpedo of World War II vintage, and it was a salvo of these that sank the *Belgrano*. The armament was later updated to include the Mk24 Tigerfish wire-guided dual-role (anti-ship and anti-submarine) torpedo, the Sub-Harpoon SSM and a new generation of 'smart' mines. The Churchills and their predecessors, *Valiant* and *Warspite*, were paid off in the late 1980s, following the full deployment of the Trafalgar-class SSNs.

Country:	Great Britain
Type:	Attack submarine
Launch date:	28 August 1969
Crew:	116
Displacement:	Surfaced: 4470 tonnes (4400 tons), submerged: 4979 tonnes (4900 tons)
Dimensions:	86.9m x 10.1m x 8.2m (285ft x 33ft 3in x 27ft)
Range:	Unlimited
Armament:	Six 533mm (21in) torpedo tubes
Powerplant:	Nuclear, one pressurized water reactor
Performance:	Surfaced: 20 knots, submerged: 29 knots

Conte di Cavour

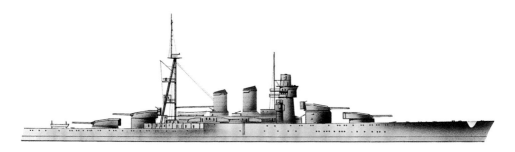

*C*onte di Cavour **was designed in 1908 as an improved version of** *Dante Alighieri.* **Completed in 1914,** *Conte di Cavour* **saw war service in the southern Adriatic, and in 1919 she engaged in a cruise to the USA. In 1923 she operated in support of Italian troops occupying the island of Corfu. She was extensively rebuilt between 1933 and 1937 and emerged as a virtually new ship. She had new machinery and her hull was lengthened. Sunk at Taranto by torpedoes launched from British aircraft flying from** *Illustrious*, *Conte di Cavour* **was later refloated and towed to Trieste. She was rebuilt but, following the Italian surrender, she was seized by the Germans in September 1943, and eventually sunk during an air raid in 1945. Her wreckage was broken up at the end of World War II.**

Country:	Italy
Type:	Battleship
Launch date:	10 August 1911
Crew:	1200
Displacement:	29,496 tonnes (29,032 tons)
Dimensions:	186m x 28m x 9m (611ft 6in x 91ft 10in x 30ft)
Range:	8640km (4800nm) at 10 knots
Armament:	10 320mm (12.6in), 12 120mm (4.7in) guns
Powerplant:	Twin screw turbines
Performance:	28.2 knots

Conyngham

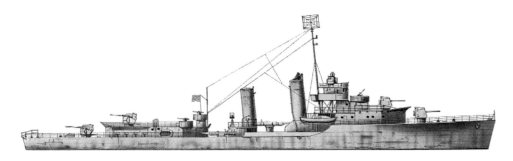

Launched in September 1935, the USS *Conyngham* was one of the Mahan class of American destroyers, closely related to the preceding Farragut class. Of the 18 ships in the class, six were lost in World War II. *Cassin* and *Downes* were virtually destroyed at Pearl Harbor but were later rebuilt; the USS *Tucker* survived the attack on Pearl Harbor but was lost in August 1942; the *Cushing* was sunk by Japanese gunfire and torpedoes off Guadalcanal on 13 November 1942; the *Preston* was sunk off Guadalcanal by a Japanese battle group on 14 November 1942; the *Perkins* went down in the Southwest Pacific on 29 November 1943; the *Mahan* was lost on 7 December 1944; and the *Reid* was lost on 11 December 1944. Another vessel, the *Lamson*, was expended at the Bikin atomic bomb tests in 1946, and the *Conyngham* herself was sunk as a target vessel on 2 July 1948.

Country:	USA
Type:	Destroyer
Launch date:	14 September 1935
Crew:	250
Displacement:	1417 tonnes (1395 tons)
Dimensions:	104m x 10.4m x 2.69m (341.25ft x 34.16ft x 8.83ft)
Range:	6482km (3500nm)
Main Armament:	Five single 127mm DP guns; two quadruple 533mm (21in) torpedo tubes
Powerplant:	Two sets of geared steam turbines
Performance:	36.5 knots

Coronel Bolognesi

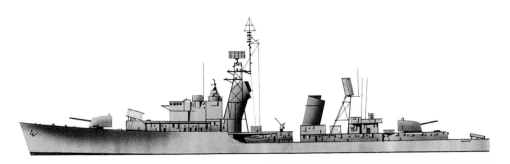

The *Coronel Bolognesi* was previously one of the Friesland class of Dutch destroyer escorts (DDE) built for the Royal Netherlands Navy. They formed the backbone of the Dutch anti-submarine groups until the late 1970s, when they were replaced by the newer Standaard-class frigate. Between 1980 and 1982, the ships were transferred to the Peruvian Navy, which had plans to arm them with Exocet missiles. The ships have side armour as well as deck protection. In Dutch service, plans were made to fit them with eight 533mm (21in) torpedo tubes, but this project was abandoned after only one ship had been so equipped (the tubes were subsequently removed). The primary anti-submarine weapon of these vessels is the Limbo-type rocket projector. Their 4.7in guns are fully automatic, with a rate of fire of 50 rounds per minute.

Country:	Netherlands
Type:	Destroyer
Launch date:	8 August 1955
Crew:	284
Displacement:	3150 tonnes (3100 tons)
Dimensions:	116m x 12m x 5m (380ft 7in x 38ft 5in x 17ft)
Range:	4632km (2500nm)
Main Armament:	Four 120mm (4.7in) guns
Powerplant:	Twin screw turbines
Performance:	36 knots

Corrientes

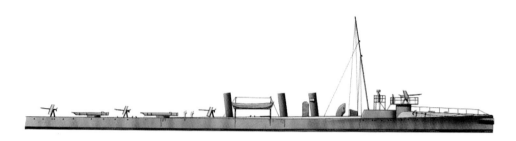

A permanent Argentine Navy was first established in 1872, when a number of vessels, including two armoured monitors, were ordered. Two small battleships were also commissioned at a later date. The contract speed for these vessels was 26 knots for three hours but they had difficulty achieving this. A border dispute with Chile in the 1890s led to a naval race, and four armoured cruisers were ordered from Italy, although two of these were cancelled when a treaty brought an end to the tension that had existed between the two countries. The two cruisers were sold to Japan. At the same time, Argentina – conscious of the threat presented to its small fleet by enemy torpedo boats – ordered four destroyers from the British company Yarrow shipbuilders on the River Clyde. *Corrientes* was one of them, and she served in the Argentinian Navy until she was taken off the active list in 1925.

Country:	Argentina
Type:	Destroyer
Launch date:	1896
Crew:	98
Displacement:	284 tonnes (280 tons)
Dimensions:	58m x 6m x 2.2m (190ft x 19ft 6in x 7ft 4 in)
Range:	1482km (800nm)
Main armament:	One 14-pounder; three six-pounders; three 457mm (18in) torpedo tubes
Powerplant:	Twin screw triple expansion engines
Performance:	22 knots

Courageous

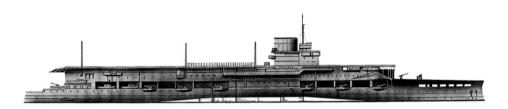

Courageous and her sister *Glorious* were completed in 1917 as fast cruisers for service in the Baltic. They were heavily armed with four 380mm (15in) guns, but had very little armour. By the 1920s, Britain was anxious to increase her carrier strength, so both vessels, and their near sister *Furious*, were converted to aircraft carriers. The conversion of *Courageous* was completed in March 1928. Her superstructure and armament were replaced by an aircraft hangar running almost the length of the ship. The forward 18m (59ft) of the hangar was an open deck, which could be used to fly off slow-flying aircraft such as the Swordfish. Above this was an open flight deck, with two large elevators set into it. All three ships served through the 1930s, and formed the backbone of the British carrier force at the start of World War II. In the opening days of the war *Courageous* was torpedoed and sunk by *U20*.

Country:	Great Britain
Type:	Aircraft carrier
Launch date:	5 February 1916
Crew:	828
Displacement:	26,517 tonnes (26,100 tons)
Dimensions:	240m x 27m x 8m (786ft 5in x 90ft 6in x 27ft 3in)
Range:	5929km (3200nm) at 19 knots
Armament:	16 120mm (4.7in) guns, six flights of aircraft
Powerplant:	Quadruple screw turbines
Performance:	31.5 knots

Couronne

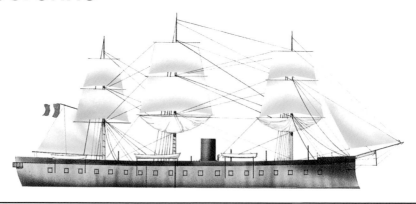

Couronne was the first iron-hulled capital ship to be laid down. Upon completion in 1862 she proved a better seaboat than her wooden-hulled contemporaries, and she was still afloat 70 years after her launch. Originally her guns were in broadside battery behind her armour, but she underwent several armament changes during her career. In 1885 she became a gunnery training ship, having had all her armour removed. *Couronne* was hulked in 1910, and was not broken up until 1934. Originally launched in March 1861, her long career compares sharply to those wooden-hulled warships of the mid-nineteenth century, and was proof, if proof were needed, that the iron-hulled warship was the future as far as warfare at sea was concerned. That said, the placing of her guns along the sides was a throwback to a bygone age.

Country:	France
Type:	Ironclad
Launch date:	23 March 1861
Crew:	570
Displacement:	6173 tonnes (6076 tons)
Dimensions:	80m x 17m x 8m (262ft 5in x 54ft 9in x 27ft)
Range:	4465km (2410nm) at 10 knots
Armament:	30 163mm (6.4in) guns
Powerplant:	Single screw, horizontal return engines
Performance:	13 knots

Crescent

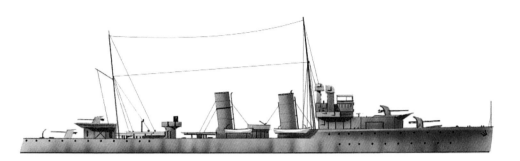

HMS *Crescent* formed part of the 1922 British naval rearmament programme, which was to be drastically curtailed due to the onset of the great worldwide economic Depression of the early 1930s. Crescent was one of the C and D classes of destroyer, which were slightly enlarged versions of the B class, having increased fuel capacity and a 76mm (3in) anti-aircraft gun in addition to the main armament of 120mm (4.7in) guns. The machinery developed 36,000hp for a designed speed of 35.5 knots. *Crescent* was launched in September 1931 and transferred to the Royal Canadian Navy in 1937, where she was renamed *Fraser*. She was lost in a collision with the British cruiser *Calcutta* off the Gironde on 26 June 1940 while taking part in Operation Aerial, in which British ships evacuated 191,870 troops from the Biscay ports.

Country:	Great Britain
Type:	Destroyer
Launch date:	29 September 1931
Crew:	190
Displacement:	1927 tonnes (1897 tons)
Dimensions:	97m x 10m x 2.6m (317ft 9in x 33ft x 8ft 6in)
Range:	3704km (2000nm)
Main Armament:	Four 120mm (4.7in) guns
Powerplant:	Twin screw turbines
Performance:	36 knots

Curlew

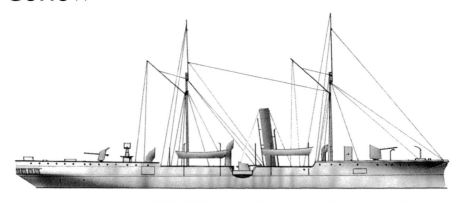

Classified as first-class gun vessels, *Curlew* and her sister *Landrail* were the last of the old-style gunboats that had filled the Royal Navy lists over the years. *Curlew* was a steel-hulled vessel with fine lines and a relatively shallow draught. Unfortunately, *Curlew* and her sister proved unsuitable as gunboats and were too slow to be cruisers. *Curlew* served in British waters until she was sold in 1906. The boats would have had much longer careers than they enjoyed had it not been for their inadequacies, since their armament was really quite formidable. Typically, their 152mm (6in) gun fired a 100lb shot and their three 127mm (5in) weapons a 60lb shot. *Curlew*'s sister ship, *Landrail*, was deployed first of all to the Cape station and spent almost all her operational life overseas. She was sunk as a target vessel in October 1906.

Country:	Great Britain
Type:	Gunboat
Launch date:	23 October 1885
Crew:	75
Displacement:	965 tonnes (950 tons)
Dimensions:	59.5m x 8.5m x 3.2m (195ft x 28ft x 10ft 6in)
Range:	1760km (950nm)
Main Armament:	One 152mm (6in) and three 127mm (5in) guns.
Powerplant:	Twin screw horizontal direct-acting compound engines
Performance:	14.5 knots

Cushing

The *Cushing* was the US Navy's first true purpose-designed torpedo boat, and was laid down in April 1888. She was built by the Herreshof company, and unlike *Stiletto*, her wooden-hulled predecessor, she was built of steel. *Cushing* had a long, slim hull with a curved deck and an anachronistic ram bow. She was used initially on experimental torpedo development work at the Newport Naval Torpedo Station. In 1897, once the technology was regarded as being well proven, she was used as a despatch boat off the coast of Cuba, and saw active service during the war with Spain in 1898. In a single action in August of that year, she intercepted and captured four small Spanish transports. After the war she was returned to Newport, where she became a target hulk. She was sunk as a target vessel in September 1920, the fate of many of her kind.

Country:	USA
Type:	Torpedo boat
Launch date:	23 January 1890
Crew:	22
Displacement:	118 tonnes (116 tons)
Dimensions:	42.6m x 4.6m x 1.5m (140ft x 15ft 1in x 4ft 10in)
Range:	926km (500nm)
Main armament:	Three 457mm (18in) torpedo tubes; three 6-pounder guns
Powerplant:	Twin screw vertical quadruple expansion engines
Performance:	23 knots

Cushing

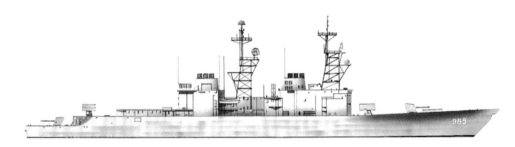

The USS *Cushing* is one of the large Spruance warships; there were 31 units in all, built by Ingalls Shipbuilding Division of Litton Industries, Pascagoula, Mississipi, as replacements for the many Gearing-class destroyers, and they were arguably the most capable anti-submarine warfare vessels ever built. On trials *Spruance* made about 32 knots. Constructed by the modular assembly technique, whereby large sections of the hull are built in various parts of the shipyard and then welded together on the slipway, these were the first large US warships to employ all gas turbine propulsion. The hull design of the Spruance-class destroyers was used, with modifications, on two other classes of US warship. All vessels in the Spruance class have undergone major weapons changes and upgrades. Although about two-thirds of the class have now been retired, *Cushing* remains on active duty.

Country:	USA
Type:	Destroyer
Launch date:	17 June 1978
Crew:	296
Displacement:	8168 tonnes (8040 tons)
Dimensions:	171.7m x 16.8m x 5.8m (563ft 4in x 55ft 2in x 19ft)
Range:	20,372km (11,000nm)
Main armament:	Two 127mm (5in) guns; Tomahawk and Harpoon missiles
Powerplant:	Twin screws, gas turbines
Performance:	32.5 knots

Dahlgren

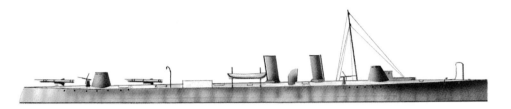

*D*ahlgren and her sister boat *Craven* were authorised in 1896, laid down in March 1897, and completed in 1899. They had closely spaced funnels, a single light pole mast, and two single torpedo tubes mounted aft. The efficiency of torpedo boats such as these was made possible by the drastic reduction in the size of powerplants that took place in the latter years of the nineteenth century. This was due to the development of new types of boiler and compound multi-cylinder engines operating at previously impossible temperatures and pressures. Such engines found application in warships and merchant vessels alike, bringing the necessary fuel economy to the latter and unheard-of speed to the former. During this period America became the world's major industrial power, a fact reflected in the strength of her navy.

Country:	USA
Type:	Torpedo boat
Launch date:	29 May 1899
Crew:	29
Displacement:	148 tonnes (146 tons)
Dimensions:	46m x 5m x 1.5m (151ft 4in x 16ft 5in x 4ft 8in)
Range:	Not known
Main armament:	Four one-pounder guns; two 457mm (18in) torpedo tubes
Powerplant:	Twin screw vertical triple expansion engines
Performance:	31 knots

Danaide

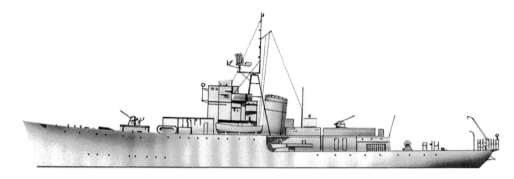

From 1942 onwards, the Italian Navy laid down a class of some 60 small escort vessels – the Gabbiano class. The last was not completed until 1948. Pressures of war caused the early ships in the class to be built extremely quickly. *Danaide* was one of the first, and was completed only four months after launching. She was originally fitted out for minesweeping, and operated extensively in the Mediterranean during World War II. Like her sister ships, she was modified extensively throughout her operational life. Many of the class survived the war, and 17 were still in Italian service in the mid-1960s. Some of the earlier vessels were seized by the Germans and pressed into service as submarine chasers; most were sunk by Allied air attack. One of the class, *Ape* (Bee) was converted to carry frogmen and commandos in the special duties role; others became target tugs.

Country:	Italy
Type:	Corvette
Launch date:	21 October 1942
Crew:	101
Displacement:	812 tonnes (800 tons)
Dimensions:	64m x 8.5m x 2.5m (209ft 7in x 27ft 6in x 8ft 1in)
Range:	2778km (1500nm)
Main armament:	Four 40mm (1.6in) anti-aircraft guns
Powerplant:	Twin screw diesel engines
Performance:	17.5 knots

Daniel Boone

Although actually two classes, the 12 Benjamin Franklin-class and the 19 Lafayette-class of nuclear-powered ballistic-missile submarines (SSBN) were very similar in appearance, the main difference being that the former were built with quieter machinery outfits. The *Daniel Boone* (SSBN629) was one of the Lafayette class. As built, the first eight Lafayettes carried the 16 Polaris A2 submarine-launched ballistic missiles (SLBMs), each with a single 800kT yield warhead, but the rest were armed with the Polaris A3, which was fitted with three independently targeted warheads; this was in turn replaced by the Poseidon C3. Between September 1978 and December 1982 12 units were converted to carry the Trident I C4 SLBM. The boats were progressively deactivated as the Trident-armed Ohio-class SSBNs entered service.

Country:	USA
Type:	Ballistic missile submarine
Launch date:	22 June 1963
Crew:	140
Displacement:	Surfaced: 7366 tonnes (7250 tons), submerged: 8382 tonnes (8250 tons)
Dimensions:	130m x 10m x 10m (425ft x 33ft x 33ft)
Range:	Unlimited
Armament:	Sixteen Polaris missiles, four 533mm (21in) torpedo tubes
Powerplant:	One water-cooled nuclear reactor, turbines
Performance:	Surfaced: 20 knots, submerged: 35 knots

Dante Alighieri

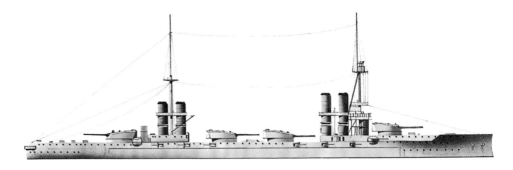

Designed by Engineering Admiral Masdea, the *Dante Alighieri* was the first battleship to mount triple turrets on the centreline; she was also the first Italian dreadnought to be built. Laid down in 1909, she was completed in 1912. She was reconstructed in 1923 and given a tripod mast. In World War I she was the flagship of the Italian Fleet in the southern Adriatic, although she saw no action. When Italy entered the war in 1915 the fleet included six dreadnoughts, with four more under construction. The main operational base was originally Trieste, but the main body of the fleet later moved to Taranto to escape Austrian air attacks. Although the Italian battle fleet did little during the war, its ships carried out a successful blockade of the eastern Adriatic coastline. *Dante Alighieri* was scrapped in 1928.

Country :	Italy
Type:	Battleship
Launch date:	20 August 1910
Crew:	981
Displacement:	22,149 tonnes (21,800 tons)
Dimensions:	168m x 26.5m x 10m (551ft 2in x 87ft 3in x 31ft 10in)
Range:	9265km (5000nm) at 10 knots
Armament:	12 304mm (12in), 20 120mm (4.7in) guns
Powerplant:	Quadruple screw turbines
Performance:	22 knots

Danton

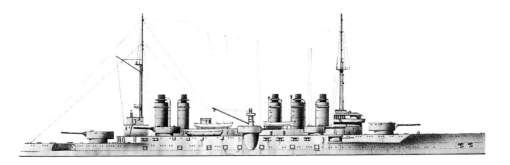

*D*anton and her five sisters were the last battleships to be built for the French Navy before the British all-big-gun battleship *Dreadnought* appeared on the scene and revolutionised naval development. Although *Danton*'s class contained powerful vessels, it was too late to provide a serious challenge to the dreadnoughts then entering service. Named after Georges Jacques Danton, a leader of the French Revolution, the battleship was laid down at Brest in 1908 and launched in July 1909. She was completed in 1911 and saw initial war service in escorting Mediterranean convoys. In 1915 she was on station in the Adriatic and in 1916 in the Aegean. On 19 March 1917, en route from Toulon to Corfu, she was hit by two torpedoes from the German submarine *U64* and sank southwest of Sardinia with the loss of 296 lives.

Country :	France
Type:	Battleship
Launch date:	4 July 1909
Crew:	753, later 923
Displacement:	19,761 tonnes (19,450 tons)
Dimensions:	146.5m x 25.8m x 9m (481ft x 84ft 8in x 28ft 8in)
Range:	6066km (3370nm) at 10 knots
Armament:	Four 304mm (12in) guns
Powerplant:	Quadruple screw turbines
Performance:	19.3 knots

Daring

During the early 1890s, the British Admiralty requested designs for small destroyers that would be faster than the rapidly growing fleet of French torpedo boats. The French had needed most of the century to recover from the total destruction of their fleet during the Napoleonic wars and, in that interlude, they concentrated on the design of small, fast craft capable of attacking enemy capital ships. Thorneycroft and Yarrow subsequently came up with the design for *Daring*, based on their successful sea-going torpedo boats. The hull at the stern had a flat floor at the waterline, so enabling the screws to be lifted to allow for navigation in relatively shallow waters. *Daring* was scrapped in 1912. Her sister boat, *Decoy*, was lost in a collision in 1904. Both vessels were built by Thorneycroft, and were stronger than contemporary vessels built by Yarrow.

Country:	Great Britain
Type:	Destroyer
Launch date:	25 November 1893
Crew:	98
Displacement:	264 tonnes (260 tons)
Dimensions:	56.6m x 5.7m (185ft 6in x 19ft.)
Range:	Not known
Main armament:	One 12-pounder; three six-pounders; three torpedo tubes
Powerplant:	Twin screw three-stage compound engines
Performance:	22 knots

Daring

Launched in 1949, *Daring* and her seven sisters were expanded and improved versions of the earlier Battle-class and Weapon-class vessels, and were able to perform a variety of tasks, including anti-submarine and reconnaissance duties. They were the largest destroyers built for the Royal Navy and had an all-welded hull construction. The 120mm (4.5in) guns were radar-controlled and automatic. The lattice foremast was built around the fore funnel, giving *Daring* an unusual and distinctive appearance. During the early years of the Cold War, the vessels of the Daring class formed an important part of NATO's hunter-killer naval forces in the Atlantic. They were the first British destroyers specifically designed to perform multi-role funtions, and set the trend for future developments that would lead to today's highly effective craft.

Country:	Great Britain
Type:	Destroyer
Launch date:	10 August 1949
Crew:	290
Displacement:	3636 tonnes (3579 tons)
Dimensions:	114m x 13m x 4m (375ft x 43ft x 13ft)
Range:	12,964km (7000nm)
Main armament:	Six 120mm (4.5in) guns
Powerplant:	Twin screw geared turbines
Performance:	31.5 knots

Davidson

The Garcia class of anti-submarine ships to which the USS *Davidson* belonged were built between 1962 and 1968 as successors to the Bronstein class of destroyer escorts. Ten were launched and were originally classed as ocean escorts, but their designation and role was soon changed to that of frigate. Gyro-driven stabilisers enabled *Davidson* to operate effectively in heavy seas, and her anti-submarine capabilities were significantly improved over earlier classes. As well as the two single gun mounts, she carried a large box launcher which held eight ASROC anti-submarine missiles. She was also equipped with twin torpedo tubes in the stern, but these were later removed. Her combat effectiveness was enhanced by an SH-2 Seasprite helicopter which is housed in a hangar towards the stern. The *Davidson* was sold to Brazil as the *Paraiba* in 1988, but has now been stricken.

Country:	USA
Type:	Destroyer escort
Launch date:	2 October 1964
Crew:	241
Displacement:	3454 tonnes (3400 tons)
Dimensions:	126m x 13.5m x 7.3m (414ft 8in x 44ft 3in x 24ft)
Range:	7585km (4096nm)
Main armament:	Two 127mm (5in) DP guns
Powerplant:	Single screw, turbines
Performance:	27 knots

Decatur

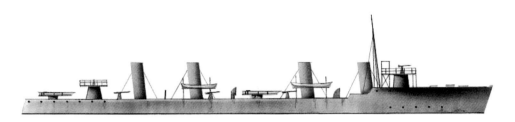

The Bainbridge class of five units was the largest destroyer class laid down before 1899. All previous destroyers had been 'one-off' vessels of between 238 and 283 tonnes (235 and 279 tons). The vessels of this class were authorized in 1898 and for most of their lives were based at Cavite in the Philippine Islands. In 1917, *Chauncey* was rammed and sunk by the steamer *Rose*, but all the remaining vessels in the class survived World War I and were sold in 1920. In general, American destroyers tended to be larger than their British counterparts, and more rakish: in fact, more like light cruisers in appearance. Some US destroyer flotillas operated from Irish bases in World War I. In fact, America's first act of war on 13 April 1917 was to deploy six destroyers to European waters to take part in the Atlantic Patrol alongside their Royal Navy counterparts.

Country:	USA
Type:	Destroyer
Launch date:	26 September 1900
Crew:	110
Displacement:	426 tonnes (420 tons)
Dimensions:	77m x 7m x 2m (252ft 7in x 23ft 6in x 6ft 6in)
Range:	2778km (1500nm)
Main armament:	Two 76mm (3in) guns; five six-pounders; two 457mm (18in) torpedo tubes
Powerplant:	Twin screw verticle triple expansion
Performance:	29 knots

Dédalo

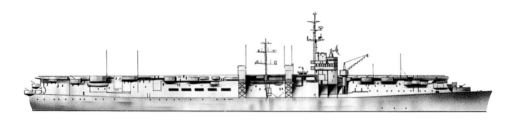

***D**édalo* was formerly the US Navy ship *Cabot*, which had been laid down in 1942 as a cruiser, but completed the following year as a carrier of the Independence class. After service in World War II, *Cabot* was decommissioned in 1947. In 1967 she was lent to Spain, who purchased her in 1972, renaming her *Dédalo*. Her normal air wing comprised four air groups, one with eight Matador (Harrier) V/STOL aircraft, one with four Sea King ASW helicopters, one with four Agusta-Bell 212 ASW/electronic warfare helicopters, and one with four specialised helicopters (for example, Bell AH-1G attack helicopters to support an amphibious landing.) A maximum of seven four-aircraft groups could be handled aboard the carrier. She remained in service until the carrier *Principe de Asturias* entered service in 1987.

Country:	USA/Spain
Type:	Aircraft carrier
Launch date:	4 April 1943
Crew:	1112
Displacement:	16,678 tonnes (16,416 tons)
Dimensions:	190m x 22m x 8m (622ft 4in x 73ft x 26ft)
Range:	13,500km (7500nm) at 12 knots
Armament:	26 40mm (1.6in) guns, seven VSTOL aircraft, 20 helicopters
Powerplant:	Quadruple screw turbines
Performance:	30 knots

Delta

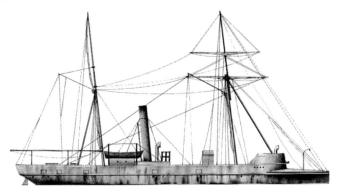

George Rendell designed a number of successful gunboats from between 1868 to 1879, starting with the British 183-tonne (180-ton) vessel, *Staunch*. Their common feature was the use of a single, very large gun mounted on a small, low profile hull with shallow draught. *Delta* was one of four units ordered by China in 1875 and completed in 1877. The other boats were named *Alpha*, *Beta* and *Gamma*. They were effectively floating gun platforms rather than warships, but were useful for coastal defence. *Delta* was armed with a single 36-tonne (35-ton) gun, which could only be traversed a few degrees from dead ahead. To aim the gun, the boat had to be pointed directly at the target, and she was fitted with twin screws to enable her to manoeuvre quickly. All four of the Chinese Rendell gunboats were captured by the Japanese in 1895 and were broken up between 1906 and 1907.

Country :	China
Type:	Gunboat
Launch date:	1876
Crew:	50
Displacement:	426 tonnes (420 tons)
Dimensions:	36.5m x 9m x 2.5m (119ft 9in x 39ft 6in x 8ft 4in)
Range:	Not known
Main armament:	One 317mm (12.5in) gun
Powerplant:	Twin screw horizontal compound engines
Performance:	9.6 knots

Delta I

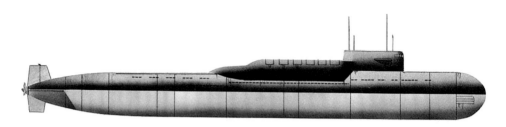

Until the early 1970s, the USA led the world in highly sophisticated and effective nuclear-missile submarines. Then the Russians deployed a new class of ballistic-missile submarine, the Delta I, or Murena-class SSBN which was a major improvement on the earlier Yankee class and which was armed with missiles that could outrange the American Poseidon. Each boat was armed with 12 two-stage SS-N-8 missiles. The first Delta was laid down at Severodvinsk in 1969, launched in 1971 and completed in the following year. With the end of the Cold War and rapidly shrinking naval budgets, the first of the class was paid off in 1992, and all have now been withdrawn from service – including the Delta II class. These were essentially Delta Is with a extra 9m (30ft) length of hull added to allow them to carry another four SS-N-8 missiles.

Country:	Soviet Union
Type:	Ballistic missile submarine
Launch date:	1971
Crew:	120
Displacement:	Submerged: 11,176 tonnes (11,000 tons)
Dimensions:	150m x 12m x 10.2m (492ft x 39ft 4in x 33ft 6in)
Range:	Unlimited
Armament:	Twelve missile tubes, six 457mm (18in) torpedo tubes
Powerplant:	Nuclear, two reactors
Performance:	Surfaced: 19 knots, submerged: 25 knots

Delta III

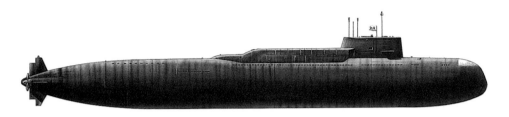

The Delta III- or Kalmar-class SSBN, completed between 1976 and 1982, had some visible differences from the earlier Delta II class from which it evolved, the most noticeable being that the missile casing was higher in order to accommodate the SS-N-18 missiles, which are longer than the SS-N-8s of the Delta II. The last of the class is the Delta IV, construction of which was first ordered in December 1975. The first of 8 boats was launched and commissioned in 1984 at Severodvinsk and the programme was completed in late 1990. Names are being allocated to the Delta IVs; *Kareliya* and *Novo Moskovsk* have been identified so far. Larger than the Delta III, the Delta IV is a new class of submarine, which has been given the name *Delfin* (Dolfin); its bases are at Saida Guba with the Northern Fleet and Rybachy in the Pacific. The Delta IIIs are all thought to be inactive.

Country:	Soviet Union
Type:	Ballistic missile submarine
Launch date:	1976
Crew:	130
Displacement:	Surfaced: 10,719 tonnes (10,550 tons, submerged: 13,463 tonnes (13,250t)
Dimensions:	160m x 12m x 8.7m (524.9ft x 39.4ft x 28.5ft)
Range:	Unlimited
Armament:	Sixteen SS-N-18 missiles; four 533mm (21in) torpedo tubes
Powerplant:	Nuclear; two pressurized water reactors, turbines
Performance:	Surfaced: 14 knots, submerged: 24 knots

Denver

*D*enver is one of the Austin class of 11 ships which are enlarged versions of the previous Raleigh group. They have increased troop and vehicle capacity, being able to carry over 900 troops and 2540 tonnes (2500 tons) of cargo. *Denver* also has a comprehensive docking facility forming the stern of the vessel, capable of holding 20 landing craft. Access to the dock is via massive lock gates in the stern. Unlike the Raleigh group, the Austin class features a helicopter hangar big enough for six helicopters in transit or two in operation. Under normal operational conditions, five Austin class ships serve with the Atlantic fleets, while six Austin class serve with the Pacific fleets. All the Austin class vessels underwent refits in the 1980s to extend their service life. *Denver* is due to decommission in 2006. The San Antonio class ships will gradually replace the Austins in service.

Country:	USA
Type:	Dock landing ship
Launch date:	23 January 1965
Crew:	447 and up to 930 troops
Displacement:	9477 tonnes (9328 tons)
Dimensions:	174m x 30.5m x 7m (570ft 3in x 100ft x 23ft)
Range:	14,824km (8000nm) at 15 knots
Armament:	Eight 76mm (3in) guns
Powerplant:	Twin screw turbines
Performance:	20 knots

Derfflinger

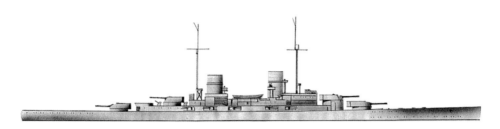

On 16 December 1914, *Derfflinger* was part of a force of German warships that bombarded Scarborough and Whitby, on the northeast coast of England; shortly afterwards, in January 1915, she was seriously damaged in the Battle of Dogger Bank. In the following year, 1916, *Derfflinger* took part in the Battle of Jutland and blew up the British battlecruiser *Queen Mary* with 11 salvos. During that same battle, however, she was hit by ten 380mm (15in) and ten 304mm (12in) shells. Despite fires on board, severe flooding and damage to her after-turrets she survived the battle. *Derfflinger* and her two sister ships, *Hindenburg* and *Lutzow*, all of which had been launched in 1913, were arguably the best capital ships of their day. *Derfflinger* was scuttled at Scapa Flow in 1919 and raised for scrap in 1934.

Country:	Germany
Type:	Battleship
Launch date:	1 July 1913
Crew:	1112
Displacement:	30,706 tonnes (30,223 tons)
Dimensions:	210m x 29m x 8m (689ft x 95ft 2in x 27ft 3in)
Range:	10,080km (5600nm) at 12 knots
Armament:	Eight 304mm (12in) guns
Powerplant:	Quadruple screw turbines
Performance:	28 knots

DE Type

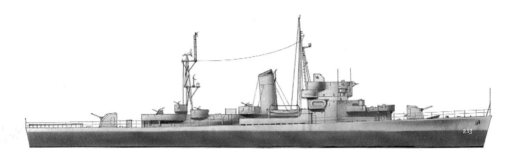

The first destroyer escorts (DEs) built in the United States were ordered under lend-lease for Britain early in 1941. The original order for 50 was expanded to 250 early in 1942, but only 55 were actually transferred. The remainder of these vessels were retained by the US Navy, which had not planned to build any. Of the 1005 destroyer escorts ordered by 1943, only 563 were completed. The DEs of this type were built after the fashion of American fleet destroyers, having a long flush deck with a prominent sheer line in place of the more commodious long forecastle decks preferred by the British. Far more emphasis was placed on gun armament. As anti-submarine warships, the DEs were extremely effective, although they arrived too late to prevent much of the carnage caused by the U-boats in the Battle of the Atlantic.

Country:	USA
Type:	Destroyer Escort
Launch date:	9 January 1943 (Buckley class, first unit)
Crew:	220
Displacement:	1748 tonnes (1720 tons)
Dimensions:	93.27m x 11.27m x 2.89m (306ft x 37ft x 9ft 6in)
Range:	15,742km (8500nm)
Main armament:	Three 76mm (3in) guns; six 40mm (1.5in) and four 20mm (0.7in) AA; three 533mm (21in) torpedo tubes; depth charges
Powerplant:	Two shafts, two steam turbines, two propulsion motors
Performance:	24 knots

D'Estienne d'Orves

Designed for coastal ASW, the D'Estienne d'Orves class could also be used for scouting missions and training. Since entering service in the mid-1970s, the design has been sold to the Argentine Navy, whose three ships the *Drummond*, *Guerrico* and *Granville* saw service in the 1982 Falklands war. In this campaign, the *Guerrico* was damaged by shore fire from small arms and 'Carl Gustav' anti-tank rocket launchers operated by a contingent of Royal Marines defending South Georgia. She was hit by 1275 rounds of rifle and machine-gun fire and three rockets, one exploding on her side, a second on her Exocet launcher, and a third on her gun turret. She had to be dry-docked for three days in order for repairs to be carried out. The French examples of the class are currently being retired or sold: *D'Estienne d'Orves* was sold to Turkey in 2000, and is now the *Beycoz*.

Country:	France
Type:	Frigate
Launch date:	1 June 1973
Crew:	105
Displacement:	1351 tonnes (1330 tons)
Dimensions:	80m x 10m x 3m (262ft 6in x 33ft 10in x 9ft 10in)
Range:	7408km (4000nm)
Main armament:	One 100mm (3.9in) DP gun; two single MM40 Exocet surface-to-surface missile launchers with two missiles (replacing earlier MM38 Exocet missiles)
Powerplant:	Twin screw diesel engines
Performance:	24 knots

Deutschland

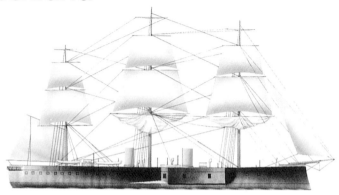

Before the foundation of the German Empire in 1871, Prussia retained only a small navy for coastal defence. It was the blockade by the French Navy during the Franco–Prussian war that finally convinced the German government of the pressing need for a larger navy. As a consequence, throughout the 1870s nine capital ships were begun, mainly in German yards. *Deutschland*, one of the Kaiser class, was an exception, and was the last German capital ship to be built abroad, being launched in Britain in 1874. She was a powerful central battery ship, with her main armament concentrated in an armoured box amidships. In 1882 her armament was altered, and in 1895 she was rebuilt as a heavy cruiser with military masts replacing her original sailing rig. *Deutschland* was taken out of service in 1906 and broken up in 1909.

Country:	Germany
Type:	Ironclad
Launch date:	9 September 1874
Crew:	656
Displacement:	8939 tonnes (8799 tons)
Dimensions:	90m x 19m x 8m (293ft x 62ft 4in x 26ft)
Range:	4576km (2470nm) at 10 knots
Armament:	Eight 254mm (10in) guns
Powerplant:	Single screw, horizontal single expansion engine
Performance:	13 knots

Deutschland

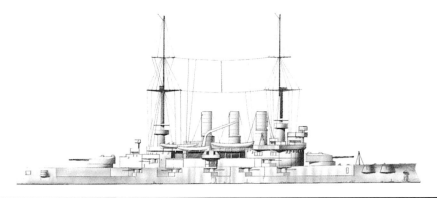

*D*eutschland was part of Germany's last pre-dreadnought class laid down between 1903 and 1905. They differed slightly from the previous class in that they had more 89mm (3.5in) guns plus improved protection, but other weaknesses remained – as was shown at the Battle of Jutland in 1916 when one vessel in the class, *Pommern*, suffered a magazine explosion after only one hit from a torpedo. Small tube boilers were used for the Deutschland class, and these became standard for all vessels employed in the German Navy. Two ships of the class, *Schlesien* and *Schleswig-Holstein*, survived to serve in World War II and were lost in action. *Schleswig-Holstein* was sunk in an air attack in December 1944, and *Schlesien* ran on a mine in the Baltic in April 1945. *Deutschland* was scrapped in 1922.

Country:	Germany
Type:	Battleship
Launch date:	19 November 1904
Crew:	743
Weight:	14,216 tonnes (13,993 tons)
Dimensions:	127.6m x 22m x 8m (418ft 8in x 73ft x 27ft)
Range:	8894km (4800nm) at 12 knots
Armament:	14 170mm (6.7in), four 279mm (11in) guns
Powerplant:	Twin screw, triple expansion engines
Performance:	18.5 knots

Deutschland

***D**eutschland* was the first West German naval ship to exceed the post-war limit of 3048 tonnes (3000 tons), and entered service in May 1963. She was a light cruiser that could also operate as a minelayer, and she carried a varied armament for training purposes, including 100mm (3.9in) and 40mm (1.6in) guns, depth-charge launchers and torpedo tubes. Two types of machinery were also installed to maximise training opportunities for the 267 cadets. *Deutschland's* total complement was 550. She would have been an important minelaying asset in a cold war. The naval mine was used by the Prussians to bar Kiel harbour against the Danes during the Schleswig-Holstein crisis of 1848–51, and mines were laid by the Russians during the Crimean War to prevent British and French naval units from shelling the Baltic naval base at Kronshtadt.

Country:	Germany
Type:	Training ship
Launch date:	5 November 1960
Crew:	172 plus cadets
Weight:	5588 tonnes (5500 tons)
Dimensions:	65m x 8.9m x 5.3m (213ft 3in x 29ft 2in x 17ft 5in)
Range:	6840km (3800nm) at 10 knots
Armament:	Four 100mm (3.9in) guns
Powerplant:	Triple screw diesel motors, turbines
Performance:	22 knots

Devonshire

*D*evonshire and *Hampshire*, designed to embody improvements in the
destroyer field, were projected between 1955 and 1956, and it was later found
possible to arm these 'super-destroyers' with guided weapons instead of anti-
aircraft guns, and to carry modern anti-submarine detection equipment. *Kent* and
London, provided under the 1956–57 estimates, had the mainmast stepped further
aft. The next four ships – *Fife*, *Glamorgan*, *Antrim* and *Norfolk* – all had the
updated Seaslug MkII SAM system, later retrofitted in the first four. All the ships
were fitted with stablisers. The County class, together with the Tribals were the first
ships to have Combined Steam and Gas turbine (COSAG) machinery. Their lengthy
endurance enabled them to operate independently, in the same way as cruisers.
The class was superseded by the Type 42 destroyer.

Country:	Great Britain
Type:	Destroyer
Launch date:	10 June 1960
Crew:	471
Displacement:	6299 tonnes (6200 tons)
Dimensions:	158.6m x 16.4m x 6m (520ft 6in x 54ft x 20ft)
Range:	12,964km (7000nm)
Main armament:	Four 114mm (4.5in) guns; twin launcher for long-range Seaslug SAM
Powerplant:	Two sets geared steam turbines, four gas turbines
Performance:	32.5 knots

Deyatelnyi

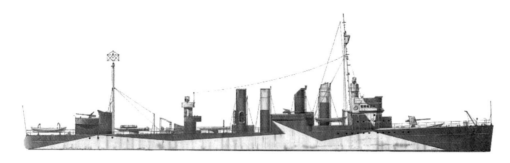

The *Deyatelnyi* was originally an American Clemson-class destroyer of 1919 vintage, the USS *Herndon*. Transferred to the Royal Navy early in World War II, she was renamed HMS *Churchill* and served on convoy escort duty in the North Atlantic until 1944, when she was handed over to the Soviet Navy and renamed *Deyatelnyi*. After some months on escort duty in the Arctic, she was escorting coastal convoy KB1 in the White Sea with the flotilla leader *Baku* and seven other destroyers, with three Pe-2 bombers providing air escort, when the convoy was attacked by German submarines. The *U997* (Lt Lehmann) sank the *Deyatelnyi* (Lt-Cdr Kravchenko) with a T-5 acoustic homing torpedo. Russian destroyers, in fact, rarely ventured outside coastal waters in World War II, leaving the burden of escort duty mostly to their Allies.

Country:	USA / Soviet Union
Type:	Destroyer
Launch date:	31 May 1919
Crew:	146
Displacement:	1209 tonnes (1190 tons)
Dimensions:	95.78m x 9.37m x 2.82m (314ft 4in x 30ft 9in x 9ft 3in)
Range:	2778km (1500nm)
Main armament:	Four single 102mm (4in) and one 76mm (2.9in) AA guns; four triple 533mm (21in) torpedo tubes
Powerplant:	Two sets of geared steam turbines
Performance:	35 knots

Dido

The 26-strong Leander class became the backbone of the Royal Navy's frigate force during the 1960s and early 1970s. Vessels of this class followed the basic pattern of the Rothesay/Whitby class, but were more versatile and had improved fighting capabilities. *Dido*, launched in December 1961, was equipped with a powerful early-warning radar, a bow-mounted sonar, and variable-depth sonar. In addition to her gun and missile armament, she carried a triple-barrelled anti-submarine mortar. She also carried a Wasp light helicopter (later replaced by a Lynx) which could be equipped with anti-submarine homing torpedoes. Some ships in this class, *Dido* included, had their guns replaced by the Ikara anti-submarine missile system. Several nations bought Leanders, or built them under licence. *Dido* was sold to New Zealand in 1983 as the *Southland*, and has now been stricken.

Country:	Great Britain
Type:	Frigate
Launch date:	22 December 1961
Crew:	263
Displacement:	2844 tonnes (2800 tons)
Dimensions:	113.3m x 12.4m x 5.4m (372ft x 41ft x 18ft)
Range:	8334km (4500nm)
Main armament:	Two 114mm (4.5in) guns; one quadruple launcher for Seacat SAMs
Powerplant:	Twin screw turbines
Performance:	30 knots

Dixmude

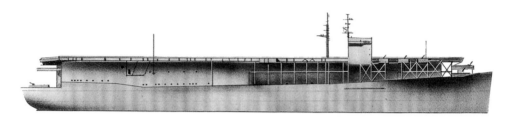

Dixmude was one of three escort carriers which were built in the USA for lease to Britain. The carrier's original name was *Rio Parana*. Launched in 1940, the flight deck was increased to 134 metres (440ft) on arrival in Britain, and in 1942 her US weapons were replaced with British 102mm (4in) Mk V guns. Renamed *Biter*, she mostly served on convoy escort duties. Escort carriers such as the *Biter* did much to turn the Battle of the Atlantic in the Allies' favour. She was returned to the USA in 1945 and handed over to France, where she became the *Dixmude* and served as an aircraft transport. She saw action in Indo-China during 1946–48. In the early 1950s she was disarmed, and in 1960 she was hulked as an accommodation ship. *Dixmude* was returned to the USA in 1966 and subsequently scrapped.

Country:	France
Type:	Aircraft carrier
Launch date:	18 December 1940
Crew:	555
Displacement:	11,989 tonnes (11,800 tons)
Dimensions:	150m x 23m x 7.6m (490ft 10in x 78ft x 25ft 2in)
Range:	7412km (4000nm) at 15 knots
Armament:	Three 102mm (4in) guns, 15 aircraft
Powerplant:	Single screw diesel engines
Performance:	16.5 knots

Dolfijn

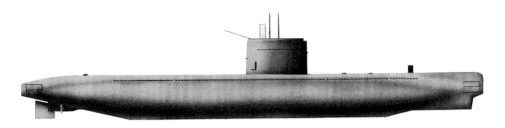

*D*olfijn was one of four diesel-electric submarines completed for the Royal Netherlands Navy in the early 1960s. She was of a triple-hulled design with a maximum diving depth of nearly 304m (1000ft). Her design represented a unique solution to the problem of internal space, the hull consisting of three cylinders arranged in a triangular shape. The upper cylinder housed the crew, navigational equipment and armament, while the lower cylinders housed the machinery. Construction of the four submarines was actually authorized in 1949, but in the case of two of them was suspended for some years because of financial constraints. *Dolfijn* and *Zeehond* were laid down in December 1954, *Potvis* in September 1962 and *Tonijn* November 1962. *Dolfijn* replaced another boat of the same name, which had a distinguished career in World War II.

Country:	Netherlands
Type:	Attack submarine
Launch date:	20 May 1959
Crew:	64
Displacement:	Surfaced: 1518 tonnes (1494 tons), submerged: 1855 tonnes (1826 tons)
Dimensions:	80m x 8m x 4.8m (260ft 10in x 25ft 9in x 15ft 9in)
Surface range:	not known
Armament:	Eight 533mm (21in) torpedo tubes
Powerplant:	Twin screw diesels. two electric motors
Performace:	Surfaced: 14.5 knots, submerged: 17 knots

Dolphin

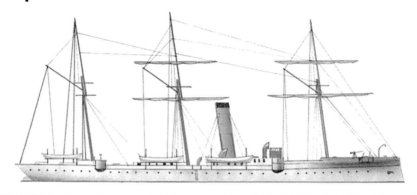

D*olphin* was the first warship of America's so-called 'New Navy', which came into being in parallel with an upsurge of overseas commercial interests. Launched in April 1884, *Dolphin* was the first all-steel warship in the US Navy. She originally had a light barque rig, but was re-rigged as a three-masted schooner before a third rig of only two masts was settled upon. She served mostly in the West Indies, but nearly became involved in hostilities with Chilean naval forces after the death of two American seamen during a revolt in Chile, which, during this period, was in a state of almost continual warfare. In a conflict with Peru, the Chilean navy was almost completely annihilated, and during the civil war which broke out in 1891, several naval actions were fought between rebel forces and government vessels. The *Dolphin* was sold in 1922.

Country:	USA
Type:	Gunboat
Launch date:	12 April 1884
Crew:	75
Displacement:	1509 tonnes (1486 tons)
Dimensions:	78m x 9.7m x 4.6m (256ft 6in x 32ft x 15ft 3in)
Range:	1852km (1000nm)
Main armament:	One 152mm (6in) gun
Powerplant:	Single screw vertical compound engines
Performance:	14 knots

Donetz

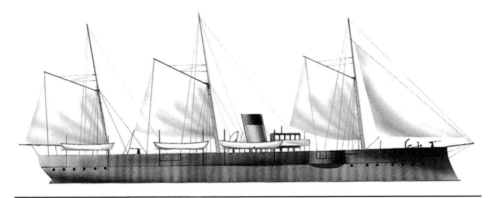

Launched in November 1887, *Donetz* was one of six ships of the Kubanetz class, all of which were built for operations in the Black Sea. They were considered to have been poorly designed and, in the case of the vessels built at Nikolaiev, to have suffered from poor workmanship. On 29 October 1914, *Donetz* was torpedoed in Odessa harbour by the Turkish destroyer *Gairet*. Although she was subsequently salvaged and repaired and put back into service, she was finally sunk in May 1919. The class leader, *Kubanetz*, saw service as an oiler during World War II as the *Krasni Kuban*, and was lost in unknown circumstances during the conflict. Another of the class, *Teretz* (renamed *Znamya Sozialisma*) was used as a school ship after the Russian Revolution. Most of the ships were rearmed with different gun calibres, and surviving vessels of the class had their fore and mizzen masts removed.

Country:	Russia
Type:	Gunboat
Launch date:	November 1887
Crew:	180
Displacement:	1219 tonnes (1200 tons)
Dimensions:	64m x 10.6m x 3m (210ft x 35ft x 10ft)
Range:	1666km (900nm)
Main armament:	One 152mm (6in) and two 203mm (8in) guns
Powerplant:	Twin screw horizontal compound engines
Performance:	14 knots

Doudart de Lagrée

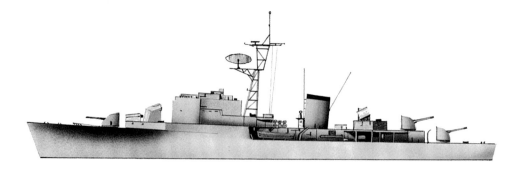

Nine vessels of the Commandant Riviere class were built under the French Navy's 1956–57 estimates by the Lorient Naval Dockyard. They were good general-purpose anti-submarine vessels of small displacement, and were intended for patrol work or escort duties. Their speed was not particularly high, but they packed a reasonable amount of equipment into a light hull. One vessel was fitted with an experimental combined gas turbine/diesel installation, which gave a dramatic increase in maximum range. *Doudart de Lagrée* had a wartime crew complement of 214, and could also carry some 80 commandos. In later life, one of her 100mm (3.9in) gun turrets was replaced by four Exocet missile launchers. The other vessels in the class were *Amiral Charner, Balny, Commandant Bory, Commandant Bourdais, Ensigne de Vaisseau Henry, Protet* and *Victor Schoelcher.*

Country:	France
Type:	Frigate
Launch date:	15 April 1961
Crew:	214
Displacement:	2235 tonnes (2200 tons)
Dimensions:	102m x 11.5m x 3.8m (334ft x 37ft 9in x 12ft 6in)
Range:	7408km (4000nm)
Main armament:	Three 100mm (3.9in) guns; twin AA weapons
Powerplant:	Twin screw diesels
Performance:	25 knots

Downes

At the time of their building, the 46 Knox-class ocean escorts, of which *Downes* was one, comprised the largest group of destroyer-escort type warships built to the same design in the West since World War II. The ships were almost identical to the earlier Garcia and Brooke classes, but slightly larger. Original planning provided for the vessels to have the Sea Mauler, a short-range anti-aircraft missile adapted from a missile being developed by the US Army, but the Mauler/Sea Mauler programme was abandoned because of technical difficulties. Mauler/Sea Mauler was a slim high-acceleration missile carried in a box of 12 and operated by a two-man crew; it could be used to spearhead amphibious assaults and engage low-flying aircraft. The ships had a very large superstructure and a distinctive cylindrical structure combining masts and engine exhaust stacks.

Country:	USA
Type:	Frigate
Launch date:	13 December 1969
Crew:	220
Displacement:	4165 tonnes (4100 tons)
Dimensions:	126.6m x 14m x 7.5m (415ft 4in x 46ft 9in x 24ft 7in)
Range:	8338km (4500nm)
Main armament:	One 127mm (5in) gun; one eight-tube Sea Sparrow missile launcher; Phalanx CIWS
Powerplant:	Single screw, turbines
Performance:	27 knots

Doyle

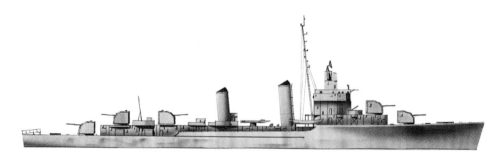

Developed from the Sims class, the large Benson-Livermore class to which *Doyle* belonged was the last destroyer class to be designed and built for the US Navy before the Americans entered World War II. Production was speeded up by the elimination of unnecessary curves in the superstructure, and many of the class were completed with straight-fronted bridge structures. Many ships in the class were transferred to friendly foreign navies after World War II, and continued to give good service for many years. The USS *Doyle*, launched in March 1942, spent her war service on convoy escort and ASW duty in the central Atlantic, and supported the Allied landings in Normandy and the south of France in June and August of 1944. Along with 23 of her sister ships, Doyle was converted to the role of high-speed minesweeper in 1945.

Country:	USA
Type:	Destroyer
Launch date:	17 March 1942
Crew:	250
Displacement:	2621 tonnes (2580 tons)
Dimensions:	106m x 11m x 5.4m (348ft 6in x 36ft x 18ft)
Range:	5556km (3000nm)
Main armament:	Four 127mm (5in) guns; five 533mm (21in) torpedo tubes
Powerplant:	Twin screw, turbines
Performance:	37 knots

Doyle

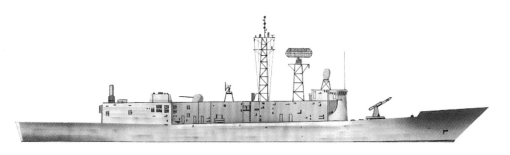

The vessels of the Oliver Hazard Perry class of guided-missile frigate, to which USS *Doyle* belongs, were tailored to cost, and as a result many limitations became apparent in service. (The British had the same problem with their Type 42 destroyers). For example, the USS *Stark* suffered intense fire damage after being hit by two Exocet missiles in the Persian Gulf on 17 May 1987. Since then, there have been many improvements in damage control procedures and equipment to cope with residual missile-propellant-induced fires. On 14 April 1988, the *Samuel B. Roberts* was mined in the Gulf. Fourteen ships of this class were active in the 1991 war with Iraq. In all, 39 units were built for the US Navy; Australia bought four of the class and has since built two more. Spain has six of the class and Taiwan is building seven, while others have been either leased or sold to Bahrain and Egypt.

Country:	USA
Type:	Frigate
Launch date:	22 May 1985
Crew:	200
Displacement:	3696 tonnes (3638 tons)
Dimensions:	135.6m x 13.7m x 7.5m (444ft 10in x 45ft x 24ft 7in)
Range:	7408km (4000nm)
Main armament:	One 76mm (3in); four Harpoon SSM; Standard SAM system
Powerplant:	Single screw, gas turbines
Performance:	29 knots

Dragone

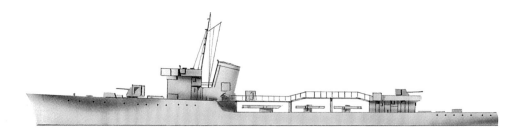

*D*ragone and her sisters were enlarged versions of the previous Spica class, but were slower, in spite of an increase in machinery power. *Dragone* was taken over by the Germans after Italy's surrender and numbered *TA30*. In May 1944, she joined other destroyers of her type in minelaying operations in the Ligurian Sea which lies between the northern tip of Corsica and Genoa, and was of strategic importance at this time. The destroyers were challenged by American PT boats, most notably in a clash on 30 May, when both sides sustained light damage. On the night of 15–16 June, *TA26* (formerly *Ardito*) and *TA30* were carrying out a mining operation when they were attacked by the American boats *PT558*, *PT552* and *PT559*. Both the *TA26* and the *TA30* were sunk in the engagement. It is sometimes stated that *Dragone* was sunk by Royal Navy light forces, which was not the case.

Country:	Italy
Type:	Destroyer
Launch date:	14 August 1943
Crew:	175
Displacement:	1117 tonnes (1100 tons)
Dimensions:	83.5m x 8.6m x 3.1m (274ft x 28ft 3in x 10ft 4in)
Range:	1851km (1000nm)
Main armament:	Two 102mm (4in) guns; six 450mm (17.7in) torpedo tubes; plus smaller weapons
Powerplant:	Twin screw, turbines
Performance:	31.5 knots

Dragonfly

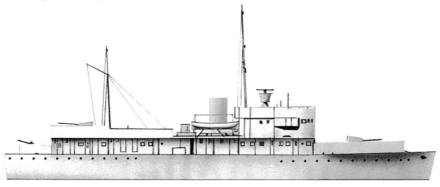

Launched in December 1938, *Dragonfly* was similar to the *Scorpion* of 1937, but slightly smaller. Five vessels were originally planned for this class of river gunboat, but one (*Bee*) was ultimately cancelled, while *Locust* and *Mosquito* were not completed until 1940. The engines developed 3800hp and carried 91.5 tonnes (90 tons). The vessels were intended primarily for river patrols in the Far East. Small and compact, with a shallow draught, they were able to navigate up most of the shallow rivers in the Malay peninsula, policing areas often unsettled by warring local chieftains. On 14 February 1942, *Dragonfly* and her sister ship HMS *Grasshopper* were bombed and sunk by Japanese aircraft south of Singapore. Another of the class, *Mosquito*, had been sunk two years previously during the evacuation of Dunkirk on 1 June 1940.

Country:	Great Britain
Type:	River gunboat
Launch date:	December 1938
Crew:	74
Displacement:	726 tonnes (715 tons)
Dimensions:	60m x 10m x 1.8m (196ft 6in x 33ft 8in x 6ft 2in)
Range:	1852km (1000nm)
Main armament:	Two 102mm (4in) guns
Powerplant:	Two-shaft geared turbines
Performance:	17 knots

Dreadnought

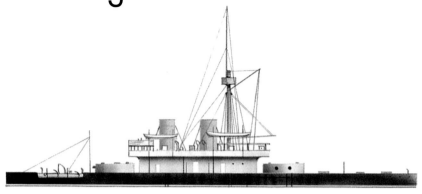

This vessel was originally designed by Edward J. Reed as a unit of the Devastation class to be called *Fury*. Work was suspended while she was on the stocks, pending a report on stability, protection and armament that was being prepared by the Committee of Designs. As *Dreadnought*, the ship was eventually completed in 1879 as a larger version of *Devastation*, and she incorporated many modifications on the earlier design. The 317mm (12.5in) guns were of a new specification, and were carried by *Dreadnought* throughout her entire career. The complete armour belt was the thickest continuous protection carried by a British warship. Commissioned in 1884, she served with the Mediterranean Fleet for 10 years before returning for a refit. She was used as a torpedo boat depot ship at Devonport, then broken up in 1908.

Country:	Great Britain
Type:	Battleship
Launch date:	8 March 1875
Crew:	369
Displacement:	11,060 tonnes (10,886 tons)
Dimensions:	104.5m x 19.4m x 8m (343ft x 63ft 10in x 26ft 3in)
Range:	9635km (5200nm) at 10 knots
Armament:	Four 317mm (12.5in) guns
Powerplant:	Twin screw, vertical compound engines
Performance:	14.5 knots

Dreadnought

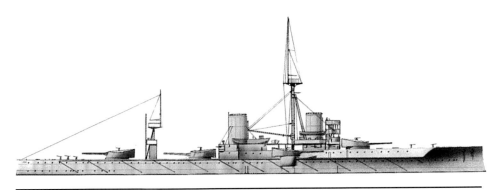

With the launching of *Dreadnought* in 1906, a new and more advanced era of warship construction began. *Dreadnought* was the first 'all-big-gun' battleship, so much so that she made all existing battleships obsolete. *Dreadnought* saw active service in World War I, being surpassed only by even larger ships of her type, to which she gave her generic name. Despite her warlike reputation, during World War I she only sank one enemy vessel, a German submarine which she rammed. The Royal Navy's Dreadnought fleet at the outbreak of World War I was thinly stretched, and after two months of hostilities ships had to be sent to their home ports on the south coast for refit. This meant that two or three of the Grand Fleet's most important vessels were absent from active duty at any one time. She was scrapped in 1923.

Country:	Great Britain
Type:	Battleship
Launch date:	10 February 1906
Crew:	695–773
Displacement:	22,194 tonnes (21,845 tons)
Dimensions:	160.4m x 25m x 8m (526ft 3in x 82ft x 26ft 3in)
Range:	11,916km (6620nm) at 10 knots
Armament:	10 304mm (12in) guns
Powerplant:	Quadruple screw turbines
Performance:	21.6 knots

Dreadnought

L aunched on Trafalgar Day, 21 October 1960, HMS *Dreadnought* was the Royal Navy's first nuclear-powered attack submarine (SSN), and was specifically designed to hunt and destroy hostile undersea craft. She was powered by an American S5W reactor, which was also used in the US Navy's Skipjack-class nuclear submarines; subsequent Royal Navy SSNs had a British-designed nuclear plant. *Dreadnought* began sea trials in 1962. The Royal Navy carried out much pioneering work with *Dreadnought,* including proving the concept of using nuclear submarines to act as escorts for a fast carrier task group; the results of this work were made available to the US Navy, which had a close relationship with the Royal Navy at this time. Although used as a trials vessel, *Dreadnought* was a fully-capable SSN.

Country:	Great Britain
Type:	Attack submarine
Launch date:	21 October 1960
Crew:	88
Displacement:	Surfaced: 3556 tonnes (3500 tons), submerged: 4064 tonnes (4000 tons)
Dimensions:	81m x 9.8m x 8m (265ft 9in x 32ft 3in x 26ft 3in)
Range:	Unlimited
Armament:	Six 533mm (21in) torpedo tubes
Powerplant:	Single screw, nuclear reactor, steam turbines
Performance:	Surfaced: 20 knots, submerged: 30 knots

Drum

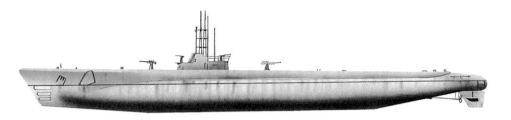

D*rum* was a double hull, ocean-going submarine with good seakeeping qualities and range. She was one of the Gato class of over 300 boats, and as such was part of the largest warship project undertaken by the US Navy. These boats, more than any others, were to wreak havoc on Japan's mercantile shipping in the Pacific war. During her first offensive patrol in April 1942 *Drum* (Lt Cdr Rice) sank the seaplane carrier *Mizuho* and two merchant ships, and later in the year she carried out vital reconnaissance work prior to the American landings in Guadalcanal.
In October 1942 she sank three more ships off the east coast of Japan, and in December she torpedoed the Japanese carrier *Ryuho*. She sank a further two ships in April 1943, another in September, one in November, and three in October 1944, with another damaged. She is now a museum exhibit.

Country:	USA
Type:	Attack submarine
Launch date:	12 May 1941
Crew:	80
Displacement:	Surfaced: 1854 tonnes (1825 tons), submerged: 2448 tonnes (2410 tons)
Dimensions:	95m x 8.3m x 4.6m (311ft 9in x 27ft 3in x 15ft 3in)
Surface range:	22236km (12,000nm) at 10 knots
Armament:	Ten 533mm (21in) torpedo tubes; one 76mm (3in) gun
Powerplant:	Twin screw diesels, electric motors
Performance:	Surfaced: 20 knots, submerged: 10 knots

Duguay-Trouin

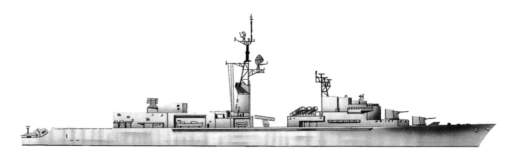

*D*uguay-Trouin was one of three vessels in a class that were designed to follow on from the earlier Aconite class destroyer. The single-screw propulsion of the earlier class had proved unsuccessful, leading to a doubling-up of the machinery in *Duguay-Trouin*. This resulted in an increase in speed of four knots. Helicopter facilities were included, plus essential backup, making the *Duguay-Trouin* and her sister vessels the first French warships of destroyer size to operate anti-submarine helicopters. The missile launcher is mounted forward of the funnel, which also carries the mast, with extensive magazines below. *Duguay-Trouin* was launched in June 1973 and retired in 1999. She was named after Admiral René Duguay-Trouin (1673-1736), who distinguished himself particularly in the wars of Louis XIV, was revered by his sailors, and died in virtual poverty.

Country:	France
Type:	Destroyer
Launch date:	1 June 1973
Crew:	250
Displacement:	5892 tonnes (5800 tons)
Dimensions:	152.5m x 15.3m x 6.5m (500ft 4in x 50ft 2in x 21ft 4in)
Range:	9630km (5200nm)
Main armament:	Two 100mm (3.9in) guns; one eight-cell Crotale missile launcher
Powerplant:	Twin screw, turbines
Performance:	32 knots

Duilio

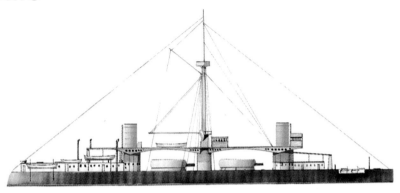

***D**uilio* and her sister *Enrico Dandolo* were turret ships designed by Benedetto
Brin, and upon completion were the most powerful warships in the world.
They were the first warships to be rigged with just a military mast and to be armed
with giant guns. Although laid down in 1873, *Duilio* was not completed until 1880.
She was modernised in 1890, and again in 1900. After providing good service,
Duilio was stripped of her armament in 1909 and became a floating oil tank.
Duilio's designer, Benedetto Brin, was a brilliant engineer whose designs did
much to keep Italy at the forefront of maritime power. Vessels such as *Duilio*
and *Dandalo*, with their massive guns, inspired competitive designs in other
countries. Several of Brin's creations were exported to other countries, such as
Spain, Argentina and Japan.

Country:	Italy
Type:	Battleship
Launch date:	8 May 1876
Crew:	420, later 515
Displacement:	12,264 tonnes (12,071 tons)
Dimensions:	109m x 19.7m x 8.3m (358ft 2in x 64ft 8in x 27ft 3in)
Range:	6768km (3760nm) at 10 knots
Armament:	Four 450mm (17.7in) guns
Powerplant:	Twin screw, vertical compound engines
Performance:	15 knots

Duilio

Completed in 1916 as members of the Doria class, *Duilio* and her sister *Andrea Doria* underwent several changes in their careers, for example, receiving seaplanes in 1925. Extensive modernisation between 1937 and 1940 upgraded both their armour and guns and turned both vessels into virtually new ships. *Duilio* was damaged in the British air attack on Taranto naval base, in November 1940. She was towed to Genoa for repair and narrowly escaped further damage when the port was bombarded by British warships in February 1941. Returned to active service later that year, she was employed on convoy interception and escort duty before being placed on the Reserve in 1942. After her surrender to the Allies at Malta in September 1943 she was used as a training ship. She was broken up at La Spezia in 1957.

Country:	Italy
Type:	Battleship
Launch date:	24 April 1913
Crew:	1198
Displacement:	29,861 tonnes (29,391 tons)
Dimensions:	187m x 28m x 8.5m (613ft 2in x 91ft 10in x 28ft 2in)
Range:	8640km (4800nm) at 12 knots
Armament:	10 320mm (12.6in) guns
Powerplant:	Twin screw turbines
Performance:	27 knots

Duncan

HMS *Duncan* was one of 14 C and D class destroyers laid down in 1931 and 1932 respectively. They were slightly enlarged versions of the B class. Whereas the C-class boats served in the Western Approaches and North Atlantic, the D class were all transferred to the Mediterranean from China when war broke out. *Duncan* was fitted out as a destroyer leader and spent two years on the Gibraltar station as apart of Force H, escorting Mediterranean convoys, and taking part in the Allied landings at Diego Suarez, Madagascar, before being transferred to the Western Approaches. In May 1943, while on convoy escort duty, she helped to sink the *U381* and damaged the *U707*. She was scrapped at Barrow in November 1945. No fewer than nine of the other ships in her class were lost during the war, including three of the five that were transferred to the Royal Canadian Navy.

Country:	Great Britain
Type:	Destroyer
Launch date:	7 July 1932
Crew:	145
Displacement:	1973 tonnes (1942 tons)
Dimensions:	100m x 10m x 4m (329ft x 32ft 10in x 12ft 10in)
Range:	2778km (1500nm)
Main armament:	Four 120mm (4.7in) guns
Powerplant:	Twin screw, turbines
Performance:	35.5 knots

Dunkerque

Based on the British Nelson class battleships, *Dunkerque* was the first French warship to be laid down after the Washington Treaty of 1922. She was the culmination of a series of design studies that resulted in an answer to the German Deutschland class of the early 1930s. A hangar and a catapult were provided for the four scout planes which she was to carry. In October 1939, as flagship of the Brest-based Force L, she joined the Royal Navy in the hunt for the German pocket battleship *Admiral Graf Spee*. She was employed on convoy escort duty until the surrender of France, and in July 1940 she was severely damaged by British warships at Mers-el-Kebir and by a torpedo attack three days later, with the loss of 210 lives. She was scuttled in Toulon harbour in 1942, and raised and sold for scrap in 1953.

Country:	France
Type:	Battleship
Launch date:	2 October 1935
Crew:	1431
Displacement:	36,068 tonnes (35,500 tons)
Dimensions:	214.5m x 31m x 8.6m (703ft 9in x 102ft 3in x 28ft 6in)
Range:	13,897km (7500nm) at 15 knots
Armament:	16 127mm (5in), eight 330mm (13in) guns
Powerplant:	Quadruple screw turbines
Performance:	29.5 knots

Dunois

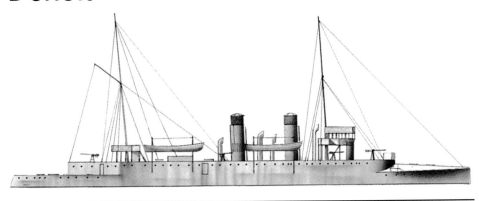

Launched in October 1897, *Dunois* was a twin-funnelled vessel with two pole masts, a straight stem and a turtle-backed foredeck. No torpedoes were fitted in this group, and the main armament was situated on the upper deck near the funnels. In service, neither *Dunois* nor her sister ship made their designed speed of 21.7 knots, but they were able to make 20 knots for lengthy periods. Although the French Navy classed the ships as contre-torpilleurs (destroyers) they were much too slow to be so rated. *Dunois* was deactivated in 1920. The French still had nine river gunboats in service at the outbreak of World War II, two of them assigned to duty in China and the others in French Indo-China. Most were laid down just after World War I and completed in the early 1920s. All were scuttled in the face of the Japanese advance, or sunk by enemy action.

Country:	France
Type:	Gunboat
Launch date:	October 1897
Crew:	75
Displacement:	903 tonnes (889 tons)
Dimensions:	78m x 8.4m x 3.8m (256ft x 27ft 10in x 12ft 8in)
Range:	2037km (1100nm)
Main armament:	Six nine-pounder guns
Powerplant:	Twin screw vertical triple expansion engines
Performance:	20 knots

Dupleix

Launched in October 1975, the *Dupleix* was one of eight ships built at Brest Naval Dockyard for service as anti-submarine vessels. The class, also known as the C70 ASW class, was actually divided into two sub-groups, the first fitted out for anti-submarine warfare and the other for air defence. A major innovation was the use of gas turbine engines. These can develop 52,000hp for a speed of 30 knots, compared with the diesels, which develop 10,400hp for 18 knots. The use of gas turbines, however, produced severe limitations on the available space amidships due to the requirement for the extensive intake and uptake trunking. This forced a choice between the Malafon anti-submarine missile and AS helicopters; the latter were chosen, and all ships in the class carry a double hangar aft. In time of war, an extra battery of four Exocet anti-ship missiles can be fitted.

Country:	France
Type:	Destroyer
Launch date:	2 December 1978
Crew:	250
Displacement:	4236 tonnes (4170 tons)
Dimensions:	139m x 14m x 5.7m (456ft x 46ft x 18ft 8in)
Range:	8334km (4500nm)
Main armament:	One 100mm (3.9in) gun; two fixed torpedo launchers
Powerplant:	Twin screw gas turbines, plus diesels
Performance:	30 knots

Duquesne

Originally classed as light cruisers, the *Duquesne* and her sister ship *Suffren* were the first French destroyers designed specifically to carry surface-to-air missiles, in this case the Masurca, mounted on a twin-round launcher. They were intended to provide both anti-aircraft and anti-submarine protection for the new generation of French aircraft carriers. *Duquesne* is also fitted with four Exocet missile launchers. *Suffren* became operational in July 1968, and *Duquesne* followed in January 1969. The structure of the ships provided the best possible resistance to atomic blast, and carefully studied habitability was a feature of the design. The *Duquesne* was named after the celebrated sixteenth-century French Admiral Abraham Duquesne (1610–1688), who achieved some notable sea victories in the Mediterranean.

Country:	France
Type:	Destroyer
Launch date:	12 February 1966
Crew:	446
Displacement:	6187 tonnes (6090 tons)
Dimensions:	157.6m x 15.2m x 7.2m (517ft x 50ft x 23ft 9in)
Range:	9260km (5000nm)
Main armament:	Two 100mm (3.9in) guns; one Malafon anti-submarine missile launcher; four torpedo launchers
Powerplant:	Twin screw turbines
Performance:	34 knots

Duncan

The second destroyer to bear the name (the earlier one was lost on 12 October 1942 of Guadalcanal), the USS *Duncan* was part of an extensive World War II building programme of ocean-going destroyers, all of which were equipped with a powerful armament and strengthened by a good radius of action. Thirty-six of the original group, known as the Gearing class, were converted in 1949 and fitted with enemy aircraft early-warning systems. Of the class of nearly 100 units, several were still in service as late as 1980. *Duncan* herself, launched in October 1944, arrived in the Pacific just in time to participate in Japan's surrender, functioning as a radar picket ship with the destroyer USS *Rogers* as part of Rear-Admiral Ballentine's Task Group 38.2. She served for many years post-war, being finally stricken from the Navy list in 1973.

Country:	USA
Type:	Destroyer
Launch date:	27 October 1944
Crew:	350
Displacement:	3606 tonnes (3550 tons)
Dimensions:	120m x 12.5m x 5.8m (390ft 6in x 41ft x 19ft)
Range:	5556km (3000nm)
Main armament:	Six 127mm (5in) guns; six torpedo tubes
Powerplant:	Twin screw, turbines
Performance:	35 knots

Durandal

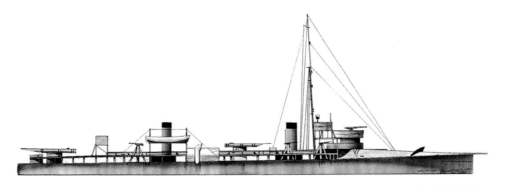

Launched in February 1899, *Durandal* was France's first destroyer, and the lead ship of a four-strong class ordered in 1896 as prototypes for a new type of anti-torpedo-boat vessel. The ships were built by Normand, who already had wide experience in building torpedo craft. Two Normand water tube boilers supplied the engines, which developed 4800hp. Coal supply was about 38 tons. *Durandal* had a flying deck which ran nearly her entire length, with funnels and gun mounts passing up through it. As originally completed, she had two masts. All vessels in the class could make 26 knots in bad weather and were generally good sea boats. *Durandal* was named after the sword of the legendary French medieval hero, Roland. According to the legend, Roland died while covering the retreat of Charlemagne's army in the Pass of Ronceveaux.

Country:	France
Type:	Destroyer
Launch date:	11 February 1899
Crew:	98
Displacement:	300 tonnes (296 tons)
Dimensions:	57.5m x 6.3m x 3.1m (188ft 8in x 20ft 8in x 10ft 5in)
Range:	1852km (1000nm)
Main armament:	One 65mm (2.6in) and six 47mm (1.85in) guns; two 380mm (15in) torpedo tubes
Powerplant:	Twin screw triple expansion engines
Performance:	26 knots

Dykkeren

Dykkeren was built in Italy by Fiat-San Giorgio, La Spezia. She was sold to the Danish Navy in October 1909. She had many teething troubles but improved at the Copenhagen Naval Yard. In 1916 she was in collision with the Norwegian steamer *Vesta* off Bergen, and sank. Salvaged in 1917, she was broken up the following year. Although a small country, Denmark maintained a strong and efficient navy for coastal defence, and in fact possessed one of the world's first ironclads – the *Rolf Krake*. A number of ironclad warships were built for coastal defence and two were purchased which had been intended for the Confederate Navy. Denmark succeeded in maintaining its neutrality throughout the various European conflicts until 1940, when the country was occupied by German forces. She acquired four patrol submarines post-World War II.

Country:	Denmark
Type:	Attack submarine
Launch date:	June 1909
Crew:	35
Displacement:	Surfaced: 107 tonnes (105 tons), submerged: 134 tonnes (132 tons)
Dimensions:	34.7m x 3.3m x 2m (113ft 10in x 10ft 10in x 6ft 6in)
Surface range:	185km (100nm) at 12 knots
Armament:	Two 457mm (18in) torpedo tubes
Powerplant:	Twin screw petrol engine, one electric motor
Performance:	Surfaced: 12 knots, submerged: 7.5 knots

E11

Completed between 1913 and 1916, the E-class submarines ran to 55 hulls whose construction, once war was declared, was shared between 13 private yards. They fell into five major groups, differences being primarily in torpedo layout and the adaptation of six boats to carry 20 mines in place of their amidships tubes. *E11*, under the command of the talented Lt Cdr Martin Nasmith, was arguably the most famous of them all; operating in the Dardanelles area she scored many successes, including the sinking of the Turkish battleship *Hairredin Barbarossa*. Many RN submariners who rose to high rank learned their trade in E-class boats. For operations in the Dardanelles, the British submarines adopted a blue camouflage to conceal themselves in the shallow, clear waters. The class was also active in the North Sea and the Baltic. In all, 22 were lost.

Country:	Great Britain
Type:	Attack submarine
Launch date:	1913
Crew:	30
Displacement:	Surfaced: 677 tonnes (667 tons), submerged: 820 tonnes (807 tons)
Dimensions:	55.17m x 6.91m x 3.81m (181ft x 22ft 8in x 12ft 6in)
Surface range:	6035km (3579nm)
Armament:	Five 457mm (18in) torpedo tubes; one 12-pounder gun
Powerplant:	Two twin-shaft diesel engines, two electric motors
Performance:	Surfaced: 14 knots, submerged: 9 knots

Eagle

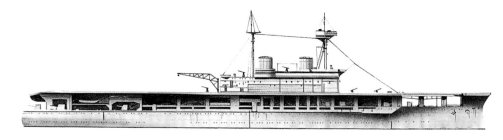

*E**agle* was originally laid down in 1913 as the Chilean Navy's super-
dreadnought *Almirante Cochrane*. With the outbreak of World War I work
stopped and it only began again in 1917 after her purchase by the Royal Navy.
Construction of the ship then continued, and the vessel was turned into an aircraft
carrier. Eventually, she entered service in 1924. When Italy entered the war on the
Axis side in June 1940, *Eagle* was the only aircraft carrier at the disposal of the
British in the Mediterranean, and she performed sterling service in ferrying
fighter aircraft to the besieged island of Malta. She had previously operated in the
Indian Ocean and the South Atlantic, based in Ceylon, her main task being to
search for German commerce raiders. In August 1942, *Eagle* was sunk in the
Mediterranean by *U73* while attempting to deliver aircraft to Malta.

Country:	Great Britain
Type:	Aircraft carrier
Launch date:	8 June 1918
Crew:	950
Displacement:	27,664 tonnes (27,229 tons)
Dimensions:	203.4m x 32m x 8m (667ft 6in x 105ft x 26ft 3in)
Range:	5559km (3000nm) at 15 knots
Armament:	Five 102mm (4in), nine 152mm (6in) guns, 21 aircraft
Powerplant:	Quadruple screw turbines
Performance:	22.5 knots

Eagle

With the completion of the naval construction programmes of 1936 and 1937 and with the construction of the Illustrious class carriers of 1938 in progress, designs were prepared in 1942 for their successors. These designs allowed for two complete hangars to be built together with the ability to handle the heavier aircraft that were expected to be introduced. *Eagle* entered service in October 1951, was decommissioned in January 1972, and was sent for breaking-up in 1978. She was the sister ship of HMS *Ark Royal*. During her service career she took part in many peacekeeping actions, but she is perhaps best remembered for her offensive role in the Anglo-French Suez operations, when her aircraft carried out numerous strikes on targets in the Suez Canal Zone in support of Anglo–French ground forces.

Country of origin:	Great Britain
Type:	Aircraft carrier
Launch date:	19 March 1946
Crew:	2740
Displacement:	47,200 tonnes (46,452 tons)
Dimensions:	245m x 34m x 11m (803ft 9in x 112ft 9in x 36ft)
Range:	7412km (4000nm) at 20 knots
Armament:	16 112mm (4.5in) guns
Powerplant:	Quadruple screw turbines
Performance:	32 knots

Echo

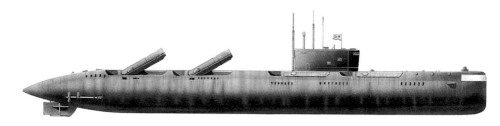

The five Echo-class SSNs were originally built at Komsomolsk in the Soviet Far East in 1960-62 as Echo I-class missile submarines (SSGNs). Armed with six tubes for the SS-N-3C Shaddock strategic cruise missile, they lacked the fire control and guidance radars of the later Echo II class, 29 of which were built. All but five of the Echo IIs served in the Northern Fleet. As the Soviet ballistic-missile submarine force was built up the need for these interim missile boats diminished, and they were converted to anti-ship attack SSNs between 1969 and 1974. The conversion involved the removal of the Shaddock tubes, the plating over and streamlining of the hull to reduce the underwater noise caused by the tube system, and modification of the sonar systems. The Echo boats were withdrawn in the 1980s.

Country:	Soviet Union
Type:	Attack submarine
Launch date:	1960
Crew:	90
Displacement:	Surfaced: 4572 tonnes (4500 tons), submerged: 5588 tonnes (5500 tons)
Dimensions:	110m x 9m x 7.5m (360ft 11in x 29ft 6in x 24ft 7in)
Range:	Unlimited
Armament:	Six 533mm (21in) and two 406mm (16 in) torpedo tubes
Powerplant:	One pressurized water reactor, two steam turbines
Performance:	Surfaced: 20 knots, submerged: 28 knots

Edinburgh

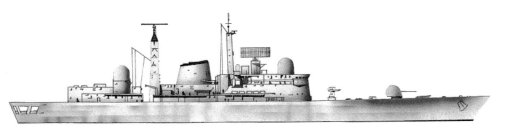

With the cancellation of a planned new generation of aircraft carriers in the mid-1960s, a Naval Staff Requirement was issued for a small fleet escort capable of providing area defence. This resulted in the Type 42 class design, which suffered considerably during gestation from constraints that were placed on the dimensions as a result of the British Treasury pressure to minimise costs. As built, the ships lacked any close-range air defence system, had reduced endurance on full power output from their gas turbines, and suffered from a short forecastle which resulted in a very wet forward section. The main armament included the Sea Dart SAM system, which proved to be a very effective area defence in the Falklands and the Gulf. The ships were built in three batches, HMS *Edinburgh* being issued as part of Batch 3. The class will be replaced by the Type 45 class from 2007.

Country:	Great Britain
Type:	Destroyer
Launch date:	14 April 1983
Crew:	300-312
Displacement:	4851 tonnes (4775 tons)
Dimensions:	141.1m x 14.6m x 5.8m (463ft x 48ft x 19ft)
Range:	5185km (2800nm)
Main armament:	One 114mm (4.5in) gun; helicopter-launched Mk44 torpedoes; two triple mounts for Mk46 AS torpedoes; one Sea Dart SAM launcher
Powerplant:	Twin screw, gas turbines
Performance:	30 knots

Ekaterina II

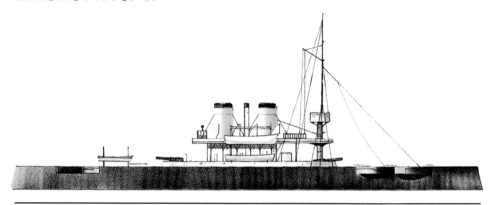

Russia's geography meant that its navy was divided into separate fleets in the Baltic, Black Sea and in the Far East, each with a different operational role. Until the 1870s the main arm of the Russian Navy comprised cruisers for commerce raiding, but as Russia sought to expand its power, so its naval strength was increased with the deployment of new warships. *Ekaterina II* was built for the Black Sea Fleet, and was one of the first major warships to have triple expansion engines. She and her sisters were among the most powerful battleships of their day, with their six guns mounted on a pear-shaped redoubt amidships. *Ekaterina II* was reclassified as a second-class battleship in 1906, and a year later became a target ship. She was sunk during target practice off Tendra harbour in 1907.

Country of origin:	Russia
Type:	Battleship
Launch date:	22 May 1886
Crew:	674
Displacement:	11,224 tonnes (11,048 tons)
Dimensions:	100.9m x 21m x 8.5m (331ft x 68ft 11in x 27ft 11in)
Range:	2500km (1350nm) at 12 knots
Armament:	Six 304mm (12in) guns
Powerplant:	Twin screw, vertical triple expansion engines
Performance:	16 knots

Elan

At the outbreak of World War II, the French fleet was poorly served for escorts in the accepted sense of the word, those available being designed primarily for colonial service. For effective anti-submarine work, therefore, the Free French Navy relied on frigates, corvettes and DEs transferred from the Royal Navy or the US Navy. The exception was the 15-strong Elan-class vessels, completed between 1939 and 1940 and fitted out as minesweepers. Those that escaped capture by Axis forces after the fall of France were pressed into service in the ASW role; despite their relatively low speed compared with that of the Royal Navy's Flower class, they had an excellent endurance. The class leader, *Elan*, captured the German cargo ship *Rostock* on 10 February 1940 and later took part in the short Syrian campaign. Afterwards, she was interned in Turkey until December 1944.

Country:	France
Type:	Corvette
Launch date:	27 July 1938
Crew:	Not known
Displacement:	752 tonnes (740 tons)
Dimensions:	78m x 8.5m x 2.4m (255ft 11in x 27ft 11in x 7ft 11in)
Range:	16,645km (8988nm)
Main armament:	Two 100mm (3.9in) guns
Powerplant:	Two shafts, two diesel engines
Performance:	20 knots

Electra

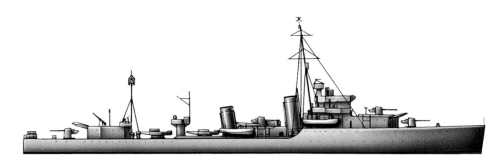

Launched on February 1934, HMS *Electra* was one of nine E-class destroyers. She saw initial action off Norway in April 1940, and a year later, as part of the escort to the battleship Prince of Wales, she took participated in the hunt for the German battleship *Bismarck*. In October 1941, together with the destroyer *Express*, she accompanied the Prince of Wales to Singapore, and was present when the battleship and the battlecruiser *Repulse* were sunk off Malaya by Japanese air attack on 10 December 1941. On 27 February 1942, she formed part of a mixed force of British, Dutch, and American warships that sailed to intercept Japanese invasion forces in the Java Sea. In a confused short-range action with eight enemy destroyers and the cruiser *Naka*, the *Electra* attacked through a smokescreen and was seen no more.

Country:	Great Britain
Type:	Destroyer
Launch date:	15 February 1934
Crew:	145
Displacement:	1397 tonnes (1375 tons)
Dimensions:	100.2m x 10.3m x 2.6m (329ft x 33ft 9in x 8ft 6in)
Range:	3889km (2100nm)
Main armament:	Four 120mm (4.7in) guns; eight 533mm (21in) torpedo tubes
Powerplant:	Two-shaft geared turbines
Performance:	35.5 knots

Emanuele Pessagno

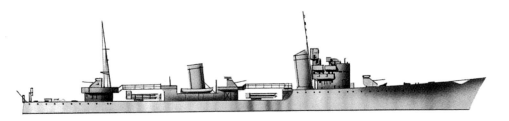

The *Emanuele Pessagno* was ordered in 1926 and laid down between 1927 and 1928. She and the other 11 vessels that made up her class all saw extensive service in World War II. Although smaller than their French rivals of the Guepard and Jaguar classes, the Italian vessels carried the same powerful armament and had a three-knot speed advantage over them. During trials, one of *Emanuele Pessagno*'s sisters was reported to have achieved 45 knots. When first completed, the vessels were classified as scouts, but by 1938 they were listed as destroyers. Only one vessel survived the war; eight were sunk in combat, two were scuttled, and one was mined. In May 1942, the *Emanuele Pessagno*, while escorting Italian supply convoys to Benghazi, was torpedoed and sunk by the British submarine HMS *Turbulent* (Cdr Linton).

Country:	Italy
Type:	Destroyer
Launch date:	12 August 1929
Crew:	225
Displacement:	2621 tonnes (2580 tons)
Dimensions:	107.3m x 10.8m x 3.4m (352ft x 33ft 6in x 11ft 2in)
Range:	3426km (1850nm)
Main armament:	Six 120mm (4.7in) guns; six 533mm (21in) torpedo tubes
Powerplant:	Twin screw, turbines
Performance:	38 knots

Engadine

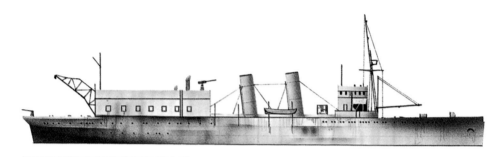

At the outbreak of World War I, the British Admiralty took over a number of fast cross-channel steamers for conversion into seaplane carriers. *Engadine* and her sister *Riviera* were two such ships and both were quickly converted to carry three aircraft. By December 1914 they were in action against the German airship sheds at Cuxhaven. *Engadine* was modified in 1915. She then served with the Grand Fleet, carrying out North Sea sweeps and anti-submarine patrols, and pursuing the German airships then beginning to increase their attacks upon the British mainland. During the Battle of Jutland in 1916, a Short 184 seaplane from *Engadine* made the first-ever air reconnaissance of a fleet in action, transmitting the position of the German warships by means of wireless telegraphy. *Engadine* later served in the Mediterranean. She was returned to her owners in 1919.

Country:	Great Britain
Type:	Seaplane carrier
Launch date:	23 September 1911
Crew:	250
Displacement:	1702 tonnes (1676 tons)
Dimensions:	96.3m x 12.5m (316 ft x 41ft)
Range:	2779km (1500nm) at 18 knots
Armament:	Two 102mm (4in), one 6-pounder gun, six seaplanes
Powerplant:	Triple screw turbines
Performance:	21 knots

Enrico Toti

Enrico Toti was the lead boat in a class of four which were the first submarines to be built in Italy since World War II. The design was revised several times, and a coastal hunter-killer type intended for shallow and confined waters was finally approved. For these operations the boats' relatively small size and minimum sonar cross-section were a great advantage. The main armament carried was the Whitehead Motofides A184 wire-guided torpedo; this was a dual ASW/anti-ship weapon with an active/passive acoustic homing head that featured enhanced ECCM to counter enemy decoys. With a range in the order of 25km (13.5nm), the weapon would have proved effective in an ambush situation at natural 'choke points' against much larger opponents such as Russian SSNs or SSGNs.

Country:	Italy
Type:	Attack submarine
Launch date:	12 March 1967
Crew:	26
Displacement:	Surfaced: 532 tonnes (524 tons), submerged: 591 tonnes (582 tons)
Dimensions:	46.2m x 4.7m x 4m (151ft 7in x 15ft 5in x 13ft)
Surface range:	5556km (3000nm) at 5 knots
Armament:	Four 533mm (21in) torpedo tubes
Powerplant:	Single screw diesel engine, electric motors
Performance:	Surfaced: 14 knots, submerged: 15 knots

Enterprise

Early *Enterprise* designs had a flush deck, but this was thought to pose a smoke threat to landing aircraft, and an island structure to carry funnel uptakes and provide control centres was devised. The aircraft hangars were light structures independent from the hull, that could be closed off with rolling shutters. *Enterprise* was refitted in 1942 after action at the Battle of Midway, during which her dive bombers helped sink three Japanese carriers. Apart from Midway, her World War II battle honours included Guadalcanal, the Eastern Solomons, the Gilbert Islands, Kwajalein, Eniwetok, the Truk raid, Hollandia, Saipan, the Battle of the Philippine Sea, Palau, Leyte, Luzon, Taiwan, the China coast, Iwo Jima and Okinawa. She received five bomb hits and survived two attacks by Kamikazes off Okinawa. She was sold in 1958, despite efforts to preserve her as a memorial.

Country:	USA
Type:	Aircraft carrier
Launch date:	3 October 1936
Crew:	2175
Displacement:	25,908 tonnes (25,500 tons)
Dimensions:	246.7m x 26.2m x 7.9m (809ft 6in x 86ft x 26ft)
Range:	21,600km (12,000nm) at 12 knots
Armament:	Eight 127mm (5in) guns
Powerplant:	Quadruple screw turbines
Performance:	37.5 knots

Enterprise

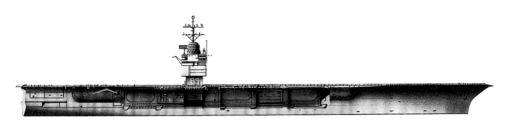

Nuclear-powered aircraft carriers had been suggested as far back as 1946, but cost delayed development of the project. *Enterprise* had a range of 643,720 kilometres (400,000 miles) at 20 knots. When completed in 1961 she was the largest vessel in the world, and was the second nuclear-powered warship to enter service. Her stowage capacity was huge, including 12,240,000 litres (2,720,000 gallons) of aviation fuel and 2560 tonnes (2520 tons) of aviation ordnance. She was refitted between 1979 and 1982 and given a revised island structure. *Enterprise* carries offensive tactical nuclear ordnance that includes 10kT B61, 20kT B57, 100kT B61, 330kT B61 and 900kT air-delivered gravity bombs, 10kT depth bombs; 1.4mT B43 and 1.1mT strategic nuclear weapons can also be carried as required. Her air group is similar in size and configuration to that of the Nimitz-class carriers.

Country:	USA
Type:	Aircraft carrier
Launch date:	24 September 1960
Crew:	3325 crew, 1891 air group and 71 marines
Displacement:	91,033 tonnes (89,600 tons)
Dimensions:	335.2m x 76.8m x 10.9m (1,100ft x 252ft x 36ft)
Range:	643,720km (400,000nm) at 20 knots
Armament:	Surface-to-air missiles, 90 aircraft
Powerplant:	Quadruple screw geared turbines, steam supplied by eight nuclear reactors
Performance:	32 knots

Erie

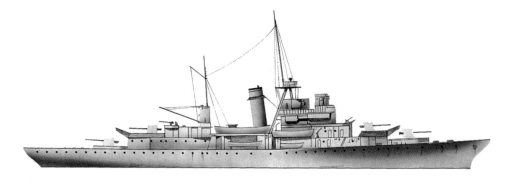

The USS *Erie* (PG50), launched in 1936, was built to an unusual design in which the needs for peacetime patrols and wartime missions were successfully combined in a vessel that also provided adequate accommodation for its crew and Marine contingent. It was also economical to run. *Erie*'s unique hull design enabled her relatively low 5941hp to drive her along at 20 knots, and her long bow helped keep the vessel dry. A scouting aircraft was carried, but it was not possible to fit a catapult and so the machine was lowered into the water and retrieved by crane. *Erie* and her sister *Charleston* were the first US ships to carry the new 152mm (6in) 47-calibre weapon with its combined shell and charge. On 12 November 1942 *Erie* weas torpedoed off Curacao by the *U163* (Cdr Engelmann); she was consequently beached and burnt out.

Country:	USA
Type:	Gunboat
Launch date:	1936
Crew:	236
Displacement:	2376 tonnes (2339 tons)
Dimensions:	100m x 12.5m x 3.4m (328ft 6in x 41ft 3in x 11ft 4in)
Range:	5556km (3000nm)
Main armament:	Four 152mm (6in) guns
Powerplant:	Two-shaft geared turbines
Performance:	20 knots

Erin

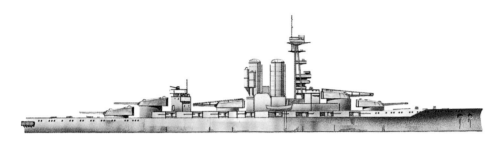

Built as the *Reshadieh* for the Turkish Navy, *Erin* was taken over by the
Royal Navy prior to her completion in 1914. She went on to serve with the
Grand Fleet for the duration of World War I. Her reduced coal capacity, which was
1,148 tonnes (1,130 tons) less than that of a contemporary British battleship of the
King George V class, did not detract from her performance which was considered
to be good. Although shorter and wider than contemporary British battleships,
nevertheless she carried the offensive power of an Iron Duke class vessel.
Her main distinguishing features were two narrow funnels and a tripod mast
with legs stepped forward. She was designed by Sir Richard Thurston and her
turbines were by Parsons (Vickers). She was refitted in 1917, placed in reserve
in 1919 and scrapped in 1921.

Country:	Great Britain
Type:	Battleship
Launch date:	3 September 1913
Crew:	1070
Displacement:	25,654 tonnes (25,250 tons)
Dimensions:	170.5m x 27.9m x 8.6m (559ft 5in x 91ft 6in x 28ft 3in)
Range:	9540km (5300nm) at 12 knots
Armament:	10 343mm (13.5in) guns
Powerplant:	Quadruple screw turbines
Performance:	21 knots

Ermanno Carlotto

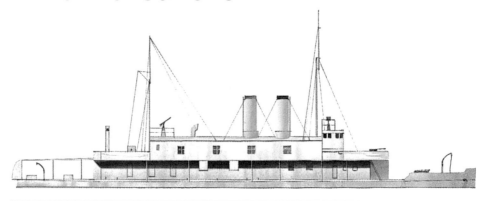

L aunched in 1918, *Ermanno Carlotto* was a shallow-draught river gunboat built by the Shanghai Dock and Engineering Company. Two Yarrow boilers provided steam for the 1100hp engines, and the twin screws operated in tunnels to achieve maximum benefit from the shallow draught. She was assigned to the Italian Far East Colonial Station and was based at Shanghai. On 9 September 1943, following the Italian armistice with the Allied powers, *Ermanno Carlotto* was scuttled in Shanghai to prevent her falling into Japanese hands. The Japanese, however, refloated her and named her *Narumi*. Enlisted into the Imperial Navy on 15 October 1943, she was used in Chinese waters before being surrendered in 1945. She was handed over to China, who renamed her *Kian Kun*, and was captured by the Chinese Communists in 1949.

Country:	Italy
Type:	Gunboat
Launch date:	19 June 1918
Crew:	75
Displacement:	221 tonnes (218 tons)
Dimensions:	48.8m x 7.5m x 0.9m (160ft x 24ft 7in x 3ft)
Range:	Not known
Main armament:	Two 76mm (3in) guns
Powerplant:	Twin screw vertical triple expansion engines
Performance:	13 knots

Erne

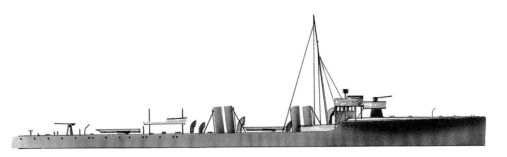

Part of the 1901–1904 naval building programme included a large group of destroyers known as the E or River class. *Erne* was the first ship of the 34-strong class to be launched, in January 1903. Experiencewith earlier types of destroyer had shown that concentrating on high trial speed was a snare and a delusion. The combination of seaworthiness with the ability to maintain a less spectacular speed when it became rough was of far more value. The larger size, sturdiness and raised forecastle of these ships made them much more seaworthy than their predecessors. These vessels thus marked the real break between the torpedo boat and the true destroyer, and set the trend for future British destroyer development. *Erne* was one of eight British destroyers wrecked during World War I; the Royal Navy's total destroyer loss, from all causes, was 64, of which one-third were the victims of mines.

Country:	Great Britain
Type:	Destroyer
Launch date	14 January 1903
Crew:	110
Displacement:	630 tonnes (620 tons)
Dimensions:	71m x 7.1m x 2.9m (233ft 6in x 23ft 6in x 9ft 9in)
Range:	2038km (1100nm)
Main armament:	One 12-pounder; two 457mm (18in) torpedo tubes
Powerplant:	Twin screw, triple expansion engines
Performance:	25.6 knots

Ersh (SHCH 303)

The Ersh (Pike) class of 88 boats, to which *Shch-303* belonged, were coastal submarines with a single hull and a maximum diving depth of 90m (295ft). Thirty-two were lost during World War II, but the survivors remained in service with the Soviet Navy until the mid-1950s. *Shch-303* operated in the Baltic, which was heavily mined and where most of the losses occurred; some of the Russian boats were sunk by Finnish submarines. The Russian submarines presented a great danger to the Germans, despite inflated claims of shipping sunk, and had to be guarded against at a cost that was unwelcome when German naval forces were badly needed elsewhere. *Shch-303*'s captain, I. V. Travkin, claimed to have sunk two large vessels in the Baltic, but the claim was never substantiated. *Shch-303* survived the war and was scrapped in 1958.

Country:	Soviet Union
Type:	Attack submarine
Launch date:	16 November 1931
Crew:	45
Displacement:	Surfaced: 595 tonnes (586 tons), submerged: 713 tonnes (702 tons)
Dimensions:	58.5m x 6.2m x 4.2m (192ft x 20ft 4in x 13ft 9in)
Surface range:	11,112km (6000nm) at 8 knots
Armament:	Six 533mm (21in) torpedo tubes, two 45mm (1.8in) guns
Powerplant:	Twin screw diesel engines, electric motors
Performance:	Surfaced: 12.5 knots, submerged: 8.5 knots

Erzherzog Karl

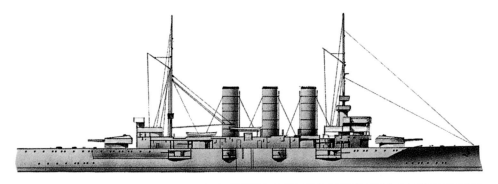

Erzherzog Karl was one of three units that formed the last of the pre-dreadnought type built for the Austrian Navy. She served in the Adriatic in World War I, and was taken over by Yugoslavia in 1919. In 1920 she was handed over to France as part of Austria's war reparations and scrapped. She is known for being the first warship to have her secondary guns housed in electrically powered turrets. The *Erzherzog Karl* and her sister ships, *Erzherzog Ferdinand Max* and *Erzherzog Friedrich*, were good vessels for their size but obsolescent by the time they were completed in 1906–10. The *Erzherzog Karl* was named after Archduke Charles, Duke of Teschen (1771–1847), field marshal and commander of the Austrian forces against Napoleon. The *Friedrich* was ceded to Britain, the *Ferdinand Max* to France.

Country:	Austria
Type:	Battleship
Launch date:	14 October 1903
Crew:	700
Displacement:	10,640 tonnes (10,472 tons)
Dimensions:	126.2m x 21.7m x 7.5m (414ft 2in x 71ft 6in x 24ft 8in)
Range:	7412km (4000nm) at 10 knots
Armament:	12 190mm (7.5in), four 240mm (9.45in) guns
Powerplant:	Twin screw, triple expansion engines
Performance:	20.5 knots

Esmereldas

Although strictly speaking rated as missile corvettes rather than small light frigates, the units of the Esmeraldas class approximate more closely to small light frigates because of their multipurpose capabilities. Ordered in 1978 from the Italian firm CNR del Tirreno, the design is based on that of the Assad class built for Libya, but with more powerful diesel engines, a helicopter landing platform amidships (but no hangar) , and a SAM launcher aft of the bridge. All six units of the class – *Esmeraldas, Manabi, Los Rios, El Oro, Galapagos* and *Laja* – are in service with the Ecuadorean Navy as the country's primary anti-ship surface strike force. *El Oro* was out of commission for two years from 1985 after a bad fire. Only self-defence ASW torpedo tubes are fitted, together with a hull-mounted sonar set for sub-surface warfare operations.

Country:	Ecuador
Type:	Corvette
Launch date:	1 October 1980
Crew:	51
Displacement:	696 tonnes (685 tons)
Dimensions:	62.3m x 9.3m x 2.5m (204ft 5in x 30ft 6in x 8ft 2in)
Range:	7037km (3800nm)
Main armament:	One 76mm gun; Exocet SSMs; Aspide SAMs
Powerplant:	Four shafts, four diesel engines
Performance:	37 knots

España

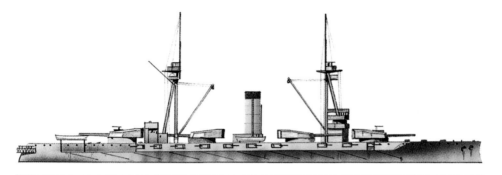

E *spaña* and her two sisters combined dreadnought armament with pre-
dreadnought dimensions. In 1923 *España* ran aground in fog off the Moroccan
coast and could not be salvaged. *Alfonso XIII*, one of *España*'s sisters, took her
name in 1931, but was sunk in 1937 when she hit a mine during the Spanish Civil
War. Ironically the mine had been laid by the Nationalists – her own side. The
Espana class of small battleships were built in Spain with British technical
assistance. They had four twin turrets, a single funnel and two tripod masts.
The completion of one of them, *Jaime I*, was held up by World War I and she was
not completed until 1921. This vessel saw more action than the others in the
Spanish Civil War; she was sunk by an explosion at Cartagena in June 1937,
with over 300 dead.

Country:	Spain
Type:	Battleship
Launch date:	5 February 1912
Crew:	845
Displacement:	15,991 tonnes (15,740 tons)
Dimensions:	140m x 24m x 7.8m (459ft x 78ft 9in x 25ft 7in)
Range:	9000km (5000nm) at 10 knots
Armament:	20 102mm (4in), eight 305mm (12in) guns
Powerplant:	Quadruple screw turbines
Performance:	19.5 knots

Espero

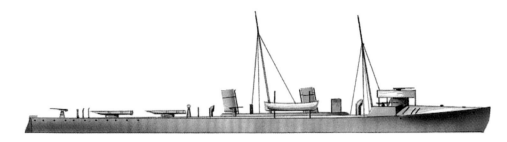

Espero was one of the six vessels of the Nembo class built for the Italian Navy by Pattison of Naples. From 1908 to 1912 all were reboilered (fuel oil) and from 1909 their armament was altered. Minelaying gear (10-16 mines) was added in 1915-18. Three of the class were sunk in action during World War I. In 1921 the three remaining vessels were reclassified as torpedo boats, and two years after that *Espero* was discarded. The confines of the Adriatic Sea, where engagments between Italian destroyers and their Austro-Hungarian counterparts were fought, lent themselves very well to actions by naval light forces, which were able to penetrate the waterways and the deep, sheltered passages that lay between the maze of islands off the coasts of Dalmatia and Albania. Italian destroyers also operated in the Dardanelles in support of the Allied naval forces deployed there.

Country:	Italy
Type:	Destroyer
Launch date:	9 July 1904
Crew:	210
Displacement:	386 tonnes (380 tons)
Dimensions:	64m x 5.9m x 2.2m (210ft x 19ft 6in x 7ft 6in)
Range:	2778km (1500nm)
Main armament:	Five 57mm (2.24in) guns; four 355mm (14in) torpedo tubes
Powerplant:	Triple expansion engines
Performance:	26 knots

Espero

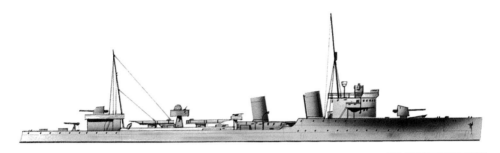

A ll eight units in the Espero class were laid down in 1925 and were slightly larger and more powerful versions of the previous Sauro class. The crew, which numbered 142 in peacetime, could be increased to 179 in time of war. All the vessels in the class underwent minor changes to their armament early in World War II. The entire class was lost during the war, with six of the group being sunk in 1940. On 28 June 1940, the Italian destroyers *Espero*, *Ostro* and *Zeffiro* were ferrying supplies from Taranto to Tobruk when they were sighted by a reconnaissance aircraft, which summoned the British 7th Cruiser Squadron to intercept. The *Espero* (Flotilla Cdr Baroni) attacked the British force to cover the withdrawal of the others, and was sunk by the Australian cruiser *Sydney*. This was one of the most gallant Italian naval actions of World War II.

Country:	Italy
Type:	Destroyer
Launch date:	31 August 1927
Crew:	142
Displacement:	1696 tonnes (1670 tons)
Dimensions:	93.2m x 9.2m x 2.9m (305ft 9in x 30ft 2in x 9ft 10in)
Range:	3890km (2100nm)
Main armament:	Four 120mm (4.7in) guns
Powerplant:	Twin screw, turbines
Performance:	36 knots

Essex

By the end of the 1930s, the increased needs of the navy for air cover led to an explosion in the size of aircraft carriers, and a larger hull was introduced to stow the aviation fuel required for the 91 aircraft now carried. There were 24 vessels in the Essex class, their designs based around an enlargement of the earlier Yorktown class carriers. *Essex* was laid down in April 1941 and entered service in 1942. She was removed from the effective list in 1969 and scrapped in 1973. *Essex*'s battle honours in World War II included raids on Marcus and Wake Islands, the Gilbert Islands and Kwajalein (1943); raids on Truk and the Marianas, Saipan, Guam, Tinian, Palau and the Battle of the Philippine Sea (1944); raids on Luzon, the China coast, the Ryukus, Iwo Jima, Okinawa and Japan (1945). In November 1944 the carrier was damaged by a kamikaze hit at Leyte, and again in April 1945 off Okinawa.

Country:	USA
Type:	Aircraft carrier
Launch date:	31 July 1942
Crew:	2687
Displacement:	35,438 tonnes (34,880 tons)
Dimensions:	265.7m x 29.2m x 8.3m (871ft 9in x 96ft x 27ft 6in)
Range:	27,000km (15,000nm) at 12 knots
Armament:	12 127mm (5in) guns, 91 aircraft
Powerplant:	Quadruple screw turbines
Performance:	32.7 knots

Étendard

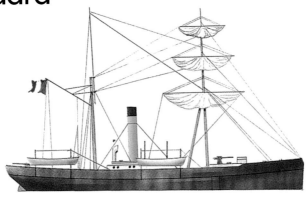

Both France and Great Britain had large colonial empires in the second half of the nineteenth century which required policing to maintain order. Consequently, both nations produced large numbers of gunboats: cheap and simple vessels able to operate for long periods away from sophisticated bases and logistic support, but powerful enough to deal with most small incidents in farflung colonies. *Étendard* (Standard) was one of an eight-strong class of gunboats built in Bordeaux. Her hull was of wooden construction, and came complete with a full brigantine rig of sail and twin screw coal-fired engines. Her bunkers could only carry a maximum of 56 tonnes (55 tons) of coal, and so she was expected to rely on sail power for most of the time. *Étendard* was one of the longest serving boats in the group, and was only removed from the effective list in 1882.

Country:	France
Type:	Gunboat
Launch date:	1868
Crew	69
Displacement:	508 tonnes (500 tons)
Dimensions:	43.4m x 7.3m x 2.7m (142ft 6in x 24ft 3in x 8ft 10in)
Range:	2592km (1400nm)
Main armament:	One 120mm (4.7in)gun; one 140mm (5.5in) gun
Powerplant:	Twin screw vertical compound engines
Performance:	9 knots

Euro

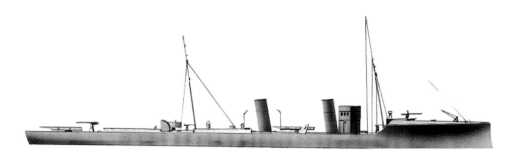

Launched in August 1900, *Euro* was one of six vessels in the first major destroyer class to be built for the Italian Navy. They were fast, strongly built ships, with a range of 551km (297 nautical miles) at 26 knots, increasing to 3792km (2048nm) at 12 knots. During World War I, five ships in the class were converted to the role of minelayer. Minelaying was a major activity of the Italian Navy in the Adriatic, where the Austro-Hungarian fleet had the benefit of many small inlets and harbours from which it could operate. The other boats in the class were *Lampo* (class leader), *Freccia, Dardo, Strale* and *Ostro*. Between 1922 and 1923, *Euro* served as a target ship. When *Strale* was discarded in January 1924 *Euro* was allocated her name so that *Euro* could be allocated to a new boat then under construction; *Euro/Strale* was discarded in November that year.

Country:	Italy
Type:	Destroyer
Launch date:	27 August 1900
Crew:	150
Displacement:	353 tonnes (348 tons)
Dimensions:	62m x 6.5m x 2.6m (203ft 5in x 21ft 4in x 8ft 6in)
Range:	3800km (2048nm)
Main armament:	One 76mm (3in) gun; two 355mm (14in) torpedo tubes
Powerplant:	Twin screw triple expansion engines
Performance:	26 knots

Euro

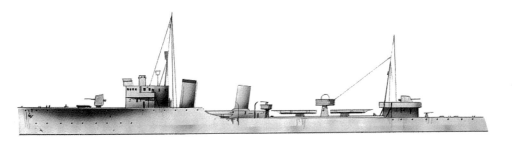

*E**uro** was part of a class of six vessels which were slightly larger versions of the previous Sauro class. All were laid down in 1925, the last unit being launched in 1928. All the vessels of this class adopted the names of their immediate predecessors. Designed to reach a speed of 36 knots with 40,000hp, *Euro* actually achieved 38.9 knots during a four-hour full-power trial. In service, however, her best sea speed was about 30 knots. After Italy's entry into World War II, she was employed on minelaying and convoy escort operations, and in November 1941 she was damaged while escorting a convoy that was attacked by the cruisers of the British Force K from Malta. All seven merchantmen were sunk, together with the destroyer *Libeccio*, which sank while under tow by the *Euro*. On 1 October 1943, following Italy's surrender, the *Euro* was sunk by German aircraft in Leros harbour.

Country:	Italy
Type:	Destroyer
Launch date:	7 July 1927
Crew:	142
Displacement:	1696 tonnes (1670 tons)
Dimensions:	93.2m x 9.2m x 3m (305ft 9in x 30ft 2in x 9ft 10in)
RAnge:	3890km (2100nm)
Main armament:	Four 120mm (4.7in) guns; six 533mm (21in) torpedo tubes
Powerplant:	Twin screw turbines
Performance:	36 knots

Euro

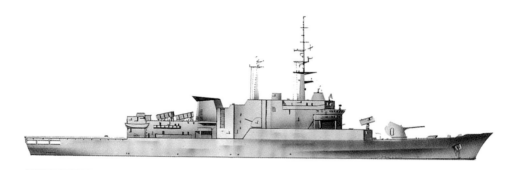

Following the success of the Lupo-class frigate, Italy decided to build an enlarged version, the Maestrale class, incorporating a hangar for two helicopters. The first six vessels were ordered in 1976 and the last pair in 1980. *Euro* entered service in 1984. The aft flight deck is 27m (88ft 6in) long and 12m (39ft 4in) wide, and there is a stern well for a new variable depth towed sonar array which is streamed out on a 600m (1968ft) long cable; this was later increased to 900m (2953ft). From 1994, hulls and sonars were modified to give better shallow water performance and a mine detection capability. The eight vessels of the Lupo class are scheduled for replacement but it is likely that they will be retained until the Horizon class enters service around 2007. The ships of this class have seen much service in the Adriatic with the NATO peacekeeping force operational in the area since 1991.

Country:	Italy
Type:	Destroyer
Launch date:	25 March 1983
Crew:	232
Displacement:	3088 tonnes (3040 tons)
Dimensions:	122.7m x 12.9m x 8.4m (402ft 6in x 42ft 4in x 27ft 6in)
Range:	7408km (4000nm)
Main armament:	One 127mm (5in) gun plus missiles
Powerplant:	Twin screw diesels and gas turbines
Performance:	29 knots (diesels), 32 knots (turbines)

Europa

Europa started life as the British merchant ship *Manila*, with a gross displacement of only 4200 tonnes (4134 tons). In 1898 her name was changed to *Salacia*. In 1911 she was sold to Germany. She then took the Italian flag under the name *Quarto*. In 1915 she was finally purchased by the Italian Navy and converted to a seaplane carrier, becoming the first Italian ship to operate fixed-wing aircraft. *Europa* emerged with two large aircraft hangars, one ahead and one aft of the low superstructure. There was a large davit mounted on the bow, which acted as a winch for launching and retrieving the aircraft. She could carry eight seaplanes, and normally operated a group of six fighters and two reconnaissance aircraft. She was based at Brindisi from October 1915 until January 1916, then transferred to Velona until 1918. She survived World War I, but was scrapped in 1920.

Country:	Great Britain
Type:	Seaplane carrier
Launch date:	4 August 1895
Crew:	394
Displacement:	8945 tonnes (8805 tons)
Dimensions:	123m x 14m x 7.6m (403ft 10in x 46ft x 25ft)
Range:	10,747km (5800nm) at 10 knots
Armament:	Two 30mm (1.2in) anti-aircraft guns, eight seaplanes
Powerplant:	Single screw, vertical triple expansion engines
Performance:	12 knots

Exeter

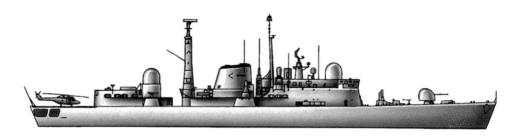

HMS *Exeter*, launched in April 1978 and commissioned in September 1980, is one of four Batch 2 Type 42 destroyers, the others being *Southampton*, *Nottingham* and *Liverpool*. The Type 42s were originally designed to provide area defence for a task force with their British Aerospace Sea Dart surface-to-air missiles; these have a range of 40km (21.5nm) under radar or semi-active radar guidance and have a height envelope of 100–18,300m (328–60,042ft). The weapons also have a limited anti-ship capability. Generally, each Type 42 is armed with 22 Sea Dart rounds. The ships' Lynx helicopter carries the Sea Skua air-to-surface missile for use against lightly defended surface-ship targets, such as fast attack craft, and has been operationally proved in the Falklands and Gulf conflicts, being especially effective against small, fast targets such as missile boats.

Country:	Great Britain
Type:	Destroyer
Launch date:	25 April 1978
Crew:	253
Displacement:	4166 tonnes (4100 tons)
Dimensions:	125m x 14.3m x 5.8m (412ft x 47ft x 19ft)
Range:	6430km (3472nm)
Main armament:	One 114mm (4.5in) gun; Sea Dart SAM; 20mm (0.7in) and Phalanx AA.
Powerplant:	Twin shafts, four gas turbines
Performance:	29 knots

Exmoor

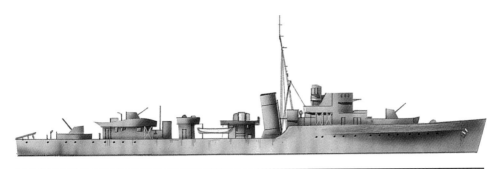

In 1941 the Type II Hunt-class destroyer HMS *Burton* was renamed *Exmoor*, following the loss of the Hunt Type I ship of that name. The choice of the original name was perhaps unfortunate, in view of the then current slang expression 'gone for a Burton', which meant that someone or something had met an untimely end. Exmoor served in the North Atlantic and in the Mediterranean with the Gibraltar-based Force H and was part of the naval support force in Operation Husky, the Allied landings on Sicily in July 1943, and the Salerno landing in September. On 10 March 1944 she participated in the destruction of the U450 off Anzio. In 1953 *Exmoor* was transferred to the Royal Danish Navy as the *Valdemar Sejr*, together with the other Hunt-class ships *Blackmore* (*Esbern Snare*) and *Calpe* (*Rolf Krake*). She was stricken in 1962.

Country:	Great Britain
Type:	Destroyer
Launch date:	12 March 1941
Crew:	168
Displacement:	1067 tonnes (1050 tons)
Dimensions:	85.3m x 9.6m x 3.7m (280ft x 31ft 6in x 12ft 5in)
Range:	3333km (1800nm)
Main armament:	Six 102mm (4in) guns
Powerplant:	Twin screw turbines
Performance:	26 knots

Exmouth

*E*xmouth** was one of the E-class destroyers that were improved versions of the C- and D-class vessels. The E class had increased fuel capacity and higher speed, plus extra stowage. Two of *Exmouth*'s sisters, *Esk* and *Express*, were fitted out as minelayers, but *Exmouth* was an enlarged version of the flotilla destroyer, with one more 120mm (4.7in) gun and a higher speed. In spite of poor weather conditions, trials run in September 1934 produced good results. At 20 knots, just over two tons of fuel oil were used per hour. In November 1939, *Exmouth* was one of the destroyers that provided an escort for the battlecruiser HMS *Hood*, searching for the German battlecruisers *Scharnhorst* and *Gneisenau* in the North Atlantic. In January 1940, *Exmouth* was sunk with all hands in the Moray Firth by the *U22* (Lt-Cdr Jenisch).

Country:	Great Britain
Type:	Destroyer (Flotilla Leader)
Launch date:	7 February 1934
Crew:	175
Displacement:	1397 tonnes (1375 tons)
Dimensions:	104.5m x 10.2m x 3.8m (342ft 10in x 33ft 9in x 12ft 6in)
Range:	3889km (2100nm)
Main armament:	Five 120mm (4.7in) guns
Powerplant:	Twin screw turbines
Performance:	35.5 knots

Falco

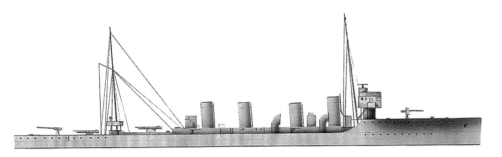

In 1913 Romania ordered four large, powerful destroyers from Pattison of Naples for service in the Black Sea where they needed to have an endurance of ten hours at full speed. *Falco* was laid down as *Viscol* but was taken over by the Italian Navy in 1916, when she was renamed and reclassified as a scout. She was completed in 1920. In 1937 she entered Spanish service for the Nationalists and was renamed *Ceuta*. The Italians were a principal supplier of arms and equipment to General Franco's forces during the Spanish Civil War, the other supplier being Nazi Germany, and much of the equipment supplied was retained after the conflict was over. The former *Falco* was discarded in 1948, when Spain received a batch of ex-American destroyers. Prior to this, the Spanish Navy was very much the same as it had been in 1939, development having stagnated during the war.

Country:	Italy
Type:	Flotilla Leader
Launch date:	16 August 1919
Crew:	150
Displacement:	1788 tonnes (1760 tons)
Dimensions:	94.7m x 9.5m x 3.6m (310ft 8in x 31ft 2in x 11ft 10in)
Range:	1667km (900nm)
Main armament:	Three 152mm (6in) guns
Powerplant:	Twin screw turbines
Performance:	35.2 knots

le Fantasque

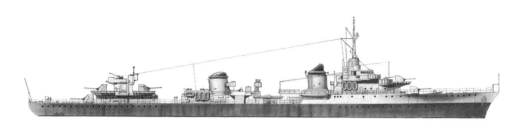

The le Fantasque class was the penultimate class in a series that set new destroyer standards, yet which had little real influence on construction abroad because it stemmed largely from naval rivalry between the French and the Italians. The six ships of the class were magnificent-looking vessels with an imposing freeboard and an extra 3m (9.84ft) in overall length that allowed for a fifth gun and three triple sets of torpedo tubes. After France's collapse, *le Fantasque* and *le Terrible* deployed to Dakar, and after a refit at Boston, USA. Subsequently, these ships and *le Malin* served with distinction in the Mediterranean, forming part of the naval force that landed in southern France in August 1944 and carried out many raiding sorties in the Aegean. At the end of the war, *le Fantasque* was deployed to the Far East to support French forces reoccupying Indo-China.

Country:	France
Type:	Destroyer
Launch date:	15 March 1934
Crew:	210
Displacement:	3404 tonnes (3350 tons)
Dimensions:	132.4m x 12.35m x 5.0m (434ft 4in x 40ft 6in x 16ft 4in)
Range:	7408km (4000nm)
Main armament:	Five single 138.6mm (5.46in) and two twin 37mm (1.4in) AA guns; three triple 553mm (21in) torpedo tubes.
Powerplant:	Two sets of geared steam turbines
Performance:	37 knots

Farragut

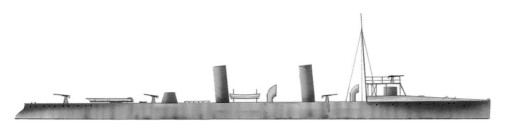

The USS *Farragut*, launched in July 1898, was the US Navy's first destroyer, although when originally authorised she was described as a torpedo boat. She was laid down in July 1897 at the Union Iron Works, and was completed in March 1899. Her engines developed 5878hp, and steam was supplied by three Thorneycroft boilers. Coal supply was 96 tonnes (95 tons). In August 1918, *Farragut* was renamed Coast Torpedo Boat No 5. She was sold in 1919. The *Farragut* entered service during an exciting period in US naval development. Victories in the Philippines had established the USA as a sea power, and with the acquisition of new territory in the Caribbean and the Far East, the prestige of the US Navy began to climb rapidly. Its development was helped by the fact that the USA was now the leading industrial nation.

Country:	USA
Type:	Destroyer
Launch date:	16 July 1898
Crew:	66
Displacement:	283 tonnes (279 tons)
Dimensions:	65m x 6.3m x 1.8m (214ft x 20ft 8in x 6ft)
Range:	1852km (1000nm)
Main armament:	Six six-pounder guns; two 457mm (18in) torpedo tubes
Powerplant:	Twin screw vertical triple expansion engines
Performance:	33.7 knots

Fasana

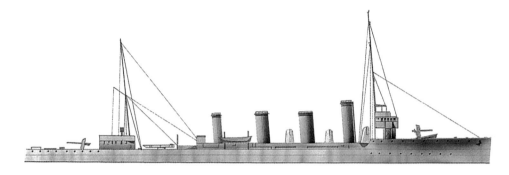

F asana was formerly the Austrian *Tatra*, one of a class of seven vessels that were the best and most powerful destroyers in the Austro–Hungarian Navy. In the years prior to World War I, the Archduke Franz Ferdinand (the heir to the Austrian throne whose assassination at Sarajevo was to precipitate the war) had made strenuous efforts to build up his country's fleet with modern warships, and the *Tatra*, launched in November 1912, was part of the building programme. As war reparations, she was transferred to the Italian Navy in August 1920 and renamed *Fasana*, though she was neither refitted nor commissioned into the Italian Navy because of her poor condition. Once in Italian service the armament of the other vessels was changed, their 533mm (21in) torpedo tubes being reduced to the standard 450mm (17.7in).

Country:	Austria
Type:	Destroyer
Launch date:	5 November 1912
Crew:	120
Displacement:	1052 tonnes (1036 tons)
Dimensions:	83.5m x 7.8m x 3m (274ft x 25ft 7in x 9ft 10in)
Range:	2778km (1500nm)
Main armament:	Two 100mm (3.9in) guns
Powerplant:	Twin screw turbines
Performance:	32.6 knots

Fatahilah class

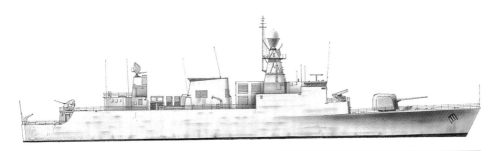

The Fatahilah class of Dutch-designed and -built ASW frigates was ordered in August 1975 as the first major new-build warship type for the Indonesian Navy since the acceptance of Soviet ships in the 1950s and 1960s. The class numbers only three, one of which, the *Nala*, has a flight deck to accommodate a light helicopter. The vessels of the Fatahilah class carry an anti-ship missile armament comprising two pairs of container-launchers for the MM39 Exocet. It is this armament which enables the ships to operate as effective supports for the considerable force of missile- and gun-armed attack units which the Indonesian Navy employs among the myriad islands which go to make up the republic. The Indonesians also use three ex-Royal Navy Tribal-class and six ex-Royal Netherlands NavyVan Speijk-class frigates, the latter a modified Leander-class design.

Country:	Indonesia
Type:	Frigate
Launch date:	22 December 1977
Crew:	89
Displacement:	1473 tonnes (1450 tons)
Dimensions:	84m x 11m x 3.3m (275ft 7in x 36ft 4in x 10ft 11in)
Range:	3333km (1800nm)
Main armament:	One 120mm (4.7in) DP gun; one 40mm (1.5in) and two 20mm (0.7in) AA guns; two triple 324mm (12.76in) torpedo tubes; ASW rockets and anti-ship missiles
Powerplant:	Two shafts, one gas turbine, two diesels
Performance:	30 knots

Faulknor

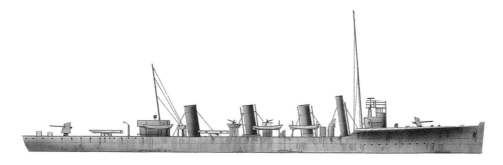

Designed by J.S. White in 1912, *Faulknor* was one of four large, powerful destroyers ordered for the Chilean Navy which was British-trained and the best in Latin America. Previously named *Almirante Simpson*, the ship was taken over by the Royal Navy in August 1914, whereupon the fore funnel was raised and a more powerful radio outfit installed. Unlike other British destroyers of the day, which had a single gun firing forward, *Faulknor* and her sisters were heavily armed with three or four guns firing forward. In 1915 *Faulknor* joined other light forces in hunting U-boats in the Irish Sea, and in November 1916, she operated intensively against enemy submarine traffic off the Norwegian coast. After World War I, *Faulknor* was refitted and returned to Chile, where she served until she was removed from the effective list in 1933.

Country:	Great Britain
Type:	Destroyer (Flotilla Leader)
Launch date:	26 February 1944
Crew:	190
Displacement:	2024 tonnes (1993 tons)
Dimensions:	100m x 10m x 6.4m (330ft 10in x 32ft 6in x 21ft 1in)
Range:	3704km (2000nm)
Main armament:	Six 102mm (4in) guns; four 533mm (21in) torpedo tubes
Powerplant:	Triple screw turbines
Performance:	29 knots

Fenian Ram

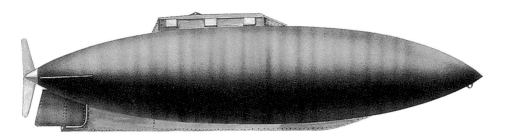

The Irish–American inventor John Philip Holland designed submarines in America, the original idea being to use them to destroy the hated British fleet on behalf of his fellow Fenians. Ironically, his business acumen overcame his nationalist sympathies and he sold his most successful design to the Royal Navy. Twenty years earlier, the *Fenian Ram* was built for the Fenian Society by the Delamater Iron Works, New York. In 1883 she was towed to Newhaven under great secrecy, so that her crew of three could familiarize themselves with her handling. The vessel was exhibited at Madison Square Gardens in 1916 in order to raise funds for the Irish uprising that took place that year. In 1927 she was housed in West Side Park, New York. John Holland has a firm place in history as the designer of the first practical submarines.

Country:	USA
Type:	Attack submarine
Launch date:	May 1881
Crew:	3
Displacement:	Surfaced: 19 tonnes (19 tons), submerged: Not known
Dimensions:	9.4m x 1.8m x 2.2m (31ft x 6ft x 7ft 3in)
Surface range:	Not known
Armament:	One 228mm (9in) gun
Powerplant:	Single screw petrol engine
Performance:	Surfaced: Not known, submerged: Not known

Ferret

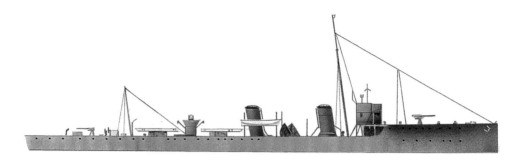

*F*errret was the lead ship in a group of destroyers that were originally intended to be repeats of the previous Acorn class. She was laid down in September 1910 and was completed in October 1911. Twenty other ships of the class were also begun in 1910, but six others were put out to private firms to see if they could improve upon the Acorn design. On trials, *Ferret* maintained slightly over 30 knots for eight hours, a credit to her builder, J.S. White. However, although the fore funnel was set well back from the bridge, the exhaust fumes still caused problems for those on the bridge. This was rectified later when the funnel was raised. Destroyers of this type performed good service with the coastal flotillas in World War I, patrolling into the Heligoland Bight and securing the Channel area. *Ferret* was scrapped in 1921.

Country:	Great Britain
Type:	Destroyer
Launch date:	12 April 1911
Crew:	98
Displacement:	762 tonnes (750 tons)
Dimensions:	75m x 7.8m x 2.6m (246ft x 25ft 8in x 8ft 9in)
Range:	2037km (1100nm)
Main armament:	Two 102mm (4in) guns
Powerplant:	Twin screw turbines
Performance:	33 knots

Fervent

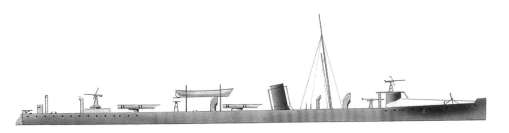

Fervent was part of the building programme of 1894–95 which was designed to combat the strength of the French Navy. The ship followed the design of earlier destroyers, but was fitted with old-style locomotive boilers and had only one funnel. At this time, new ideas and inventions in shipbuilding were emerging so quickly that a new vessel could be obsolete before it was launched. Much of this problem was created by Britain's own naval policy, which was described as a 'two-power standard' and which kept the Royal Navy equal in numbers to any two foreign navies. In simple terms, warships were being built at too fast a rate to incorporate the latest technological advances. *Fervent* and her sister ship, *Zephyr*, failed entirely to meet their contract speed, and their builder eventually went out of business. She was scrapped in 1920.

Country:	Great Britain
Type:	Destroyer
Launch date:	20 March 1895
Crew:	80
Displacement:	280 tonnes (275 tons)
Dimensions:	61m x 5.7m x 2.4m (200ft 4in x 19ft 1in x 8ft)
Range:	1760km (950nm)
Main armament:	Three six-pounders; one 12-pounder
Powerplant:	Twin screw triple expansion engines
Performance:	22 knots

Feth-I-Bulend

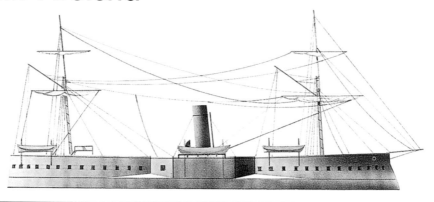

In a bid to support the backward Turkish Empire against Russian expansionist policies, Britain gave considerable aid to the Turkish in their efforts to build a powerful and modern naval fleet. In the 1860s and 1870s, so many modern ironclad warships were built on behalf of Turkey by both Britain and France that the Ottoman Empire became the world's third largest naval fleet. Much of this development occurred under the administration of a British naval officer, Hobart Pasha. Vessels of this era included *Feth-I-Bulend*, an iron-hulled, central battery ship built at Blackwall in London. *Feth-I-Bulend* was laid down in 1868 and completed in 1872. She was reconstructed between 1903 and 1907. In 1912, during the Balkans war, *Feth-I-Bulend* was sunk by the Greek torpedo vessel *No. 11*.

Country:	Turkey
Type:	Ironclad
Launch date:	1870
Crew:	220
Displacement:	2805 tonnes (2761 tons)
Dimensions:	72m x 12m x 5.5m (236ft 3in x 39ft 4in x 18ft)
Range:	1927km (1040nm) at 10 knots
Armament:	Four 229mm (9in) guns
Powerplant:	Single screw, horizontal compound engines
Performance:	13 knots

Flamingo

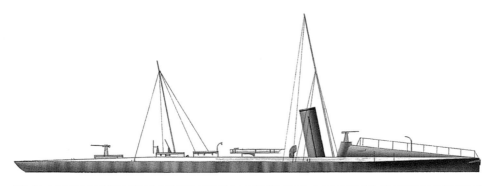

Flamingo was one of a group of 20 small torpedo boats built for the Austrian Navy in the late 1880s and 1890s. They were based on the earlier and successful *Schichau* design, and incorporated a number of improvements. *Flamingo* herself was laid down in 1888 and completed in the following year. All the boats of this design underwent major reconstruction between 1900 and 1910. During this refit, *Flamingo* had her boiler replaced by two Yarrow units, and eventually re-entered service bearing pennant number 26. She was mined and sunk off Pola on 23 August 1914. Eighteen remaining boats were converted to the minesweeping role in 1917, and 16 of these were transferred to Italy in 1920. Most were scrapped soon after, but four operated as customs patrol boats until 1925. The Austro-Hungarian fleet had dozens of similar craft at this time.

Country:	Austria
Type:	Torpedo boat
Launch date:	1889
Crew:	15
Displacement:	91.4 tonnes (90 tons)
Dimensions:	39.9m x 4.8m x 1.9m (130ft 11in x 15ft 9in x 6ft 3in)
Range:	2276km (1229nm)
Main armament:	Two 350mm (13.8in) torpedo tubes
Powerplant:	Single screw triple expansion engine
Performance:	19 knots

Flandre

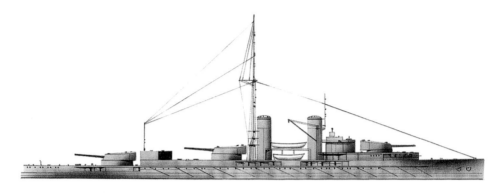

F*landre* was laid down in October 1913 as one of a class of five units built in response to the increased gun calibres being used by other countries. It was decided to fit the 340mm (13.4in) guns in three quadruple turrets, which were in reality two twin mounts placed side by side in a single well-armoured barbette. Work halted on the class in 1914 and they were launched to clear the docks. Four were scrapped in 1924–25; one of the class, *Béarn*, was completed as an aircraft carrier. Impounded by the Americans at Martinique after going aground, she was towed to Puerto Rico. In 1943–44 she was refitted at New Orleans, rearmed, had her flight deck shortened, and was reclassified as an aircraft transport. Handed over to the Free French Navy, she saw service in the Far East in 1945–46, supporting the French reoccupation of Indo-China.

Country:	France
Type:	Battleship
Launch date:	20 October 1914
Crew:	1200
Displacement:	25,230 tonnes (24,833 tons)
Dimensions:	176.4m x 27m x 8.7m (578ft 9in x 88ft 7in x 28ft 6in)
Range:	11,700km (6500nm) at 12 knots
Armament:	12 340mm (13.4in), 24 140mm (5.5in) guns
Powerplant:	Quadruple screws - two for turbines and two for vertical triple expansion engines
Performance:	21 knots

Fletcher

Though the extensive Benson class achieved the aim of putting the US destroyer-building industry on to a war footing, the design had limitations for a Pacific war, both in terms of endurance and its curtailed weapons fit. Even before the end of the programme, therefore, the first of an improved class were coming off the slipways. The first two of this Fletcher class went down the ways in February 1942 and the last four of 175 ships on the same day in September 1944 at Puget Sound Navy Yard. Although the vessels in the Fletcher class were generally rushed out to the Pacific on completion, those built on the Atlantic seaboard saw some service in that ocean. The USS *Fletcher* herself served on convoy protection duty in the western Atlantic before being deployed to the Pacific in time for the naval actions off Guadalcanal. She was reclassified as a destroyer escort (DDE) in 1949.

Country:	USA
Type:	Destroyer
Launch date:	3 May 1942
Crew:	295
Displacement:	2083 tonnes (2050 tons)
Dimensions:	114.76m x 12.04m x 5.41m (376ft 6in) x 39ft 6in x 17ft 9in)
Range:	7412km (4000nm)
Main armament:	Five single 127mm (5in) D; three twin 40mm (1.5in) AA and four single 20mm(0.7in) AA guns; two quintuple 533mm (21in) torpedo tubes
Powerplant:	Two sets of geared steam turbines, two shafts
Performance:	37 knots

Floréal

*F*loréal is the leader of a class of six ships, all commissioned between 1992 and 1994. Officially described as 'Ocean Capable Patrol Vessels', they are designed to operate in the offshore zone in low-intensity operations. The frigates, all of which were built at the Chantiers de l'Atlantique, St Nazaire, were constructed to merchant passenger ship standards, with air conditioning and stabilisers, which enables them to operate a helicopter up to Sea State 5. The ships proved to have a better range than expected during their sea trials, and have an endurance of 50 days. *Floréal* is stationed in the South Indian Ocean and the others at various points in the Far East where the French have interests, such as the sensitive nuclear test site at Mururoa. The ships are named after the months of the French Revolutionary Calendar.

Country:	France
Type:	Frigate
Launch date:	6 October 1990
Crew:	86
Displacement:	2997 tonnes (2950 tons)
Dimensions:	93.5m x 14m x 4.3m (306ft 10in x 45ft 11in x 14ft 1in)
Range:	16,075km (8680nm)
Main armament:	One 100mm (3.9in) gun; Exocet SSMs; Matra Simbad SAMs
Powerplant:	Two shafts, four diesel engines
Performance:	20 knots

Florida

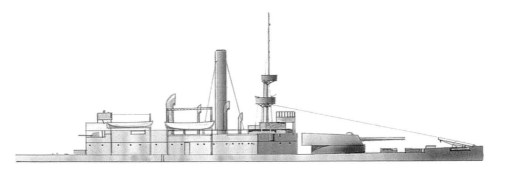

Launched in 1901, *Florida* was one of the Arkansas class of four that were the last of the big-gun monitors built for the US Navy. The maximum thickness of the belt armour was at the 37.5mm (1.5in) armoured-deck level only, tapering to 127mm (5in) at the lower edge and at the ends. The 305mm (12in) guns were in a single turret forward. Four 102mm (4in) guns were also carried, two at the rear of the superstructure and two under the bridge. All vessels of the class at some time served as submarine tenders. In 1908 she was renamed *Tallahassee* and was successively employed as an experimental ordnance ship and submarine tender. During World War I she served in the Panama Canal Zone, the Virgin Islands and Bermuda, and from 1920 to 1922 she was used as a Reserve training ship. She was sold and broken up in 1922, but her sister, *Wyoming* was not sold until 1939.

Country:	USA
Type:	Monitor
Launch date:	30 November 1901
Crew:	270
Displacement:	3277 tonnes (3225 tons)
Dimensions:	77.75m x 15.25m x 3.8m (255ft x 50ft x 12ft 6in)
Range:	3113km (1680nm) at 10 knots
Armament:	Two 306mm (12in) and four 102mm (4in) guns
Powerplant:	Twin screw, vertical triple expansion engines
Performance:	12.5 knots

Flower class

Possibly because of their homely names or their rather unwarlike appearance, the units of the Flower class (45 built in the UK and 113 in Canada for launch between 1940 and 1942) came to be regarded by the British as the archetypal escort ship. Though they made their reputation in the early days of the Battle of the Atlantic, they were not really suited to the job, this type having been developed primarily as a coastal escort fitted for minesweeping. Paradoxically, however, the design was based on that of a commercial whale-catcher, a hull form meant to withstand the worst of weathers. They were superb seaboats, but being so short, were horribly lively and wet in the deep ocean, so that crews quickly became exhausted. Thirty-one were lost in World War II, and the Flower class was immortalised by the fictitious *Compass Rose* in the book and film, *The Cruel Sea*.

Country:	Great Britain
Type:	Corvette
Launch date:	14 January 1940 (HMS *Gladiolus*, first unit)
Crew:	85
Displacement:	179 tonnes (1160 tons)
Dimensions:	62.5m x 10.1m x 3.5m (205ft 1in x 33ft 1in x 11ft 6in)
Range:	6389km (3450nm)
Main armament:	One 102mm (6in) gun; one two-pounder or one quadruple 12.7mm (0.5in) AA mounting; depth charges
Powerplant:	Single shaft, triple expansion steam engine
Performance:	16 knots

Foch

L aid down in 1957 and completed in 1963, *Foch* is the second of the Clémenceau class carriers. She underwent a refit between 1981 and 1982 which enabled her to carry tactical nuclear weapons, and in 1984 received a satellite communications system. Further improvements included the introduction of a point-defence missile system in place of 100mm (3.9in) guns, a new catapult mechanism and a laser landing system for her flight deck. Her missile system was improved again in 1996. Despite these upgrades, *Foch* failed to retain a full air group. From 1975 onwards she shared one with her sister *Clémenceau* and spent part of her time as a helicopter carrier. Her strike component consisted of the Super Etendard attack aircraft, which can be armed with AN52 15kT tactical nuclear bombs. She was sold to the Brazilian Navy in 2001 as the *São Paulo*.

Country:	France
Type:	Aircraft carrier
Launch date:	28 July 1960
Crew:	1338 (as aircraft carrier), 984 (as helicopter carrier)
Displacement:	32,255 tonnes (32, 780 tons)
Dimensions:	265m x 31.7m x 8.6m (870ft x 104ft x 28ft)
Range:	13,500km (7500nm) at 12 knots
Armament:	Eight 100mm (3.9in) guns, Crotale and Sadral surface-to-air missile systems, 40 aircraft
Powerplant:	Two shaft, geared steam turbines
Performance:	32 knots

Folaga

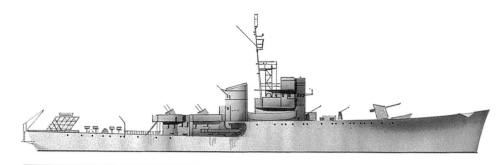

Launched in November 1942, *Folaga* was one of a class of 60 vessels designed early in World War II as cheap anti-submarine escorts for service in the Mediterranean. They could be quickly built, some being completed in less than seven months, and had a range of 4822km (2604nm). To allow for silent running during anti-submarine operations, two electric motors were fitted, although endurance in this mode was only 25.5km (13.8nm). *Folaga's* wartime career was quite unremarkable. She escaped the fate of many of her sister vessels, which were seized by the Germans after Italy's armistice with the Allies, pressed into service as submarine hunters, and later sunk in action or scuttled. Some of the latter were raised by the Italians and recommissioned in the post-war years. *Folaga* survived the war and was stricken in 1965.

Country:	Italy
Type:	Corvette
Launch date:	14 November 1942
Crew:	150
Displacement:	740 tonnes (728 tons)
Dimensions:	64m x 8.7m x 2.5m (210ft x 28ft 7in x 8ft 4in)
Range:	4822km (2604nm)
Main armament:	One 100mm (3.9in) gun
Powerplant:	Twin screw diesel engines
Performance:	19 knots

Folgore

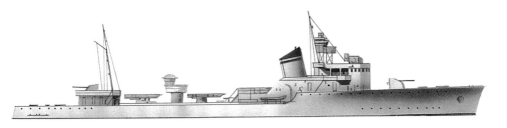

*F*olgore was one of a class of four fast destroyers which were developed from the
earlier Freccia class. The new ships had a narrower beam than before, which
reduced hull drag and ensured a high sustained speed. The penalty for this was less
internal storage space, which reduced the amount of weapons, equipment and fuel
they could carry. All four ships had their armament upgraded at various times, and
were eventually modified to carry 52 mines. They were popular as minelaying
vessels, as their high speed enabled them to transit to and from the mining area
quicker than most other ships, leaving them less vulnerable to detection and
interception. The whole class saw extensive active service during World War II.
Three were sunk in action, including *Folgore*, which was destroyed by British
cruisers in December 1942.

Country:	Italy
Type:	Destroyer
Launch date:	26 April 1931
Crew:	175
Displacement:	2123 tonnes (2090 tons)
Dimensions:	96m x 9.2m x 3.3m (315ft x 30ft 2in x 10ft 10in)
Range:	6840km (3693nm)
Main armament:	Four 119mm (4.7in) guns; six 533mm (21in) torpedo tubes
Powerplant:	Twin screw turbines
Performance:	38.8 knots

Forban

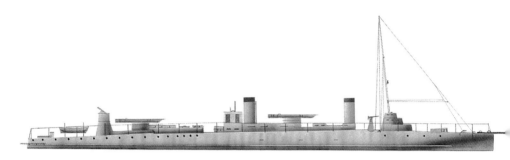

Launched in July 1895, *Forban* was a major milestone in the development of torpedo boats, being the first vessel to exceed 30 knots. Ordered in 1893, she was designed and built by Normand. She followed on from the three vessels in the Filibustier class, which possessed fine sea-keeping qualities and were ideal for service in the Bay of Biscay and English Channel areas. Indeed, the threat posed by these vessels persuaded the British Admiralty to build the first true destroyers in reply. *Forban* was a superb sea boat, with more powerful engines than the vessels of the Filibustier class. In 1907 her torpedo tubes were replaced by 457mm (18in) ones. She was sold in 1920. *Forban* was followed into service by *Mangini*, which was one of the most successful torpedo boats of the period. She could reach a top speed of 24 knots, and once averaged 18 knots for 24 hours.

Country:	France
Type:	Torpedo boat
Launch date:	25 July 1895
Crew:	57
Displacement:	152 tonnes (150 tons)
Dimensions:	44m x 4.6m x 1.3m (144ft 4in x 15ft 3in x 4ft 5in)
Range:	1852km (1000nm)
Main armament:	Two 355mm (14in) torpedo tubes
Powerplant:	Twin screw triple expansion engines
Performance:	30+ knots

Formidable

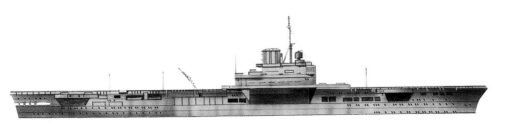

The 1936 Royal Navy programme called for the construction of two 23,368-tonne (23,000-ton) carriers, and at first plans were drawn up based on *Ark Royal*. With the realisation that war in Europe was coming ever closer, and that such carriers would be subject to constant air attack, armour protection and defensive armament was seen as important. The aircraft hangar was set in an armoured box intended to be proof against 227kg (500lb) bombs and 152mm (6in) gunfire. *Formidable* was completed in Belfast in 1940. She received serious damage from air attack while transporting aircraft to Malta in 1941. After being repaired, she went on to serve in the Pacific and survived several kamikaze attacks. British fleet carriers had armoured flight decks, unlike their US counterparts, and were consequently far less vulnerable to air attack. She was scrapped in 1953.

Country:	Great Britain
Type:	Aircraft carrier
Launch date:	17 August 1939
Crew:	1997
Weight:	28,661 tonnes (28,210 tons)
Dimensions:	226.7m x 29.1m x 8.5m (743ft 9in x 95ft 9in x 28ft)
Range:	20,383km (11,000nm) at 14 knots
Armament:	16 112mm (4.5in) guns, 36 aircraft
Powerplant:	Triple screw turbines
Performance:	30.5 knots

Forrestal

*F*orrestal* and her three sisters of the Forrestal class were authorised in 1951. Large size was needed to operate fast combat jets, which needed more fuel than their piston-engined predecessors. Designed with an angled flight deck and four steam catapults, *Forrestal* had space for around 3.4 million litres (750,000 gallons) of aviation fuel and 1670 tonnes (1650 tons) of aviation ordnance. She served with the Atlantic Fleet until 1965, when she underwent a refit before being transferred to the Pacific Fleet for operations off Vietnam. In July 1967 she was severely damaged by fire and explosion when fire broke out on the flight deck as aircraft were being readied for operations, touching off bombs and ammunition and killing 132 crew. *Forrestal* underwent a major refit between 1983–85. She was stricken in September 1993 and is currently in storage at Newport, RI.

Country:	USA
Type:	Aircraft carrier
Launch date:	11 December 1954
Crew:	2764 crew, 1912 air crew
Displacement:	80,516 tonnes (79,248 tons)
Dimensions:	309.4m x 73.2m x 11.3m (1,015ft x 240ft x 37ft)
Range:	21,600km (12,000nm) at 10 knots
Armament:	Eight 127mm (5in) guns, 90 aircraft
Powerplant:	Quadruple screw turbines
Performance:	33 knots

Foudre

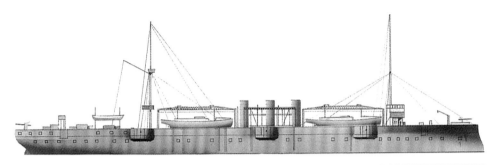

*F*oudre was built as a special depot ship for 10 small 18m (60ft) torpedo boats, each fitted with one 380mm (15in) torpedo tube. These boats were carried on cradles positioned in groups on either side of the central superstructure. *Foudre* had three funnels, close together, and was fitted with overhead gear for handling her torpedo boats, nine of which were built.*Foudre* underwent many conversions including to repair ship, minelayer, aircraft depot ship and seaplane carrier. She served in the latter role during World War I. Before that, she had demonstrated the feasibility of aircraft operation during the 1913 manoeuvres, hoisting out one seaplane and launching the other from a ramp. She carried armour ranging from a maximum of 16mm (0.6in) on the slopes to 58mm (2.3in) on the flat. She was scrapped in 1921.

Country:	France
Type:	Torpedo depot ship
Launch date:	October 1895
Crew:	410
Displacement:	6186 tonnes (6089 tons)
Dimensions:	118.7m x 17.2m x 7.2m (389ft 5in x 56ft 5in x 23ft 7in)
Range:	Not known
Main armament:	Eight 100mm (3.9in) guns; four nine-pounder guns
Powerplant:	Twin screw triple expansion engines
Performance:	19 knots

Foxtrot class

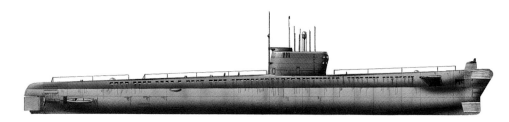

Built in the periods 1958–68 (45 units) and 1971–74 (17 units), the Foxtrot-class diesel-electric submarine remained in production at a slow rate for export, the last unit being launched in 1984. The class proved to be the most successful of the post-war Russian conventional submarine designs, 62 serving with the Soviet Navy. Three Soviet Navy Fleet Areas operated Foxtrot, and the Mediterranean and Indian Ocean Squadrons regularly had these boats deployed to them. The Foxtrots were used more regularly for long-range ocean patrols than the Soviet Union's SSNs. The first foreign recipient of the type was India, which received eight new boats between 1968 and 1976. India was followed by Libya, with six units received between 1976 and 1983, and Cuba, three boats being handed over between 1979 and 1984. All Soviet Foxtrots were withdrawn by the late 1980s.

Country:	Soviet Union
Type:	Attack submarine
Launch date:	1959 (first unit)
Crew:	80
Displacement:	Surfaced: 1950 tonnes (981 tons), submerged: 2500 tonnes (2540 tons)
Dimensions:	91.5m x 8m x 6.1m (300ft 2in x 26ft 3in x 20ft)
Surface range:	10,190km (5500nm) at 8 knots
Armament:	Ten 533mm (21in) torpedo tubes
Powerplant:	Three shafts, three diesel engines and three electric motors
Performance:	Surfaced: 18 knots, submerged: 16 knots

Framée

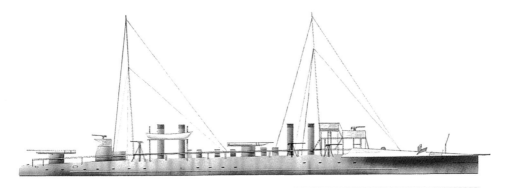

The threat posed by small torpedo boats was the catalyst for the development of a new class of warship: the destroyer. These were supposed to be powerful enough to overcome such boats, but light and fast enough to catch them. They used the new pattern of watertube boiler to feed fast-running engines. Full design speed was rarely achieved. A more critical problem was that of weight distribution. By packing the necessary weapons and equipment into a narrow hull, the designers produced a ship which was top-heavy and rolled excessively. Later modifications were removal of the main mast and aft control area, but the problem remained. The class to which *Framée* belonged was never repeated, although lessons learned were incorporated in later designs. Launched in October 1899, *Framée* was accidentally rammed and sunk off Cape St Vincent on 11 August 1900 by the battleship *Brennus*.

Country:	France
Type:	Destroyer
Launch date:	21 October 1899
Crew:	66
Displacement:	354 tonnes (348 tons)
Dimensions:	58.1m x 6.3m x 3m (190ft 7in x 20ft 8in x 9ft 10in)
Range:	1482km (800nm)
Main armament:	One 65mm (2.56in) gun
Powerplant:	Twin screw triple expansion engines
Performance:	26 knots

Francesco Caracciolo

Work started on *Francesco Carracciolo* and three sister units of the Carraciola class in 1914, but was halted in 1916 so that materials and labour could be devoted to building destroyers, submarines and light craft. Work recommenced in October 1919, but after the launch, the hull was sold in October 1920 to the Navigazione Generale Italiana which intended to convert her into a merchant ship. Lack of funds stopped this and a plan to turn her into an aircraft carrier was also dropped, and she was scrapped in 1921. The three sister ships were less advanced when work was halted and they were scrapped on the stocks. *Francesco Carracciolo*'s design gave her four widely spaced turrets, with the 152mm (6in) guns in two groups near the centre of the vessel. The other vessels in this class were the *Cristoforo Colombo*, *Francesco Morosini*, and *Marcantonio Colonnal*.

Country:	Italy
Type:	Battleship
Launch date:	12 May 1920
Crew:	1200
Displacement:	34,544 tonnes (34,000 tons)
Dimensions:	212m x 29.6m x 9.5m (695ft 6in x 97ft x 31ft 2in)
Range:	14,824km (8000nm) at 10 knots
Armament:	Eight 380mm (15in), 12 152mm (6in) guns
Powerplant:	Quadruple screw turbines
Performance:	28 knots

Francesco Mimbelli

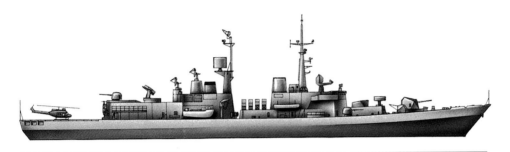

The Italian guided-missile destroyers *Luigo Durand de la Penne* and *Francesco Mimbelli* were originally named *Animoso* and *Ardimentoso*. Their names were changed in 1992 to honour former Italian naval heroes. On 10 June 1942 Cdr Francesco Mimbelli lost his life while commanding Italian MTB units in action against Soviet shipping attempting to supply the fortress of Sevastopol. It was Lt Cdr de la Penne who led the small force of Italian frogmen when they successfully placed explosive charges under the British battleships *Valiant* and *Queen Elizabeth* in Alexandria harbour in December 1941. Both vessels are fitted with Kevlar armour plating. Their three super-rapid fire 76mm (3in) guns are used as a combined medium-range anti-surface weapon and as a close-in defence system against missiles. Weapons of this kind were first developed during the Pacific war.

Country:	Italy
Type:	Destroyer
Launch date:	13 April 1991
Crew:	377
Displacement:	5486 tonnes (5400 tons)
Dimensions:	148.5m x 16.1m x 8.6m (487ft 5in x 52ft 10in x 28ft 2in)
Range:	11,252km (6076nm)
Main armament:	One 127mm (5in) and three 76mm (3in) guns; antiship missiles and ASW rockets; six 324mm (12.75in) torpedo tubes
Powerplant:	Two shafts, two gas turbines and two diesels
Performance:	31 knots

Francesco Nullo

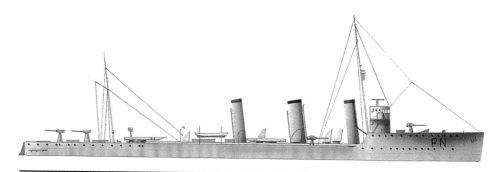

*F*rancesco Nullo** was one of a class of eight destroyers laid down between 1913 and 1914. She was the first Italian destroyer to have a single-calibre gun armament. Built by Pattison of Naples, she was completed in 1915 and this design set the pattern for the next major destroyer groups. The armament of these ships underwent several changes and, during World War I, they were all fitted out as minelayers. They were reclassified as torpedo boats in 1929 and *Francesco Nullo* herself was renamed *Fratelli Cairoli* so that the original name could be passed on to a modern destroyer. She was finally sunk by an enemy mine in December 1940. The other ships in the class serving in World War II were the *Giuseppe Cesare Abba*, *Giuseppe Dezza* (formerly *Pilade*), *Giuseppe Missori*, *Antonio Mosto*, *Rosolino Pilo* and *Simone Schiaffino*.

Country:	Italy
Type:	Destroyer
Launch date:	24 July 1915
Crew:	145
Displacement:	914 tonnes (900 tons)
Dimensions:	73m x 7.3m x 2.7m (239ft 6in x 24ft x 9ft)
Range:	2222km (1200nm)
Main armament:	Five 76mm (3in) guns
Powerplant:	Twin screws, turbines
Performance:	28 knots

Freccia

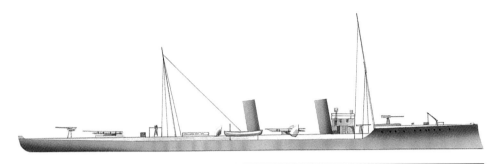

Laid down in 1899 and completed in 1902, *Freccia* was designed and constructed by the German builders Schichau. She and her five sisters formed the first major group of destroyers built for the Italian Navy. She was lost on 12 October 1911, in the Italo-Turkish war, when she went aground at the entrance to Tripoli harbour. The Italian Navy played a key part in this bitter little conflict, bombarding Turkish strongpoints at Benghazi and other coastal locations. The naval bombardment of Tripoli, in fact, was the first action of the war, and for some time the Italian Navy bore the brunt of the fighting because the Italian Army was not ready. After bombarding the forts of Tripoli in late September 1911, Italian warships disembarked 1700 sailors, who occupied the town and pushed the Turkish troops back towards the interior.

Country:	Italy
Type:	Destroyer
Launch date:	23 November 1899
Crew:	102
Displacement:	354 tonnes (4348 tons)
Dimensions:	62.1m x 6.5m x 2.6m (203ft 7in x 21 ft 4in x 8ft 6in)
Range:	2778km (1500nm)
Main armament:	One 76mm (3in) gun
Powerplant:	Twin screw, triple expansion engines
Performance:	31 knots

Freccia

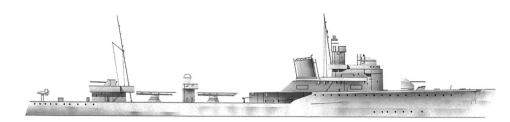

Freccia was one of a class of four units, which were a complete break with the previous classes of two- and three-funnelled destroyers of the Italian Navy, and set the pattern for destroyer design in Italy for several years. Two sets of triple 533mm (21in) torpedo tubes were carried between the single, raked funnel and the main mast. During World War II, *Freccia* served with the 7th Destroyer Flotilla, her first major battle being the 'Action off Calabria' in July 1940. She subsequently saw action against the British Mediterranean convoys, in between escorting axis convoys to North Africa. One of the most hectic actions in which she fought took place in June 1942, when all available Italian warships were thrown against two vital Malta convoys. On 9 August 1943, she was sunk during an air raid while lying off Genoa.

Country:	Italy
Type:	Destroyer
Launch date:	3 August 1930
Crew:	175
Displacement:	2134 tonnes (2100 tons)
Dimensions:	96m x 9.75m x 2.3m (315ft x 32ft x 10ft 4in)
Range:	3592km (1940nm)
Main armament:	Four 119mm (4.7in) guns
Powerplant:	Twin screw, turbines
Performance:	36 knots

Frimaire

*F**rimaire** was one of the Brumaire class of 16 submarines launched in 1911-13. All 16 boats operated in the Mediterranean during World War I. One of them, *Bernouilli*, infiltrated into Cattaro harbour on 4 April 1916 and torpedoed the Austrian destroyer *Csepel*, blowing off her stern, and another, *Le Verrier*, accidentally rammed the German *U47* on 28 July 1918 after an unsuccessful torpedo engagement. Three were lost; *Fourcault* was sunk off Cattaro by Austrian aircraft, *Curie* was captured at Pola after becoming trapped in the harbour and recommissioned by the Austrians as the *U14* (she was recovered by the French at the end of the war) and *Joule* was mined in the Dardanelles. *Frimaire* was stricken from the navy list in 1923. The boats of this class were all named after the months of the French Revolutionary calendar.

Country:	France
Type:	Attack submarine
Launch date:	26 August 1911
Crew:	29
Displacement:	Surfaced: 403 tonnes (397 tons), submerged: 560 tonnes (551 tons)
Dimensions:	52.1m x 5.14m x 3.1m (170ft 11in x 17ft 9in x 10ft 2in)
Surface range:	3150km (1700nm) at 10knots
Armament:	Six 450mm (17.7in) torpedo tubes
Powerplant:	Two-shaft diesel engines, electric motors
Performance:	Surfaced: 13 knots, submerged: 8 knots

Frithjof

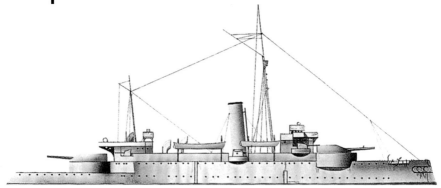

F<i>rithjof</i> was one of a class of eight vessels of the Siegfried class, designed for coastal defence in the Baltic Sea. The main guns were carried in three turrets – two forward side by side on a raised barbette, with the third aft on the centreline. The 86mm (3.4in) secondary weapons were carried, all behind shields, at the corners of the superstructure and in the waist on sponsons. The class underwent a rebuild between 1900 and 1904, which included reboilering, the vessels receiving two funnels. In 1915 she was used for coastal defence and in the following year she became an accommodation ship at Danzig. The ships of her class were all named after heroes of Teutonic mythology – *Siegfried, Beowulf, Hagen, Heimdall* and *Hildebrand. Frithjof* was sold in 1919, becoming a cargo ship, and was broken up in 1930.

Country:	Germany
Type:	Battleship
Launch date:	22 April 1925
Crew:	276
Displacement:	3750 tonnes (3691 tons)
Dimensions:	78.9m x 14.9m x 5.8m (258ft 10in x 48ft 11in x 19ft)
Range:	2760km (1490nm) at 10 knots
Armament:	Three 239mm (9.4in) guns
Powerplant:	Twin screw, triple expansion engines
Performance:	14.5 knots

Frunze

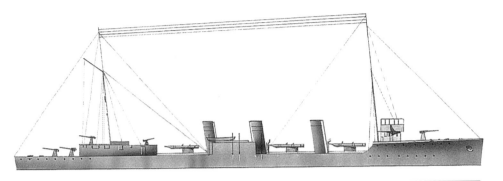

Originally named *Bystry*, the *Frunze* belonged to a class whose design was heavily influenced by the successful *Novik* design. The original specification called for a destroyer which would be capable of 35 knots and which would be armed with two 102mm (4in) and four 457mm (18in) torpedo tubes. This in fact was altered before the ships were ordered, and additional armament of a single gun and six torpedo tubes was fitted. Out of the nine ships in the class, three, including the *Bystry*, were scuttled by loyalist crews during the Russian Revolution. *Bystry* was later raised by the Soviet Government and renamed *Frunze*. Two 47mm guns were added as anti-aircraft armament. On 21 September 1941, while on active service with the Black Sea Fleet, *Frunze* was finally sunk off the Tendra peninsula by Ju87 Stuka divebombers of StG77, together with the gunboat *Krasnaya Armeniya*.

Country:	Soviet Union
Type:	Destroyer
Launch date:	7 June 1914
Crew:	160
Displacement:	1321 tonnes (1300 tons)
Dimensions:	93m x 9.3m x 2.8m (305ft x 30ft 6in x 9ft 2in)
Range:	3333km (1800nm)
Main armament:	Three 102mm (4in) guns; one 75mm (3in) gun
Powerplant:	Twin shaft geared turbines
Performance:	34 knots

Fubuki

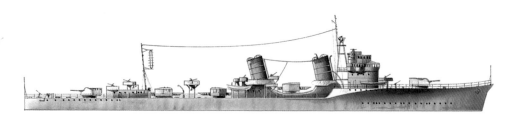

At the time of their construction between 1927 and 1931, the Fubuki-class ships were among the trend-setters of the destroyer world. Previously, Japanese destroyers had been influenced by British and German designs but now, Japanese designers went their own way to produce a destroyer so advanced that it was still formidable at the end of World War II. In 1943, the X turret was removed from surviving Fubuki-class destroyers in favour of more light AA guns. The original AA armament of two 13mm (0.5in) machine guns was changed to four 13mm (0.5in) and 14 25mm (0.9in) weapons. The class served widely in all theatres of war. Only the *Ushio* survived the conflict. Badly damaged in Manila Bay on 14 November 1944, she was towed to Yokosuka, and surrendered there at the war's end. *Fubuki* herself was sunk by US warships off Guadalcanal on 11 October 1942.

Country:	Japan
Type:	Destroyer
Launch date:	15 November 1927
Crew:	197
Displacement:	2123 tonnes (2090 tons)
Dimensions:	118.35m x 10.36m x 3.2m (388ft 3in x 34ft x 10ft 6in)
Range:	8684km (4689nm)
Main armament:	Three twin 127mm (5in) guns; three triple 610mm (24in) torpedo tubes
Powerplant:	Two sets of geared steam turbines
Performance:	37 knots

Fuji

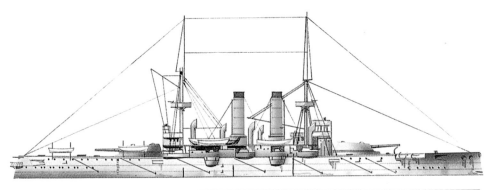

In the early 1890s, Japan anticipated war with China, and placed an order with Britain for two modern battleships. *Fuji*, and her sister *Yashima*, were improved versions of the Royal Sovereign class, although they carried lighter but equally effective 304mm (12in) guns instead of the 344mm (13.5in) weapons of the British ships. Their main armament was placed fore and aft of the vessel, while four of the 152mm (6in) guns were mounted in casements on the main deck. These were the first modern battleships in the Japanese Navy. They were completed too late for the 1894–95 Sino-Japanese war, but took part in the 1904–05 Russo–Japanese conflict. *Yashima* was sunk by a Russian mine in May 1904, but *Fuji* survived the war. She fought in the Battle of the Yellow Sea in August 1904 and sunk the Russian battleship *Borodino* at the Battle of Tsushima in 1905. She was stricken in 1923.

Country:	Japan
Type:	Battleship
Launch date:	31 March 1896
Crew:	637
Weight:	12,737 tonnes (12,533 tons)
Dimensions:	125.3m x 22.3m x 8.1m (411ft x 73ft x 26ft 7in)
Range:	7412km (4000nm) at 10 knots
Armament:	Four 254mm (10in), eight 152mm (6in) guns
Powerplant:	Twin screw, vertical triple expanion engines
Performance:	18 knots

Fu Lung

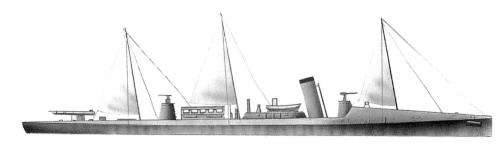

In the 1890s, the Chinese were making frantic efforts to modernize their fleet, which was then a collection of four autonomous navies based at Canton, Foochow, Shanghai and in the Yellow Sea. The *Fu Lung* was a steel-hulled, first-class ocean-going torpedo boat, with two torpedo tubes mounted side by side in the bows, for which two reloads were carried. She was one of two torpedo boats with the barbette ships *Ting Yuen* and *Kwang Ting* in the Chinese Inshore Squadron at the battle of the Yalu in 1894, and the presence of such vessels contributed to the Japanese decision not to carry on the naval action into the night. Nevertheless, the 1894–95 war with Japan saw the loss of China's only capital ships, when the Yellow Sea Fleet was destroyed. *Fu Lung* was captured by the Japanese on 8 February 1895 at the fall of Wei-Hai-Wei and renamed *Fukuryu*. She was broken up in 1908.

Country:	China
Type:	Torpedo boat
Launch date:	1885
Crew:	25
Displacement:	130 tonnes (128 tons)
Dimensions:	44m x 5m x 2.3m (144ft 4in x 16ft 5in x 7ft 6in)
Range:	Not known
Main armament:	Two 356mm (14in) torpedo tubes
Powerplant:	Single screw, triple expansion engine
Performance:	19 knots

Fulmine

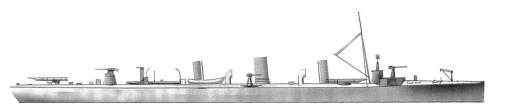

In July 1897, at the Odero yard at Sestri Ponente, Italy laid down the first
destroyer to join the Italian Navy. Designed by Engineering Inspector General
Martinez, it followed the standard destroyer design of the period, with a long, sleek
hull and a turtleback forecastle. The design speed was 26.5 knots, but initially only
24 knots was achieved. In fact, by 1908 *Fulmine* had been credited with as many as
28 knots. Much experience was gained with this vessel and Italy went on to produce
the fastest destroyers in the world. Despite this, however, she purchased her next
batch from Germany. The *Fulmine* underwent some significant changes during her
career. The number of torpedo tubes was reduced from three to two and her gun
armament was changed to one 76mm (3in) and three 57mm (2.25in) guns. *Fulmine*
was essentially an experimental ship, and was stricken in 1921.

Country:	Italy
Type:	Destroyer
Launch date:	4 December 1898
Crew:	120
Displacement:	347 tonnes (342 tons)
Dimensions:	62m x 6.5m x 2.25m (204ft x 21ft x 7ft 6in)
Range:	2224km (1200nm)
Main armament:	Five 57mm (2.25in) guns; three 356mm (14in) torpedo tubes
Powerplant:	Twin screw triple expansion engines
Performance:	26 knots

Fulmine

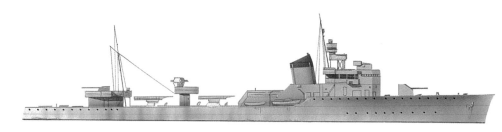

The *Fulmine* was one of a class of eight vessels divided into two sub-groups, one ordered in 1928 and the other, to which she belonged, ordered a year later. They were among the few single-funnel destroyers built prior to World War II and all were good sea boats with a splendid turn of speed. As originally designed, the boats had two funnels and a straight bow, but during construction this was changed to one wider funnel and an overhang on the bow to improve sea-keeping. Six vessels of this class were lost in action during World War II, including the *Fulmine* herself: she was sunk during a skirmish with Royal Navy warships. At the time she was one of six destroyers escorting a large Italian supply convoy bound for North Africa; as well as *Fulmine*, the two British cruisers and two destroyers sank all seven merchant ships.

Country:	Italy
Type:	Destroyer
Launch date:	2 August 1931
Crew:	174
Displacement:	2124 tonnes (2090 tons)
Dimensions:	94.5m x 9.25m x 3.35m (309ft 6in x 30ft 6in x 11ft)
Range:	3952km (2134nm)
Main armament:	Four 12mm (4.7in) guns
Powerplant:	Twin screw turbines
Performance:	38 knots

Fulton

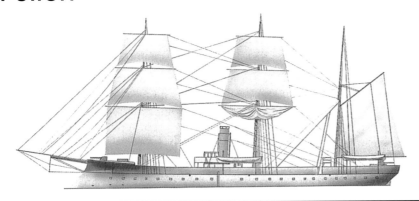

L aid down in 1882, *Fulton* was a wooden-hulled sloop with iron beams, rigged as a barque. She had a short, high forecastle, a pronounced ram bow, overhanging stern, and single, tall funnel. One of her 140mm (5.5in) guns was mounted on the forecastle and two amidships on the centreline, with the 100mm (3.9in) aft on a raised platform. She was not completed until 1888, the delay being caused by problems over the supply of engines. This occurred at a time when naval development was making rapid, dramatic strides and a long construction time could lead to vessels becoming dated before completion. *Fulton* was scrapped in 1900, but sister vessels *Inconstant* and *Papin* served in Ecuador's navy from 1901 to 1920. At about this time Ecuador also had a 19.8m (65ft) Yarrow-built torpedo boat in service; she was called the *Tungurahua*.

Country:	France
Type:	Gunboat
Launch date:	January 1887
Crew:	116
Displacement:	838 tonnes (825 tons)
Dimensions:	60.8m x 8.7m x 3.9m (199ft 5in x 28ft 5in x 12ft 8in)
Range:	Not known
Main armament:	Three 140mm (5.5in) guns; one 100mm (3.9in) gun
Powerplant:	Single screw horizontal compound engine
Performance:	13 knots

Furious

The origin of one of the best-known British aircraft carriers of World War II dates back to pre-1914 when Jack Fisher, then First Sea Lord, planned for a fleet of fast, powerful cruisers with shallow draught to operate in the Baltic. *Furious* was one of three such vessels built. Launched in 1916, she was converted to a carrier in 1917 to increase the Grand Fleet's aircraft support. Originally her flight deck and hangar were built over her forward gun positions. After undergoing a more complete rebuild, she served with the Home and Mediterranean fleets in World War II. Together with HMS *Eagle*, she was an invaluable asset in the early months of the Mediterranean war, flying off fighter aircraft to Malta. Her aircraft attacked *Tirpitz* in 1944 and she was taken out of operational service the same year. She was scrapped in 1948.

Country:	Great Britain
Type:	Aircraft carrier
Launch date:	15 August 1916
Crew:	1218
Displacement:	22,758 tonnes (22,400 tons)
Dimensions:	239.6m x 27.4m x 7.3m (786ft 4in x 90ft x 24ft)
Range:	5929km (3200nm) at 19 knots
Armament:	Six 102mm (4in) guns, 36 aircraft
Powerplant:	Quadruple screw turbines
Performance:	30 knots

Furor

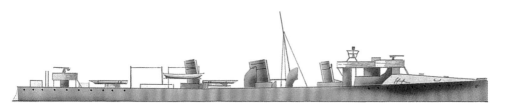

Built at Clydebank, Scotland, *Furor* was the first destroyer to go into service with the Spanish Navy, and formed part of Admiral Ceveras's squadron which was sent to Cuba in 1898. The USA, following the destruction of their battleship USS *Maine* in Havana harbour on 21 February 1898, had decided on armed intervention in Cuba where the Spanish were attempting to crush a rebellion. There was little fierce resistance against the American intervention force, and when Admiral Ceveras attempted to escape from Santiago, whose garrison had held out for some time, he was resoundingly defeated by the American warships waiting to ambush him offshore. Three of his ships, including the *Furor*, were run ashore in flames, and another, with the Americans in hot pursuit, got as far as the Rio Turquino, where she was beached.

Country:	Spain
Type:	Destroyer
Launch date:	1896
Crew:	98
Displacement:	376 tonnes (370 tons)
Dimensions:	67m x 6.7m x 1.7m (219ft 10in x 22ft x 5ft 7in)
Range:	1667km (900nm)
Main armament:	Two 14-pounder guns; two 356mm (14in) torpedo tubes
Powerplant:	Twin screw triple expansion engines
Performance:	28 knots

Fuso

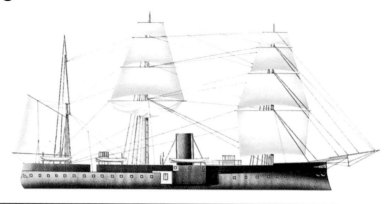

In 1875, Japan ordered three armoured vessels. Two were armoured broadside cruisers; the other was a powerful central battery ironclad named *Fuso*. All were designed by Sir Edward Reed, one of the world's leading naval architects. Rebuilt in 1894, just before the war with China, *Fuso* emerged with eight 152mm (6in) guns and two military masts, and fought at the Battle of the Yalu where she was damaged. She suffered further damage in 1897, when she was beached after colliding with the cruiser *Matsushima* in a gale. She was salvaged and repaired in the following year. She was the mother of the modern Japanese Navy and the first ironclad to be built in Japan; prior to her construction, Japan's only ironclad vessel was the former Confederate ram *Stonewall*. She was reclassified as a coastal defence ship in 1903 and broken up in 1910.

Country :	Japan
Type:	Ironclad
Launch date:	14 April 1877
Crew:	250
Displacement:	3777 tonnes (3837 tons)
Dimensions:	67m x 14.6m x 5.6m (220ft x 48ft x 18ft 3in)
Range:	8100km (4500nm)
Armament:	Four 236mm (9in) guns
Powerplant:	Twin screw, compound horizontal, surface-condensing engines
Performance:	13 knots

Fuso

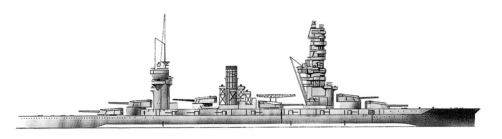

With the laying down of this vessel in March 1912 in a home yard, Japan confirmed her position as a leading naval power in the Pacific. Up until then, all Japanese battleships had been built in British yards. Although *Fuso* and her sister *Yamarisho* were less heavily armoured than contemporary US battleships, they carried a heavier armament and were two knots faster. As originally completed in 1915, *Fuso* had two funnels, with the first between the bridge and third turret. In an extensive refit in the 1930s, this was removed and replaced by a massive bridge structure. Underwater protection was greatly improved and new machinery fitted. *Fuso* served in the Aleutians and at Leyte during World War II, and it was during the Battle of Leyte Gulf that she and the *Yamashiro* were sunk by gunfire and torpedoes from US battleships in October 1944.

Country:	Japan
Type:	Battleship
Launch date:	28 March 1914
Crew:	1193
Displacement:	36,474 tonnes (35,900 tons)
Dimensions:	205m x 28.7m x 8.6m (672ft 6in x 94ft x 28ft)
Range:	14,400km (8000nm)
Armament:	12 356mm (14in), 16 152mm (6in) guns
Powerplant:	Quadruple screw turbines
Performance:	23 knots

Fuyutsuki

The *Fuyutsuki* was ordered in 1939 as part of the large Akitsuki class of ocean-going destroyers, originally planned as fast anti-aircraft escorts to work with the Japanese carrier task forces. However, the design was modified to incorporate one quadruple torpedo mount. At the end of the war, *Fuyutsuki* was surrendered at Moji in a badly damaged condition, and her sister ship *Suzutsuki* was surrendered at Sasebo in a similar state. Of the other four surviving ships, all of which surrendered at Kure, *Hanatsuki* was handed over to the Americans for use as a target ship; *Natsutsuki* was given to the British in June 1947 and subsequently scapped; *Harutsuki* was handed over to the Russians and served for a time in the Soviet Navy; and *Yoitsuki* was impressed by Nationalist China and renamed *Fen Yang*.

Country:	Japan
Type:	Destroyer
Launch date:	20 January 1944
Crew:	175
Displacement:	3759 tonnes (3700 tons)
Dimensions:	134.2m x 11.6m x 4.2m (440ft 3in x 38ft x 13ft 9in)
Range:	7408km (4000nm)
Main armament:	Eight 96mm (3.8in) guns; four 607mm (23.9in) torpedo tubes in one quadruple mount
Powerplant:	Twin screw turbines
Performance:	33 knots

G1

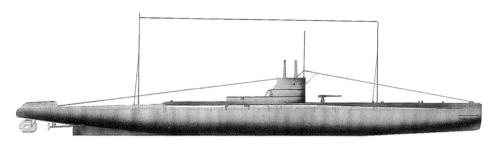

The G class of 14 boats, based on the E-class design, was ordered by the British Admiralty in 1914 in response to information that Germany was about to build a fleet of double-hulled, oceangoing submarines. Two of the G-class boats were lost in action during World War I and two more through accidental causes. One of their main tasks during the war was to ambush U-boats trying to pass through the Channel. The boats had an unusual armament arrangement in that they were fitted with torpedo tubes of different calibres: one 533mm (21in) and four 457mm (18in), the larger-calibre weapon being intended for use against armoured targets. One G-class boat, *G7*, had the unhappy distinction of being the last British submarine lost in World War I, failing to return from a North Sea patrol on 1 November 1918.

Country:	Great Britain
Type:	Attack submarine
Launch date:	August 1915
Crew:	31
Displacement:	Surfaced: 704 tonnes (693 tons), submerged: 850 tonnes (836 tons)
Dimensions:	57m x 6.9m x 4.1m (187ft x 22ft x 13ft 6in)
Surface range:	4445km (2400nm) at 12.5 knots
Armament:	Four 457mm (18in) torpedo tubes, one 533mm (21in) torpedo tube, one 76mm (3in) gun
Powerplant:	Twin screw diesel-electric motors
Performance:	Surfaced: 14.25 knots, submerged: 9 knots

G5

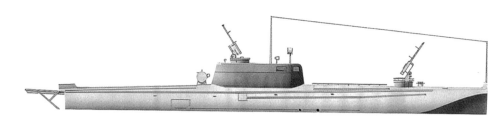

G5 was one of a class of about 295 vessels, first conceived in the early 1930s. As the series progressed, their displacement grew, until finally it reached 17 tons (16.7 tonnes). Some units claimed to have reached 60 knots. Many were fitted with Isotta Fraschini engines, which proved very reliable, but those fitted with Russian-built versions had a poorer record. Torpedoes were launched from tubes aft of the conning tower, and as they struck the water, the boat had to make a sharp turn to veer out of their way. At the time of the German invasion in June 1941, there were a total of 44 boats in this class in commission with the Baltic Fleet, 77 with the Black Sea, and 135 with the Pacific Fleet. During the German invasion, 73 were lost and 31 were discarded or decommissioned. A few were transferred to North Korea after the war.

Country:	Soviet Union
Type:	Torpedo gunboat
Launch date:	1934
Crew:	6–7
Displacement:	14 tonnes (13.7 tons
Dimensions:	19.1m x 3.3m x 0.76m (62ft 6in x 11ft x 2ft 6in)
Range:	Not known
Main armament:	Two 533mm (21in) torpedo tubes; two 12.7mm (0.5in) guns
Powerplant:	Twin screw petrol engines
Performance:	45 knots

G40

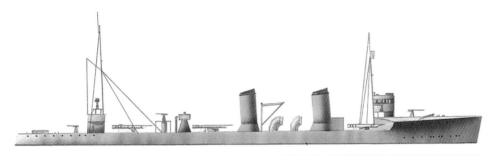

Although successful, *G40* and her three sister ships, launched between 1914 and 1915, were regarded as too big to act in concert with a tight battleline, and many later groups were scaled-down versions. The high, long forecastle made for good seaworthiness. A large bridge structure was positioned at the aft end of the forecastle, and almost level with this were two single torpedo tubes, one on each side. The rest of the torpedo tubes were placed in pairs in the centreline. All ships saw active wartime service. Of the four ships in this class, *G37* was mined and sunk in the North Sea on 4 November 1917; the others were all scuttled by their own crews at Scapa Flow on 21 June 1919, and were later raised and scrapped. The Germans consistently failed to exploit their destroyer force to the full in World War I, except during the final months.

Country:	Germany
Type:	Destroyer
Launch date:	27 February 1915
Crew:	87
Displacement:	1068 tonnes (1051 tons)
Dimensions:	79.5m x 8.36m x 3.74m (261ft x 27ft 6in x 12ft 1in)
Range:	3335km (1800nm)
Main armament:	Three 85mm (3.3in) guns; six 508mm (20in) torpedo tubes
Powerplant:	Twin screw turbines
Performance:	34.5 knots

G101

One of a quartet laid down for Argentina at the yard of Germaniawerft, Kiel, in 1914 and completed in 1915 (but subsequently taken over by the German Navy), *G101* was originally named *Santiago,* the other three *San Luis, Santa Fe* and *Tecuman.* Had these vessels entered service with the Argentinian Navy, they would have been among the most powerful destroyers in South American waters. The turbines of *G101* and her sisters developed 29,500hp. All four were interned after the war and scuttled by their crews at Scapa Flow on 21 June 1919. *G101* was raised and scrapped at Charleston, USA, in 1926; *G102* was salved and sent to the USA, where she was sunk as a bombing target by US aircraft off Cape Henry; *G103* was raised and foundered in a storm north of Scotland while en route to the breakers in November 1925, and *G104* was also scrapped at Charleston.

Country:	Germany
Type:	Destroyer
Launch date:	12 August 1914
Crew:	104
Displacement:	1873 tonnes (1843 tons)
Dimensions:	98m x 9.4m x 3.9m (321ft 6in x 30ft 9in x 12ft 9in)
Range:	(3704km) 2000nm
Main armament:	Four 85mm (3.3in) guns; six 508mm (20in) torpedo tubes
Powerplant:	Twin screw turbines
Performance:	36.5 knots

G132

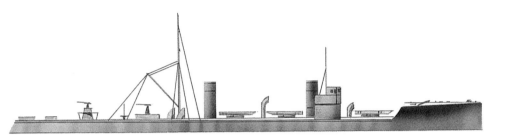

A n improved version of the basic German destroyer design, *T132* and her four
sisters (originally designated *G132–G136*, but re-lettered in 1916) were built
by Germaniawerft, Kiel, in 1906. A follow-on boat, *G137* (*T137*) had a greater
displacement and and was used in experiments with Parsons turbine engines. Six
were fitted: one high pressure, two low pressure, one cruising and two reverse.
G137 was two knots faster than *T132* but burnt more fuel. At the time, Germany
was building up a large force of destroyers designed to act with the Battle Fleet by
breaking through the enemy battleline and attacking it with torpedoes. This tactic
would leave attacks on enemy destroyers as a secondary function for the German
vessels, and was thereby in accordance with the aggressive doctrine of Admiral von
Tirpitz, which failed somewhat in its actual implementation during WWI.

Country:	Germany
Type:	Destroyer
Launch date:	12 May 1906
Crew:	102
Displacement:	553 tonnes (544 tons)
Dimensions:	65.7m x 7m x 2.6m (215ft 6in x 23ft 1in x 8ft 6in)
Range:	1575km (850nm)
Main armament:	Four 51mm (2in) guns; three 450mm (17.7in) torpedo tubes
Powerplant:	Twin screw triple expansion engines
Performance:	28 knots

Gabbiano

The lead ship of a very large class of Italian corvettes laid down between 1942 and 1943, *Gabbiano* was heavily involved in escorting Axis convoys that were taking desperately needed supplies and reinforcements from Italy to Tunisia. They were also involved in evacuating the wounded on the return trip. The convoys were heavily attacked by Allied aircraft and British submarines, which sank several merchantmen with severe loss of life. However, on 16 April, *Gabbiano* (Cdr Ceccacci) attacked and sank HM submarine *Regent*, and then, on 24 April, she also attacked HM submarine *Sahib* near the Lipari Islands. As a result, the British boat was forced to the surface and sunk by a German Junkers 88 dive-bomber. *Gabbiano* and a dozen of her sister ships served in the Italian Navy until the mid-1970s.

Country:	Italy
Type:	Corvette
Launch date:	23 June 1942
Crew:	109
Displacement:	740 tonnes (728 tons)
Dimensions:	64.3m x 9m x 2.5m (211ft x 28ft 7in x 8ft 4in)
Range:	5556km (3000nm)
Main armament:	One 102mm (4in) gun; depth charges
Powerplant:	Twin screw diesel engines
Performance:	18 knots

Gadfly

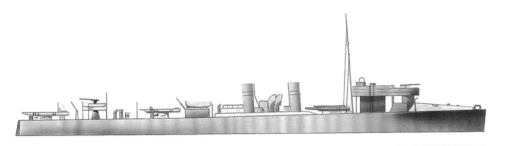

Gadfly was one of a large class of 36 coastal-defence destroyers, built as a cheap alternative to the Tribal-class destroyers, which were primarily intended for service with the fleet. The design followed that of the large first-class torpedo boats of the period, and was an economical way of creating a large fleet of destroyers for coastal defence and coastal roles. *Gadfly* was numbered TB6 soon after completion, and scrapped in 1920. During World War I, boats of this type were used to patrol the flanks of the Dover Barrage, which was intended to prevent the passage of U-boats through the Straits of Dover into the Western Approaches. The Dover passage could save a small U-boat based in Flanders nearly eight days on its 14-day cruise, and a larger boat from the German Bight six days out of 25. By 1917, the U-boat campaign was causing Britain serious problems.

Country:	Britain
Type:	Destroyer
Launch date:	24 June 1906
Crew:	120
Displacement:	406 tonnes (400 tons)
Dimensions:	54.9m x 5.3m x 1.8m (180ft x 17ft 4 in x 5ft 11in)
Range:	4076km (2200nm)
Main armament:	Two 12-pounder guns; three 457mm (18in) torpedo tubes
Powerplant:	Triple screw turbines
Performance:	26 knots

Gal

Gal is one of three German-designed Type 206 boats built by Vickers of
Barrow in the UK in the mid-1970s, following a contract signed in April 1972.
Gal, laid down in 1973 and commissioned in December 1976, ran aground on her
delivery voyage, but was repaired. The other two boats, *Tanin* and *Rahav,* were
commissioned in June and December 1977 respectively. The Type 206 is a
development of the Type 205; built of high tensile non-magnetic steel, it was
intended for coastal operations and had to conform with treaty limitations on the
maximum tonnage allowed for West Germany. New safety devices for the crew
were fitted, and the weapons fit allowed for the carriage of wire-guided torpedoes.
The Type 206 was just one of a range of similar boats offered for export.

Country:	Israel
Type:	Attack submarine
Launch date:	2 December 1975
Crew:	22
Displacement:	Surfaced: 427 tonnes (420 tons), submerged: 610 tonnes (600 tons)
Dimensions:	45m x 4.7m x 3.7m (147ft 8in x 15ft 5in x 12ft 2in)
Surface range:	7038km (3800nm) at 10 knots
Armament:	Eight 533mm (21in) torpedo tubes
Powerplant:	Single shaft, two diesels, one electric motor
Performance:	Surfaced: 11 knots, submerged: 17 knots

Galatea

One of the Leander class designed in the late 1950s, planned as improved versions of the Type 12 Rothesay class, and intended to be built in five batches spread over 10 years, *Galatea* was part of the first group of seven vessels. In all, 24 were to be constructed, with the later ships increasing in size and carrying a greater amount of equipment, including Exocet and updated electronics. The hull had a long, unbroken form, with a raised forecastle. The hangar for one or two ASW helicopters was situated aft. The Ikara ASW missile system in *Galatea* was housed forward on the extended superstructure in front of the bridge. The class was updated in batches during the 1970s and 1980s, and progressively withdrawn from 1988 onwards. The success of the class was measured by the fact that it sold overseas, and was built under licence in some countries.

Country:	Great Britain
Type:	Frigate
Launch date:	23 May 1963
Crew:	263
Displacement:	2906 tonnes (2860 tons)
Dimensions:	113.4m x 12.5m x 4.5m (372ft x 41ft x 14ft 9in)
Range:	8519km (4600nm)
Main armament:	One anti-submarine Ikara missile launcher
Powerplant:	Twin screws, turbines
Performance:	28 knots

Galerna

Galerna was a medium-range submarine built to the design of the French Agosta class. She marked a major step forward in Spanish submarine technology. This submarine and her three sisters can carry 16 reload torpedoes or nine torpedoes and 19 mines. A full sonar kit is carried, comprising one active and one passive set. The first two boats, *Galerna* and *Siroco,* were ordered in May 1975, and a second pair (*Mistral* and *Tramontana*) in June 1977. The Spanish Agosta-class boats are armed with four bow torpedo tubes which are fitted with a rapid-reload pneumatic ramming system that can launch the weapons quickly but with a minimum of noise. The boats have a diving depth of 350m (1148ft). They were built with some French help, and all were upgraded in the mid-1990s.

Country:	Spain
Type:	Attack submarine
Launch date:	5 December 1981
Crew:	54
Displacement:	Surfaced: 1473 tonnes (1450 tons), submerged: 1753 tonnes (1725 tons)
Dimensions:	67.6m x 6.8m x 5.4m (221ft 9in x 22ft4in x 17ft 9in)
Surface range:	13,672km (7378nm) at 9 knots
Armament:	Four 551mm (21.7in) torpedo tubes
Powerplant:	Single screw diesel/electric motors
Performance:	Surfaced: 12 knots, submerged: 20 knots

Gambier Bay

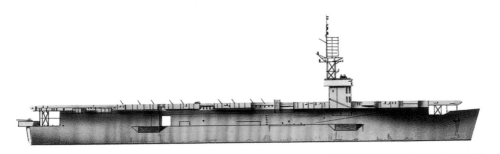

Gambier Bay was one of a 50-strong group of light escort carriers, completed from the unfinished hulls of a standard type of merchant ship mass-produced by Henry J. Kaiser in 1942. All 50 vessels were completed in under one year. The class was designed to carry an air group of nine fighters, nine bombers and nine torpedo bombers. The first mission for *Gambier Bay* was in early 1944, when she ferried aircraft to USS *Enterprise* and then supported US forces off Saipan, in the Marianas, and later at Leyte. She was sunk by gunfire during action off Samar in October 1944. Her loss occurred during one of the most epic sea-fights of the war, when the lightly armed escort carrier groups supporting the invasion of the Philippines fought off the main Japanese battle fleet in a surface action. The survivors of the class were all laid up at the end of the war.

Country:	USA
Type:	Aircraft carrier
Launch date:	22 November 1943
Crew:	860
Displacement:	11,074 tonnes (10,900 ton)
Dimensions:	156.1m x 32.9m x 6.3m (512ft 3in x 108ft x 20ft 9in)
Range:	18,360km (10,200nm) at 12 knots
Armament:	One 127mm (5in), 16 40mm (1.6in) guns, 27 aircraft
Powerplant:	Twin screw, reciprocating engines
Performance:	19 knots

Gangut

Designed at a time when the battle line was likely to be in line abreast , instead of a line ahead, *Gangut* had her single 305mm (12in) gun mounted forward in a centreline turret on the foredeck. The four 229mm (9in) guns were concentrated in a battery amidships, protected by 127mm (5in) armour. Two 152mm (6in) guns were placed forward on the same level alongside the turret, but these could only fire straight ahead. Two more 152mm (6in) guns were positioned right aft and these also lacked broadside fire. Laid down in 1889, *Gangut* was completed in 1894. Whilst returning from gunnery practice in 1897, she struck an uncharted rock off Transund harbour and sank. In her short career she had served with the Baltic Fleet, where conditions were suited to vessels of her size. Russia made very little use of large battleships in these confined waters, as they would have presented easy targets.

Country:	Russia
Type:	Battleship
Launch date:	October 1890
Crew:	521
Displacement:	6697 tonnes (6592 tons)
Dimensions:	88.3m x 18.9m x 6.4m (289ft 8in x 62ft x 21ft)
Range:	4632km (2500nm) at 10 knots
Armament:	One 305mm (12in), four 229mm (9in) and four 152mm (6in) guns
Powerplant:	Twin screw, vertical compound engines
Performance:	14.7 knots

Gangut

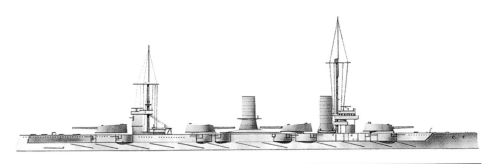

L aunched in 1911, *Gangut* and her three sisters were Russia's first dreadnoughts. The contract was won by Blohm and Voss, Hamburg, but the Russian government refused funds unless they were built in Russia. As Russian industry could not produce enough high tensile steel, an ingenious construction method was used, based upon the Italian *Dante Alighieri*. Building time was lengthy, and Gangut was not ready until 1914, by which time she was largely obsolete. Her main guns, however, were the largest then at sea. She was renamed *Oktyabrskaya Revolutsia* in 1919. In the 'Winter War' against Finland (1939–40) she was used to bombard Finnish shore positions. In September 1941, while taking part in the defence of Leningrad, she was severely damaged by six bombs during a Stuka attack, and was again hit by four bombs in April 1942. She was scrapped in 1956–59.

Country:	Russia
Type:	Battleship
Launch date:	17 October 1911
Crew:	1126
Displacement:	26,264 tonnes (25,850 tons)
Dimensions:	182.9m x 26.9m x 8.3m (600ft x 88ft 3in x 27ft 3in)
Range:	7412km (4000nm) at 16 knots
Armament:	12 305mm (12in), 16 120mm (4.7in) guns
Powerplant:	Quadruple screw turbines
Performance:	23 knots

Garibaldino

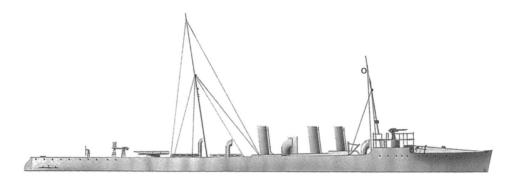

Originally intended as a follow-on group to the Nembo class, launched in 1901, *Garibaldino* incorporated improvements gained through operational experience. The six vessels in this class were all laid down in 1905 and completed between 1907 and 1910. *Garibaldino* was one of the group laid down in 1905. All in this 1905 group were coal burners, but a second group, known as the Soldato or Alpino class, were oil burners. *Garibaldino*'s engines developed 6000hp, and the ship had an endurance of 2894km (1536nm) at 12 knots, or 760km (410nm) at 23.5 knots. She was sunk on 16 July 1918, after colliding with the British destroyer HMS *Cygnet* off Villefranche in southern France. In effect, the Garibaldino class formed a stepping-stone between the coal-burning pre-war destroyers and the oil-burning postwar ones.

Country:	Italy
Type:	Destroyer
Launch date:	12 February 1910
Crew:	98
Displacement:	419 tonnes (412 tons)
Dimensions:	65m x 6.1m x 2.1m (213ft 3in x 20ft x 7ft)
Range:	1890km (1020nm)
Main armament:	Three 76mm (3in) guns; three 450mm (17.7in) torpedo tubes
Powerplant:	Twin screw triple expansion
Performance:	28 knots

Garland

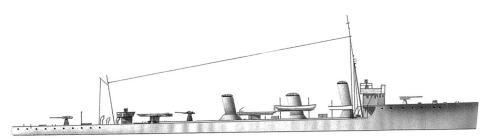

HMS *Garland* was one of a class of 20 destroyers which originated in the British naval construction programme of 1911–12. Designed to counter the considerable threat posed by the latest German destroyers, they were to be armed with two 102mm (4in) guns, plus four 12-pounders, but three 102mm (4in) guns were chosen instead, making them the most powerful destroyers of that period. Ships of this class were normally deployed in support of the Royal Navy's light cruiser forces, which were based at locations such as Harwich, from where they could readily intercept German excursions into the North Sea area. After Jutland, such excursions were rare. However, there were some spirited engagements between opposing destroyer forces in the Heligoland Bight, particularly in March and April 1918.

Country:	Great Britain
Type:	Destroyer
Launch date:	23 April 1913
Crew:	147
Displacement:	1005 tonnes (989 tons)
Dimensions:	81.5m x 8.2m x 2.8m (267ft 6in x 27ft x 9ft 3in)
Range:	3335km (1800nm)
Main armament:	Three 102mm (4in) guns; two 533mm (21in) torpedo tubes
Powerplant:	Twin screw semi-geared turbines
Performance:	28 knots

Gatineau

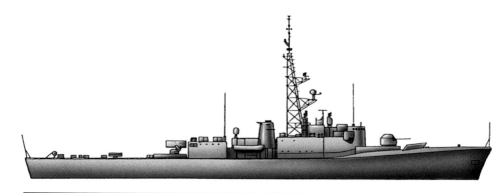

Gatineau, completed in February 1959, was one of seven escort destroyers of the Restigouche class built for the Royal Canadian Navy, the others being *Chaudiere, Colombia, Kootenay, St Croix* and *Terra Nova*. The class was converted in order to carry variable-depth sonar, advanced electronics, and ASROC in the early 1970s, the latter supplementing the ASW mortars. The ships were developed from the original St Laurent class and were generally similar to other destroyer escorts completed at about the same time, namely the *Annapolis, Nipigon, Mackenzie, Saskatchewan, Qu'appelle* and *Yukon*. All ships of the Restigouche, Annapolis, and Mackenzie classes were capable of operating a Sea King ASW helicopter. Surviving ships of the Restigouche class were in reserve in the late 1990s.

Country:	Canada
Type:	Destroyer
Launch date:	3 June 1957
Crew:	246
Displacement:	2946 tonnes (2900 tons)
Dimensions:	111.5m x 12.8m x 4.1m (366ft x 42ft x 13ft 6in)
Range:	12,970km (7003nm)
Main armament:	Two 76mm (3in) DP guns; Limbo 3-barrelled depth charge mortars
Powerplant:	Two shafts, geared turbines
Performance:	28 knots

Gatling

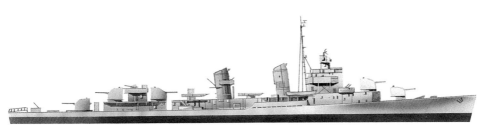

The USS *Gatling* was a Fletcher-class destroyer and, as such, was one of the largest classes built for the US Navy. Launched in June 1943, she went into action in the Pacific in late January 1944, when she formed part of a US naval task force attacking Japanese bases in the Marshall Islands. In June 1944, she was operating in support of US carriers attacking enemy bases in the Marianas, and in October of that same year she was conducting similar operations off Formosa along with 13 other destroyers of Task Group 38.3. From 30 December 1944 to 25 January 1945, her Task Group carried out many attacks on Japanese airfields in the Central and Southwest Pacific, and fought on to the Japanese surrender. A highly successful design, the Fletcher class formed the backbone of the Pacific Fleet. Many were sold after the war. *Gatling* was stricken from the Navy List in 1974.

Country:	USA
Type:	Destroyer
Launch date:	20 June 1943
Crew:	300
Displacement:	2971 tonnes (2924 tons)
Dimensions:	114.7m x 12m x 4.2m (376ft 5in x 39ft 4in x 13ft 9in)
Range:	8334km (4500nm)
Main armament:	Five 127mm (5in) guns
Powerplant:	Twin screw turbines
Performance:	37 knots

Gearing

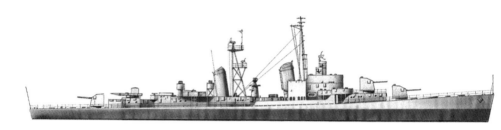

Yet more space and endurance requirements stretched the hull of the Sumner class of US destroyers – which had evolved from the Fletcher class – by 4.27m (14ft) to produce the Gearing class. This development into the Gearing class was to prove the ultimate stage in this family of closely related warships. Externally, these larger ships were distinguishable primarily through their more widely spaced funnels. Although the backbone of the Japanese surface fleet had been broken by 1945, the air threat remained considerable, and some of the Gearing class were fitted with a braced tripod bearing an air surveillance radar or an extra quadruple 40mm (1.5in) mounting. However, the 76.2mm (3in) automatic guns that could literally disintegrate a low-flying suicide aircraft did not generally become available until peacetime when they were fitted to most warships.

Country:	USA
Type:	Destroyer
Launch date:	18 February 1945
Crew:	350
Displacement:	2971 tonnes (2924 tons)
Dimensions:	114.7m x 12.5m x 5.79m (376ft 5in x 41ft x 19ft)
Range:	8338km (4500nm)
Main armament:	Three twin 127mm (5in) DP and three quadruple 40mm (1.5in) AA guns; two quintuple 533mm (21in) torpedo tubes
Powerplant:	Two sets of geared steam turbines
Performance:	36.5 knots

Gemlik

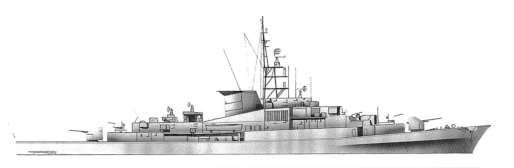

The *Gemlik* started life as the *Emden*, a Köln-class frigate of the West German Navy. She and her sisters were among the first modern warships built for the Federal German Navy after World War II. She was laid down in 1958 and completed in October 1961. She is of a compact design, and is equipped with a wide range of anti-submarine weapons, sophisticated sensors, and electronic countermeasures. Her 100mm (3.9in) guns can fire a 13.5kg (30lb) projectile up to 15km (9 miles), at a maximum rate of 60–80 shells per minute. She has four launch tubes used for anti-submarine acoustic homing torpedoes, supplemented by four twin-barrelled anti-submarine mortars. She is also capable of carrying up to 80 anti-ship and anti-submarine mines. She was transferred from Germany to the Turkish Navy in September 1983.

Country:	Germany
Type:	Frigate
Launch date:	21 March 1959
Crew:	210
Displacement:	2743 tonnes (2700 tons)
Dimensions:	109.9m x 11m x 5.1m (360ft 7in x 36ft x 16ft 9in)
Range:	5662km (3052nm)
Main armament:	Two 100mm (3.9in) guns; four 533mm (21in) torpedo tubes
Powerplant:	Twin screw gas turbines/diesel engines
Performance:	28 knots

General Admiral Apraksin

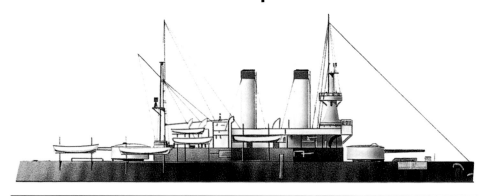

Launched in 1896, *General Admiral Apraksin* was one of three in a class of coastal defence ships intended for service in the Baltic, to counter the threat from Sweden. The 1.8m (6ft) deep armour belt ran for 53.6m (176ft) of the length of the vessel, or just over half way, with 203mm–153mm (8in–6in) thick bulkheads at each end. In February 1905 she sailed for the Far East as part of the 3rd Pacific Squadron, and on 28 May she surrendered to the Japanese in the aftermath of Tsushima – one of the most complete naval victories of all time, in which the Japanese sank six battleships and captured two for the loss of three destroyers. Of eleven assorted Russian cruisers and armoured ships, only three escaped to be interned in neutral ports. *General Admiral Apraksin* was taken into Japanese service as the *Okinoshima*. She was scrapped in 1926.

Country:	Russia
Type:	Battleship
Launch date:	1896
Crew:	404
Displacement:	4192 tonnes (4126 tons)
Dimensions:	84.6m x 15.8m x 5.2m (277ft 6in x 51ft 10in x 17ft)
Range:	4818km (2600nm) at 10 knots
Armament:	Three 254mm (10in), four 120mm (4.7in) guns
Powerplant:	Twin screw, triple expansion engines
Performance:	16.2 knots

George Washington

In 1955, the Soviet Union began modifying six existing diesel submarines to carry nuclear-tipped ballistic missiles. America was simultaneously developing the Jupiter missile, which was to equip a projected 10,160-tonne (10,000-ton) nuclear submarine. Jupiter used a mix of highly volatile liquids for its propellant, and was posing immense problems of safety and operation. The smaller, lighter Polaris A1 presented a more suitable alternative. The nuclear submarine *Scorpion*, then building, was chosen as the delivery platform for the new weapon and a new 40m (13ft) hull section was added just aft of the conning tower to house 16 missiles in vertical launch tubes. Renamed *George Washington*, she was the first of a new type of weapons platform, and put the USA far ahead in the nuclear arms race.

Country:	USA
Type:	Ballistic missile submarine
Launch date:	June 1959
Crew:	112
Displacement:	Surfaced: 6115 tonnes (6019 tons), submerged: 6998 tonnes (6888 tons)
Dimensions:	116.3m x 10m x 8.8m (381ft 7in x 33ft x 28ft 10in)
Range:	Unlimited
Armament:	Sixteen Polaris missiles, six 533mm (21in) torpedo tubes
Powerplant:	Single screw, one pressurized water-cooled reactor, turbines
Performance:	Surfaced: 20 knots, submerged: 30.5 knots

George Washington

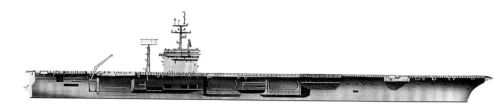

*G*eorge Washington is one of nine Nimitz class supercarriers built to date. She was laid down in August 1986, 17 years after *Nimitz*, the first of the class. *George Washington* carries extensive damage-control systems, including 63mm-(2.5in-) thick armour over parts of the hull, plus box protection over the magazines and machinery spaces. Aviation equipment includes four lifts and four steam catapults, and over 2540 tonnes (2500 tons) of aviation ordnance. The life of the nuclear reactors is 15 years. *George Washington's* air wing, like that of all Nimitz class carriers, comprises around 85 aircraft, with two squadrons of Grumman F-14 Tomcats forming the interceptor element. The F-14s are currently being phased out of service and replaced by the F/A-18 Super Hornet. The big carriers form the nucleus of a US fleet's Battle Force, the principal task force.

Country:	USA
Type:	Aircraft carrier
Launch date:	21 July 1990
Crew:	5621 crew and air group
Displacement:	92,950 tonnes (91,487 tons)
Dimensions:	332.9m x 40.8m x 11.3m (1,092ft 2in x 133ft 10in x 37ft)
Range:	Unlimited
Armament:	Four Vulcan 20mm guns plus three Sparrow surface-to-air missile launchers
Powerplant:	Quadruple screw turbines, two water-cooled nuclear reactors
Performance:	30 knots+

George Washington Carver

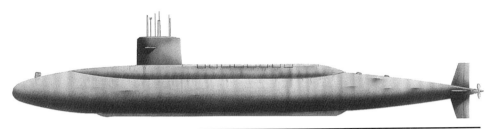

George Washington Carver was one of 29 vessels of the Lafayette class, enlarged versions of the Ethan Allen class, and all were refitted with Poseidon missiles. She was laid down in April 1964 and was completed in August 1966. This class of submarine could dive to depths of up to 300m (985ft) and the nuclear reactor core provided enough energy to propel the vessel for 760,000km (347,200nm), which to all intents and purposes gave it an unlimited endurance. Like all American SSBNs, *George Washington Carver* had two crews which carried out alternate 68-day patrols, with 32-day refit periods between patrols. The vessels underwent an extensive refit, which took nearly two years to complete, every six years in rotation. *George Washington Carver* was deactivated on 2 November 1992.

Country:	USA
Type:	Ballistic missile submarine
Launch date:	14 August 1965
Crew:	140
Displacement:	Surfaced: 7366 tonnes (7250 tons), submerged: 8382 tonnes (8250 tons)
Dimensions:	129.5m x 10m x 9.6m (424ft 10in x 32ft 10in x 31ft 10in)
Range:	Unlimited
Armament:	Sixteen Trident C4 missiles, four 533mm (21in) torpedo tubes
Powerplant:	Single screw, one pressurized water-cooled nuclear reactor
Performance:	Surfaced: 20 knots, submerged: 30 knots

Georges Leygues

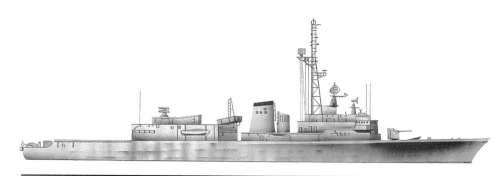

There are seven ships in the Georges Leygues class of guided-missile destroyer, all of which were commissioned between 1979 and 1990. Primary missile armament is the Exocet; anti-aircraft missile armament is the Thomson-CSF Crotale, which has a range of 13km (7 miles) and a speed of 2.4 Mach. Some of the vessels have undergone an air defence upgrade, the various weaponry and sensors (Matra Sadral sextuple SAM launchers; Breda-Mauser 30mm guns; and jammers) being controlled from a large command structure fitted above the bridge. Sea trials were conducted by the *Jean de Vienne* in 1996. Apart from the *Georges Leygues* and *Jean de Vienne*, the other vessels in this class are the *Dupleix, Montcalm, Primauguet, La Motte-Picquet* and *Latouche-Tréville*. The main role of the Georges Leygues class is surface-to-surface attack.

Country:	France
Type:	Destroyer
Launch date:	17 December 1976
Crew:	218
Displacement:	4236 tonnes (4170 tons)
Dimensions:	139m x 14m x 5.7m (456ft x 46ft x 18ft 8in)
Range:	14,816km (8000nm)
Main armament:	One 100mm (3.9in) gun; Exocet missiles
Powerplant:	Twin screw, gas turbines and diesel engines
Performance:	30 knots

Georgia

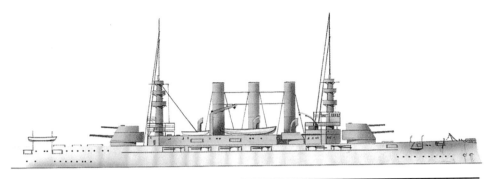

G *eorgia* and her four sisters of the Virginia class were a major development in
US battleship design. They were well-protected and carried the heaviest
possible armament on a relatively modest displacement. To reduce the risk of fire
damage, wood was eliminated wherever possible. Launched in 1904, *Georgia* was
given cage masts in 1909–10, and was later reboilered. In 1906–07 she served with
the Atlantic Fleet, and in 1907 she was damaged by a powder explosion in one of
her 8in turrets while in Cape Cod Bay. She supported US action in Mexico in 1914
and worked with the Atlantic Fleet throughout World War I; in 1919 she made five
voyages as a troop transport, bringing US personnel home from Europe, and was
then transferred to the Pacific Fleet, in which she served from 1919 to 1920. She
was sold in 1923.

Country:	USA
Type:	Battleship
Launch date:	11 October 1904
Crew:	812
Displacement:	16,351 tonnes (16,094 tons)
Dimensions:	134.5m x 23.2m x 7.2m (441ft 3in x 76ft 2 in x 23ft 9in)
Range:	9117km (4920nm) at 10 knots
Armament:	12 152mm (6in), eight 203mm (8in), four 305mm (12in) guns turrets
Powerplant:	Twin screw, vertical triple expansion engines
Performance:	19.2 knots

Gillis

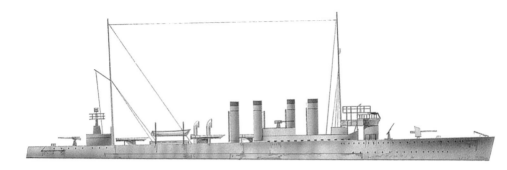

Launched on 29 May 1919, *Gillis* was one of a large class of vessels that were improved versions of the Wickes class of destroyer. Between 1938 and 1940 Gills and 13 other old flush-deck destroyers were converted as seaplane tenders, having two of their boilers and their torpedo tubes removed. The USS *Williamson, George E. Badger, Clemson, Goldsborough, Hulbert, Belknap, Osmond Ingram, Greene* and *McFarland* reverted to destroyers in November 1943, but *Gillis* (AVD12) continued to serve as a seaplane tender together with the USS *Childs, William B. Preston, Ballard* and *Thornton*. Between 11 and 13 June 1942, Catalina aircraft, supported by the *Gillis*, attacked Japanese ships and installations on Kiska in the Aleutians in an intense 48-hour attack, exhausting the tender's bomb and fuel supplies, but failing to drive the enemy from the island. *Gillis* was scrapped in 1946.

Country:	USA
Type:	Destroyer
Launch date:	29 April 1919
Crew:	150
Displacement:	1328 tonnes (1308 tons)
Dimensions:	95.8m x 9.4m x 3m (314ft 4in x 30ft 10in x 9ft 10in
Range:	4741km (2560nm)
Main armament:	Four 102mm (4in) guns; 12 533mm (21in) torpedo tubes
Powerplant:	Twin screw geared turbines
Performance:	25 knots

Giulio Cesare

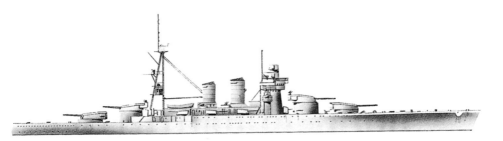

Designed in 1908 by Engineer-General Masdea, *Giulio Cesare* and her two sisters were the first large group of Italian dreadnoughts. *Giulio Cesare* was completely rebuilt between 1933 and 1937, and emerged from this lengthy transformation with improved protection, new machinery and revised armament. She served in the Adriatic during World War I and saw early action against the British Mediterranean Fleet in World War II, being hit by the battleship *Warspite* in the Ionian Sea in July 1940. She was damaged by a near miss in an air raid on Naples in January 1941, and in December took part in the Battle of Sirte. In September 1943 she sailed for Malta to surrender to the Allies. At the end of World War II the ship was handed over to the Soviet Union and was re-named *Novorossisk*. She served in the Black Sea until 1955.

Country:	Italy
Type:	Battleship
Launch date:	15 October 1911
Crew:	1235
Displacement:	29,496 tonnes (29,032 tons)
Dimensions:	186.4m x 28m x 9m (611ft 6in x 92ft x 30ft)
Range:	8640km (4800nm) at 10 knots
Armament:	12 120mm (4.7in), 10 320mm (12.6in) guns
Powerplant:	Quadruple screw turbines
Performance:	28.2 knots

Giuseppe la Masa

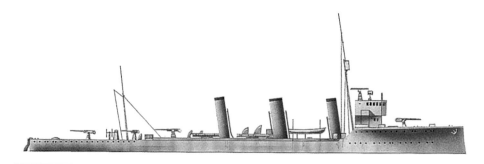

Launched in 1917, the *Giuseppe la Masa* was one of eight ships that formed the third series of the Indomito class destroyers. In 1929, she was reclassified as a torpedo boat. During World War II, her anti-aircraft armament was increased. Only one ship in the class, the *Giacinto Carini*, survived the war. Italy's fleet at the end of World War I depended to a great extent on its destroyers, which, with some 50 in service, were by far the most numerous of any of its warship categories. The vessels, like the *Giuseppe la Masa* that were still in commision at the outbreak of World War II were used as harbour defence vessels, whereas the first-line destroyer forces were composed of fast, modern ships which were laid down during the inter-war 'treaty years'. *Giuseppe la Masa* was scuttled in September 1943 while in dock at Naples, where she was undergoing repairs, after Italy's armistice with the Allies.

Country:	Italy
Type:	Destroyer
Launch date:	6 September 1917
Crew:	174
Displacement:	823 tonnes (810 tons)
Dimensions:	72.5m x 7.3m x 2.9m (238ft x 24ft x 9ft 6in)
Range:	3333km (1800nm)
Main armament:	Six 102mm (4in) guns; four 450mm (17.7in) torpedo tubes
Powerplant:	Twin screw, turbines
Performance:	34 knots

Glasgow

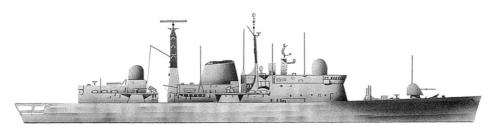

Oone of the first batch of Type 42 destroyers, HMS *Glasgow* was deployed to the South Atlantic in 1982 as part of the British task force assembled to retake the Falkland Islands. One of her sister ships, HMS *Sheffield*, was sunk by an Exocet missile launched by an Argentine Navy Super Etendard, while another, HMS *Coventry*, sustained three bomb hits on 25 May and sank within 45 minutes. Earlier, on 12 May, the *Glasgow* herself had narrowly missed serious damage – and perhaps even destruction – when a bomb passed through her hull amidships from side to side without exploding. The lack of any close-range air defence systems was a significant factor in each case, and was one of many shortcomings caused by economic restraints. On the credit side, the ships' Sea Dart missiles were credited with the destruction of five enemy aircraft.

Country:	Great Britain
Type:	Destroyer
Launch date:	14 April 1976
Crew:	253
Displacement:	4165 tonnes (4100 tons)
Dimensions:	125m x 14.3m x 5.8m (410ft x 47ft x 19ft)
Range:	8334km (4500nm)
Main armament:	One 115mm (4.5in) gun; one twin Sea Dart launcher
Powerplant:	Twin screw, gas turbines
Performance:	30 knots

Glatton

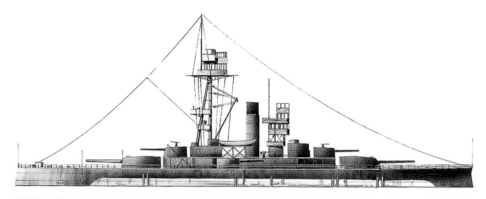

Glatton was one of two coast defence ships ordered by Norway in 1913 and laid down in Britain later that year. In November 1914 both vessels were bought by the Royal Navy for service in World War I, and modified to take standard British shells. Due to more pressing building work, *Glatton* was not completed until 1918. In that year she was assigned to the Dover patrol, which was intended to prevent German U-boats passing through the English Channel from their North Sea bases. German destroyers from Ostend and Zeebrugge attempted to break down the patrols by sudden raids, but they were repulsed in fierce night actions. Thirteen U-boats were destroyed in the Dover area in 1918. *Glatton* had been on station for only a short time when she was wrecked by an internal explosion on 16 September 1918 with the loss of 77 crew.

Country:	Great Britain
Type:	Monitor
Launch date:	8 August 1914
Crew:	305
Displacement:	5831 tonnes (5740 tons)
Dimensions:	94.5m x 22.4m x 5m (310ft x 73ft 6in x 16ft 5in)
Range:	5003km (2700nm) at 11 knots
Armament:	Four 152mm (6in), two 233mm (9.2in) guns
Powerplant:	Twin screw, triple expansion engines
Performance:	12 knots

Gloire

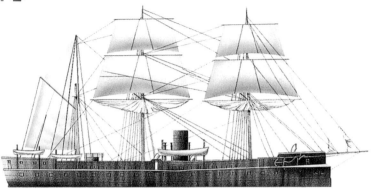

Designed by Dupuy de Lome, *Gloire* was the first armoured ship of-the-line (in other words, the first modern battleship) in the world. She was constructed with a wooden hull and armour plating to the upper deck because French manufacturers were unable to provide sufficient plating and armour in time to construct an iron hull. The battleship's design was based on the steam frigate *Napoleon* in that it had a full-length battery along the hull. Plans showed 68-pounder, smoothbore guns, although the battleship was fitted with rifled versions of the same weapon and was later rearmed with modern guns. Her barquentine rig was later changed to full ship rig. *Gloire* was launched in 1859 and discarded in 1879, being broken up four years later. Other ships in her class included *Invincible* and *Normandie*.

Country:	France
Type:	Ironclad
Launch date:	24 November 1859
Crew:	570
Displacement:	5720 tonnes (5630 tons)
Dimensions:	77.8m x 17m x 8.4m (255ft 6in x 55ft 9in x 27ft 10in)
Range:	7412km (4000nm) at 8 knots
Armament:	36 162.5mm (6.4in) guns
Powerplant:	Single screw, horizontal return engines
Performance:	13 knots

Glorious

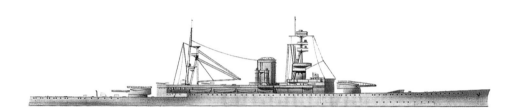

One of the Courageous class of cruisers, *Glorious*, her sister *Courageous*, and near sister *Furious* combined maximum firepower with speed. Completed in 1917, *Glorious* was laid up in 1919, but along with her sister ships she was converted into an aircraft carrier during the 1920s. In the afternoon of 8 June 1940, *Glorious* and her escorts were intercepted by *Scharnhorst* and *Gneisenau*, out on a sortie against the Allied troop transports west of Harstad, Norway. The carrier was caught completely unaware; for reasons that were never explained, none of her reconnaissance Swordfish aircraft were airborne. Desperate attempts were made to arm and launch them as the enemy battlecruisers came in sight, but she was overwhelmed and was sunk before this could be accomplished. Her escorting destroyers, *Ardent* and *Acasta*, were also sunk.

Country:	Great Britain
Type:	Battleship
Launch date:	20 April 1916
Crew:	842
Displacement:	23,327 tonnes (22,960 tons)
Dimensions:	239.5m x 24.7m x 6.7m (786ft x 81ft x 22ft 3in)
Range:	5929km (3200nm) at 19 knots
Armament:	18 102mm (4in), four 380mm (15in) guns
Powerplant:	Quadruple screw, turbines
Performance:	33 knots

Gneisenau

Both launched in 1936, *Gneisenau* and her sister *Scharnhorst* were completed with straight stems, but the bows were later lengthened. Both vessels served in World War II, attacking British commerce and sinking the British aircraft carrier *Glorious*. Both ships received damage from air attacks in 1941 while in Brest harbour, and in February 1942, together with the cruiser *Prinz Eugen*, they broke out and made an epic dash across the English Channel, for the north German ports. *Gneisenau* reached Kiel without incident only to be damaged in an RAF bombing raid two weeks later, after which she was moved to Gdynia (Gdansk). She was decommissioned in July 1942 and her turrets were removed for coastal defence. A planned refit was abandoned in 1943 and her hulk was sunk as a blockship at Gdynia in March 1945. Salvaged by the Russians, she was broken up in 1947–51.

Country:	Germany
Type:	Battleship
Launch date:	8 December 1936
Crew:	1840
Displacement:	39,522 tonnes (38,900 tons)
Dimensions:	226m x 30m x 9m (741ft 6in x 98ft 5in x 30ft)
Range:	16,306km (8800nm) at 18 knots
Armament:	14 104mm (4.1in), 12 150mm (5.9in), nine 279mm (11in) guns
Powerplant:	Triple screw turbines, with diesels for cruising
Performance:	32 knots

Godavari

L aunched in May 1980, the *Godavari* is a modified version of the British Leander class. Two helicopters are housed in a large hangar aft, and the vessel carries a unique mixture of Russian, European, and Indian weapons. The Styx missiles with active radar or infrared homing capability have a range of 69km (43 miles) at 0.9 Mach with a 500kg (1100lb) warhead. Gecko has semi-active radar homing to 13km (8 miles) at 2.5 Mach with a 50kg (110lb) warhead. The Godavari class are longer and wider than the basic vessels of the Leander class. The other two vessels are the *Ganga* and *Gomati*. India has always maintained strong naval forces, based on carrier task groups, and used her naval power to good effect in the wars with Pakistan which took place in 1965 and 1971, when she used both naval gunfire and aircraft to attack shore targets.

Country:	India
Type:	Frigate
Launch date:	15 May 1980
Crew:	330
Displacemenmt:	4064 tonnes (4000 tons)
Dimensions:	126.5m x 14.5m x 9m (415ft x 47ft 7in x 29ft 6in)
Range:	8334km (4500nm)
Main armament:	Two 57mm (2.25in) guns; four SS-N-2C Styx missiles; plus SA-N-4 Gecko missiles
Powerplant:	Twin screw, turbines
Performance:	27 knots

Goeben

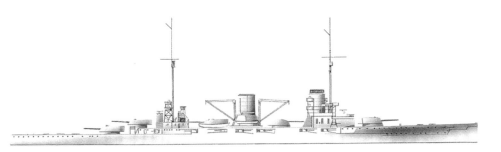

Goeben was one of two ships in the Moltke class that formed the second group of battlecruisers built for the rapidly expanding German Imperial Navy before World War I. With the outbreak of war, *Goeben* and her sister ship *Breslau* were pursued across the Mediterranean by British ships *Indomitable* and *Indefatigable*, but they easily outran the British and put into the Turkish port of Constantinople. Both ships were transferred to the Turkish Navy, and *Goeben* was renamed *Yavuz Sultan Selim* on 16 August 1914. In November 1914 she was seriously damaged in action with Russian battleships off Samsoun; in December she struck two mines on the approaches to the Bosphorus; and she was again damaged by Russian warships in May 1915. In January 1918 she sank the British monitors *Raglan* and *M28* at Mudros, and was again damaged by mines afterwards. She was broken up in 1954.

Country:	Germany
Type:	Battleship
Launch date:	28 March 1911
Crew:	1053
Displacement:	25,704 tonnes (25,300 tons)
Dimensions:	186.5m x 29.5m x 9m (611ft 10in x 96ft 9in x 29ft 6in)
Range:	7634km (4120nm) at 14 knots
Armament:	12 150mm (5.9in), 10 280mm (11in) guns
Powerplant:	Quadruple screw turbines
Performance:	28 knots

Golf I

By the 1950s, the Soviet Union had embarked upon a massive submarine programme that would initially give her a larger fleet of submarines than any other country. Twenty-three Golf I-class boats were completed between 1958 and 1962, and entered service at a rate of six or seven a year. One unit was built in China from Russian-supplied components. The ballistic missiles were housed vertically in the rear section of the extended fin, which produced a great deal of resistance underwater and reduced speed, as well as generating high noise levels; however, the boats could be driven by a creep motor, giving quiet operation and very long endurance. Thirteen Golf I boats were modified to Golf II standard starting in 1965, using the SS-N-5 ballistic missile. Code-named Sark by NATO, this was a single-stage, liquid-fuelled missile with a range of 1400km (750nm).

Country:	Soviet Union
Type:	Ballistic missile submarine
Launch date:	1958
Crew:	86
Displacement:	Surfaced: 2336 tonnes (2300 tons), submerged: 2743 tonnes (2700 tons)
Dimensions:	100m x 8.5m x 6.6m (328ft x 27ft 11in x 21ft 8in)
Surface range:	36,510km (19,703nm) at 10 knots
Armament:	Three SS-N-4 ballistic missiles; ten 533mm (21in) torpedo tubes
Powerplant:	Triple screws, diesel/electric motors
Performance:	Surfaced: 17 knots, submerged: 14 knots

Gossamer

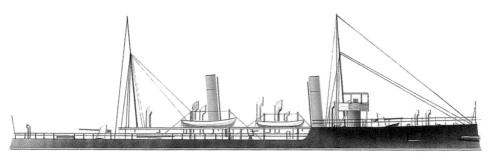

*G*ossamer and her 12 sisters were built to counter the threat posed by France's expanding torpedo boat fleet. To improve seakeeping qualities, the extended forecastle deck ran aft to the main mast, but initially the class suffered from hull weakness. One torpedo tube was carried in the bows; the others in paired mounts on either side amidships. The 120mm (4.7in) quick-firing guns eventually installed in this class had five times the rate of fire as the earlier breechloaders. Although properly titled the Sharpshooter class, the 13 boats were often called the Gossamer class. Four of the boats were allocated to colonial stations: two to the Royal Indian Marine, and two to the Australian station. Between 1908 and 1909, *Gossamer*, *Seagull*, *Skipjack* and *Spanker* were converted to the minesweeping role. *Gossamer* was sold in 1920.

Country:	Great Britain
Type:	Torpedo gunboat
Launch date:	9 January 1890
Crew:	91
Displacement:	746 tonnes (735 tons)
Dimensions:	70m x 8.2m x 3.2m (230ft x 27ft x 10ft 6in)
Range:	Not known
Main armament:	Five 355mm (14in) torpedo tubes; two 120mm (4.7in) guns
Powerplant:	Twin screws, triple expansion engines
Performance:	19 knots

Göteborg

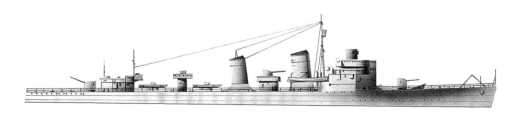

By 1934, it was clear that Sweden's destroyer force needed modernizing. The ships already in service with the Swedish Navy were being outclassed by those coming off the slips in Germany and elsewhere. A new construction programme was begun and a class of six units began building, with the aim that they would be completed by 1941. The 120mm (4.7in) guns were housed in single mounts, one forward, one aft, and one on a raised platform amidships. Göteborg was sunk by an internal explosion in 1941, but was raised and continued in service until 1958. She was expended as a gunnery target on 14 August 1962. In effect, Sweden's navy is essentially a coastal force, and as such, its task is to defend the neutral country's long and rugged coastline against infiltration by hostile vessels. It was not until the Cold War era that the perceived threat to her security became serious.

Country:	Sweden
Type:	Destroyer
Launch date:	14 October 1935
Crew:	220
Displacement:	1219 tonnes (1200 tons)
Dimensions:	94.6m x 9m x 3.8m (310ft 4in x 29ft 6in x 12ft 6in)
Range:	3333km (1800nm)
Main armament:	Three 120mm (4.7in) guns; six 533mm (21in) torpedo tubes
Powerplant:	Twin screws, turbines
Performance:	35 knots

Goubet I

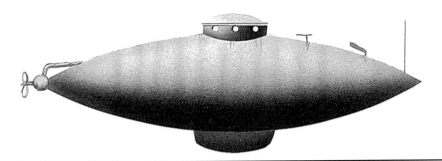

At the end of the nineteenth century, Great Britain was considered France's main enemy, and, since British industry was stronger, the French tried to build up a navy of small but numerous coastal combatants such as torpedo boats and submarines. The greatest difficulty facing early submarine designers was to find an acceptable form of underwater propulsion. Steam power and compressed air were being tested, but they had limitations. An answer appeared in 1859 when Plante invented the lead accumulator. By 1880, this had been improved by coating the surface with red lead. At long last, the submarine designers had access to a power source that no longer relied on oxygen to function. *Goubet I* had a pointed, cylindrical hull with an observation dome. She was one of the first successful submarines, but was discarded because of her small size.

Country:	France
Type:	Attack submarine
Launch date:	1887
Crew:	Two
Displacement:	Surfaced: 1.6 tonnes /tons, submerged: 1.8 tonnes /tons
Dimensions:	5m x 1.7m x 1m (16ft 5in x 5ft 10in x 3ft 3in)
Surface range:	Not known
Armament:	None
Powerplant:	Single screw electric motor
Performance:	Surfaced: 5 knots, submerged: Not known

Graf Spee

Graf Spee** was to have been an improved version of the powerful *Hindenburg* battlecruiser launched in 1917. The main armament of *Graf Spee* was updated, the weapons being positioned in four twin turrets, two superfiring fore and aft. The secondary armament was concentrated on the upper deck in a long battery that was a continuation of the raised foredeck. The Germans hoped to complete all four vessels in the class by 1918, but although *Graf Spee* was launched in 1917 she was never completed and was scrapped in 1921–23. Other vessels in her class were the *Mackensen, Prinz Eitel Friedrich* and *Furst Bismarck*; work on all of these was suspended in 1917 and the last two were never launched. By this time the German Fleet was virtually inactive, except in the Baltic, and materials intended for new-build warships were urgently needed in other sectors of the war industry.

Country:	Germany
Type:	Battlecruiser
Launch date:	30 June 1934
Crew:	1186
Displacement:	36,576 tonnes (36,000 tons)
Dimensions:	223m x 30.4m x 8.4m (731ft 8in x 99ft 9in x 27ft 7in)
Range:	14,400km (8000nm) at 10 knots
Armament:	12 150mm (5.9in), eight 350mm (13.8in) guns
Powerplant:	Quadruple screw turbines
Performance:	28 knots

Graf Zeppelin

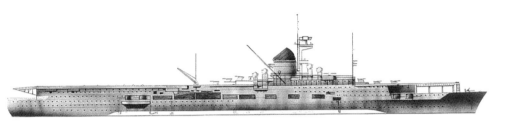

After World War I Germany was denied any opportunity of developing a carrier force as a result of restrictions imposed upon them in 1919. By 1933 Wilhelm Hadelar had prepared a basic design for a full deck carrier able to operate 40 aircraft, but lack of construction experience delayed the project. In 1935 work began, but *Graf Zeppelin*'s completion was delayed to make way for the U-boat programme. The incomplete carrier was scuttled a few months before the end of World War II. She was raised by the Soviet Union, but sank on her way to Leningrad. *Graf Zeppelin* was originally intended to carry an air group of 12 Ju87D dive-bombers and 30 Me109F fighters; this was later amended to 28 Ju87Ds and 12 Me109s. Half of a sister ship was also completed; it was speculated that this vessel would be named *Peter Strasser*, after the commander of the German Naval Airship Division in World War I.

Country:	Germany
Type:	Aircraft carrier
Launch date:	8 December 1938
Crew:	1760 (estimated)
Displacement:	28,540 tonnes (28,090 tons)
Dimensions:	262.5m x 31.5m x 8.5m (861ft 3in x 103ft 4in x 27ft 10in)
Range:	14,842km (8000nm) at 19 knots
Armament:	12 104mm (4.1in), 16 150mm (5.9in) guns, 43 aircraft
Powerplant:	Quadruple screw turbines
Performance:	35 knots

Grafton

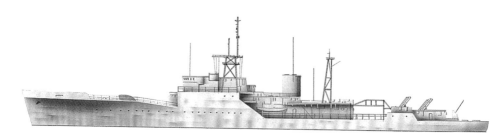

One of the Blackwood class of 12 post-World War II frigates, *Grafton* was built in pre-fabricated sections before final assembly on the launching ramp. The Blackwood-class vessels were very lightly gunned, having only two 40mm (1.6in) Bofors AA weapons. Their anti-submarine weaponry consisted of two Limbo three-barrelled depth charge launchers which could fire a pattern of large depth charges with great accuracy over a wide area. Three ships of this class – *Duncan, Palliser* and *Russell* – originally formed the 1st Division of the Fishery Protection Squadron, later incorporated in the Western Fleet. Some vessels incorporated four 533mm (21in) torpedo tubes, but these were removed. Between 1958 and 1959, all the Blackwoods had their hulls strengthened to withstand prolonged and severe conditions on fishery protection duty in Icelandic waters.

Country:	Great Britain
Type:	Frigate
Launch date:	13 September 1954
Crew:	175
Displacement:	1480 tonnes (1456 tons)
Dimensions:	94.5m x 10m x 4.7m (310ft x 33ft x 15ft 6in)
Range:	7037km (3800nm)
Main armament:	Two 40mm (1.6in) guns
Powerplant:	Single screw, turbines
Performance:	27.8 knots

Grasshopper

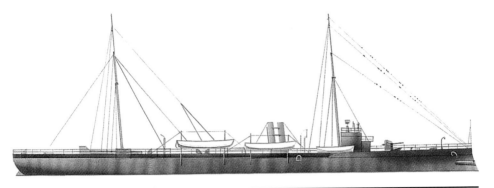

Grasshopper and her two sister vessels, *Sandfly* and *Spider*, formed the first true class of British torpedo gunboats. They were similar to the one-off *Rattlesnake*, but were somewhat larger and their performance was not as good. By the time they entered service there had been a steady increase in the range, speed reliability and explosive power of the torpedo, and the 355mm (14in) weapon, standard for some time, was being supplanted in the early 1890s by the 457mm (18in). *Grasshopper* was sold in 1905. The end of the nineteenth century saw the introduction of gyroscopic torpedo guidance and internal combustion in torpedoes, leading to still further improvements in range and accuracy. The combination of gun and torpedo was seen as the ideal mix of naval armament, and the torpedo gunboat was about to enjoy its brief but heady day.

Country:	Great Britain
Type:	Torpedo gunboat
Launch date:	30 August 1887
Crew:	66
Displacement:	558 tonnes (550 tons)
Dimensions:	60.9m x 7m x 3m (200ft x 23ft x 10ft 4in)
Range:	7585km (4096nm) at 10 knots
Main armament:	One 102mm (4in) gun; four 355mm (14in) torpedo tubes
Powerplant:	Twin screws, triple expansion engines
Performance:	17 knots

Grasshopper

In 1907 the British Admiralty obtained plans of the latest German destroyers.
Immediately, the Admiralty set a new construction programme in motion to
counter these German designs. Initial plans for *Grasshopper* and her 15 sisters
specified oil fuel, but this was soon changed to the more readily available coal fuel.
The class carried a new torpedo, which was fitted with a heater to improve
performance and which had a range of 10,972m (12,000yd) at 30 knots.
Grasshopper, launched in November 1909, served with the Harwich Force on
North Sea patrol duty during World War I, and was the second ship to bear the
name. The first was a torpedo gunboat, launched in 1887, which carried a single
102mm (4in) gun and had four 355mm (14in) torpedo tubes. The second
Grasshopper was withdrawn in 1921.

Country:	Great Britain
Type:	Destroyer
Launch date:	23 November 1909
Crew:	150
Displacement:	937 tonnes (923 tons)
Dimensions:	82.6m x 27.5m x 9.7m (271ft x 27ft 10in x 9ft 6in)
Range:	2407km (1300nm)
Main armament:	One 102mm (4in) and three 12-pounder guns
Powerplant:	Triple screws, turbines
Performance:	27 knots

Gravina

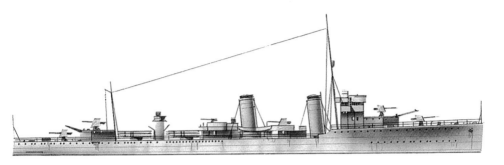

ravina belonged to the largest class of destroyers built for the Spanish Navy. The class of 16 vessels was made up of two groups, *Gravina* being part of the second group. The destroyers were virtual copies of the British Scott-class flotilla leaders. All vessels in *Gravina*'s class were built at Cartagena and launched between 1926 and 1933. The ships of the second group all featured large gun shields. Engines developed 42,000hp, and oil fuel capacity was 548 tonnes (540 tons). Range at 14 knots was 8550km (5312 miles). One ship in *Gravina*'s group, the *Ciscar*, was sunk in the Spanish Civil War in October 1957. All ships in this class were withdrawn from use in the late 1950s and early 1960s, *Gravina* herself being stricken from the Navy List in 1964. By this time, Spain had launched an ambitious naval expansion scheme.

Country:	Spain
Type:	Destroyer
Launch date:	24 December 1931
Crew:	275
Displacement:	2209 tonnes (2175 tons)
Dimensions:	101.5m x 9.6m x 3.2m (333ft x 31ft 9in x 10ft 6in)
Range:	8534km (4608nm)
Main armament:	Five 120mm (4.7in) guns; six 533mm (21in) torpedo tubes
Powerplant:	Twin screws, turbines
Performance:	35 knots

Grayback

*G*rayback and her sister vessel, *Growler,* were originally intended to be attack submarines, but in 1956 their design was modified to provide a missile-launching capability using the Regulus, a nuclear-tipped high-altitude cruise missile which was launched by solid-fuel boosters and then guided to its target by radio command signals from the submarine, cruising at periscope depth. Both submarines were withdrawn from service in 1964, when the Regulus programme ended, but *Grayback* was subsequently converted to an Amphibious Transport Submarine (LPSS), capable of carrying 67 Navy SEALs and their assault craft. Her torpedo tubes and attack capability were retained. *Growler* was also to have been converted, but this was deferred because of rising costs. As a command ship, Grayback had a crew of 96 and could accommodate 10 officers and 75 men.

Country:	USA
Type:	Transport submarine
Launch date:	2 July 1957
Crew:	84
Displacement:	Surfaced: 2712 tonnes (2670 tons), submerged: 3708 tons (3650 tons)
Dimensions:	102m x 9m x (335ft x 30ft)
Surface range:	14,824km (8000nm) at 10 knots
Armament:	Four Regulus missiles, eight 533mm (21in) torpedo tubes
Powerplant:	Twin screws, diesel/electric motors
Performance:	Surfaced: 20 knots, submerged: 17 knots

Grisha class

Built as a small anti-submarine ship between 1968 and 1974, the Grisha-class vessels had a relatively short production run, ending after only 14 units had been built. They were followed by eight Grisha II border patrol ships, which were assigned to the Maritime Border Directorate of the KGB. These differed from the Grisha I class in having a second twin 57mm (2.2in) anti-aircraft mounting in place of the SAM launcher. The main Soviet Navy production model was the Grisha III, with a construction rate of about five per year in the early 1980s. Two vessels of the Grisha II class went to Lithuania in 1992, and four were transferred to the Ukraine in 1994. The latest variant is the Grisha V class, one of which was also delivered to the Ukraine in 1996. With their relatively shallow draught the Grishas are ideal craft for patrolling the shallow waters of river estuaries.

Country:	Soviet Union
Type:	Frigate
Launch date:	1968 (first unit)
Crew:	80
Displacement:	1219 tonnes (1200 tons)
Dimensions:	72m x 10m x 3.7m (236ft 2in x 32ft 10in x 12ft)
Range:	2779km (1500nm)
Main armament:	One twin 57mm (2.2in) and one 30mm (1.2in) AA gun; ASW rocket launchers; SAMs
Powerplant:	Twin shafts, one gas turbine, four diesels
Performance:	30 knots

Grom

The *Grom* ('Thunderbolt') was the former Soviet Skory-class destroyer *Smetlivy*. This was the largest class of Soviet destroyers to be built after World War II, and the ships, which were adapted from a pre-war design, incorporated many of the best design features of Nazi Germany's later destroyers. The other ex-Russian destroyer, the *Wicher* ('Hurricane') was in fact the class prototype, the *Skory* herself. More than 70 Skory-class units were completed between 1950 and 1953. At a later date, the two Polish vessels were augmented by the transfer of a Kotlin-class destroyer. During the years of the Cold War, the Polish Navy, as a satellite of the Soviet Union, would have had an important part to play in operations in the Baltic. By the early 1980s, its strength was centred on fast-attack craft and patrol boats, together with five submarines all supplied by the Soviet Union.

Country:	Soviet Union
Type:	Destroyer
Launch date:	17 November 1951
Crew:	280
Displacement:	3150 tonnes (3100 tons)
Dimensions:	120.5m x 11.8m x 4.6m (395ft 4in x 38ft 9in x 15ft)
Range:	7037km (3800nm)
Main armament:	Four 130mm (5.1in) guns; two 76mm (3in) AA guns
Powerplant:	Twin screws, turbines
Performance:	36 knots

Gromki

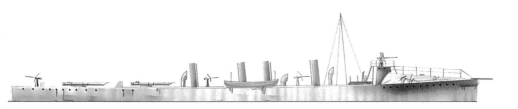

The *Gromki* belonged to the Boykiy class – one of the largest group of destroyers built for the Imperial Russian Navy – and formed part of the Second Pacific Squadron. During the Battle of Tsushima in 1905, she was attacked by a group of Japanese warships. After a two-hour running battle, she was crippled and dead in the water. She sank at midday on 28 May 1905, two-thirds of her crew having been killed or wounded. Another vessel of this class, the *Byedovi*, which was carrying the badly wounded Russian Admiral Rozhdestvensky, was also captured by Japanese ships after the Battle of Tsushima and was recommissioned into the Japanese Navy as the Satsuki. All of the destroyers in this class, including *Gromki*, were built at the Nevsky yards in St Petersburg, apart from five which were constructed by the Belgian Works yard at Nicolaiev.

Country:	Russia
Type:	Destroyer
Launch date:	1904
Crew:	68
Displacement:	355 tonnes (350 tons)
Dimensions:	64m x 6.4m x 2.5m (210ft x 21ft x 8ft 6in)
Range:	2222km (1200nm)
Main armament:	One 11-pounder, five three-pounder guns; three 350mm (15in) torpedo tubes
Powerplant:	Twin screws, vertical triple expansion engines
Performance:	26 knots

Gromki

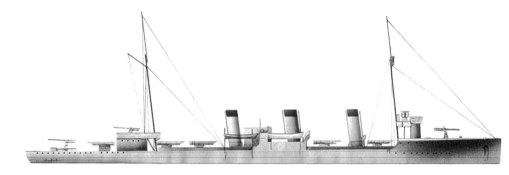

The *Gromki* of 1913 was one of the Bespokoiny class of nine destroyers that were reduced versions of the 1300-tonne (1280ton) *Novik*. They were part of a new naval construction programme whose primary aim was to increase the size of the Black Sea Fleet. Design studies had begun in 1907, and revised designs showed a 50.8-tonne (50-ton) increase in displacement to enable the vessels to carry more armament. Five twin torpedo tubes were carried on the centreline, with one 102mm (4in) gun forward and two aft. The engines developed 25,500hp, but not all vessels in the class reached the designed top speed, and other faults became apparent in service. All the ships served in World War I. Some vessels were built at Nikolaiev on the Black Sea, but *Gromki* was built at the Nevski yard. She was scuttled at Novorossisk on 18 June 1918.

Country:	Russia
Type:	Destroyer
Launch date:	18 December 1913
Crew:	160
Displacement:	1483 tonnes (1460 tons)
Dimensions:	98m x 9.3m x 3.2m (321ft 6in x 30ft 6in x 10ft 5in))
Range:	3333km (1800nm)
Main armament:	Three 102mm (4in) guns; 10 457mm (18in) torpedo tubes
Powerplant:	Two-shaft geared turbines
Performance:	34 knots

Gromkiy

Gromkiy was one of the Russian Type 7 destroyers designed with Italian assistance, something that clearly shows in her lines. As with all pre-World War II designs, the anti-aircraft armament was inadequate, but this was updated during the war. *Gromkiy* was laid down at Leningrad in 1936 and completed in 1939. Her engines developed 48,000hp and oil fuel capacity was 548 tonnes (540 tons), enough for 1529km (826nm) at full speed and 4944km (2670nm) at 19 knots. *Gromkiy* spent her war career in the Arctic, and in November 1941, she was attached to a British naval force (the cruiser *Kenya* and the destroyers *Bedouin* and *Intrepid*) searching for German ships operating off the north coast of Norway. Her principal tasks were escorting coastal convoys, minelaying, and providing fire support for Soviet troops on the Murmansk Front. She survived the war and was discarded in the 1950s.

Country:	Soviet Union
Type:	Destroyer
Launch date:	18 December 1937
Crew:	220
Displacement:	2070 tonnes (2039 tons)
Dimensions:	112.8m x 10.2m x 3.8m (370ft 3in x 33ft 6in x 12ft 6in)
Range:	4944km (2670nm)
Main armament:	Four 130mm (5.1in) and two 76mm (3in) guns; six 533mm (21in) torpedo tubes
Powerplant:	Twin screws, turbines
Performance:	36 knots

Grondeur

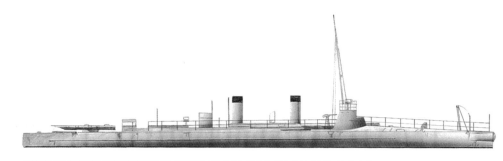

Launched in December 1892, *Grondeur* was a development of the *Coureur*, launched in 1888 to test the new Thorneycroft Watertube Boiler. This type of boiler gave the vessel a very high power output compared to weight. *Grondeur* was slightly larger and more strongly constructed than *Coureur*, and living accommodation for the crew was greatly improved. The torpedo tubes were positioned forward and aft. She was sold in 1926. France's torpedo boats suffered heavily during World War I, particularly in the Dardanelles. Little attention was paid to the development of this type of craft between the wars, and altough a building programme of MTBs was launched in the late 1930s, only a handful saw action before France's collapse. A few of the latter found their way into the Royal Navy in World War II and were manned by British, French and Polish crews.

Country:	France
Type:	Torpedo boat
Launch date:	13 December 1892
Crew:	75
Displacement:	133 tonnes (131 tons)
Dimensions:	45m x 4.4m x 1.3m (147ft 10in x 14ft 6in x 4ft 6in)
Range:	3333km (1800nm)
Main armament:	Two 47mm (1.85in) guns; two 355mm (14in) torpedo tubes
Powerplant:	Twin screws, triple expansion engines
Performance:	23.5 knots

Gröningen

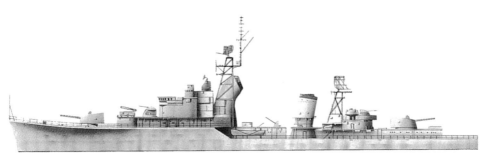

Completed in September 1956, *Gröningen* was one of of eight Friesland-class post-war destroyers that resembled the light cruisers of the war years. They were among the few destroyers to be built with side armour as well as deck protection. Their armament consisted mainly of conventional dual-purpose guns. These guns had a rate of fire of 50 rounds per minute, which demanded sophisticated automatic ammunition winching and handling systems. Originally, two of the class were installed with eight tubes for anti-submarine torpedoes, but these were removed in 1961. The Friesland-class vessels were never armed with torpedoes, and were among the first destroyers ever to be deployed with no torpedo capability. These ships represented the final development of the gun-armed destroyer, as missiles were on the horizon for this class of vessel.

Country:	Netherlands
Type:	Destroyer
Launch date:	9 January 1954
Crew:	287
Displacement:	3119 tonnes (3070 tons)
Dimensions:	116m x 11.7m x 3.9m (380ft 3in x 38ft 6in x 13ft)
Range:	8334km (4500nm)
Main armament:	Four 120mm (4.7in) guns
Powerplant:	Twin-shaft geared turbines
Performance:	36 knots

Grosser Kurfürst

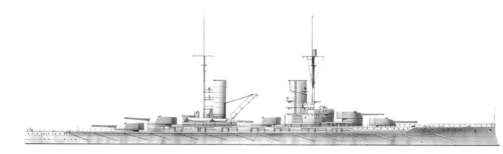

Turbines were used in German battleships for the first time on *Grosser Kurfürst* and her three sisters. The ships were greatly improved versions of *Helgoland*, and had superfiring guns aft, allowing the broadside to be increased from six to ten 305mm (12in) guns. Vessels of this class were contemporaries of the first British 343mm (13.5in) gunned battleships with similar displacement, but where the British had adopted the heavier guns and had only moderate protection, *Grosser Kurfürst* and her sisters retained the 305mm (12in) guns and used more armour. Launched in 1913, *Grosser Kurfürst* saw action at the Battle of Jutland, taking eight hits. She surrendered at the end of World War I, and was scuttled with the rest of the German fleet in 1919. She was raised and scrapped in 1934. Her sister ships were *König*, *Kronprinz* and *Markgraf*. Of these, only *König* was not raised after being scuttled.

Country:	Germany
Type:	Battleship
Launch date:	15 May 1913
Crew:	1136
Displacement:	28,598 tonnes (28,148 tons)
Dimensions:	175.7m x 29.5m x 8.3m (576ft 5in x 96ft 9in x 27ft 3in)
Range:	12,240km (6800nm) at 10 knots
Armament:	Eight 86mm (3.4in) and 14 150mm (5.9in) guns
Powerplant:	Triple screw turbines
Performance:	21 knots

Grouper

*G*rouper was originally completed as one of the Gato class, and ten years later she was converted into one of the first hunter/killer submarines (SSK) dedicated specifically to tracking down and destroying enemy submarines. The concept required that the hunter/killer submarine be very quiet and carry long-range listening sonar with high bearing accuracy. So equipped, the submarine could lie in wait off enemy bases, or in narrow straits, and intercept the enemy boats as they moved out to patrol. *Grouper* was converted in 1951, and in 1958 she became the sonar test submarine for the Underwater Sound Laboratory at New London. The work she did in this respect was vital in building up a library of underwater 'sound signatures'. The submarine was decommissioned in 1968, and was scrapped in 1970.

Country:	USA
Type:	Attack submarine
Launch date:	7 October 1941
Crew:	80
Displacement:	Surfaced: 1845 tonnes (1816 tons), submerged: 2463 tonnes (2425 tons)
Dimensions:	94.8m x 8.2m x 4.5m (311ft 3in x 27ft x 15ft)
Surface range:	19,300km (10,416nm) at 10 knots
Armament:	Ten 533mm (21in) torpedo tubes
Powerplant:	Twin screws, diesel/electric motors
Performance:	Surfaced: 20.25 knots, submerged: 10 knots

Grozyashchi

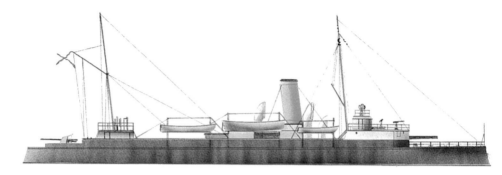

***G**rozyashchi* was an armoured gunboat with a well-balanced design for a small ironclad. The single 228mm (9in) gun was sited forward in a protected mounting beneath the bridge, allowing for a training arc of 100 degrees, while the 152mm (6in) gun was mounted aft in a shield. The ship was fitted with a steel armoured belt extending from the stern to within 9.15m (30ft) of the bow. During World War I, *Grozyashchi* was rearmed with four 152mm (6in) guns, one firing ahead and three aft. Further armour plating was also added. Of *Grozyashchi*'s two sister ships, *Gremyashchi* was mined at Port Arthur on 18 August 1904, while *Otvajni* was scuttled at the same location on 2 January 1905. *Grozyashchi* was scrapped in 1922. The crippling losses sustained in the war of 1904–5 left the Russians short of almost every type of warship except gunboats.

Country:	Russia
Type:	Gunboat
Launch date:	May 1890
Crew:	178
Displacement:	1653 tonnes (1627 tons)
Dimensions:	72.2m x 12.6m x 3.7m (237ft x 41ft 6in x 12ft 2in)
Range:	Not known
Main armament:	One 152mm (6in) and one 228mm (9in) gun
Powerplant:	Twin screws, vertical triple expansion engines
Performance:	15 knots

Guadiana

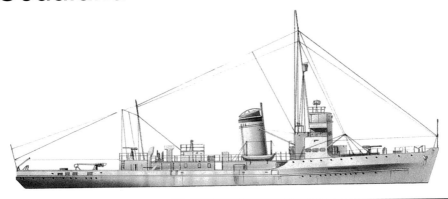

The *Guadiana* was one of four destroyers prefabricated by Yarrow shipbuilders on the Tyne and assembled in Portugal. At the time, the group comprised the largest number of warships to be ordered by the Portuguese Navy for many years. The 102mm (4in) gun was mounted on a platform on the forecastle, with the two twin torpedo mounts located aft on the centreline separated by two small structures, one of which carried a 76mm (3in) gun. The *Guadiana*'s engines developed 11,000hp, and her range at 15 knots was 3033km (1638nm). She was discarded in 1934. Between 1895 and World War II, the Portuguese Government proposed several schemes to increase the size of the navy in defence of its neutrality, and there were even plans to acquire small battleships, but these plans came to nothing mainly because the country's economy could not support a large fleet.

Country:	Portugal
Type:	Destroyer
Launch date:	21 September 1914
Crew:	170
Displacement:	670 tonnes (660 tons)
Dimensions:	73.2m x 7.2m x 2.3m (240ft 2in x 23ft 8in x 7ft 6in)
Range:	3040km (1638nm)
Main armament:	One 102mm (4in) and two 76mm (3in) guns; four 457mm (18in) torpedo tubes
Powerplant:	Twin screws, turbines
Performance:	33 knots

Guam

*G*uam and her sister ship *Alaska,* were built to combat the fast raiders of the
German *Scharnhorst* type believed in 1940 to be under construction for the
Imperial Japanese Navy. *Guam* was an enlarged version of the cruiser *Baltimore,*
with three triple turrets housing specially designed 305mm (12in) guns and
upgraded armour. Completed in 1944, she was flush-decked, with a single funnel
flanked by the cranes for the two catapults which launched the scout planes.
Range at 15 knots was 22,800km (12,000 miles). In March 1945 she was part of a
covering force of warships operating in support of US carriers making a series of
air strikes on the Japanese island of Kyushu, and in April–June she again
supported naval task forces attacking Okinawa. Her last operations, in August
1945, were against shipping in the East China Sea. *Guam* was scrapped in 1961.

Country:	USA
Type:	Battlecruiser
Launch date:	12 November 1943
Crew:	1517
Displacement:	34,801 tonnes (34,253 tons)
Dimensions:	246m x 27.6m x 9.6m (807ft 5in x 90ft 9in x 31ft 9in)
Range:	22,800km (12,000nm) at 15 knots
Armament:	12 127mm (5in), nine 305mm (12in) guns
Powerplant:	Quadruple screw turbines
Performance:	33 knots

Guglielmo Pepe

Designed and built by Ansaldo of Genoa, the *Guglielmo Pepe* was a large and powerful flotilla leader and was one of three boats laid down in 1913. Originally, she was to have been given eight torpedo tubes, but on completion she was fitted with only four. In 1916 she was given two 76mm (3in) anti-aircraft guns, but these were removed in the following year. In 1921 the ship was reclassified as a destroyer and in June 1938 she was transferred to Spain, where she was renamed *Teruel*. She continued to serve until 1947, at which time the Spanish Navy, whose development had stagnated during World War II which was now desperately in need of a modern shipbuilding programme to expand its resources. A programme soon began to replace its pre-war destroyer force with modern, indigenous warships like the Audaz class of the early 1950s.

Country:	Italy
Type:	Destroyer
Launch date:	17 September 1914
Crew:	174
Displacement:	1235 tonnes (1216 tons)
Dimensions:	85m x 8m x 2.8m (278ft 10in x 26ft 3in x 9ft 2in)
Range:	2592km (1400nm)
Main armament:	Six 102mm (4in) guns; four 450mm torpedo tubes
Powerplant:	Twin screws, turbines
Performance:	31.5 knots

Gurkha

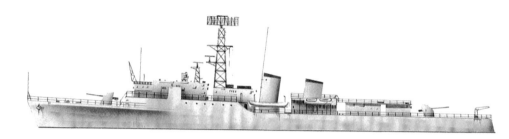

Launched in 1960, *Gurkha* was one of seven general-purpose frigates in the Tribal class. These vessels were among the first ships to be fully air-conditioned in all crew areas and most working spaces. The standard steam turbine developed 12,500hp, and this could be boosted by a gas turbine which increased output to 20,000hp. The ships were very seaworthy and made good speed even in unfavourable sea states. Of the ships in this class, *Ashanti*, *Eskimo* and *Gurkha* were ordered under the 1955–56 British Navy Estimates, *Nubian* and *Tartar* under the 1956–57 programme, and *Mohawk* and *Zulu* under the 1957–58 programme. The ships were of welded prefabricated construction and were all completed between 1961 and 1964. They were the first frigates designed to carry a helicopter for anti-submarine reconnaissance. *Gurkha* was sold to Indonesia in 1984.

Country:	Great Britain
Type:	Frigate
Launch date:	11 July 1960
Crew:	253
Displacement:	2743 tonnes (2700 tons)
Dimensions:	109m x 12.8m x 5.3m (360ft x 42ft x 17ft 6in)
Range:	7778km (4200nm)
Main armament:	Two 114mm (4.5in) guns; one Limbo three-barrelled anti-submarine mortar
Powerplant:	Single screw, turbine and gas turbine
Performance:	28 knots

Gustave Zédé

After overcoming some initial problems of inadequate power from the 720-cell batteries, together with their excessive weight which gave her uneven diving characteristics, *Gustave Zédé* became one of the world's first successful submarines, completing over 2500 dives without incident. During her trials she made the 66km (35nm) journey from Toulon to Marseille underwater. *Gustave Zédé* was probably the first submarine to be fitted with an effective periscope, and this innovation put France at the forefront of submarine technology. She was given a tall conning tower with a platform for surface lookouts. The hull was made up from 76 sections of Roma-bronze, and all the controls in the boat were placed centrally under the conning tower. *Gustave Zédé* was stricken from the Navy List in 1909.

Country:	France
Type:	Attack submarine
Launch date:	June 1893
Crew:	19
Displacement:	Surfaced: 265 tonnes (261 tons), submerged: 274 tonnes (270 tons)
Dimensions:	48.5m x 3.2m x 3.2m (159ft x 10ft 6in x 10ft 6in)
Surface range:	Not known
Armament:	One 450mm (17.7in) torpedo tube
Powerplant:	Single screw, electric motor
Performance:	Surfaced: 9.2 knots, submerged: 6.5 knots

Gwin

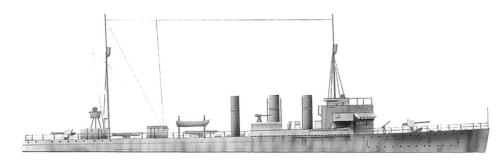

The USS *Gwin*, launched in December 1917, was an early 'flushdecker', many of which served alongside modern counterparts in World War II. She had three funnels and a raised superstructure amidships that carried two of the 102mm (4in) guns. She was sold in 1939. At the time of the Japanese attack on Pearl Harbor in December 1941, of the 171 US destroyers in commission, over one-third were of World War I vintage: the famous 'flushdeckers', of which 272 had been built. Twelve had been lost between the wars and 93 more had been scrapped under the terms of the London Naval Disarmament Treaty of 1930. Another 46 were serving in subsidiary duties, and 50 were transferred to the Royal Navy in 1940. All the Royal Navy's ex-American destroyers were named after British towns. The name *Gwin* was later allocated to a light minelayer in 1944.

Country:	USA
Type:	Destroyer
Launch date:	22 December 1917
Crew:	175
Displacement:	1205 tonnes (1187 tons)
Dimensions:	96.2m x 9.1m x 2.7m (315ft 7in x 30ft x 9ft)
Range:	2779km (1500nm)
Main armament:	Four 102mm (4in) guns; 12 533mm (21in) torpedo tubes
Powerplant:	Twin screws, turbines
Performance:	32 knots

H4

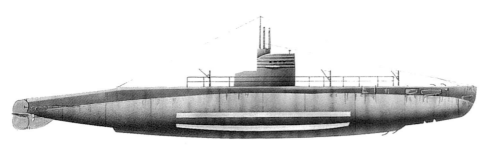

*H*4 was one of 17 boats ordered for the Imperial Russian Navy under the 1915 Emergency Programme. With the collapse of Tsarist Russia, a few were seized by the Bolsheviks and commissioned. Eleven were actually delivered to Russia in sections for assembly at the Baltic Shipyards. *H4*'s contract was cancelled, however, and she was purchased for the United States Navy from her builders, the Electric Boat Company, in 1918. The boats had been built to a Holland design identical with the boats built for Britain, Italy and the USA. In 1920 *H4* was renumbered *SS147*. The US H class had a designed depth limit of 6m (20ft) and, despite engine problems, were considered successful boats. *H4* was stricken in 1930 and broken up in 1931. This class should not be confused with the British and Chilean H class, also built by the Electric Boat Company.

Country:	USA
Type:	Attack submarine
Launch date:	October 1918
Crew:	35
Displacement:	Surfaced: 398 tonnes (392 tons), submerged: 529 tonnes (521 tons)
Dimensions:	45.8m x 4.8m x 3.8m (150ft 3in x 15ft 9in x 12ft 6in)
Surface range:	3800km (7041nm)
Armament:	Four 457mm (18in) torpedo tubes
Powerplant:	Twin screws, diesel/electric motors
Performance:	Surfaced: 14 knots, submerged: 10 knots

Ha 201 class

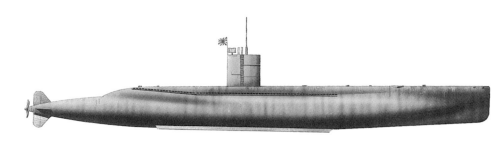

Ordered under a crash programme of 1943–44, these small submarines had a high underwater speed and excellent manoeuvrability, and were designed for the sole purpose of defending the Japanese Home Islands against American warships. Large numbers were planned, and it was hoped that the production schedule could be met by prefabricating parts of the hull in the workshops and assembling them on the slipway. Electric welding was extensively used, and the first unit, *Ha 201*, was laid down in the Sasebo Naval Yard on 1 May 1945 and completed on 31 May 1945. Owing to the critical shortage of materials and to American bombing, only 10 units had been completed by the end of the war, and none carried out any active patrols. *Ha 201* was scuttled by the US Navy in April 1946.

Country:	Japan
Type:	Attack submarine
Launch date:	May 1945
Crew:	22
Displacement:	Surfaced: 383 tonnes (377 tons), submerged: 447 tonnes (440 tons)
Dimensions:	50m x 3.9m x 3.4m (164ft x 13ft x 11ft 3in)
Surface range:	5559km (3000nm) at 10 knots
Armament:	Two 533mm (21in) torpedo tubes; one 7.7mm AA gun
Powerplant:	Single shaft diesel/electric motor
Performance:	Surfaced: 10.5 knots, submerged: 13 knots

Habana

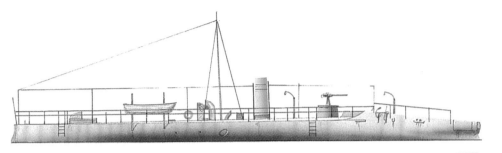

Launched in 1886, *Habana* was built in London by Thorneycroft and was one of 13 first-class boats constructed up to 1887 for the Spanish Navy. Spain had always been in the forefront of naval development, especially in the 1880s, when she possessed a powerful fleet of ironclads that placed her navy sixth in the world. *Habana* carried her machine gun on the conning tower; the two torpedo tubes were mounted in the bow. There is no record of *Habana* being involved in any action during the war with America in 1898, when several gunboats were deployed to Manila and to the Caribbean. The war, which was won decisively by the Americans, destroyed Spain's credibility as a leading naval power and saw the beginning of the USA's rapid rise as a major maritime nation. Two world wars would pass before Spain again became a maritime nation.

Country:	Spain
Type:	Torpedo boat
Launch date:	1886
Crew:	24
Displacement:	68 tonnes (67 tons)
Dimensions:	38.8m x 3.8m x 1.5m (127ft 7in x 12ft 7in x 5ft)
Range:	Not known
Main armament:	Two 355mm (14in) torpedo tubes; one machine gun
Powerplant:	Single screw, vertical triple expansion engine
Performance:	24.5 knots

Habsburg

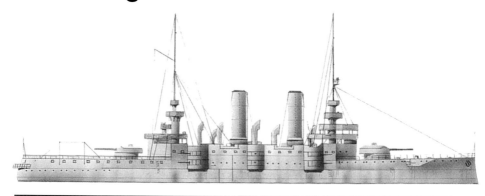

Habsburg was one of a trio of vessels that were the first true Austrian ocean-going battleships since the launching of *Tegetthoff* in 1878. Launched in 1900, she later underwent a reconstruction, having her top superstructure removed in 1910–11. By now Austria was starting to build new ships at a faster rate, but lack of funds hindered development. During the period before World War I, however, the navy had two staunch supporters, the heir to the throne – Archduke Franz Ferdinand – and the navy commander, Admiral Montecuccoli. It was the latter who ordered Austria's first and only class of Dreadnought in 1911; construction was begun even before the government had actually approved it. After World War I, all three of *Habsburg*'s class (the others being *Arpad* and *Babenberg*) were handed over to Britain and scrapped in 1921.

Country:	Austria
Type:	Battleship
Launch date:	9 September 1900
Crew:	638
Displacement:	8964 tonnes (8823 tons)
Dimensions:	114.5m x 19.8m x 7.4m (376ft x 65ft 2in x 24ft 6in)
Range:	6670km (3600nm) at 10 knots
Armament:	12 150mm (5.9in), three 240mm (9.4in) guns
Powerplant:	Twin screw, vertical triple expansion engines
Performance:	19.6 knots

Hachijo

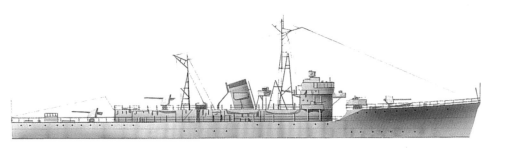

*H*achijo and her three sister ships (*Ishigaki*, *Kunashiri* and *Shumushu*) were ordered under the Imperial Japanese Navy's 1937 programme and were designed as general purpose escorts fitted out for coastal patrol, convoy escort, anti-submarine and minesweeping duties. The design proved very satisfactory, and all the later classes of escorts stemmed from it. *Ishigaki* was lost in May 1944; *Shumushu* and *Kunashiri* were surrendered to the Allies at the end of World War II and used to repatriate prisoners. *Shumushu* was handed over to Russia as war reparation, but *Kunashiri* was wrecked in June 1946 when she ran aground on a reef. *Hachijo* was also surrendered, but was in such a bad state of repair that she saw no further service and was scrapped in 1946. In all, very few Japanese vessels survived to be surrendered at the war's end.

Country:	Japan
Type:	Destroyer Escort
Launch date:	10 April 1940
Crew:	Not known
Displacement:	1020 tonnes (1004 tons)
Dimensions:	77.7m x 8.8m x 3m (255ft x 29ft x 9ft 10in)
Range:	Not known
Main armament:	Three 120mm (4.7in) guns
Powerplant:	Twin screws, diesel engines
Performance:	19.5 knots

Halifax

Frigates are the most important class of warship in the Canadian Navy, which is an integrated component of the Canadian Armed Forces. *Halifax* is one of 12 frigates of her class, all commissioned between 1992 and 1996. Most have been built by St John Shipbuilding of New Brunswick, who won the competition for the first six of this new class of patrol frigate in 1983. Combat-system design and integration was sub-contracted to Loral Canada; three ships were sub-contracted to Marine Industries Ltd. It was planned to fit a towed integrated active/passive sonar array from 2002 onwards, and there were also plans to convert four of the vessels to the air-defence role from 2002. Five of the class – *Vancouver, Regina, Calgary, Winnipeg* and *Ottawa* – are based in the Pacific. All ships carry either the CH-124A or CH-124B Sea King helicopter.

Country:	Canada
Type:	Frigate
Launch date:	30 May 1988
Crew:	198
Displacement:	4847 tonnes (4770 tons)
Dimensions:	134.7m x 16.4m x 7.1m (441ft 11in x 53ft 9in x 16ft 5in)
Range:	15,280km (8246nm)
Main armament:	One 57mm (2.25in) gun; Harpoon SSM; four 324mm (12.75in) torpedo tubes
Powerplant:	Two shafts, two gas turbines, one diesel
Performance:	29 knots

Hamakaze

Hamakaze was the first Japanese destroyer to be fitted with radar. When completed in 1941, she and her 17 sister ships were armed with six 152mm (6in) guns in twin turrets, but between 1943 and 1944, the turret on top of the aft superstructure was removed and replaced by additional anti-aircraft guns. The torpedo tubes were positioned amidships in enclosed quadruple mounts. *Hamakaze* was involved in almost every Japanese naval operation in the Pacific during World War II, and right from the beginning, she was part of the escort to the aircraft carrier task force that launched the air strike on Pearl Harbor. She was sunk on 7 April 1945, when large numbers of US carrier aircraft attacked a Japanese battle group – including the massive battleship *Yamato* – which was sailing to intercept American forces at Okinawa.

Country:	Japan
Type:	Destroyer
Launch date:	25 November 1940
Crew:	240
Displacement:	2489 tonnes (2450 tons)
Dimensions:	118.5m x 10.8m x 3.7m (388ft 9in x 35ft 5in x 12ft 4in)
Range:	8338km (4500nm)
Main armament:	Four 152mm (6in) guns; eight 610mm (24in) torpedo tubes
Powerplant:	Two-shaft geared turbines
Performance:	35.5 knots

Hamayuki

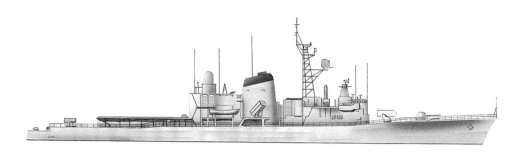

The modern Japanese Navy is a well-handled, efficient fighting force, the core of its strength being submarines, destroyers and frigates. *Hamayuki* was a radical departure from previous Japanese anti-submarine destroyer designs. Although the weapons systems are of US origin, the concept and general layout closely resemble the successful French Georges Leygues class. The British propulsion machinery consists of two groups of gas turbines, one set developing 56,780hp, the other 10,680hp. *Hamayuki* is one of 12 guided-missile destroyers of the Hatsuyuki class. *Shirayuki* was the first to be fitted with the Phalanx CIWS, early in 1992, and all the other ships had been retrofitted by 1996. The last three of the class – *Setoyuki*, *Asayuki* and *Shimayuki* – are equipped with the Canadian Beartrap landing aid. All vessels carry the Sikorsky SH-60J Seahawk.

Country:	Japan
Type:	Destroyer
Launch date:	27 May 1982
Crew:	250
Displacement:	3760 tonnes (3700 tons)
Dimensions:	131.7m x 13.7m x 4.2m (432ft x 45ft x 14ft)
Range:	9260km (5000nm)
Main armament:	One 76mm (3in) gun; one eight-cell Sea Sparrow launcher; two Phalanx CIWS
Powerplant:	Twin screws, gas turbines
Performance:	30 knots

Han

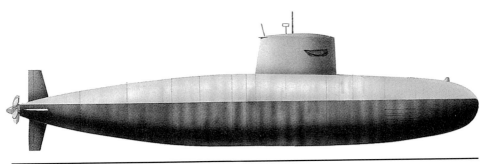

The Chinese Navy took a massive leap forward in the early 1970s with its Han-class nuclear-attack submarines (SSNs). The highly streamlined hull shape was based on the design of the USS *Albacore,* and was a radical departure from previous Chinese submarine designs. While the Russians cut many corners to get their first SSNs into service, China proceeded at a more leisurely pace, and although the Han class of four boats is fairly basic, with little of the high technology that is standard on American and British vessels, it provided a solid basis for further development. From the Hans came the Xia class, which was China's first nuclear ballistic-missile submarine. According to some reports, however, China's SSN/SSBN programme has suffered its fair share of accidents, which have been concealed from the rest of the world.

Country:	China
Type:	Attack submarine
Launch date:	1972
Crew:	120
Displacement:	Surfaced: Not known, submerged: 5080 tonnes (5000 tons)
Dimensions:	90m x 8m x 8.2m (295ft 3in x 26ft 3in x 27ft)
Range:	Unlimited
Armament:	Six 533mm (21in) torpedo tubes
Powerplant:	Single screw, pressurized water nuclear reactor
Performance:	Surfaced: 20 knots, submerged: 28 knots

Hansa

*H*ansa **was the first battleship to be built in Germany. She was laid down at the Danzig dockyard in 1868 and took seven years to complete, by which time her iron hull had badly corroded. The 210mm (8.25in) guns were carried in a two-tier casemate, with two guns on each side in the lower level, and four firing from corner positions in the upper level. Classed as an armoured corvette,** *Hansa* **was a small central battery ship built for foreign service. She was the first German-designed armoured vessel, and she had a wooden hull. In 1878–80 she served in South American waters as a trade protection vessel, the Germans having substantial commercial interests in Latin America, and for eight years after that she was used as a guard ship at Kiel.** *Hansa* **became a training hulk in 1888 and was scrapped in 1906.**

Country:	Germany
Type:	Battleship
Launch date:	22 April 1925
Crew:	399
Displacement:	4403 tonnes (4334 tons)
Dimensions:	73.4m x 14.1m x 6.7m (241ft x 46ft 3in x 22ft 3in)
Range:	2465km (1330nm) at 10 knots
Armament:	Eight 210mm (8.25in) guns
Powerplant:	Single screw, horizontal single expansion engines
Performance:	12.5 knots

Harbin

Harbin was the first of a class of two destroyers – the other being the *Qingdao* – ordered in 1985. Construction was delayed because priority had already been given to warship construction for Thailand, and the vessels were not commissioned until July 1994 and March 1996 respectively. The most notable features are the forward-mounted octuple launcher for the HQ-7 (Crotale) SAM system, improved radar and fire-control systems, and a modern twin 100mm (3.9in) gun which can be elevated to 85 degrees and which fires a 15kg (33lb) shell up to 22km (12nm). *Harbin* is based with the North Sea Fleet at Guzhen Bay, while *Qingdao* is with the East Sea Fleet at Jianggezhuang. The gas turbines for the latter warship were manufactured in the Ukraine. Chinese warships have frequently been criticized for poor quality construction.

Country:	China
Type:	Destroyer
Launch date:	October 1991
Crew:	230
Displacement:	4267 tonnes (4200 tonnes)
Dimensions:	142.7m x 15.1m x 5.1m (468ft 2in x 49ft 6in x 16ft 8in)
Range:	8042km (4340nm)
Main armament:	Two 100mm (3.9in) guns; YJ-1 Eagle Strike SSMs; 324mm (12.75in) torpedo tubes
Powerplant:	Two shafts, two gas turbines, two diesels
Performance:	31 knots

Haruna

*H*aruna was one of the first dreadnought-type warships to be laid down in a Japanese yard, and her sister *Kongo* was the last major Japanese warship to be built abroad. The four ships in *Haruna*'s class originally had three funnels and light military masts. In 1927–28 *Haruna* underwent a major refit and was reclassified as a battleship. The fore funnel was removed, and the second enlarged and heightened. Sixteen new boilers were installed, bulges were fitted and the armour thickened, increasing the total weight from 6606 tonnes (6502 tons) to 10,478 tonnes (10,313 tons). In December 1941 she formed part of the distant covering force for the Japanese landings in Malaya and the Philippines and then took part in every major action of the Pacific War. *Haruna* was sunk by US aircraft in July 1945. She was raised and broken up in 1946.

Country:	Japan
Type:	Battleship
Launch date:	14 December 1913
Crew:	1221
Displacement:	32,715 tonnes (32,200 tons)
Dimensions:	214.5m x 28m x 8.4m (703ft 9in x 91ft 10in x 27ft 6in)
Range:	14,400km (8000nm) at 12 knots
Armament:	16 152mm (6in), eight 355mm (14in) guns
Powerplant:	Quadruple screw turbines
Performance:	27.5 knots

Harushio

The six submarines of the Harushio class were a natural progression from the previous Yushio class, with improved noise reduction and ZQR-1 towed array sonar. They are also equipped with the Hughes/Oki ZQQ-5B hull sonar. All five boats are capable of firing the Sub-Harpoon anti-ship missile from their torpedo tubes. Beginning with *Harushio* in 1989, the boats were built at the rate of one a year to replace the vessels of the Uzushio class. The other five boats, in order of their launch date, are named *Natsushio, Hayashio, Arashio, Wakashio* and *Fuyushio*. Their excellent endurance means that they can be deployed in a defensive screen well out from their home bases. The class will provide the Japanese Navy with a very effective conventional underwater attack capability until well into the 21st century.

Country:	Japan
Type:	Attack submarine
Launch date:	26 July 1989
Crew:	75
Displacement:	Surfaced: 2489 tonnes (2450 tons), submerged: n/a
Dimensions:	77m x 10m x 7.75m (252ft 7in x 32ft 10in x 25ft 4in)
Surface range:	22,236km (12,000nm) at 10 knots
Armament:	Six 533 mm (21in) torpedo tubes, Sub-Harpoon SSM
Powerplant:	Single shaft, diesel/electric motors
Performance:	Surfaced: 12 knots, submerged: 20 knots

Hatakaze

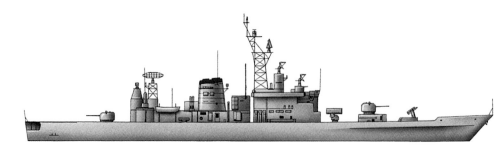

Hatakaze is the lead vessel of a two-ship class, her sister vessel being the *Shimakaze*. Both ships carry a platform for a Sikorsky SH-60J Seahawk helicopter. They are fitted with the Standard SM-1MR surface-to-air missile, which has command guidance and semi-active radar homing out to 46km (25nm) at Mach 2 and a height envelope of 45–18,288m (150-60,000ft). Principal anti-submarine weapon is the Honeywell ASROC Mk112 multiple launcher, which has inertial guidance to 1.6–10km (15.4nm); its payload is the Mk46 Mod 5 torpedo. The ships are also armed with the General Dynamics 20mm(0.7in) Phalanx Mk15 CIWS six-barrelled gun, which fires 3000 rounds per minute and has a range of 1.6km (1 mile). Phalanx is a 'last ditch' air defence weapon, laying down a lethal cone of fire capable of destroying sea-skimming missiles.

Country:	Japan
Type:	Destroyer
Launch date:	9 November 1984
Crew:	260
Displacement:	5588 tonnes (5500 tons)
Dimensions:	150m x 16.4m x 4.8m)
Range:	8042km (4342nm)
Main armament:	Two 127mm (5in) guns; Harpoon SSM; ASROC: 324mm (12.75in) Mk46 Neartip torpedoes
Powerplant:	Twin shafts, four gas turbines
Performance:	30 knots

Havock

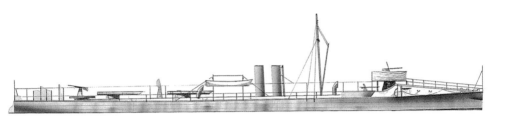

HMS *Havock* was the world's first true destroyer. In 1892 Alfred Yarrow of Tyneside was asked by the Admiralty to prepare an answer to the French torpedo craft then being built: *Havock*, launched in August 1893 and completed in 1894, was his response. Ten watertight bulkheads divided the vessel into 11 compartments. Her 12-pounder gun was mounted on a platform forward, and there were two six-pounders in the waist and one aft. On trials, *Havock* proved to be a very good, fast sea vessel with very little vibration or heel under full helm. She was eventually scrapped in 1912. In years to come, other destroyers would bear the name of their progenitor, and one of them would achieve everlasting fame in battle at Narvik in April 1940, when most of Germany's existing destroyers were annihilated.

Country:	Great Britain
Type:	Destroyer
Launch date:	12 August 1893
Crew:	68
Displacement:	243.8 tonnes (240 tons)
Dimensions:	54.8m x 5.6m x 3.3m (180ft x 18ft 6in x 11ft)
Range:	1482km (800nm)
Main armament:	One 12-pounder and three six-pounder guns; three torpedo tubes
Powerplant:	Twin screws, triple expansion engines
Performance:	26 knots

Helgoland

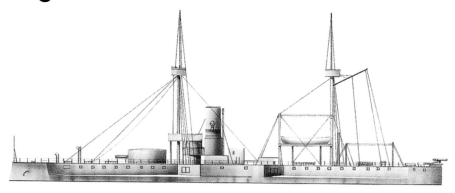

For many years, *Helgoland* was Denmark's largest warship. The battery housing the four 260mm (10.2in) guns was situated amidships, with the sides of the hull on each side of the battery recessed to allow for end-on fire. A single turret forward housed the 304mm (12in) gun. Two 127mm (5in) guns were also carried, one fore and one aft. A small outfit of sails could be carried on the two masts. Designated as a coast defence torpedo ram, she was named after the Danish naval victory over the combined forces of Prussia and Austria off Heligoland on 9 May 1864. Laid down at Copenhagen in 1876, she was completed in 1879 and underwent a refit in 1884. Denmark maintained a fleet of small coastal defence ships and also guarded its neutrality throughout the later European conflicts until 1940. *Helgoland* was removed from the effective list in about 1907.

Country:	Denmark
Type:	Battleship
Launch date:	9 May 1878
Crew:	331
Displacement:	5417 tonnes (5332 tons)
Dimensions:	79m x 18m x 5.8m (259ft 7in x 59ft x 19ft 4in)
Range:	2594km (1400nm) at 9 knots
Armament:	One 304mm (12in), four 260mm (10.2in) guns
Powerplant:	Twin screws
Performance:	13.7 knots

Helgoland

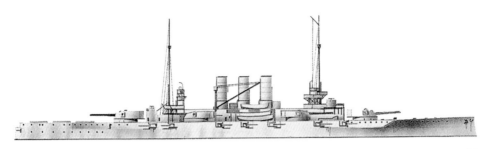

L aunched in 1909, *Helgoland* was the last three-funnelled German battleship, and the first to adopt the 304mm (12in) gun as a main armament. All ships in her class served in World War I, two being damaged at the Battle of Jutland in 1916. *Helgoland* herself was hit by one shell. After this decisive battle, the German High Seas Fleet never again contested possession of the North Sea. It sortied on three further occasions, twice in 1916 and once in 1918. None resulted in action, and the low level of activity resulted in disillusionment and, ultimately, open rebellion. The crew of *Helgoland*, in command with most of their compatriots, mutinied in 1918. This turn of events might have been avoided if the High Seas Fleet had embarked on an all-out war against Allied commerce. *Helgoland* was broken up in 1924.

Country:	Germany
Type:	Battleship
Launch date:	25 September 1909
Crew:	1113
Displacement:	24,700 tonnes (24,312 tons)
Dimensions:	166.4m x 28.5m x 8.3m (546ft x 93ft 6in x 27ft 6in)
Range:	6670km (3600nm) at 18 knots
Armament:	14 150mm (5.9in), 12 304mm (12in) guns
Powerplant:	Triple screw, triple expansion engines
Performance:	20.3 knots

Henri IV

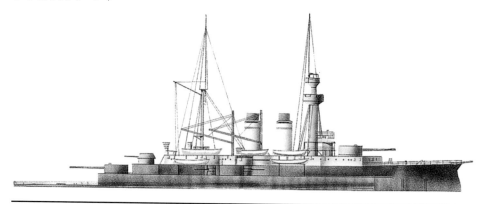

Henri IV was unusual in that weight was saved by cutting down the aft hull leaving very little freeboard. The 270mm (10.8in) guns were carried one forward on the raised superstructure 8.5m (28ft) above the water, and one in the aft turret 4.8m (16ft) above the water. The belt was 2m (7ft) deep, with just over half the depth below the waterline. The decks were flat and armoured. She also had lateral armoured bulkheads. Total weight of armour was about 3556 tonnes (3500 tons). In 1907 she was damaged off Algiers in a collision with the destroyer *Dard*, which lost its bow. In March 1915 she was sent to the Dardanelles, where a French naval squadron was operating under the orders of Admiral Carden. She subsequently took part in the bombardment of Turkish forts, and in May she covered the landing of General Bailloud's Algerian Division. *Henri IV* was stricken in 1921.

Country:	France
Type:	Battleship
Launch date:	23 August 1899
Crew:	464
Displacement:	8948 tonnes (8807 tons)
Dimensions:	108m x 22.2m x 6.9m (354ft 4in x 73ft x 23ft)
Range:	11,118km (600nm) at 10 knots
Armament:	Seven 140mm (5.5in), two 274mm (10.8in) guns
Powerplant:	Triple screw, triple expansion engines
Performance:	17 knots

Hermes

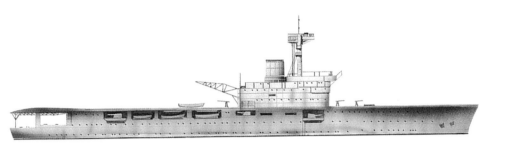

*H*ermes was the first true purpose-designed aircraft carrier to be ordered by any navy. She was laid down in 1917, but was not completed until 1924, and was thus beaten into service by the Japanese carrier *Hosho*. Her hull had a cruiser form, with the main deck providing the strength. Above this was a 122m (400ft) hangar deck, surmounted by the flight deck. Her bridge, funnel, command centre and masts were all grouped in a large island on the starboard side of the flight deck. Her 150mm (5.9in) guns were set in the hull, while the smaller weapons were mounted on the starboard edge of the flight deck. She could not carry many aircraft, and in 1940 her air wing comprised only 12 fighters. She was sunk by Japanese carrier aircraft off Ceylon on 9 April 1942, together with the Australian destroyer *Vampire*, the corvette *Hollyhock* and two tankers, during an enemy sortie towards Ceylon.

Country:	Great Britain
Type:	Aircraft carrier
Launch date:	11 September 1919
Crew:	664
Displacement:	13,208 tonnes (13,000 tons)
Dimensions:	182.9m x 21.4m x 6.5m (600ft x 70ft 2in x 21ft 6in)
Range:	7412kt (4000nm) at 15 knots
Armament:	Three 102mm (4in), six 140mm (5.5in) guns
Powerplant:	Twin screw turbines
Performance:	25 knots

Hermes

In 1943 designs were drawn up for a class of eight carriers, with machinery twice as powerful as that installed in the earlier *Colossus* class. Armour was to be improved, and a stronger flight deck was planned to handle the new, heavier aircraft then entering service. Eventually, only four ships were laid down, and the Admiralty decided to scrap these while they were still on the stocks at the end of World War II. However, due to the inability of many existing carriers to handle the new jet aircraft, construction was continued. After several design changes, *Hermes* was completed in 1959. During a scheduled refit in 1979 she was given a 12-degree ski ramp to operate the British Aerospace Sea Harrier FSR.1 V/STOL strike aircraft, two squadrons of six being embarked. In 1982 she served as flagship during the Falklands War. She was put on reserve in 1984, and later sold to India.

Country:	Great Britain
Type:	Aircraft carrier
Launch date:	16 February 1953
Crew:	1830 and 270 air group
Displacement:	25,290 tonnes (24,892 tons)
Dimensions:	224.6m x 30.4m x 8.2m (737ft x 100ft x 27ft)
Range:	7412km (4000nm) at 15 knots
Armament:	32 40mm (1.6in) guns
Powerplant:	Twin screw turbines
Performance:	29.5 knots

Hibiki

It is worthy of note that a full decade earlier than the British J class, the Japanese had destroyers in their Fubiki class, which were of a superior specification. This sudden leap in capability was bound to bring problems, as succeeding classes demonstrated. The four Akatsuki-class ships of 1931–33 kept the same arrangement on a slightly shorter hull but reduced the forward funnel to a thick pipe to save topweight. They also featured lightweight masting and a reduction in depth charges. The *Hibiki* of this group was the first all-welded Japanese destroyer; she was also the only Akatsuki-class ship to survive the war. Her X turret was replaced with more light anti-aircraft weapons in 1942, and by the end of the war, she was carrying 28 25mm anti-aircraft cannon. In 1947 she went to the Soviet Union as war booty.

Country:	Japan
Type:	Destroyer
Launch date:	16 June 1932
Crew:	240
Displacement:	2530 tonnes (2490 tons)
Dimensions:	118.45m x 10.8m x 3.76m (388ft 7in x 35ft 4in x 12ft 4in)
Range:	9250km (4986nm)
Main armament:	Three twin 127mm (5in) and two twin 25mm (1in) AA guns; two quadruple 610mm (24in) torpedo tubes
Powerplant:	Two sets of geared steam turbines
Performance:	35 knots

H L Hunley

H *L Hunley* was the first true submersible craft to be used successfully against an enemy. The main part of the hull was shaped from a cylindrical steam boiler, with the tapered ends added. Armament was a spar torpedo, an explosive charge on the end of a pole. The craft had a nine-man crew, eight to turn the handcranked propeller and one to steer. On 17 February 1864, commanded by Lt George Dixon, she slipped into Charleston Harbor and sank the newly commissioned Union corvette *Housatonic*, but was dragged down by the wave caused by the explosion of the torpedo. Years later, when the wreck was located on the sea bed, the skeletons of eight of the crew were discovered, still seated at their crankshaft. Named after her inventor, H L Hunley was one of a number of small submersibles built for the Confederate Navy.

Country:	Confederate States of America
Type:	Attack submersible
Launch date:	1863
Crew:	9
Displacement:	Surfaced: 2 tonnes/2 tons approx, submerged: Not known
Dimensions:	12m x 1m x 1.2m (40ft x 3ft 6in x 4ft)
Surface range:	Not known
Armament:	One spar torpedo
Powerplant:	Single screw, hand-cranked
Performance:	Surfaced: 2.5 knots, submerged: Not known

Hood

After the Battle of Jutland in 1916, in which three of Britain's battlecruisers
blew up, designs were put in hand for a better-protected vessel. *Hood* was to
have been the first of four such ships, but was the only one completed. Her engines
developed 144,000hp, and range was 7600km (4000 miles) at 10 knots. Despite
being designed to avoid the fate of her predecessors, whilst engaging the German
battleship *Bismarck* and the cruiser *Prinz Eugen* on 21 May 1941, her upper armour
was breached by a shell which reached her magazine, blowing her in two. There
were only three survivors; 1338 were lost. The sinking of *Hood* was keenly felt by
the British people, who held her in great affection. She had 'shown the flag' for
Britain several times, most notably in 1923, when she embarked on a world cruise.
Her assailant, *Bismarck*, survived her by just three days before she too was sunk.

Country:	Great Britain
Type:	Battlecruiser
Launch date:	22 August 1918
Crew:	1477
Displacement:	45,923 tonnes (45,200 tons)
Dimensions:	262m x 31.7m x 8.7m (860ft x 104ft x 28ft 6in)
Range:	7200km (4000nm) at 10 knots
Armament:	12 140mm (5.5 in), eight 381mm (15in) guns
Powerplant:	Quadruple screw turbines
Performance:	32 knots

Hunt

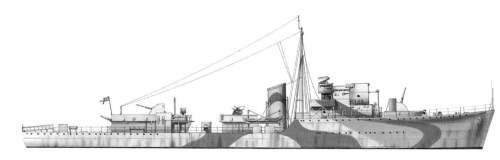

Aware of the shortage of escorts as early as 1938, the British Admiralty designed what was termed a Fast Escort Vessel (FEV) to give convoys both anti-aircraft and anti-submarine coverage without tying down the precious, and, as it turned out, inadequate, fleet destroyers. Rather shortsightedly, there was perceived the need for speed – in order to prosecute sonar contacts more smartly – but not endurance, as the latter requirement was deemed to be met by true escort vessels such as the Flower-class corvettes. To improve them as gun platforms, the Hunt-class ships were fitted initially with active stabilisers as standard. However, their power demands and their poor control systems made them so unpopular that later ships had extra bunker space instead, which considerably improved their endurance. In all, 83 Hunt Types I-, II- and III-class destroyers were built.

Country:	Great Britain
Type:	Destroyer
Launch date:	12 December 1939 (HMS Atherstone, first unit)
Crew:	170
Displacement:	1107 tonnes (1090 tons)
Dimensions:	85.7m x 9.6m x 2.36m (281ft 3in x 31ft 6in x 7ft 9in)
Range:	4626km (2498nm)
Main armament:	Two twin 102mm (4in) guns; two 533mm (21in) torpedo tubes
Powerplant:	Two shafts, geared steam turbines
Performance:	25 knots

Hydra

The Greek Government announced its decision to buy four Meko 200 Mod 3HN frigates from what was then West Germany, on 18 April 1988. The West German Government was to offset the cost of the purchase by supplying tanks and aircraft, whereas US credits contributed to the cost of electronics and weapon systems. The first ship, *Hydra*, was built by Blohm & Voss at Hamburg, with the remainder scheduled to be built by the Hellenic Shipyards at Skaramanga. However, construction of the second vessel, *Spetsai*, was delayed by financial constraints, so some of the construction work was completed in Hamburg. The design closely follows that of the Portuguese Vasco da Gama class. All four ships were commissioned between November 1992 and January 1999, and all four carry the Sikorsky Aegean Hawk ASW helicopter.

Country:	Greece
Type:	Frigate
Launch date:	25 June 1991
Crew:	173
Displacement:	3251 tonnes (3200 tons)
Dimensions:	117m x 14.8m x 4.1m (383ft 11in x 48ft 7in x 13ft 6in)
Range:	6591km (3559nm)
Main armament:	One 127mm (5in) DP gun; Harpoon SSM; six 324mm (12.75in) Mk46 torpedoes; Sea Sparrow SAM
Powerplant:	Two shafts, two gas turbines, two diesels
Performance:	31 knots

I7

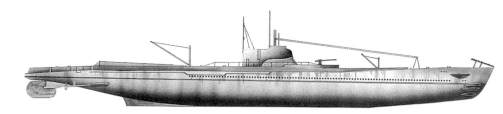

At the time of their construction, *I7* and her sister boat *I8* were the largest submarines built for the Japanese Navy. They were intended for the scouting role, and carried a reconnaissance seaplane. They could stay away from base for 60-day periods, cruising for over over 14,000nm at 16 knots, and could dive to a depth of 99m (325ft). Between them, the two boats sank seven Allied merchant ships totalling 42,574 (41,902 tons). *I7* was sunk by the American destroyer *Monaghan* on 22 June 1943. *I8* was modified to carry four Kaiten suicide submarines in place of her aircraft hangar. She was sunk by the destroyers USS *Morrison* and *Stockton* on 30 March 1945 while attempting to attack American ships involved in the Okinawa landings. Many Japanese warships were lost in suicide attacks during this campaign.

Country:	Japan
Type:	Attack submarine
Launch date:	3 July 1935
Crew:	100
Displacement:	Surfaced: 2565 tonnes (2525 tons), submerged: 3640 tonnes (3583 tons)
Dimensions:	109.3m x 9m x 5.2m (358ft 7in x 29ft 6in x 17ft)
Surface range:	26,600km (14,337nm) at 16 knots
Armament:	Six 533mm (21in) torpedo tubes, one 140mm (5.5in) gun
Powerplant:	Twin screws, diesel/electric motors
Performance:	Surfaced: 23 knots, submerged: 8 knots

I15

The I15-class submarines were highly specialized scouting boats, with streamlined hulls and conning towers. Compared with earlier classes of scouting submarines, the seaplane hangar was also streamlined, being a smooth, rounded fairing that extended forward as part of the conning tower. Although designed to mount four 25mm AA guns, they were completed with a single twin 25mm mounting. During World War II some vessels had their hangar and catapult removed and replaced by a second 140mm (5.5in) gun, being reclassed as attack submarines. Only one boat of the fairly large class, *I36*, survived the war, being surrendered at Kobe. *I15* (Cdr Ishikawa) was lost on 2 November 1942. As the war progressed and the Americans recaptured the Pacific islands the Japanese submarine fleet was penned into its home bases, its radius of action reduced.

Country:	Japan
Type:	Attack submarine
Launch date:	1939
Crew:	100
Displacement:	Surfaced: 2625 tonnes (2584 tons), submerged: 3713 tonnes (3654 tons)
Dimensions:	102.5m x 9.3m x 5.1m (336ft x 30ft 6in x 16ft 9in)
Surface range:	45,189km (24,400nm) at 10 knots
Armament:	Six 533mm (21in) torpedo tubes; one 140mm (5.5in) and two 25mm AA guns
Powerplant:	Two shafts, diesel/electric motors
Performance:	Surfaced: 23.5 knots, submerged: 8 knots

I21

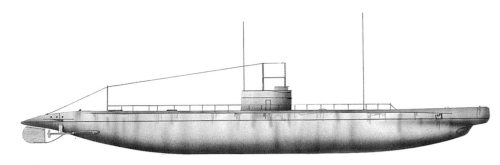

One of two vessels that were Japan's first ocean-going submarines, *I21* was built from Italian plans of the Fiat-Laurenti *F1* type. She was built at the Kawasaki yard in Kobe and completed in 1920. Her number was changed to *RO2* in 1924, and she was stricken in 1930. In the meantime, the *I21* number had been re-allocated to a new submarine, launched in March 1926; the design of this vessel was based on the German submarine *UB125*, which had been given to Japan after surrendering in 1918. The new *I21* was leader of a class of four boats, all of which went on to see service in the Pacific War. In 1939 they received new designations, *I21* becoming *I121* and so on. *I21/I121* was scrapped; the others were lost in action. Very few Japanese submarines survived until the final surrender.

Country:	Japan
Type:	Attack submarine
Launch date:	November 1919
Crew:	45
Displacement:	Surfaced: 728 tonnes (717 tons), submerged: 1063 tonnes (1047 tons)
Dimensions:	65.6m x 6m x 4.2m (215ft 3in x 19ft 8in x 13ft 9in)
Surface range:	19,456km (10,500nm) at 8 knots
Armament:	Five 457mm (18in) torpedo tubes
Powerplant:	Two screws, diesel/electric motors
Performance:	Surfaced: 13 knots, submerged: 8 knots

I400

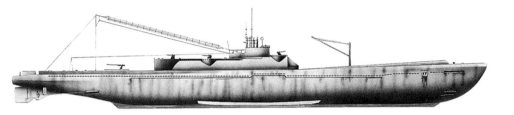

Prior to World War II, several navies tried to build an effective aircraft-carrying submarine. Only the Japanese managed to produce a series of workable vessels, the most notable being the STO class. Of the 19 planned vessels only two, the *I400* and *I401*, were completed for their intended role. A third, *I402*, was completed as a submersible tanker transport. *I400* was a huge vessel, with a large aircraft hangar offset to starboard, to hold three M6A1 Seiran floatplanes, plus components for a fourth. To launch the aircraft, *I400* would surface, then the machines would be warmed up in the hangar, rolled out, wings unfolded, and launched down a 26m (85ft) catapult rail. It was planned to attack the locks on the Panama Canal, but the mission was never flown. The I400 class was not rivalled in size until the emergence of the Ethan Allen class of SSBN.

Country:	Japan
Type:	Attack submarine
Launch date:	1944
Crew:	100
Displacement:	Surfaced: 5316 tonnes (5233 tons), submerged: 6665 tonnes (6560 tons
Dimensions:	122m x 12m x 7m (400ft 1in x 39ft 4in x 24ft)
Surface range:	68,561km (37,000nm) at 14 knots
Armament:	Eight 533mm (21in) torpedo tubes; one140mm (5.5in) gun
Powerplant:	Twin screws, diesel/electric motors
Performance:	Surfaced: 18.7 knots, submerged: 6.5 knots

Ibuki

Ibuki was the first Japanese warship to be fitted with turbine engines. Laid down in May 1907, she was quickly built, but her launch was delayed due to other construction work already in hand. The delay enabled her design to be modified, prior to completion, to include the installation of turbine machinery, which developed 24,000hp. Coal supply was 2032 tonnes (2000 tons), plus 221 tonnes (218 tons) of oil fuel. *Ibuki* served as an escort for Australian troops on their way to the Dardanelles during World War I, and also took part in the search for the German cruiser *Emden*, which was engaged in commerce raiding in the Indian Ocean. *Emden* took 21 Allied ships and also destroyed a small Russian cruiser and a French destroyer, as well as destroying a signal station, before being sunk by the cruiser HMAS *Sydney*. *Ibuki* was scrapped in 1924.

Country:	Japan
Type:	Cruiser
Launch date:	21 November 1907
Crew:	844
Displacement:	15,844 tonnes (15,595 tons)
Dimensions:	148m x 23m x 8m (465ft x 75ft 4in x 26ft 1in)
Range:	6485km (3500nm) at 15 knots
Armament:	Four 305mm (12in), eight 203mm (8in) guns
Powerplant:	Twin screw turbines
Performance:	21 knots

Idaho

Idaho was one of a trio of battleships of the New Mexico class that introduced a new 356mm (14in) gun which could be elevated independently; with previous guns, all weapons in a turret had been locked into the same elevation. The main guns were housed in triple turrets. Originally 22 127mm (5in) guns were planned. The number was reduced to 14, allowing extra armour in some areas. *Idaho* was extensively rebuilt in 1930–31. From 1919 to 1941 she served with the Pacific Fleet, being transferred to the Atlantic Fleet for a brief period before returning to the Pacific. She subsequently fought actions off Attu, the Gilbert Islands, Kwajalein, Saipan, Guam, Palau, Iwo Jima and Okinawa, running aground off the latter island in June 1945. By 1943 she had had all her 127mm (5in) guns removed. *Idaho* was stricken in 1947; her sister ships were *New Mexico* and *Mississippi*.

Country:	USA
Type:	Battleship
Launch date:	30 June 1917
Crew:	1084
Displacement:	33,528 tonnes (33,000 tons)
Dimensions:	190.2m x 29.7m x 9.1m (624ft x 97ft 6in x 29ft 10in)
Range:	14,400km (8000nm) at 10 knots
Armament:	12 356mm (14in), 14 127mm (5in) guns
Powerplant:	Quadruple screw turbines
Performance:	21 knots

Impavido

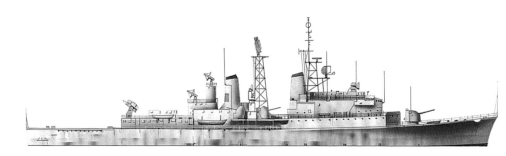

Impavido and her sister ship, *Intrepido*, were the first missile-armed destroyers in the Italian Navy. Derived from the conventional gun-armed Impetuoso-class destroyers, they retained the forward 127mm (5in) twin gun turret, but the after turret was replaced with a US Mk13 launcher for Tartar surface-to-air missiles. The Tartar area defence weapon, similar in concept to Britain's Sea Dart, was developed in response to a 1952 requirement for a weapon capable of engaging targets at all altitudes. The after funnel was made taller to keep exhaust away from the fire-control tracker on top of the aft structure. *Impavido* ws fitted with four 76mm (3in) anti-aircraft guns, and anti-submarine capability was provided by two triple torpedo tubes. *Impavido* was modernized between 1976 and 1977, and was stricken on 30 June 1992.

Country:	Italy
Type:	Destroyer
Launch date:	25 May 1962
Crew:	344
Displacement:	4054 tonnes (3990 tons)
Dimensions:	131.3m x 13.7m x 4.4m (430ft 9in x 45ft x 14ft 5in)
Range:	9260km (5000nm)
Main armament:	Two 127mm (5in) guns; one Tartar missile launcher
Powerplant:	Twin screws, turbines
Performance:	34 knots

Imperator Pavel I

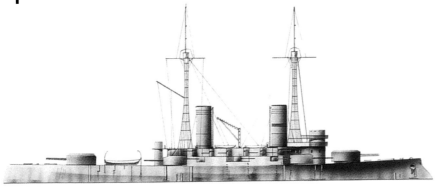

*I*mperator Pavel I was laid down in April 1904, but construction was delayed to incorporate lessons learned in the Russo–Japanese War of 1904–05. The hull was completely armoured and was flush-decked. The superstructure housed six of the 203mm (8in) guns and all the 120mm (4.7in) guns, with twin 203mm (8in) turrets mounted on the upper deck at each corner of the superstructure. The 304mm (12in) guns were in turrets. She saw action in the Baltic during World War I and was renamed *Respublika* after the second Russian revolution in 1917. She was scrapped in 1923. The Baltic, where this vessel spent its operational service, was the scene of a number of fierce naval actions during World War I, as the Russians attempted to contest German domination of the Baltic states. Most actions were fought against warships of the German 3rd High Sea Squadron.

Country:	Russia
Type:	Battleship
Launch date:	7 September 1907
Crew:	933
Displacement:	17,678 tonnes (17,400 tons)
Dimensions:	140.2m x 24.4m x 8.2m (460ft x 80ft x 27ft)
Range:	11,118km (6000nm) at 12 knots
Armament:	Four 305mm (12in), 14 203mm (8in) and 12 119mm (4.7in) guns
Powerplant:	Twin screw, vertical triple expansion engines
Performance:	17.5 knots

Independence

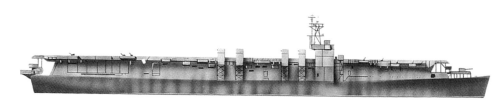

During 1942 the US Navy lost four aircraft carriers, and for a time had only *Enterprise* in the Pacific. The first of the large Essex-class carriers were not expected to enter service until the following year, so plans were put in hand to convert some of the 39 light cruisers of the Cleveland class then under construction. Emergency work was carried out on nine of the vessels and they all entered service in 1943. *Independence* had 45 aircraft, but she had room to 'ferry' up to 100. Her World War II battle honours included raids on the Gilbert Islands, Palau, Leyte, Luzon, Taiwan, Okinawa, the China coast, the Ryukus and the Japanese Home Islands. During the invasion of the Gilbert Islands in November 1943 the carrier was severely damaged by an aerial torpedo off Tarawa. She was used as a target in the Bikini atomic bomb tests, and was finally sunk as a target ship in 1951.

Country:	USA
Type:	Aircraft carrier
Launch date:	22 August 1942
Crew:	1569
Displacement:	14,980 tonnes (14,751 tons)
Dimensions:	189.78m x 33.3m x 7.4m (622ft 6in x 109ft 2in x 24ft 3in)
Range:	23,400km (13,000nm) at 12 knots
Armament:	Two 40mm (1.5in), 22 20mm (0.78in) guns, 30 aircraft
Powerplant:	Quadruple screw turbines
Performance:	31.6 knots

Indiana

Indiana was one of a class of four units of the South Dakota class that were the last US battleships designed within the weight limits of the 1922 London Treaty. Completed in 1942, all *Indiana*'s secondary 127mm (5in) guns were concentrated on two levels in twin turrets amidships, and her single funnel was faired into the rear of the bridge. The class carried over 100 40mm (1.5in) and 20mm (0.78in) anti-aircraft guns. *Indiana* saw extensive service in the Pacific during World War II. She saw action in the Southwest Pacific, the Gilbert Islands, Kwajalein, the Philippine Sea, Saipan, Guam, Palau, Iwo Jima and Okinawa. In February 1944 she was damaged in collision with the battleship *Washington* off Kwajalein; in June that year she was hit by a suicide aircraft off Saipan; and in June 1945 she was further damaged by a typhoon off Okinawa. She was sold in 1963.

Country:	USA
Type:	Battleship
Launch date:	21 November 1941
Crew:	1793
Displacement:	45,231 tonnes (44,519 tons)
Dimensions:	207.2m x 32.9m x 10.6m (680ft x 108ft x 35ft)
Range:	27,000km (15,000nm) at 12 knots
Armament:	20 127mm (5in), nine 406mm (16in) guns
Powerplant:	Quadruple screw turbines
Performance:	27.5 knots

Inflexible

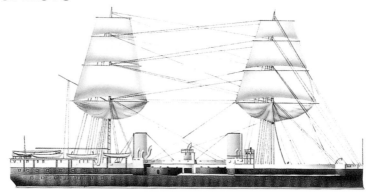

Designed by Nathaniel Barnaby, *Inflexible* was one of the most powerful vessels of her time. Laid down in 1881 in direct response to the giant Italian battleships *Duilio* and *Dandolo*, and to French moves towards arming their new ships with large guns. As completed in 1874, *Inflexible* had the heaviest muzzle-loading rifled guns of any vessel in the Royal Navy – and the thickest armour. The 81-tonne (80-ton) guns were positioned in turrets at opposite corners of the citadel. As they were too long to be reloaded in the turrets, the guns were designed to depress into an armoured glacis for reloading on the main deck. In 1881 she was assigned to the Mediterranean Fleet, and in 1882 she was damaged by shellfire during the bombardment of Alexandria following anti-foreign riots there. This led to conflict between the British and Egyptians. She was scrapped in 1903.

Country:	Great Britain
Type:	Battleship
Launch date:	27 April 1876
Crew:	440
Displacement:	12,070 tonnes (11,880 tons)
Dimensions:	104.8m x 22.8m x 7.7m (344ft x 75ft x 25ft 6in)
Range:	6300km (3400nm) at 10 knots
Armament:	Four 406mm (16in) guns
Powerplant:	Twin screw, compound engines
Performance:	14.7 knots

Inflexible

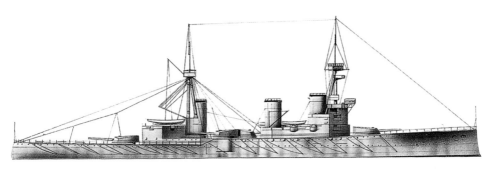

In 1904 the powerful Japanese *Tsukuba* and *Ibuki* classes convinced the British Admiralty of the need for a vessel combining the speed of a cruiser with the firepower of a battleship. The answer was *Inflexible* and her sisters of the Invincible class. *Inflexible* was launched in 1907 and completed in 1908. In May 1911 she suffered a damaged bow in collision with the battleship *Bellerophon* in the English Channel. Early in World War I she took part in the naval action off the Falklands and the hunt for the German cruiser *Goeben*; in 1915 she was one of the vessels covering the Dardanelles landings, and while carrying out a bombardment operation in March she was severely damaged by shore batteries and a mine. She was at Jutland in 1916 but received no damage, unlike her sister *Invincible* which was blown up by German shell fire. *Inflexible* and *Indomitable* were sold for scrap in 1922.

Country:	Great Britain
Type:	Battlecruiser
Launch date:	26 June 1907
Crew:	784
Displacement:	20,320 tonnes (20,000 tons)
Dimensions:	172.8m x 23.9m x 8m (567ft x 78ft 6in x 26ft 10in)
Range:	5562km (3090nm) at 10 knots
Armament:	16 102mm (4in), eight 305mm (12in) guns
Powerplant:	Quadruple screw turbines
Performance:	25.5 knots

Inhauma

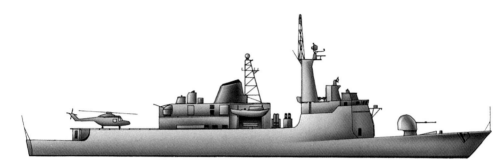

Inhauma is the lead ship of a class of four corvettes designed by the Brazilian Naval Design Office with the assistance of the German privately-owned Marine Technik design company. *Inhauma* was commissioned in December 1989, and the other corvettes between 1991 and 1994. Originally, it had been intended to order a class of 16 ships, but this was reduced to four because of financial considerations. As a country with a long coastline, Brazil has always endeavoured to maintain a substantial navy. Her first dreadnoughts, built in Britain in 1907, came about as a response to the growth of the Argentine Navy, and as a consequence, she had ships of this type in commission even before larger powers such as France, Italy and Russia. Corvettes such as *Inhauma* are ideally suited to the task of defending Brazil's coast.

Country:	Brazil
Type:	Corvette
Launch date:	13 December 1986
Crew:	122
Displacement:	2002 tonnes (1970 tons)
Dimensions:	95.83m x 11.4m x 3.7m (314ft 2in x 37ft 5in x 12ft 1in)
Range:	6434km (3474nm)
Main armament:	One 115mm (4.5in) gun; Exocet SSMs; six 324mm (12.75in) torpedo tubes
Powerplant:	Two shafts, one gas turbine, two diesels
Performance:	27 knots

Invincible

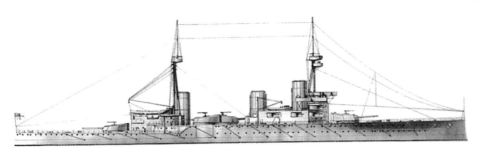

Completed in 1908, *Invincible* was the world's first battlecruiser, and so was the first of an entirely new type of warship. It sacrificed armoured protection for speed, range and battleship-sized armament, and could outrun and outfight its prey – the armoured cruiser. However, as the disastrous loss of *Invincible* and two other battlecruisers at Jutland was to show, when up against a battleship's firepower, the lack of armour, particularly around the magazines, was a fatal flaw. Despite being refitted with more armour as a result of the this débâcle, events had proved the obsolescence of this type of vessel and development was stopped. *Invincible* blew up and sank with the loss of 1026 lives, including Rear-Admiral H.L.A. Hood. The battlecruiser *Queen Mary* suffered the same fate at Jutland, exploding with the loss of 1266 lives after a direct hit from the battlecruiser *Derfflinger*.

Country:	Great Britain
Type:	Battlecruiser
Launch date:	13 April 1907
Crew:	784
Displacement:	20,421 tonnes (20,100 tons)
Dimensions:	175.5m x 23.9m x 7.7m (576ft x 78.5ft x 25.5ft)
Range:	5559km (3000nm) at 25 knots
Armament:	Eight 305mm (12in), 16 102mm (4in) guns
Powerplant:	Four shaft geared turbines
Performance:	25 knots

Iowa

Designs for the Iowa class of fast battleships were started in 1936 in response to rumours that the Japanese were laying down battleships of 46,736 tonnes (46,000 tons). *Iowa* was laid down in 1940 and commissioned in 1943. The class including the *New Jersey* and *Missouri,* had greater displacement than the previous South Dakota class, and had more power and protection. The *Iowa* class served as escort for carriers in World War II, being the only battleships fast enough to keep up with carrier groups. She was used to bombard shore positions during the Korean War. The last of the Iowas, *Kentucky*, was not launched until 1950. They were the fastest battleships ever built, with a high length to beam ratio; the armour belt was inside the hull. Two of the class, *Illinois* and *Kentucky*, were not completed. *Iowa* was damaged by gunfire from shore batteries on Mili Island in March 1944.

Country:	USA
Type:	Battleship
Launch date:	27 August 1942
Crew:	1921
Displacement:	56,601 tonnes (55,710 tons)
Dimensions:	270.4m x 33.5m x 11.6m (887ft 2in x 108ft 3in x 38ft)
Range:	27,000km (15,000nm) at 12 knots
Armament:	Nine 406mm (16in), 20 127mm (5in) guns
Powerplant:	Quadruple screw turbines
Performance:	32.5 knots

Iron Duke

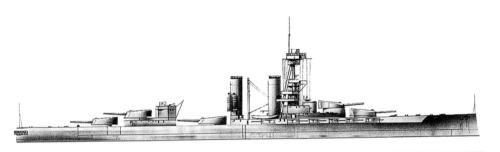

Launched in 1912, *Iron Duke* was the British flagship at the Battle of Jutland in 1916, and was one of the longest serving pre-World War I dreadnought battleships. She was a member of a class of four vessels that formed the third group of super-dreadnoughts. They were all armed with 343mm (13.5in) guns, and were the first major capital ships to revert to 152mm (6in) guns for anti-torpedo boat defence. Minor changes were later made to the secondary armament. The rest of her class was scrapped to comply with the Washington Treaty in the 1920s, but *Iron Duke* herself became a training ship in 1931, and was a depot ship at Scapa Flow between 1939–45. On 17 October 1939 she was attacked by four Junkers Ju88 dive-bombers of I/KG30 while at anchor in Scapa Flow and had to be beached after sustaining damage from near-misses. She was finally scrapped in 1946.

Country:	Great Britain
Type:	Battleship
Launch date:	12 October 1912
Crew:	1022
Displacement:	30,866 tonnes (30,380 tons)
Dimensions:	189.8m x 27.4m x 9m (622ft 9in x 90ft x 29ft 6in)
Range:	14,000km (7780nm) at 10 knots
Armament:	12 152mm (6in), 10 342mm (13.5in) guns
Powerplant:	Quadruple screw turbines
Performance:	21.6 knots

Iroquois

Launched between 1970 and 1971, *Iroquois* and her three sisters – *Athabaskan*, *Algonquin* and *Huron*, all four named after Indian tribes of the Great Lakes region – were designed specifically for anti-submarine warfare operations in Arctic waters, where much naval warfare would have taken place in any East-West conflict. They have the same hull design, dimensions, and basic characteristics as an earlier class of large, general-purpose frigates which had been cancelled in the early 1960s. Properly designated Destroyer Helicopter Escorts (DDH), they carry two Sea King ASW helicopters. They are equipped with anti-rolling tanks to stabilise them at low speed, a pre-wetting system to counter radioactive fallout, and an enclosed citadel from which control of all machinery is exercised. A comprehensive electronics system includes an effective, long-range radar warning device.

Country:	Canada
Type:	Destroyer
Launch date:	28 November 1970
Crew:	246
Displacement:	4267 tonnes (4200 tons)
Dimensions:	129.8m x 15.5m x 4.5m (426ft x 51ft x 15ft)
Range:	8338km (4502nm)
Main armament:	One 127mm (5in) gun; one triple A/S mortar
Powerplant:	Twin screw, gas turbines
Performance:	30 knots

Isaac Peral

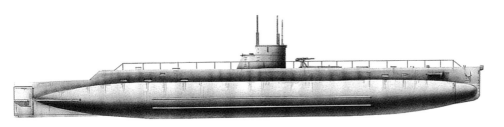

Isaac Peral was Spain's first major submarine. She was built by the Fore River Company in the United States and modelled on the Holland design. She attained 15.36 knots on the surface during trials. Surface range was 5386km (2835 statute miles and 2903 nautical miles) at 11 knots; range submerged was 130km (70nm) at full power from her 480hp electric motors. She was renumbered *O1* in 1930, later being reduced to a hulk and numbered *AO*. Her single 76mm (3in) gun was fixed to a collapsible mount, and was not a permanent feature. Spain did not maintain a substantial submarine force; after General Franco's victory in the Civil War, boats were obtained from Italy. The Civil War created an enormous drain on Spain's resources, one of the reasons why Franco chose to remain neutral in World War II.

Country:	Spain
Type:	Attack submarine
Launch date:	July 1916
Crew:	35
Displacement:	Surfaced: 499 tonnes (491 tons), submerged: 762 tonnes (750 tons)
Dimensions:	60m x 5.8m x 3.4m (196ft 10in x 19ft x 11ft 2in)
Surface range:	5386km (2903nm) at 11 knots
Armament:	Four 457mm (18in) torpedo tubes, one 76mm (3in) gun
Powerplant:	Twin screws, diesel/electric motors
Performance:	Surfaced: 15 knots, submerged: 8 knots

Ise

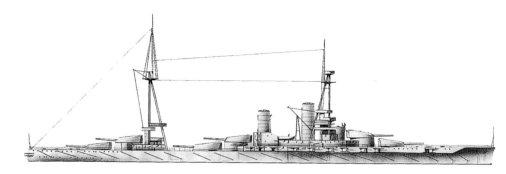

L aunched in 1916, *Ise* was an improved version of the previous Fuso class, and
carried two twin superfiring guns amidships. She was extensively modernised
between World Wars I and II, and by 1937 had been lengthened aft by 7.6m (25ft).
Following the large loss of Japanese aircraft carriers at Midway in June 1942, *Ise*
was converted to a hybrid battleship-carrier in 1943 when a hangar and flight
deck were built on her quarter deck. Because of a lack of space, her complement
of 22 seaplanes were launched by catapult but had to be retrieved by crane. She
took part in the battles of Midway and Leyte Gulf, and was deactivated after being
damaged by mines laid by American aircraft. She was sunk at Kure in July 1945 in
a two-day series of air strikes that also destroyed the battleships *Hyuga* and
Haruna and the aircraft carrier *Amagi*. She was raised and scrapped in 1946.

Country:	Japan
Type:	Battleship
Launch date:	12 November 1916
Crew:	1376 as battleship, 1463 as carrier
Displacement:	32,576 tonnes (32,063 tons) as battleship
Dimensions:	208.2m x 28.6m x 8.8m (683ft x 94ft x 29ft)
Range:	7412km (4000nm) at 15 knots
Armament:	12 356mm (14in), 20 140mm (5.5in) guns
Powerplant:	Quadruple screw turbines
Performance:	23 knots

Italia

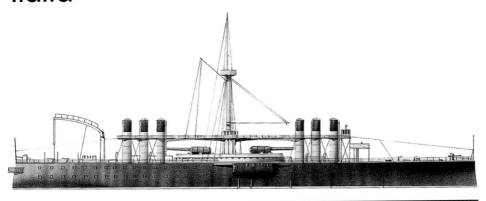

At the time of her completion in 1880, *Italia* and her sister *Lepanto* were among the fastest vessels afloat. This was partially due to the lack of side armour, these ships having no armoured belt. Instead they had a thick armoured deck which curved down to the waterline, and which was supplemented by an extensive honeycomb of watertight compartments. Their 104-tonne (102-ton) main guns were mounted in pairs on turntables, which were placed on a huge single oval-shaped armoured barbette. Ammunition had to be trundled up from below the armoured deck, and each gun could only fire one shell every five minutes. In the event technology overtook these vessels, and by the time they entered service the quick-firing gun and improved high-explosive shell had rendered them obsolete. *Italia* was transferred to harbour duties in 1914, and was scrapped in 1921.

Country:	Italy
Type:	Battleship
Launch date:	29 September 1880
Crew:	701
Displacement:	15,904 tonnes (15,654 tons)
Dimensions:	124.7m x 22.5m x 8.7m (409ft 2in x 73ft 10in x 28ft 6in)
Range:	9000km (5000nm) at 10 knots
Armament:	Four 431mm (17in) guns
Powerplant:	Twin screw, vertical compound engines
Performance:	17.8 knots

Iwo Jima

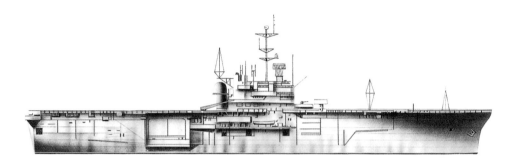

*I*wo Jima – first of a class of seven – and was the world's first ship designed to carry and operate helicopters. She can also carry a Marine battalion of 2000 troops, plus their artillery and support vehicles. The flight deck allows for the simultaneous take-off of up to seven helicopters, and *Iwo Jima* has hangar facilities for up to 20 helicopters. The two lifts are situated at the very edges of the deck, so as not to reduce the flight-deck area. Storage capacity is provided for 1430 litres (6500 gallons) of petrol for the vehicles, plus over 88,000 litres (400,000 gallons) for the helicopter force. In 1970 a Sea Sparrow missile launcher was installed, followed by a second three years later. Iwo Jima and her six sisters have extensive medical facilities, including operating theatres and a large hospital. Other vessels in the class are *Guadalcanal, Guam, Inchon, Okinawa, Tripoli* and *New Orleans*.

Country:	USA
Type:	Helicopter carrier
Launch date:	17 September 1960
Crew:	667, plus 2000 troops
Displacement:	18,330 tonnes (18,042 tons)
Dimensions:	183.6m x 25.7m x 8m (602ft 8in x 84ft x 26ft)
Range:	11,118km (6000nm) at 18 knots
Armament:	Four 76mm (3in) guns
Powerplant:	Single screw turbines
Performance:	23.5 knots

Izumrud

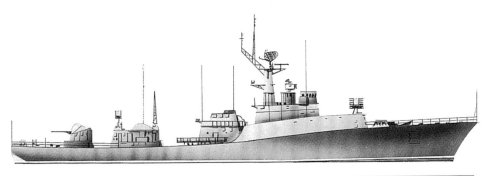

Izumrud ('Emerald') was one of a large group of small anti-submarine Grisha-class frigates built at the rate of three per year, and divided into five sub-groups according to the equipment carried. *Izumrud* was in the first group. Her twin 57mm (2.25in) gun turret was mounted aft, and the SA-N-4 SAM missiles were mounted forward of the bridge and were fired upward through a circular hatchway in the deck. Two twin, multi-barrel rocket launchers were also fitted in front of the bridge, and twin 533mm (21in) torpedo tubes were mounted amidships. *Izumrud*'s turbines developed 24,000hp, and the diesels produced 16,000hp. Range was 1800km (972nm) at 27 knots and 8550km (4616nm) at 10 knots. *Izumrud* was used for inshore anti-submarine patrols, where her principal targets would be small and very quiet diesel-electric boats (SSKs) engaged in special operations.

Country:	Soviet Union
Type:	Frigate
Launch date:	1970
Crew:	250
Displacement:	1219 tonnes (1200 tons)
Dimensions:	72m x 10m x 3.7m (236ft 3in x 32ft 10in x 12ft 2in)
Range:	8550km (4608nm)
Main armament:	Two 57mm (2.25in) guns; SAMs
Powerplant:	Triple screws, one gas turbine, two diesel engines
Performance:	27 knots

J1

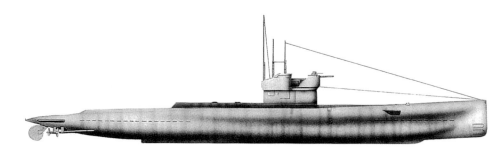

*J*1 was built in response to a perceived threat from German submarines then entering service and reputed to be capable of 22 knots. As first completed, *J1*'s large forward free-flooding tank brought the bows down in the water, causing loss of speed when surfaced. Later the bows were raised, curing this pitching tendency, and the submarine was then able to maintain 17 knots surfaced in heavy seas. Range at 12.5 knots surfaced was 9500km (5120nm). Later, a 102mm (4in) gun was positioned high up at the front of the conning tower in place of the 76mm (3in) weapon. On 5 November 1916, *J1* torpedoed and damaged the German battleships *Grosser-Kurfurst* and *Kronprinz*. *J1* was handed over to Australia in 1919, and was broken up in 1924. Only seven J-class boats were built, one of which was lost accidentally.

Country:	Great Britain
Type:	Attack submarine
Launch date:	November 1915
Crew:	44
Displacement:	Surfaced: 1223 tonnes (1204 tons), submerged: 1849 tonnes (1820 tons)
Dimensions:	84m x 7m x 4.3m (275ft 7in x 23ft x 14ft)
Surface range:	9500km (5120nm) at 12.5 knots
Armament:	Six 457mm (18in) torpedo tubes; one 76mm (3in) gun
Powerplant:	Triple screws, diesel/electric motors
Performance:	Surfaced: 17 knots, submerged: 9.5 knots

Jacob van Heemskerck

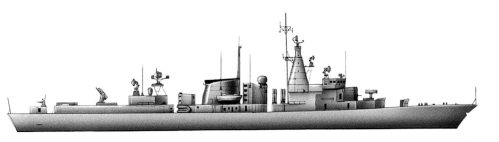

The *Jacob van Heemskerck* is the leader of a two-ship class, the other being the *Witte de With*. Commissioned in 1986, the ships were planned to alternate as the flagship of the Royal Netherlands Navy's 3rd ASW hunter-killer group, assigned to NATO's Channel Command in wartime. The two vessels were originally designed to replace two Kortenaer-class frigates which had been sold to Greece, and were intended to be an air-defence variant. In addition to the Goalkeeper CIWS, they are armed with the Standard and Sea Sparrow SAMs, and are thus capable of providing effective area defence of a task group out to a range of 46km (25nm) with the Standard SM-1MR SAM, the Raytheon Sea Sparrow providing medium-range backup to 14.6km (7.8nm). The Standard missile replaced the Tartar in NATO service.

Country:	Netherlands
Type:	Frigate
Launch date:	5 November 1983
Displacement:	3810 tonnes (3750 tons)
Dimensions:	130.5m x 14.6m x 6.2m (428ft x 47ft 11in x 20ft 4in)
Range:	7560km (4082nm)
Main armament:	One 30mm (1.1in) Goalkeeper; two 20mm (0.7in) guns; Harpoon SSM; Standard and Sea Sparrow SAMs; four 324mm (12.75in) torpedo tubes
Powerplant:	Two shafts, four gas turbines
Performance:	30 knots

Jauréguiberry

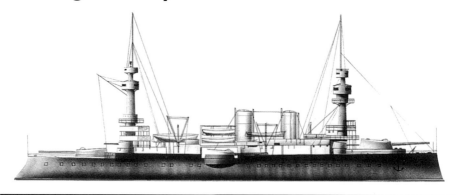

*J*auréguiberry was designed by Lagane as an enlarged version of his successful small battleship *Capitan Prat*, launched in 1890. After initial problems with her boilers, *Jauréguiberry* became a good steamer and was able to maintain high speed for long periods. Though in poor condition, she saw service in the early months of World War I. At the time of the warship's launch France was still obsessed with the view that Great Britain was her traditional enemy, and so was developing her fleet in a manner that threatened British trade and also aimed to offset the size of the Royal Navy by innovative technology. British policy of the day was to maintain a so-called 'two-power standard', which kept the Royal Navy equal in numbers to any two foreign navies and consequently saw large numbers of battleships built in the years up to 1906. *Jauréguiberry* was hulked in 1920 and scrapped in 1934.

Country:	France
Type:	Battleship
Launch date:	27 October 1893
Crew:	631
Displacement:	11,823 tonnes (11,637 tons)
Dimensions:	108.5m x 22m x 8.4m (356ft x 72ft 8in x 27ft 8in)
Range:	6485km (3500nm) at 10 knots
Armament:	Two 305mm (12in), two 270mm (10.8in), eight 140mm (5.5in) guns
Powerplant:	Twin screw, vertical triple expansion engines
Performance:	17.7 knots

Jeanne D'Arc

Originally to be named *La Résolue*, this ship was authorised in 1957 as a training cruiser to replace the pre-World War I *Jeanne D'Arc*. Due to the cancellation of a large carrier, *La Résolue* underwent major design changes, emerging in 1964 as *Jeanne D'Arc*, a combination of cruiser, helicopter carrier and assault ship. Her superstructure is situated forward, with the aft of the vessel being a helicopter deck below which is housed the narrow hangar. In her role as a troop carrier, *Jeanne D'Arc* can transport 700 men and eight large helicopters. In 1975 Exocet missiles were fitted, giving her a full anti-ship role. In peacetime she reverts to a training role, providing facilities for up to 198 cadets. The ship has a modular type action information and operations room with a computerised tactical data handling system, and a combined command and control centre for amphibious warfare operations.

Country:	France
Type:	Helicopter carrier
Launch date:	30 September 1961
Crew:	627, plus 198 cadets
Displacement:	13,208 tonnes (13,000 tons)
Dimensions:	180m x 25.9m x 6.2m (590ft 6in x 85ft x 20ft 4in)
Range:	10,800km (6000nm) at 12 knots
Armament:	Four 100mm (3.9in) guns, Exocet missiles, 4 – 8 helicopters
Powerplant:	Twin screw turbines
Performance:	26.5 knots

Jebat

On 31 March 1992, it was announced that a contract had been signed for the construction of two corvettes, subsequently classed as light frigates, between Yarrow Shipbuilders of Glasgow and the Malaysian Navy. The two ships, named *Jebat* and *Lekiu*, were launched between 1994 and 1995 and commissioned in 1998, but delivery dates were delayed because of problems with integrating the weapon system. Basically, the vessels are a GEC Naval Systems Frigate 2000 design with a modern combat data system and automatic machinery control. Missile armament is the Aerospatiale Exocet MM40 Block II sea skimmer and the British Aerospace Vertical Launch Seawolf. Malaysia's long coastline makes it imperative for her to maintain strong patrol forces. As well as three frigates and two corvettes, she has some 40 patrol craft of various types.

Country:	Malaysia
Type:	Frigate
Launch date:	May 1995
Crew:	146
Displacement:	2306 tonnes (2270 tons)
Dimensions:	105.5m x 12.8m x 3.6m (346ft x 42ft x 11ft 9in)
Range:	9650km (5208nm)
Main armament:	One 57mm (2.25in) and two 30mm (1.1in) guns; Exocet SSM; Seawolf SAM; six 324mm (12.75in) torpedo tubes
Powerplant:	Two shafts, four diesel engines
Performance:	28 knots

Jianghu class

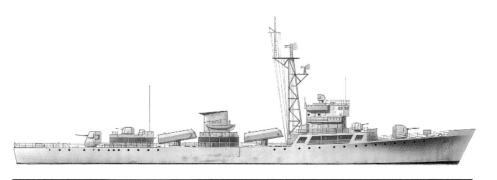

The first three or four units of what became known as the Jianghu I class were laid down between 1973 and 1974 at Hutung, launched in 1975, and commissioned in 1976. The vessels were a follow-on from the Jiangdong class, the first frigate design to emerge from China after the Cultural Revolution. A second shipyard, the Tungmang at Shanghai, subsequently joined the programme. About 20 ships were built, and one of them (pennant No 544) was modified and redesignated *Jianghu II*, the after part of the ship being rebuilt to take a hangar and flight deck for a single helicopter. Several of the class were expected to be converted, but 544 may have been a one-off helicopter trials ship for the improved Luhu and Jiangwei designs. There is also a Jianghu III class, fitted with improved weaponry and electronics.

Country:	China
Type:	Frigate
Launch date:	1975 (Chang De, first unit)
Crew:	195
Displacement:	1900 tonnes (1930 tons)
Dimensions:	103.2m x 10.2m x 3.1m (338ft 7in x 33ft 6in x 10ft 2in)
Range:	7408km (4000nm)
Main armament:	Two single 100mm (3.9in) DP and six twin 37mm (1.4in) AA guns; plus anti-ship missiles
Powerplant:	Two shafts, two diesels
Performance:	30 knots

Jianghu III

Based on the Jianghu II, the Jianghu III class reverted to the rounded stack of the first of the class, the Jianghu I, but was armed with twin 57mm (2.25in) DP guns mounted fore and aft plus six twin 37mm anti-aircraft guns, four RBU 1200 ASW rocket launchers, four BMB-2 depth charge projectors and two depth charge racks. The first two units were sold to Egypt in 1984 and 1985 as the *Najim az Zaffer* and the *El Nasser*, and four more to Thailand in 1991-92. Two units are currently in service with the Chinese fleet; the first is the *Huangshi*, commissioned in December 1986, and the other is the *Wuhu*. Two more vessels, one of which is identified as the *Zhoushan* (completed in early 1993) are improved Type IVs. The Types III and IV are referred to as New Missile Frigates. The Type IVs are the first all-enclosed, air conditioned ships to be built in China.

Country:	China
Type:	Frigate
Launch date:	1986 (Huangshi, first unit commisioned)
Crew:	200
Displacement:	1955 tonnes (1924 tons)
Dimensions:	103.2m x 10.8m x 3.1m (338ft 6in x 35ft 3in x 10ft 2in)
Range:	6434km (3474nm)
Main armament:	Four 100mm (3.9in) guns; YJ-1 Eagle Strike SSMs; depth charges; AS mortars and mines
Powerplant:	Two shafts, two diesel engines
Performance:	28 knots

Jiangwei class

The programme to construct four Jiangwei I frigates began in 1988, and the ships were commissioned between 1991 and 1994. The vessels are named *Anquing*, *Huainan*, *Huaibei* and *Tongling*, and all are based in the East Sea Fleet at Dinghai. They were followed by three ships of the Jiangwei II class, launched between 1997 and 1998. These vessels have an improved SAM system, updated fire-control radars, and a redistribution of the aft-mounted anti-aircraft guns. They are equipped with a hangar and helicopter platform aft to accommodate one Harbin Z-9A (Dauphin) helicopter for ASW and general-purpose work. A hull-mounted, active search-and-attack medium-frequency Echo Type 5 sonar is fitted. The first of the class began sea trials in early 1998 which was somewhat later than planned, unspecified delays having arisen.

Country:	China
Type:	Frigate
Launch date:	completed December 1991 (*Anqing*. first unit)
Crew:	170
Displacement:	2286 tonnes (2250 tons)
Dimensions:	111.7m x 12.1m x 4.8m (366ft 6in x 39ft 8in x 15ft 8in)
Range:	6437km (3472nm)
Main armament:	Two 100mm (3.9in) guns; Eagle Strike or C-802 SSMs; RF-61 SAMs; AS mortars
Powerplant:	Two shafts, two diesel engines
Performance:	25 knots

Kaiser

Launched in 1911 and completed in 1912, *Kaiser* was the first of a new type of German dreadnought that was to set the style for following vessels and eventually develop into *Bismarck* and *Tirpitz* of World War II. There were five units in the Kaiser class. All had superfiring turrets aft and diagonally offset wing turrets. Machinery developed 31,000hp, coal supply was 3000 tonnes (2953 tons), and range at 12 knots was nearly 15,200km (8000 miles). *Kaiser* was in action at the Battle of Jutland, and all vessels in the class were interned at Scapa Flow and scuttled in 1919. From 1929–1937 the class was salvaged and broken up. *Kaiser* was originally laid down as *Ersatz Hildebrand*. Other vessels in her class were *Friedrich der Grosse*, *Kaiserin*, *König Albert* and *Prinzregent Luitpold*. They were the first German battleships to be equipped with turbines.

Country:	Germany
Type:	Battleship
Launch date:	22 March 1911
Crew:	1278 (at Jutland)
Displacement:	26,998 tonnes (26,573 tons)
Dimensions:	172.4m x 29m x 8.3m (565ft 8in x 95ft 2in x 27ft 3in)
Range:	15,200km (8000nm) at 12 knots
Armament:	10 304mm (12in), 14 150mm (5.9in) guns
Powerplant:	Triple screw turbines
Performance:	23.5 knots

Kaiser Friedrich III

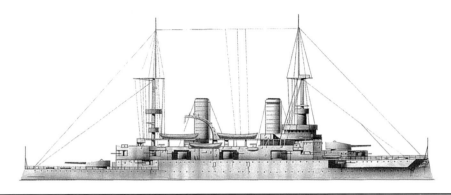

Kaiser Friedrich III was laid down in 1895 and completed in 1898. Six of her 152mm (6in) guns were in single turrets high on the superstructure, with the remainder in casemates. The 86.3mm (3.4in) guns were carried singly behind shields on the upper deck. She set a pattern for German pre-dreadnoughts of the period with their light main armament and triple screws. *Kaiser Friedrich III's* total armour weight was 3860 tonnes (3800 tons). She was fleet flagship in 1906, and was reconstructed between 1907–10. By 1916, however, she was hulked as being obsolete and was eventually scrapped in 1920. Other vessels in her class, all named after German emperors, were *Kaiser Barbarossa*, *Kaiser Wilhelm der Grosse*, *Kaiser Wilhelm II* and *Kaiser Karl der Grosse*. All except the last were modernised; new funnels and casemates were fitted, and pole masts replaced military masts.

Country:	Germany
Type:	Battleship
Launch date:	31 July 1896
Crew:	651
Displacement:	11,784 tonnes (11,599 tons)
Dimensions:	125.3m x 20.4m x 8.2m (411ft x 67ft x 27ft)
Range:	4170km (2250nm) at 12 knots
Armament:	Four 238mm (9.4in), 18 152mm (6in), 12 86.3mm (3.4in) guns
Powerplant:	Triple screw, triple expansion engines
Performance:	17 knots

Kamikaze

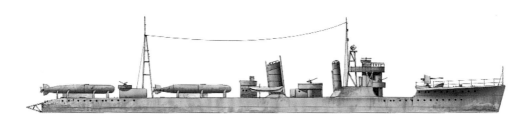

The name *Kamikaze* means 'Divine Wind', and was first applied to the typhoon that destroyed the fleet of Kubla Khan, sailing to invade Japan in 1281. Ordered between 1921 and 1922, the nine Kamikaze-class destroyers actually formed Group II of the preceding Minekaze class. They were the first destroyers in the Imperial Japanese Navy to be built with a bridge strengthened by steel plating. This gave them a high centre of gravity, which was counterbalanced by an increased displacement and slightly wider beam. The ships of this class had a distinguished record in World War II. In 1944 four were sunk by American submarines and a fifth in an air attack on Truk. *Kamikaze* survived the war and was surrendered at Singapore, but in June 1946, while trying to assist the repatriation ship *Kunashiri*, she became stranded on the same reef and was scrapped where she lay.

Country:	Japan
Type:	Destroyer
Launch date:	25 September 1922
Crew:	148
Displacement:	1676 tonnes (1650 tons)
Dimensions:	102.6m x 9m x 2.89m (336ft 3in x 29ft 6in x 9ft 6in)
Range:	6670km (3601nm)
Main armament:	Four 120mm (4.7in) guns; six 533mm (21in) torpedo tubes
Powerplant:	Two shafts, geared steam turbines
Performance:	37.5 knots

Kapitan Saken

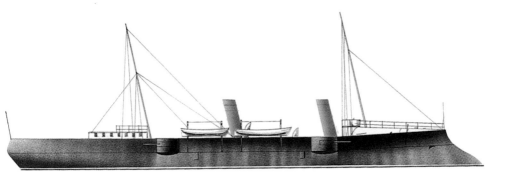

The *Kapitan Saken* was a powerful-looking vessel with twin funnels and a pronounced bow ram. She had two masts, the foremost of which was sited just in front of the forward funnel. Five of the torpedo tubes were in fixed positions: two facing ahead; one on each bow; one in the stern; and with the other two tubes on swivel mounts. Spare torpedoes were housed in racks on the lower deck and moved to the torpedo tubes on railway tracks that ran the whole length of the ship to loading poisitions at the rear of the tubes, an arrangement that saved a great deal of labour. The *Kapitan Saken*'s design was virtually identical to that of the previous torpedo gunboat, *Leitenant Ilin*, except that fewer guns were carried. She was scrapped in 1907. At this time, Russia's gunboats were considered a serious threat by other European navies.

Country:	Russia
Type:	Torpedo gunboat
Launch date:	12 May 1889
Crew:	125
Displacement:	610 tonnes (600 tons)
Dimensions:	64m x 7.3m x 3.3m (210ft x 24ft x 10ft)
Range:	Not known
Main armament:	Four 431mm (17in) torpedo tubes; four three-pounder guns
Powerplant:	Twin screws, vertical triple expansion engines
Performance:	18.5 knots

Kashin

Built as the world's first major class of warships to be powered by gas turbines, the Kashin class was produced from 1959 onwards at the Zhdanov shipyard in Leningrad (five units between 1962 and 1966) and at the 61 Kommuna (North) shipyard at Nikolaiev (15 units between 1959 and 1972). In 1972, one of the Nikolaiev-built ships, *Otvzhny*, foundered in the Black Sea following a catastrophic explosion and fire that raged out of control for five hours until the destroyer sank. Over 200 of her crew lost their lives, making this the worst peacetime naval disaster since the end of World War II. The last of the class, *Sderzhanny*, was completed to a revised design designated Kashin II, and three further units were built in the late 1970s for the Indian Navy, named *Rajput*, *Rana* and *Ranjit*. The Kashin class was prolific in all the Soviet Navy's operational areas.

Country:	Soviet Union
Type:	Destroyer
Launch date:	31 December 1960 (Komsomolets Ukrainy, first unit)
Crew:	280
Displacement:	4572 tonnes (4500 tons)
Dimensions:	144m x 15.8m x 4.8m (472ft 5in x 51ft 10in x 15ft 9in)
Range:	15,750km (8504nm)
Main armament:	Two twin 76mm (3in) guns; 4 533mm (21in) torpedo tubes; SA-N-1 SAMs; ASW rockets
Powerplant:	Two shafts, four gas turbines
Performance:	36 knots

Kaszub

Kaszub's design is based on that of the Russian Grisha class, but with many alterations. Built by the Northern Shipyard in Gdansk, *Kaszub* was to have been followed by a second vessel, but this was cancelled in 1989. However, there are still tentative plans to construct a class of up to seven more ships based on the *Kaszub* hull and carrying specialized equipment for anti-submarine warfare when funds become available. *Kaszub* was commissioned in March 1987 but was not fully fitted out until 1991, when the 76mm (3in) gun was installed. The ship also carries a 23mm (0.9in) gun aft, but there are plans to replace this with a vertical-launch SAM system in due course. *Kaszub* became operational in 1990 and was initially based with the Border Guard, but was transferred to the Polish Navy in 1991. She now exercises regularly with NATO forces in the Baltic.

Country:	Poland
Type:	Frigate
Launch date:	4 October 1986
Crew:	67
Displacement:	1202 tonnes (1183 tons)
Dimensions:	82.3m x 10m x 3.1m (270ft x 32ft 10in x 10ft 2in)
Range:	5629km (3038nm)
Main armament:	One 76mm (3in) gun; four 533mm (21in) torpedo tubes
Powerplant:	Two shafts, four diesel engines
Performance:	27 knots

Kelly

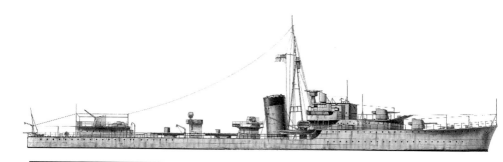

Launched in October 1938, HMS *Kelly* was one of a class which marked a considerable change in British destroyer design. The first single-funnelled class this century, the J, K, and I classes adopted the guns and the turrets used in the big vessels of the Tribal class, but mounted on a more easily built hull. The six 119mm (4.7in) Mk XII guns had a maximum elevation of 40 degrees, leaving air defence to the quadruple two-pounder 'pompom' abaft the funnel. This was a weakness that was to be highlighted by the loss early in the war of several vessels, including *Kelly*, to air attack, particularly dive-bombing. By the end of the war, survivors of this class were to mount up to 10 20mm (0.7in) cannon, giving a much more effective air defence. *Kelly* and her sister ship, *Kashmir*, were bombed and sunk by German dive-bombers off Crete on 23 May 1941.

Country:	Great Britain
Type:	Destroyer
Launch date:	25 October 1938
Crew:	218
Displacement:	1722 tonnes (1695 tons)
Dimensions:	108.7m x 10.9m x 2.75m (356ft 6in x 35ft 9in x 9ft)
Range:	4444km (2400nm)
Main armament:	Six 119mm (4.7in) guns
Powerplant:	Two-shaft geared turbines
Performance:	36 knots

Kidd

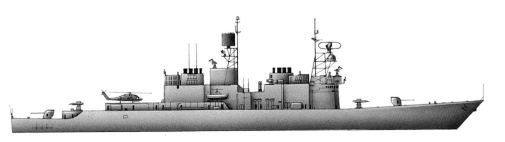

In 1974 the Iranian Government ordered six SAM-equipped versions of the Spruance-class destroyer for service in the Persian Gulf and the Indian Ocean. However, following the revolution in Iran (then Persia), two were cancelled in 1979 while the remaining four under construction were taken over by the US Navy as the Kidd class. These were the world's most powerfully armed, general-purpose destroyers at the time of their commissioning, and because of their origins, they were generally known in the US Navy as the Ayatollah class. The four ships were the *Kidd*, *Callaghan*, *Scott* and *Chandler*. The Kidd-class vessels were optimized for the area defence role, but they also had a powerful surface-to-surface and anti-submarine capability. The principal SAM armament is the Standard missile. They were all decommissioned by 1999 and have now been sold to Taiwan.

Country:	USA
Type:	Destroyer
Launch date:	11 August 1979
Crew:	368
Displacement:	9728 tonnes (9574 tons)
Dimensions:	171.6m x 16.8m x 9.1m (563ft x 55ft x 30ft)
Range:	14,824km (8004nm)
Main armament:	Two 127mm (5in) DP guns; Harpoon SSM; Standard SAM; six 324mm (12.75in) torpedo tubes
Powerplant:	Two shafts, four gas turbines
Performance:	32 knots

Kiev

Kiev was the first Soviet aircraft carrier to be built with a full flight deck and a purpose-built hull. She was laid down in September 1970 in the Black Sea Nikolayev Dockyard and completed in May 1975. The flight deck is angled, with most of the armament carried forward, comprising a full range of anti-ship, anti-air and anti-submarine missiles. Twenty-four of the SS-N-12 Shaddock type missiles were carried. The large bridge structure is set on *Kiev*'s starboard side, and housed an array of radar equipment. The ship joined the Soviet Northern Fleet in 1976. *Kiev* carried an air group of Yakovlev Yak-38 Forger VTOL fighter-bombers and anti-submarine helicopters. She is now a museum in China. Other vessels in the Kiev class were *Minsk*, *Novorossiysk* (both stricken) and *Admiral Gorshkov*, which has been refitted and sold to India.

Country:	Soviet Union
Type:	Aircraft carrier
Launch date:	26 December 1972
Crew:	1700
Displacement:	38,608 tonnes (38,000 tons)
Dimensions:	273m x 47.2m x 8.2m (895ft 8in x 154ft 10in x 27ft)
Range:	24,300km (13,500nm) at 10 knots
Armament:	Four 76.2mm (3in) guns, plus up to 136 missiles
Powerplant:	Quadruple screw turbines
Performance:	32 knots

Kilo class

Built at the river shipyard of Komsomolsk in the Russian Far East, the first medium-range Kilo-class submarine was launched early in 1980. By 1982 construction had also started at the Gorki shipyard, while export production began in 1985 at Sudomekh. In August 1985 the first operational Kilo deployed to the vast Vietnamese naval base at Cam Ranh Bay for weapon systems trials under tropical conditions, and in the following year the first sighting of a Kilo in the Indian Ocean was made by a warship of the Royal Australian Navy. The Kilo class has a more advanced hull form than the other contemporary Russian conventional submarine designs, and is more typical of western 'teardrop' submarine hulls. About 50 Kilos were still in service with seven navies in 2001, and Kilo production was continuing at the rate of two a year for export.

Country:	Soviet Union
Type:	Attack submarine
Launch date:	Early 1980 (first unit)
Crew:	45-50
Displacement:	Surfaced: 2494 tonnes (2455 tons), submerged: 3193 tonnes (3143 tons)
Dimensions:	69m x 9m x 7m (226ft 5in x 29ft 6in x 23ft)
Surface range:	11,112km (6000nm) at 7 knots
Armament:	Six 533mm (21in) torpedo tubes
Powerplant:	Single shaft, three diesels, three electric motors
Performance:	Surfaced: 15 knots, submerged: 24 knots

King Edward VII

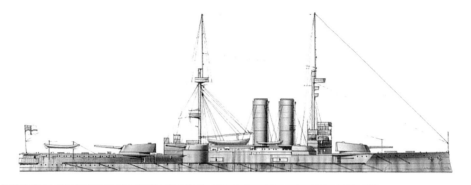

King Edward VII has the historical distinction of being the first British battleship built in the 20th century. She was laid down in 1902, completed three years later, and was first in a class of eight. Known throughout the service for her eccentric steering, she also suffered in having a mixed secondary armament which prevented her employing large enough weapons in high enough numbers. *King Edward VII* hit a German mine off northern Scotland in 1916 and sank after a 12-hour struggle. Other ships in this class were *Africa, Britannia, Commonwealth, Dominion, Hibernia, Hindustan* and *New Zealand*. In 1912 *Hibernia* was fitted with a flying-off platform, and on 9 May 1912 Lt C.R. Samson became the first pilot in the world to take off in an aircraft from a ship under way, flying a Short seaplane off the platform as *Hibernia* steamed into the wind at 10kt.

Country:	Great Britain
Type:	Battleship
Launch date:	27 July 1903
Crew:	777
Displacement:	17,566 tonnes (17,290 tons)
Dimensions:	138.3m x 23.8m x 7.72m (453ft 9in x 78ft x 25ft 8in)
Range:	12,970km (7000nm) at 10 knots
Armament:	Four 304mm (12in), four 230mm (9.2in) guns
Powerplant:	Twin shaft vertical triple expansion engine
Performance:	18.5 knots

Kirishima

Launched in 1913 as a Kongo class battlecruiser, *Kirishima* underwent reconstruction between 1927–1930 and, like the rest of the class, was reclassified as a battleship. Further rebuilding between 1934–1936 completely altered her aft, added over 393 tonnes (400 tons) of armour to her barbettes and increased her anti-aircraft armament. In December 1941 she was part of the escort to the carriers whose aircraft attacked Pearl Harbor; she subsequently covered Japanese landings at Rabaul and in the Dutch East Indies, and on 1 March 1942 she sank the destroyer USS *Edsall* south of Java. During the second Battle of Guadalcanal in November 1942, she fell victim to the accurate radar-directed gunfire of USS *Washington*. At night over a range of 7677m (8400yds) she was hit by nine 400mm (16in) and 40 127mm (5in) shells and had to be scuttled.

Country:	Japan
Type:	Battlecruiser
Launch date:	1 December 1913
Crew:	1437 (after 1936 re-fit)
Displacement:	32,491 tonnes (31,980 tons) as battleship
Dimensions:	219.6m x 222.1m x 9.7m (720ft 6in x 738ft 7in x 31ft 11in)
Range:	14,824km (8000nm) at 14 knots
Armament:	Eight 356mm (14in), 14 152mm (6in), eight 127mm (5in) guns
Powerplant:	Four shaft turbines
Performance:	30.4 knots

Kniaz Suvarov

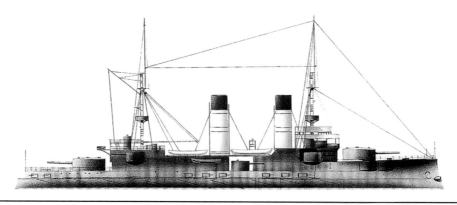

Launched in 1902 and completed in September 1904, *Kniaz Suvarov* was the Russian flagship at the Battle of Tsushima in May 1905, and was sunk by Japanese torpedoes. She was one of five vessels of the Borodino class. Her sister ships, *Borodino* and *Alexander,* were also sunk at Tsushima, while *Orel* surrendered to Japanese forces, later being renamed *Iwami.* The remaining ship in the class, *Slavia*, was not completed in time to join her ill-fated sisters. While en route to their fatal rendezvous, the Russian ships created a major diplomatic incident by opening fire on some British trawlers (which the crews mistook for Japanese torpedo boats!) in the North Sea. Gibraltar was put on a war footing and 28 British warships stood ready to intercept and destroy the Russian Pacific Squadron for several hours before the situation was defused.

Country:	Russia
Type:	Battleship
Launch date:	25 September 1902
Crew:	835
Displacement:	13,730 tonnes (13,513 tons)
Dimensions:	121m x 23m x 7.9m (397ft x 76ft 2in x 26ft 2in)
Range:	12,274km (6624nm) at 10 knots
Armament:	12 152mm (6in), four 304mm (12in), 20 11-pounder guns
Powerplant:	Twin screw, vertical triple expansion engines
Performance:	17.5 knots

Knox class

The Knox class is similar to the Garcia and Brooke designs from which it is developed, but is slightly larger because of the use of non-pressure fired boilers. It was designed in the early 1960s. The first vessels entered US Navy service in 1969, the last units of the 46-strong class being delivered in 1974. They are specialized ASW ships and have been heavily criticised because of their single propeller and solitary 127mm (5in) gun armament. A five-ship class based on the Knox design but with a Mk22 missile launcher for 16 Standard SM-1MR missiles was built for the Spanish Navy. Knox-class frigates have been used over the years to test individual prototype weapon and sensor systems, such as the Phalanx close-range anti-aircraft system. Some units were assigned to the US Naval Reserve Force in the late 1980s as replacements for ageing destroyers.

Country:	USA
Type:	Frigate
Launch date:	19 November 1966
Crew:	283
Displacement:	3939 tonnes (3877 tons)
Dimensions:	133.5m x 14.3m x 4.6m (438ft x 46ft 10in x 15ft)
Range:	9260km (5000nm)
Main armament:	One 127mm (5in) DP gun; SAMs; ASW and anti-ship missiles
Powerplant:	Geared steam turbines
Performance:	27 knots

Kongo

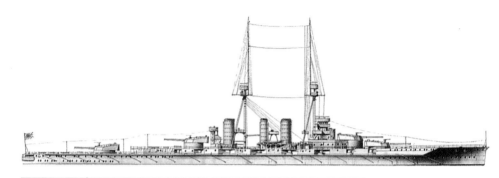

Completed in 1912, *Kongo* and her sisters, *Hiei*, *Haruna* and *Kirishima*, were inspired by the design and performance of British battlecruisers, *Kongo* herself being built in a British yard. Following the lessons of World War I and the naval treaties of the 1930s, the class was rebuilt with greater deck armour and anti-torpedo bulges. The development of fast carrier groups also led to further remodelling, including an improvement of machinery which took the speed of the class up to 30 knots. All four vessels were sunk during World War II. *Kongo* was torpedoed by the US submarine *Sealion* in November 1944. Of the others, *Hiei* and *Kirishima* were both sunk in the battle for Guadalcanal, the former receiving 50 shell hits, one bomb hit from a B-17, and two torpedo hits from aircraft operating from the USS *Enterprise*. *Haruna* was sunk by US aircraft at Kure in July 1945.

Country:	Japan
Type:	Battleship
Launch date:	18 May 1912
Crew:	1221
Displacement:	27,940 tonnes (27,500 tons)
Dimensions:	214.7m x 28m x 8.4m (704ft x 92ft x 27ft 7in)
Range:	14, 824km (8000nm) at 14 knots
Armament:	Eight 356mm (14in), 16 152mm (6in) guns
Powerplant:	Four shaft geared turbines
Performance:	27.5 knots

Kongo

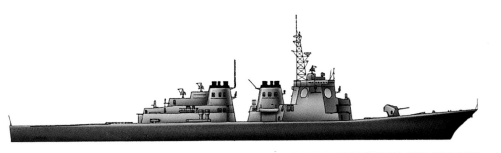

The *Kongo* was commissioned in March 1983 and was followed by four more vessels of her class, the *Kirishima*, *Myoko*, and *Choukai*, the latter being commissioned in March 1998. The ships are enlarged and improved versions of the American Arleigh Burke destroyers and are armed with a lightweight version of the Aegis air defence system. As well as providing area air defence for the fleet, the ships also contribute towards the air defence of mainland Japan, standing well out from the Home Islands in the role of air defence picket ships. Although designated as destroyers, the vessels are in fact of cruiser size. Their entry into Japanese Navy service was slowed down by a combination of cost and the reluctance of the US Congress to release Aegis technology. The highly sophisticated Aegis is the US Navy's primary air defence system.

Country:	Japan
Type:	Destroyer
Launch date:	26 September 1991
Crew:	307
Displacement:	9637 tonnes (9485 tons)
Dimensions:	161m x 21m x 10m (528ft 2in x 68ft 11in x 32ft 9in)
Range:	7238km (3908nm)
Main armament:	One 127mm (5in) gun; Harpoon SSM; Standard SAM; six 324mm (12.75in) torpedo tubes; vertical launch ASROC
Powerplant:	Two shafts, four gas turbines
Performance:	30 knots

Koni class

Although constructed in the Soviet Union at the Zelenodolsk shipyard on the Black Sea, the Koni class of frigate was intended solely for export, only one unit being retained by the Russians as a crew training ship for the naval personnel from those countries whose navies bought the vessels. There were two distinct sub-classes, the Koni Type II class differing from the Koni Type I class in having the space between the funnel and the aft superstructure occupied by an extra deckhouse believed to contain air-conditioning units for use in tropical climates. Two units sold to Yugoslavia were locally modified to carry SS-N-2B Styx anti-ship cruise missiles. Others were sold to Cuba and the former German Democratic Republic. It appears, however, that sales of the type never reached the level that the Soviet Union had anticipated.

Country:	Soviet Union
Type:	Frigate
Launch date:	completed 1978 (Delfin)
Crew:	110
Displacement:	1930 tonnes (1900 tons)
Dimensions:	95m x 12.8m x 4.2m (311ft 8 in x 42ft x 13ft 8in)
Range:	4076km (2200nm)
Main armament:	Two twin 76mm (3in) guns and two twin 30mm(1.1in) guns; SAMs
Powerplant:	Three shafts, two gas turbines and one diesel
Performance:	27 knots

Korietz

Korietz was laid down in 1885 at Stockholm. She was a barquentine-rigged vessel, with the two 203mm (8in) guns firing forward from sponsons protected by armour shields. The 152mm (6in) guns were mounted aft, and four 107mm (4.2in) weapons were mounted on the broadside. She and her sister *Mandjur* were heavily armed for their size, and ideal for patrol work, although they were considered to be poor sailers, possibly because they carried too great a weight of canvas for their size. Both featured a ram bow, which was much more pronounced in *Korietz* than in her sister ship. On 9 February 1904 *Korietz* was heavily damaged in action with the Japanese armoured cruiser squadron at Port Arthur, and was subsequently scuttled in Korea. The name *Korietz* was later allocated to a vessel of the 1905 Gilyak class.

Country:	Russia
Type:	Gunboat
Launch date:	August 1886
Crew:	179
Displacement:	1290 tonnes (1270 tons)
Dimensions:	66.7m x 10.6m x 3.7m (219ft x 35ft x 12ft 4in)
Range:	Not known
Main armament:	One 152mm (6in) and two 203mm (8in) guns
Powerplant:	Twin screws, horizontal compound engines
Performance:	13.3 knots

Krivak II class

In 1970 the first unit of the Krivak I class of large anti-submarine warfare vessel entered service with the Soviet Navy. Built at the Zhdanov shipyard in Leningrad, the Kaliningrad shipyard and the Kamysh-Burun shipyard in Kerch between 1971 and 1982, 21 units of this variant were constructed. In 1976 the Krivak II class, of which 11 were built at Kaliningrad between that year and 1981, was first seen. This differed from the previous class in having single 100mm (3.9in) guns substituted for the twin 76mm (3in) turrets of the earlier version, and a larger variable-depth sonar at the stern. Both classes were re-rated to patrol ship status in the late 1970s, possibly in the light of what some observers considered to be deficiencies in terms of limited endurance for ASW operations in open waters. An improved Krivak III class was later developed, and three export versions have been sold to India.

Country:	Soviet Union
Type:	Frigate
Launch date:	1975 (Rezvyy)
Crew:	220
Displacement:	3759 tonnes (3700 tons)
Dimensions:	123.5m x 14m x 4.7m (405ft 2in x 45ft 11in x 15ft 5in)
Range:	5188km (2800nm)
Main armament:	Two single 100mm (3.9in) DP guns; SAMs; ASW missiles; eight 533mm (21in) torpedo tubes
Powerplant:	Two shafts, four gas turbines
Performance:	32 knots

Kurfürst Friedrich Wilhelm

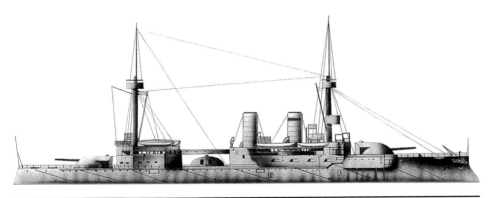

Kurfürst Friedrich Wilhelm of the Brandenburg class was one of four powerful pre-dreadnoughts that formed the basis of the German Navy in the early 1900s. Laid down in 1890 and completed in 1893, she was one of the first German warships to be fitted with wireless telegraph. Her main armament was installed in three twin turrets on the centreline; an amidships turret with guns of shorter calibre had a restricted field of fire. She was sold to Turkey in 1910, becoming *Heireddin Barbarossa*. In Turkish service she took part in the bombardment of Varna in 1912, and in December that year she was damaged in action with a Greek naval squadron off the Dardanelles. She was again damaged in the same area a week later, and on 8 August 1915 she was torpedoed and sunk by the British submarine *E11* in the Dardanelles with the loss of 253 lives.

Country:	Germany
Type:	Battleship
Launch date:	30 June 1891
Crew:	568
Displacement:	10,210 tonnes (10,050 tons)
Dimensions:	115.7m x 19.5m x 7.9m (379ft 7in x 64ft x 26ft)
Range:	8338km (4500nm) at 10 knots
Armament:	Six 280mm (11in), six 105mm (4.1in), eight 88mm (3.4in) guns
Powerplant:	Twin screw, triple expansion engines
Performance:	14 knots

L3

L3 was one of a large class of Russian submarines. On the night of 16 April 1943, commanded by Capt 3rd Class Konovalov, she intercepted a German convoy of eight ships evacuating refugees from the Hela peninsula in the Baltic to the west, and sank the large steamship *Goya*. Of the 6385 persons on board, only 165 were rescued. It was the climax of a long and successful operational career that began with minelaying operations in the Baltic in June 1941, days after the German invasion of Russia. Russian submarine operations in the Baltic were a considerable threat to German supply and reinforcement traffic. Minelaying continued to be *L3*'s principal occupation, and she did not register her first success until August 1942, when she sank the 5580-tonne (5492-ton) steamer *C.F. Liljevalch*. *L3* served for several years after the war, and was scrapped in 1959.

Country:	Soviet Union
Type:	Attack submarine
Launch date:	July 1931
Crew:	50
Displacement:	Surfaced: 1219 tonnes (1200 tons), submerged: 1574 tonnes (1550 tons)
Dimensions:	81m x 7.5m x 4.8m (265ft 9in x 24ft 7in x 15ft 9in)
Surface range:	11,112km (6000nm) at 9 knots
Armament:	Six 533mm (21in) torpedo tubes; one 100mm (3.9in) gun
Powerplant:	Twin screws, diesel/electric motors
Performance:	Surfaced: 15 knots, submerged: 9 knots

L23

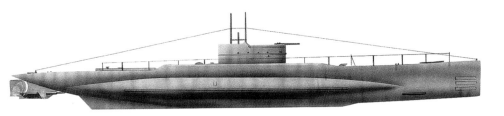

L23 was one of the last surviving units of the large L class of submarines, 17 of which were built after the end of World War I. One of the L-class boats, *L12*, torpedoed and sank the German submarine *UB90* on 16 October 1918 while the enemy boat was recharging her batteries on the surface of the North Sea at night. The second boat of the class, *L2*, was subjected to a fierce gunfire and depth charge attack by American warships escorting a convoy in February 1918, one shell scoring a direct hit on the pressure hull just behind the conning tower as the boat re-surfaced. Fortunately, the Americans realised their mistake in time to avert a tragedy. Three boats, *L23*, *L26* and *L27*, served on training duties in World War II; *L23* foundered under tow off Nova Scotia en route to the breaker's yard in May 1946.

Country:	Great Britain
Type:	Attack submarine
Launch date:	1 July 1919
Crew:	36
Displacement:	Surfaced: 904 tonnes (890 tons), submerged: 1097 tonnes (1080 tons)
Dimensions:	72.7m x 7.2m x 3.4m (238ft 6in x 23ft 8in x 11ft 2in)
Surface range:	8338km (4500nm)
Armament:	Four 533mm (21in) torpedo tubes; one 102mm (4in) gun
Powerplant:	Twin screws, diesel/electric motors
Performance:	Surfaced: 17.5 knots, submerged: 10.5 knots

La Fayette

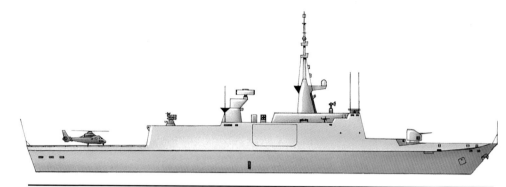

The first three of five La Fayette-class frigates were ordered in July 1988, but construction was delayed because of funding problems. *La Fayette* was commissioned in March 1996, followed by *Surcouf, Courbet, Aconit* and *Guepratte*. The La Fayette class-frigates are intended for out-of-area operations on overseas stations, and the first three are assigned to the Indian Ocean. Super Frelon helicopters may be operated from the flight deck, and the vessels can launch inflatable boats from a hidden hatch in the stern. The ships incorporate many stealth features, and extensive use is made of radar-absorbent paint. Protruding equipment is either hidden or fitted as flush as possible. Exports include an anti-submarine warfare version for Taiwan (Kang Ding), an anti-air version for Saudi Arabia (F3000S) and six Project Delta stealth frigates for Singapore.

Country:	France
Type:	Frigate
Launch date:	13 June 1992
Crew:	139
Displacement:	3658 tonnes (3600 tons)
Dimensions:	124.2m x 15.4m x 5.9m (407ft 6in x 50ft 6in x 19ft 5in)
Range:	14,467km (7812nm)
Main armament:	One 100mm (3.9in) DP gun; Exocet SSM; Crotale SAM
Powerplant:	Two shafts, four diesel engines
Performance:	25 knots

Leberecht Maass

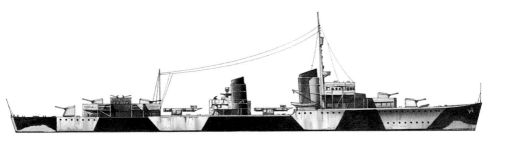

The Type 34 or Maass class were the first German destroyers to be built since World War I. Of conventional layout, their only major problem was lack of freeboard, which had disagreeable consequences in heavy seas. All 16 ships were launched between 1937 and 1939. Five were sunk by Royal Navy destroyer forces in the Second Battle of Narvik in April 1943. Of the remainder, *Leberecht Maass* and *Max Schulz* were mined and sunk in the North Sea on 22 February 1940; *Hermann Schoemann* was sunk in Arctic waters by the RN cruiser HMS *Edinburgh* on 2 May 1942; *Bruno Heinemann* was mined and sunk in the English Channel on 25 January 1942; *Friedrich Eckoldt* was sunk in the Barents Sea by the RN cruisers *Jamaica* and *Sheffield* on 31 December 1942; one was broken up post-war in the UK; and two went to the Soviet Union in 1946.

Country:	Germany
Type:	Destroyer
Launch date:	18 August 1935
Crew:	315
Displacement:	3211 tonnes (3160 tons)
Dimensions:	119m x 11.3m x 3.8m (390ft 5in x 37ft 1in x 12ft 6in)
Range:	8135km (4393nm)
Main armament:	Five single 127mm (5in) guns; two quadruple 533mm (21in) torpedo tubes; up to 60 mines
Powerplant:	Two-shaft geared turbines
Performance:	30 knots

Leonardo Da Vinci

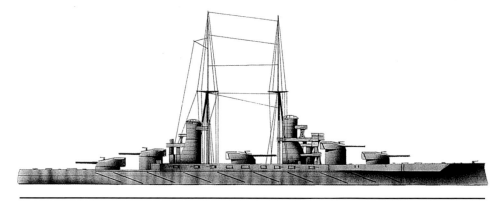

*L*eonardo da Vinci and her two sisters were an improvement on the previous Dante Alighieri class, having 13 big guns mounted in five centreline turrets, with superfiring twin turrets fore and aft. Instead of carrying the secondary armament in twin turrets, the battery was concentrated amidships in casemates. Machinery developed 31,000hp, and range at 10 knots was 8640km (4800 miles). *Leonardo da Vinci* was completed in 1914, and spent her war service in the Adriatic. On 2 August 1916 she caught fire, blew up and capsized at Taranto. The explosion, which was caused either by unstable cordite or Austrian sabotage, left 249 dead. In September 1919 she was refloated upside down and was righted in January 1921. However, she was not repaired and was broken up in 1923. Her two sister ships were *Conte de Cavour* and *Giulio Cesare*.

Country:	Italy
Type:	Battleship
Launch date:	14 October 1911
Crew:	1235
Displacement:	25,250 tonnes (25,086 tons)
Dimensions:	176m x 28m x 9.3m (577ft 9in x 91ft 10in x 30ft 10in)
Range:	8640km (4800nm) at 10 knots
Armament:	13 304mm (12in), 18 120mm (4.7in) guns
Powerplant:	Quadruple screw turbines
Performance:	21.6 knots

Lexington

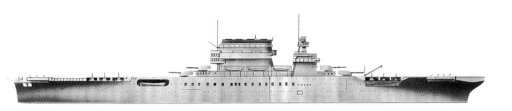

exington was the first fleet aircraft carrier completed for the US Navy. She was laid down in 1921 as a battlecruiser, but work was stopped as a result of the 1922 Washington Naval Treaty. Her design was then changed to that of an aircraft carrier, though her cruiser-type hull form was retained. A 137m x 21m (450ft x 70ft) hangar was installed and for many years she remained the largest aircraft carrier afloat. In May 1942 she was operating as part of Task Force 11, one of three Allied naval task forces which combined to thwart a Japanese landing at Port Moresby, New Guinea, in the Battle of the Coral Sea. On the morning of 8 May the opposing carrier forces sighted one another and flew off their aircraft (90 Japanese and 78 American) to attack. *Lexington* (Capt F.C. Sherman) was hit by two torpedoes and three bombs and was abandoned, being sunk later by the destroyer USS *Phelps*.

Country:	USA
Type:	Aircraft carrier
Launch date:	3 October 1925
Crew:	2327
Displacement:	48,463 tonnes (47,700 tons)
Dimensions:	270.6m x 32.2m x 9.9m (88ft x 105ft 8in x 32ft 6in)
Range:	18,900km (10,500nm) at 10 knots
Armament:	Eight 203mm (8in), 12 127mm (5in) guns, 80 aircraft
Powerplant:	Quadruple screw turbo electric drive
Performance:	33.2 knots

Lion

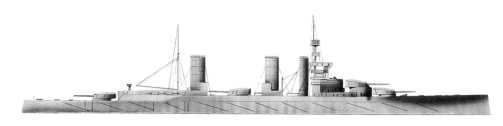

The Lion class of ship were the first battlecruisers to surpass battleships in terms of size. Launched in 1910 and completed in 1912, *Lion* had eight 343mm (13.5in) guns, and these were mounted in twin turrets, two forward with one superfiring, one aft and one amidships (the latter having a restricted arc of fire) between the second and third funnels. During World War I *Lion* was the flagship of the Grand Fleet's Battlecruiser Fleet (commanded by Admiral Sir David Beatty). On 24 January 1915 *Lion* received a total of 21 shell hits during the Battle of Dogger Bank, and during the Battle of Jutland in 1916 she narrowly escaped destruction when she was severely damaged by twelve shells, with the loss of 99 of her crew. She was eventually sold and broken up at Blyth, Northumberland, in 1924.

Country:	Great Britain
Type:	Battlecruiser
Launch date:	6 August 1910
Crew:	997
Displacement:	30,154 tonnes (29,680 tons)
Dimensions:	213.3m x 27m x 8.7m (700ft x 88ft 6in x 28ft 10in)
Range:	10,098km (5610nm) at 10 knots
Armament:	16 102mm (4.2in), eight 343mm (13.5in) guns
Powerplant:	Quadruple screw turbines
Performance:	27 knots

Littorio

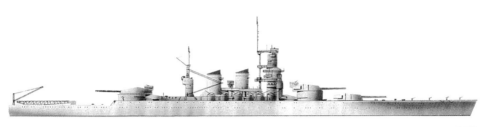

ittorio was one of the last battleships to be built for the Italian Navy. Completed in 1940, she was also the first Italian battleship to be commissioned after World War I. Her impressive outline was all the more striking due to the raised height of the aft turret, which was designed to avoid blast damage to the two fighter planes carried on the poop deck. On 12 November 1940 she was severely damaged by three torpedoes dropped by Swordfish aircraft during the Royal Navy's attack on Taranto, and she received further damage in June 1942 when she was torpedoed by British aircraft during an attack on a Malta convoy. In 1943 she was renamed *Italia*, and after the Italian surrender she was damaged by a German radio-controlled bomb. She was interned on the Suez Canal's Great Bitter Lake until February 1946. Stricken in 1948, she was broken up in 1960.

Country:	Italy
Type:	Battleship
Launch date:	22 August 1937
Crew:	1950
Displacement :	46,698 tonnes (45,963 tons)
Dimensions:	237.8m x 32.9m x 9.6m (780ft 2in x 108ft x 31ft 6in)
Range:	8487km (4580nm) at 16 knots
Armament:	Nine 380mm (15in), 12 152mm (6in), four 120mm (4.7in) 11 89mm (3.5in) guns
Powerplant:	Quadruple screw turbines
Performance:	28 knots

Lord Nelson

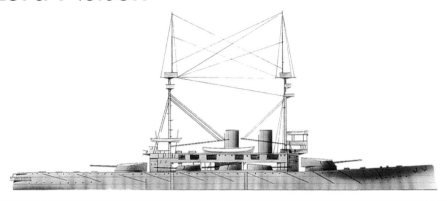

*L*ord Nelson and her sister *Agamemnon* were the last pre-dreadnoughts built for the Royal Navy. *Lord Nelson* was completed in October 1908. The 305mm (12in) guns were in twin turrets, with the 233mm (9.2in) guns in a mix of twin and single turrets on the broadside. The main belt ran her full length, supplemented by an upper belt which ran to the base of the 'Y' turret. She was further protected by a number of solid bulkheads, the first to be fitted to a British battleship. She saw extensive service during World War I, a notable action being the bombardment of the Narrows at the Dardanelles on 7 March 1915. *Lord Nelson* and *Agamemnon* had engaged Turkish forts with direct gunfire at a range of 12,000 – 14,000 yd, putting two forts out of action. The British ships were covered by the French battleships *Gaulois*, *Charlemagne*, *Bouvet* and *Suffren*. *Lord Nelson* was broken up in 1920.

Country:	Great Britain
Type:	Battleship
Launch date:	4 September 1906
Crew:	900
Displacement :	17,945 tonnes (17,663 tons)
Dimensions:	135m x 24m x 7.9m (443ft 6in x 79ft 6in x 26ft)
Range:	17,010km (9180nm) at 10 knots
Armament:	Four 304mm (12in), ten 233mm (9.2in) guns
Powerplant:	Twin screw, triple expansion engines
Performance:	18.7 knots

Los Angeles

The lead ship of this class, *Los Angeles*, was commissioned on 13 November 1976. She was followed by 52 more, the last of which, *Cheyenne*, was commissioned on 13 September 1996. They are nuclear attack submarines (SSN), fulfilling a variety of roles: land attack with onboard GDC/Hughes Tomahawk TLAM-N missiles, anti-ship with the Harpoon SSM and anti-submarine Mk48 and ADCAP (Advanced Capability) torpedoes, first fired by the USS *Norfolk* on 23 July 1988. Nine of the class were involved in the Gulf War of 1991, two firing Tomahawk missiles at targets in Iraq from stations in the eastern Mediterranean. From SN719 (USS *Providence*) onwards all are equipped with the vertical launch system. Eleven of the Los Angeles class have already been retired; most of the class will be withdrawn from service from 2010 onwards.

Country:	USA
Type:	Attack submarine
Launch date:	6 April 1974
Crew:	133
Displacement:	Surfaced: 6180 tonnes (6082 tons), submerged: 7038 tonnes (6927 tons)
Dimensions:	110.3m x 10.1m x 9.9m (362ft x 33ft x 32ft 3in)
Range:	Unlimited
Armament:	Four 533mm (21in) torpedo tubes; Tomahawk Land Attack Cruise Missiles, Harpoon SSM
Powerplant:	Single shaft, nuclear PWR, turbines
Performance:	Surfaced: 20 knots, submerged: 32 knots

Lupo

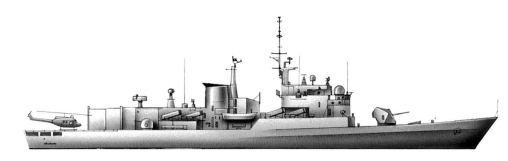

Commissioned between September 1977 and March 1980, and originally described as modified Alpinos, the four ships of the Lupo class – *Lupo, Sagittario, Perseo* and *Orsa* – underwent a mid-life update between 1991 and 1994. This included the installation of a low-altitude CORA SPS-702 search radar, new gyros, and new communications, including SATCOM. Similar vessels were built for Peru (4), Venezuela (6), and Iraq (4), but the Iraqi ships were not delivered because of the international situation and were taken over by the Italian Navy as the Artigliere class. They are the *Artigliere* (Iraqi name *Hittin*), *Aviere* (*Thi Qar*), *Bersagliere* (*Al Yarmouk*) and *Granatiere* (*Al Qadsiya*). The vessels are officially described as Fleet Patrol Ships. Two are based at Augusta and two at Brindisi, and they exercise regularly with units of the US Sixth Fleet.

Country:	Italy
Type:	Frigate
Launch date:	29 July 1976
Crew:	185
Displacement:	2565 tonnes (2525 tons)
Dimensions:	113.2m x 11.3m x 3.7m (371ft 4in x 37ft 1in x 12ft 1in)
Range:	6997km (3778nm)
Main armament:	One 127mm (5in) gun; OTO Melara Taseo SSM; Sea Sparrow SAM; six 324mm (12.75in) torpedo tubes, 1 helicopter
Powerplant:	Two shafts, two gas turbines, two diesels
Performance:	35 knots

Lutjens

The three ships of the Lutjens class – *Lutjens*, *Mölders* and *Rommel* – are modified Charles F. Adams class destroyers, fitted out to meet West German requirements. *Mölders* (named after Major Werner Mölders, a leading wartime Luftwaffe ace who was killed in 1941) was completed in March 1984; *Rommel* (named after Field Marshal Erwin Rommel, the 'Desert Fox') in July 1985; and *Lutjens* herself, named after Admiral Günther Lutjens, who went down with the battleship *Bismarck* in May 1941. All three ships underwent a substantial weapons upgrade in the early 1990s. The vessels show some diferences from the Charles F. Adams class in general outline, especially in the shape of the funnels. They were expected to have a life of at least 30 years, but *Rommel* was decommissioned in June 1999.

Country:	USA/Germany
Type:	Destroyer
Launch date:	11 August 1967
Crew:	337
Displacement:	4572 tonnes (4500 tons)
Dimensions:	132.2m x 14.3m x 6.1m (437ft x 47ft x 20ft)
Range:	7238km (3908nm)
Main armament:	Two 127mm (5in) guns; Harpoon SSM; Standard SAM; six 324mm (12.75in) torpedo tubes
Powerplant:	Two shafts, two turbines
Performance:	32 knots

Madina class

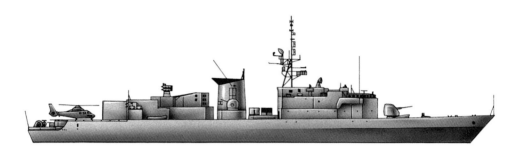

Frigates form the core of Saudi Arabia's navy, which also has some corvettes and fast attack craft armed with missiles. The four frigates of the Madina class – *Madina*, *Hofouf*, *Abha* and *Taif* – were ordered from France by Saudi Arabia in 1980 under a programme called Sawari I. The agreement specified that as well as carrying out the contruction work, France was to provide supplies and technical assistance. The vessels, all of which were delivered between 1985 and 1986, have been progressively upgraded during the 1990s. Work on *Madina* began in December 1995 and was completed in April 1997; work on *Hofouf* started in October 1996 and was completed in 1998. The other two ships were expected to be returned to service between 1999 and 2000. The vessels carry a Dauphin 2 helicopter which can provide mid-course guidance for SSMs.

Country:	France/Saudi Arabia
Type:	Frigate
Launch date:	1997
Crew:	179
Displacement:	2906 tonnes (2870 tons)
Dimensions:	115m x 12.5m x 4.9m (377ft 4in x 41ft x 16ft)
Range:	12,867km (6947nm)
Main armament:	One 100mm (3.9in) gun; four 40mm (1.5in) AA; OTO Melara/Matra Otomat SSM; Crotale SAM; four 533mm (21in) torpedo tubes
Powerplant:	Two shafts, four diesel engines
Performance:	30 knots

Maestrale class

The first six Maestrale-class vessels were ordered in 1976 and completed in 1980. All but one (*Grecale*) were built at Rio Trigoso. The Maestrale class is essentially a stretched version of the Lupo design, with fewer weapons and a greater emphasis on anti-submarine warfare. The increase in length and beam over the earlier Lupo ships was to provide for a fixed hangar installation and a variable-depth sonar housing at the stern. The improvements resulted in better seaworthiness and habitability, plus the space required to carry and operate a second light helicopter. However, to compensate for this, the class carries four fewer SSMs, and because of the extra tonnage has suffered a speed reduction of about three knots. There are eight vessels in the class: *Maestrale, Grecale, Libeccio, Schirocco, Aliseo, Euro, Espero* and *Zeffiro*.

Country:	Italy
Type:	Frigate
Launch date:	2 February 1981
Crew:	224
Displacement:	3251 tonnes (3200 tons)
Dimensions:	122.7m x 12.9m x 8.4m (402ft 7in x 42ft 4in x 27ft 7in)
Range:	8334km (4500nm)
Main armament:	One 127mm (5in) DP gun; two twin 40mm (1.5in) CIWS; two triple 324mm (12.75in) torpedo tubes
Powerplant:	Two shafts, two gas turbines and two diesels
Performance:	32 knots

Magenta

Launched in 1861, *Magenta* and her sister *Solferno* were the only two-decker, broadside ironclads to be built. The armour was concentrated amidships where the guns were housed on main and upper decks, with shotproof transverse bulkheads. The two-tier placing gave the upper-deck guns increased elevation and range, as well as lightening the ends of the vessel. *Magenta* was an imposing-looking ship, with a pronounced tumble-home to the hull and a prominent ram. On 31 October 1875 she blew up as a result of a fire that started in the wardroom galley. *Magenta*'s sister vessel, *Solferino* – named after the bloody French and Sardinian victory over Austria in June 1859 – remained in first-line service for ten years before being placed in reserve in 1871 and broken up in 1884. She was the only French ironclad with a figurehead, a golden eagle.

Country:	France
Type:	Ironclad
Launch date:	22 June 1861
Crew:	674
Displacement :	6832 tonnes (6715 tons)
Dimensions:	86m x 57.7m x 8.4m (282ft x 56ft 8in x 27ft 8in)
Range:	2913km (1840nm) at 10 knots
Armament:	Two 223mm (8.8in) howitzers, 34 162mm (6.4in) and 16 55-pounder guns
Powerplant:	Single screw, horizontal return connecting rod engine
Performance:	13 knots

Maine

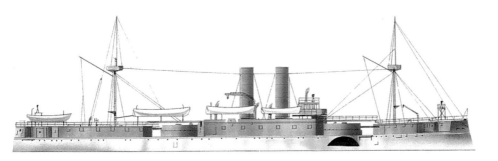

Launched in 1889, initial designs for *Maine* showed a three-masted sail rig, but this was abandoned and she entered service in 1895 with two military masts instead. In January 1898 she was sent to Havana, Cuba, to protect US interests there, but in February she was sunk by an explosion in her forward magazine. This was thought to be the result of Spanish sabotage, and war began between the USA and Spain the following month. The wreck was raised in 1912 and evidence suggested that a coal bunker fire had been the cause of the tragedy. The war with Spain gained the USA a number of territories. Cuba was occupied until 1902, after which America was guaranteed political control and commercial dominance; Hawaii was annexed; and the Philippines, although at first seen as a major prize, cost over 4000 American lives in suppressing a rebellion that lasted three years.

Country:	USA
Type:	Battleship
Launch date:	18 November 1889
Crew:	374
Displacement :	6789 tonnes (7180 tons)
Dimensions:	98.9m x 17.4m x 6.9m (318ft x 57ft x 21ft 6in)
Range:	6670km (3600nm) at 10 knots
Armament:	Four 254mm (10in), six 152mm (6in) guns
Powerplant:	Twin screw, triple expansion engines
Performance:	16.4 knots

Majestic

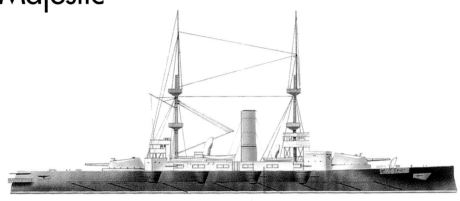

Completed in 1895, *Majestic*, together with her eight sisters, proved to be the best battleships of the 1890s, and set the pattern for all battleship design until the coming of *Dreadnought* in 1905. Designer Sir William White used improved armour, allowing for adequate protection at less cost in weight. The armoured hull curved down to meet the lower edge of the belt, so increasing internal protection. In December 1904 she suffered a coal gas explosion while in the Channel, and in July 1912 she was damaged in a collision with her sister ship *Victorious* (the others were *Caesar, Hannibal, Illustrious, Jupiter, Magnificent, Mars* and *Prince George*). After escort duty and Channel patrols, she was sent to the Mediterranean. *Majestic* was sunk in the Dardanelles on 27 May 1915, after being struck by two torpedoes from the German submarine *U21*.

Country:	Great Britain
Type:	Battleship
Launch date:	31 January 1895
Crew:	672
Displacement:	16,317 tonnes (16,060 tons)
Dimensions:	128.3m x 22.8m x 8.2m (421ft x 75ft x 27ft)
Range:	14,082km (7600nm) at 10 knots
Armament:	Four 304mm (12in), 12 152mm (6in) guns
Powerplant:	Twin screw, triple expansion engines
Performance:	17 knots

Marsopa

***M**arsopa* is one of four Daphne-class boats of French design manufactured under licence in Spain, the others being *Delfin, Tonina* and *Narval*. All the Spanish boats underwent updates and modifications similar to those applied to the French vessels. The Daphne class, dogged by misfortune in its early operational days, went on to be an export success; in addition to the 11 French and four Spanish units, Portugal received the *Albacore, Barracuda, Cachalote* and *Delfin,* while Pakistan took delivery of the *Hangor, Shushuk* and *Mangro* (and also, later, Portugal's *Cachalote,* which was renamed *Ghazi*). In 1971 the *Hangor* made the first submarine attack since World War II, sinking the Indian frigate *Khukri* during the Indo-Pakistan war. South Africa also received three boats of this type.

Country:	Spain
Type:	Attack submarine
Launch date:	15 March 1974
Crew:	45
Displacement:	Surfaced: 884 tonnes (870 tons), submerged: 1062 tonnes (1045 tons)
Dimensions:	58m x 7m x 4.6m (189ft 8in x 22ft 4in x 15ft)
Surface range:	8338km (4300nm) at 5 knots
Armament:	Twelve 552mm (21.7in) torpedo tubes
Powerplant:	Two diesels, two electric motors
Performance:	Surfaced: 13.5 knots, submerged: 16 knots

MAS 9

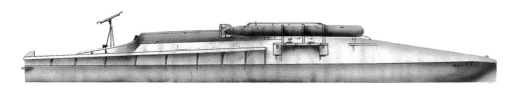

L aunched in 1916, *MAS 9* was one of a group of unusual vessels designed for
rapid attack by Engineer Bisio, and built by SVAN in Venice. Total crew for each
vessel numbered eight. The small size of the boats made them very difficult targets
for the enemy, espcially when manouevring at high speed. Torpedoes were carried
one each side amidships, on the whaleback foredeck. One night in December 1917,
MAS 9, commanded by Luigi Rizzo, successfully penetrated Trieste harbour and
sank the Austrian battleship *Wien*. The latter was an elderly second-class
battleship, launched in 1895, which had been used as a gunnery training ship
during the early years of World War I. *MAS 9* was discarded in 1922. Another boat
of this class, MAS 15, torpedoed and sank the Austro-Hungarian dreadnought Szent
Istvan off Premuda Island, on 10 June 1918.

Country:	Italy
Type:	Torpedo boat
Launch date:	1916
Crew:	8
Displacement:	16 tonnes (16 tons)
Dimensions:	16m x 2.6m x 1.2m (52ft 6in x 8ft 8in x 4ft)
Range:	Not known
Main armament:	One 47mm (1.85in) gun; two 450mm (17.7in) torpedo tubes
Powerplant:	Twin screws, petrol engines
Top speed:	25.2 knots

Masséna

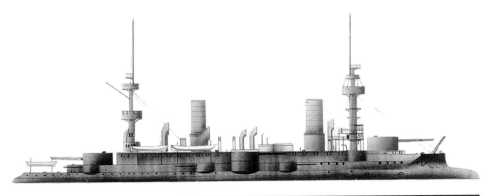

Completed in 1898, *Masséna* was the first French warship to be constructed with triple screws. The ship itself had a long, sleek hull, a pronounced tumble-home and a prominent bow ram. Her 304mm (12in) guns were housed in single turrets, one high up on the bows and the other placed right aft, at main deck level. The 270mm (10.8in) guns were mounted singly on each side of the ship, and were on deep barbettes which protruded outwards from the hull so that the guns could fire in line with the keel. *Masséna* was hulked in 1913 and on 9 November 1915 was subsequently sunk as a breakwater at Seddulbahir in the Dardanelles. The ship was similar in construction to another French ship *Charles Martel*, which was laid down a year earlier, discarded in 1915 and then broken up in 1922.

Country:	France
Type:	Battleship
Launch date:	24 July 1895
Crew:	667
Displacement :	11,922 tonnes (11,735 tons)
Dimensions:	112.6m x 20.2m x 8.8m (369ft 7in x 66ft 6in x 29ft)
Range:	8524km (4600nm) at 10 knots
Armament:	Two 304mm (12in), two 274mm (10.8in), 140mm (5.5in), eight 100mm (3.9in) guns
Powerplant:	Triple screw, triple expansion engines
Performance:	17 knots

MEKO 140A16 class

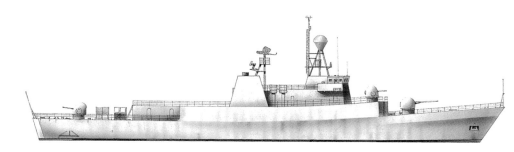

As part of the Argentine Navy's modernization plans, a contract was signed in October 1980 with the German firm, Blohm & Voss, for six MEKO 140A16 ships, to be built under licence at the AFNE shipyard in Rio Santiago, Ensenada, to a light frigate design based on the Portuguese Joao Coutinho class. Known locally as the Espora class, its lead ship, *Espora*, was commissioned into the Argentine Navy in 1983. A trio comprising the *Rosales*, *Spiro* and *Parker* followed in 1985, with a final pair, the *Robinson* and *Seaver*, in 1986 and 1987 respectively. The first three differed from the last three units in initially having only a helicopter landing platform amidships; the others had a telescopic hangar to allow the permanent carriage of a light helicopter. Although designed primarly for use on coastal operations, the class also forms a powerful offensive force.

Country:	Germany/Argentina
Type:	Frigate
Launch date:	23 January 1982 (Espora, first unit)
Crew:	93
Displacement:	1727 tonnes (1700 tons)
Dimensions:	91.2m x 12.2m x 3.3m (299ft 2in x 40ft x 10ft 10in)
Range:	5559km (3000nm)
Main armament:	One 76mm (2.9in) DP and two 40mm (1.5in) AA guns; two triple 324mm (12.76in) torpedo tubes
Powerplant:	Twin shafts, two diesels
Performance:	27 knots

Michigan

Completed in 1910, *Michigan* was designed before, but built after, the epoch-making *Dreadnought*. One of the South Carolina class, her design introduced the concept of all-big-guns on the centreline. Most of the 76mm (3in) guns were concentrated in a box battery amidships, with the rest on the upper deck. Cage masts greatly reduced the target area offered to enemy gunners and were a characteristic of US dreadnoughts. As the turbine was still in the development stage, triple expansion engines were installed instead. *Michigan* served with the Atlantic Fleet between 1910 and 1916 and in 1917–18 was employed on convoy escort duty. In January 1918 she lost her cage foremast in a storm off Cape Hatteras, and in 1919 she made two voyages as a troop transport, bringing US servicemen home from Europe. She was decommissioned in 1922 and broken up at Philadelphia in 1924.

Country:	USA
Type:	Battleship
Launch date:	25 May 1908
Crew:	869
Displacement:	18,186 tonnes (17,900 tons)
Dimensions:	138.2m x 24.5m x 7.5m (453ft 5in x 80ft 4in x 24ft 7in)
Range:	9000km (5000nm) at 10 knots
Armament:	Eight 305mm (12in), 22 76mm (3in) guns
Powerplant:	Twin screw, vertical triple expansion engines
Performance:	18.5 knots

Mikasa

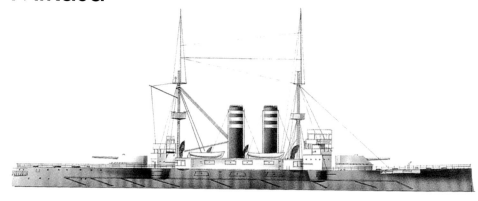

Completed in 1902, *Mikasa* was the last battleship built under the Japanese naval expansion programme of 1896, and was the flagship of Vice-Admiral Togo during the Russo-Japanese War of 1904–05. In February 1904 she was hit three times during the bombardment of Port Arthur, and in August she was again damaged by gunfire in the Battle of the Yellow Sea, receiving 22 hits. She took yet more serious damage at the Battle of Tsushinma on 27 May 1905, when she was hit 32 times. On 12 September that year she sank at her moorings at Sasebo after an ammunition explosion in her after magazine that left 114 crew dead, but was refloated and recommissioned in August 1906. In 1921 she was reclassified as a coastal defence ship. She retired in 1923 after running aground, and is now on permanent public display as the last surviving battleship of her period.

Country:	Japan
Type:	Battleship
Launch date:	8 November 1900
Crew:	830
Displacement:	15,422 tonnes (15,179 tons)
Dimensions:	131.7m x 23.2m x 8.2m (432ft x76ft 3in x 27ft 2in)
Range:	16,677km (9000nm) at 10 knots
Armament:	Four 305mm (12in), 14 152mm (6in) guns
Powerplant:	Twin screw, vertical triple expansion engines
Performance:	18 knots

Minas Gerais

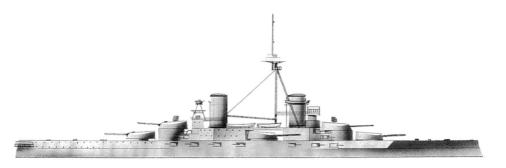

***M**inas Gerais* was originally designed as a pre-dreadnought battleship in
answer to the powerful vessels then being built for Chile. Her design was
later modified and she became the first powerful dreadnought to be built for a
minor navy. She was constructed in Britain and completed in 1910. She was
extensively modernised in the USA in 1923, and again in Brazil from 1934 to 1937.
Minas Gerais was scrapped in 1954. Brazil offered the services of both ships of
this class (the other being *Sao Paulo*) for service with the British Grand Fleet in
1917, after the country revoked its neutrality and seized German ships in
Brazilian ports, but the offer was declined because of fuel problems. Tentative
plans for Brazilian warships to serve in European waters in 1918 under the
command of Admiral Bonti did not materialise.

Country:	Brazil
Type:	Battleship
Launch date:	10 September 1908
Crew:	900
Displacement:	21,540 tonnes (21,200 tons)
Dimensions:	165.8m x 25.3m x 8.5m (544ft x 83ft x 27ft 10in)
Range:	18,000km (10,000nm) at 10 knots
Armament:	12 304mm (12in), 22 120mm (4.7in) guns
Powerplant:	Twin screw, vertical triple reciprocating engines
Performance:	21 knots

Minekaze

At the end of World War I, the Japanese applied the concept of first- and second-class destroyers, one being a scaled-up version of the other. Before then, the Japanese either bought or copied British ships, but with the 21-Momi class and 13 Minekaze-class second- and first-class destroyers, they produced something more original, fitting 533mm (21in) torpedo tubes (twins in the Momis and triples in the Minekazes). Both types carried their 120mm (4.72in) guns high on deck-houses and forecastle, enabling them to fight in poor conditions when the weather deck could be swept by water. By World War II standards, the vessels of the Minekaze class were both old and small, and despite their high speed, many fell victim to US submarines. Eight of them were lost in action during World War II. The *Minekaze* was sunk by the submarine USS *Pogy* in the East China Sea on 10 February 1944.

Country:	Japan
Type:	Destroyer
Launch date:	8 February 1919
Crew:	148
Displacement:	1676 tonnes (1650 tons)
Dimensions:	102.6m x 9m x 2.9m (336ft 6in x 29ft 8in x 9ft 6in)
Range:	6657km (3595nm)
Main armament:	Four single 120mm (4.72in) guns; two triple 533mm (21in) torpedo tubes; up to 20 mines
Powerplant:	Two sets of geared steam turbines
Performance:	39 knots

Minsk

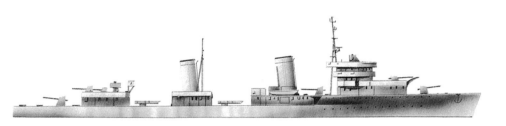

During World War I, the Imperial Russian Navy had conducted some outstandingly successful operations with the large, fast destroyer *Novik*. The type was later repeated, but with a reduced displacement. By the early 1930s the Soviet Navy decided that a type of super destroyer would be ideal for raiding operations in the Baltic, and *Minsk* was built between 1932 and 1934 with technical assistance from Italy and France. She saw early action, being flotilla leader of a bombardment force involved in a gun duel with Finnish shore batteries in December 1939, and in August 1941 her gunfire supported the defenders of Tallinn and covered their subsequent retreat to Kronstadt. The *Minsk* was bombed and sunk in a Stuka attack on Kronstadt harbour in September 1941, but was raised and refloated in 1942. She served as a training ship until the early 1960s.

Country:	Soviet Union
Type:	Destroyer
Launch date:	6 November 1935
Crew:	160
Displacement:	2623 tonnes (2582 tons)
Dimensions:	127.5m x 11.7m x 4m (418ft 4in x 38ft 4in x 13ft 4in)
Range:	4076km (2200nm)
Main armament:	Five 130mm (5.1in) and two 76mm (3in) guns
Powerplant:	Triple screws, turbines
Performance:	33 knots

Mirka class

Built between 1964 and 1965 at the Kaliningrad shipyard, the nine Mirka I class vessels were followed on the stocks during the latter half of 1965 and 1966 by nine Mirka II class units. The various vessels of the two Mirka classes served only with the Soviet Baltic and Black Sea Fleets, where their task was to search for infiltrating SSKs. The later Mirka II units had the 'Strut Curve' air search radar in place of the 'Slim Net' array of the earlier ships. Almost all units of both classes were retrofitted with dipping sonar in place of the internal depth charge rack on the port side of the stern to improve their ASW capability in their operational areas. This was particularly true in the Baltic, where oceanographic conditions make ASW operations very difficult. The Mirka class had been reduced to five units by 1990, all of which had been laid up or scrapped by 1998.

Country:	Soviet Union
Type:	Frigate
Launch date:	1964 (first unit)
Crew:	98
Displacement:	1168 tonnes (1150 tons)
Dimensions:	82.4m x 9.1m x 3m (270ft 4in x 29ft 11in x 9ft 10in)
Range:	6300km (3400nm)
Main armament:	Two twin 76mm (3in) guns; five or 10 533mm (21in) torpedo tubes; ASW rocket launchers
Powerplant:	Two shafts, two gas turbines and two diesels
Performance:	35 knots

Moltke

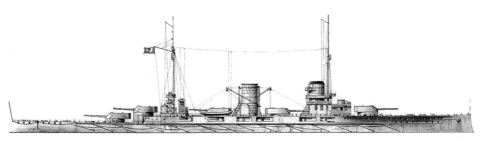

Moltke was laid down in 1909 and completed in 1911, and like her sister *Goeben* was the successor to the battlecruiser *Von der Tann*, having two more 280mm (11.1in) guns in a second aft turret. *Moltke* served with Admiral Hipper's squadron in World War I and had a remarkable war, surviving two torpedo strikes from British submarines as well as 304mm (12in) shell hits at Jutland. She saw action at Dogger Bank and the Heligoland Bight and took part in the bombardment of English east coast towns. The bombardment of these 'soft' targets, which took place at intervals between November 1914 and the spring of 1916, caused much outrage among the British public, and added to the wealth of stories about German atrocities of the time. *Moltke* was torpedoed by the British submarine *E42* but survived. In 1919 she was scuttled with the rest of the German fleet. In 1927 she was raised and scrapped.

Country:	Germany
Type:	Battleship
Launch date:	7 April 1910
Crew:	1355 (at Jutland)
Displacement :	25,704 tonnes (25,300 tons)
Dimensions:	186.5m x 29.5m x 9m (611ft 11in x 96ft 10in x 26ft 11in)
Range:	7416km (4120nm) at 12 knots
Armament:	Ten 280mm (11.1in), 12 150mm (5.9in) guns
Powerplant:	Four shaft geared turbines
Performance:	28 knots

Monarch

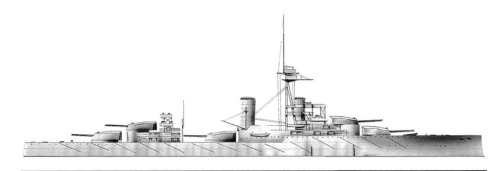

*M*onarch was one of four units that were the first vessels to carry 343mm (13.5in) guns since the days of the Royal Sovereign class of 1889. With a massive increase of 2540 tonnes (2500 tons) displacement over contemporary dreadnoughts, *Monarch* and her three sisters of the Orion class were called 'super-dreadnoughts'. They were the first capital ships of the dreadnought era to carry all the main guns on the centreline. Armour protection was thorough, the side armour rising to upper deck level 5m (17ft) above the waterline. All ships in the class served at Jutland in 1916. *Monarch* was sunk as a target in 1925. Of the other three, *Conqueror* (damaged in a collision with *Monarch* in December 1914) was broken up at Upnor, Kent in December 1922, as was *Orion*; and *Thunderer*, which ended her career as a seagoing cadet training ship, was broken up at Blyth in 1924.

Country:	Great Britain
Type:	Battleship
Launch date:	30 March 1911
Crew:	752
Displacement :	26,284 tonnes (25,870 tons)
Dimensions:	177m x 26.9m x 8.7m (580ft x 88ft 6in x 28ft 9in)
Range:	12,114km (6730nm) at 10 knots
Armament:	10 343mm (13.5in), 16 102mm (4in) guns
Powerplant:	Quadruple screw turbines
Performance:	20.8 knots

Moon

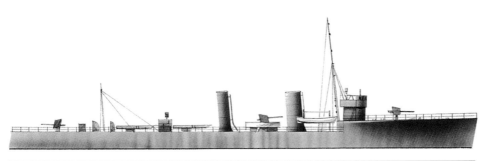

Moon was one of four special boats built by Alfred Yarrow. They formed part of the massive World War I emergency programme which was put in hand in September 1914, in which repeats of the M class were ordered in large numbers. *Moon* and her three sisters had increased length over the rest of the M class, and had raked stems and sloping sterns to improve seakeeping qualities. The central gun was on a raised platform to improve local fire control. There were also two twin mounts for 533mm (21in) torpedo tubes. Construction of the ships was subject to delay because of a shortage of zinc. *Moon* was sold for scrap in 1921. Many of these ships served with the Harwich Force, which made constant forays into the German Bight. At Jutland in May 1916, the British mustered 85 destroyers to the German 72.

Country:	Great Britain
Type:	Destroyer
Launch date:	23 April 1915
Crew:	160
Displacement:	910 tonnes (895 tons)
Dimensions:	114m x 8m x 2.9m (375ft x 26ft 8in x 9ft 6in)
Range:	2594km (1400nm)
Main armament:	Three 102mm (4in) guns
Powerplant:	Twin screws, turbines
Performance:	35 knots

Moreno

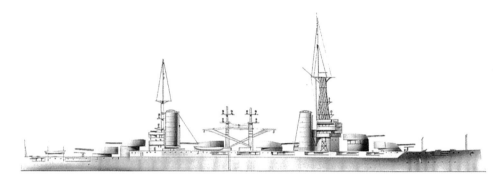

Rivalry between South American republics reached a new height around 1910, when Brazil ordered two powerful dreadnoughts from British yards. Argentina answered with a programme of three dreadnoughts, but owing to financial limitations only two were ordered, from US yards. *Moreno* and her sister *Rivadavia* were modernised in 1924–25. They were converted to run on oil, the lattice mast forward was shortened and the pole mast aft was replaced by a tripod. Displacement increased by 1016 tonnes (1000 tons). In 1937 *Moreno* went on a cruise to Europe, and after service in territorial waters in World War II she successively became a depot ship and a prison ship. Together with her sister ship, *Rivadavia* (which accompanied *Moreno* on her European cruise) she remained Argentina's largest warship until the 1950s. *Moreno* was sold in 1956.

Country:	Argentina
Type:	Battleship
Launch date:	23 September 1911
Crew:	1130
Displacement:	30,500 tonnes (30,000 tons)
Dimensions:	173.8m x 29.4m x 8.5m (270ft 3in x 96ft 9in x 27ft 10in)
Range:	19,800km (11,000nm) at 12 knots
Armament:	12 304mm (12in), 12 152mm (6in), guns
Powerplant:	Three shaft geared turbines
Performance:	22.5 knots

Moskva

*M*oskva was the first helicopter carrier built for the Soviet Navy. She was laid down in 1962 and completed in 1967. She was designed to counteract the growing threat from the US nuclear-powered missile submarines that first entered service in 1960, and to undertake search and destroy missions. However, by the time *Moskva* and *Leningrad* had been completed at the Nikolayev South shipyard, they were incable of coping with both the numbers and capabilities of NATO submarines, so the building programme was terminated. Classed by the Russians as *PKR* (*Protivolodochnyy Kreyser*, or anti-submarine cruiser) the ships proved to be poor sea boats in heavy weather. *Moskva* had a massive central block which dominated the vessel and housed the major weapons systems and a huge sonar array. *Leningrad* was stricken in 1991, *Moskva* in 1996. Both were scrapped.

Country:	Soviet Union
Type:	Helicopter carrier
Launch date:	14 January 1965
Crew:	850
Displacement:	14,800 tonnes (14,567 tons)
Dimensions:	191m x 34m x 7.6m (626ft 8in x 111ft 6in x 25ft)
Range:	8100km (4500nm) at 12 knots
Armament:	One twin SUW-N-1 launcher, two twin SA-N-3 missile launchers, 14 – 20 helicopters
Powerplant:	Twin screw turbines
Performance:	30 knots

Mount Whitney

A merica's Pacific battles during World War II convinced the US Navy and Marine Corps of the value of specialised amphibious assault forces. There was a core of experience in mounting amphibious operations, which was used to construct the Guam class assault ships. *Mount Whitney*, launched in 1969, and her sister ship *Blue Ridge*, use the same hull form and machinery as the Guam class, and have flat open decks to allow maximum antenna placement. There is a helicopter flight deck aft. These ships are crammed with communications equipment, while there are briefing areas, planning facilities and command spaces. They have space for 200 staff officers and 500 men. Their engines develop 22,000hp, and range at 16 knots is 25,650km (13,500 miles). They have limited self-defence weapons, and normally rely on an escorting task force for protection. They now serve as fleet flagships.

Country:	USA
Type:	Command ship
Launch date:	8 January 1970
Crew:	720, plus 700 fleet staff
Displacement:	19,598 tonnes (19,290 tons)
Dimensions:	189m x 25m x 8.2m (620ft 5in x 82ft x 27ft)
Range:	25,650km (13,500) at 16 knots
Armament:	Two 76mm (3in) guns, two 8-tube Sea Sparrow missile launchers (removed in 1992)
Powerplant:	Single screw turbines
Performance:	23 knots

Mourad Rais

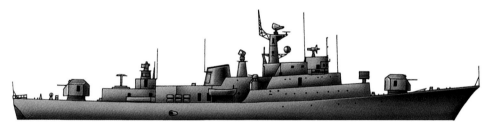

Although constructed in the Soviet Union at the Zelenodolsk shipyard on the Black Sea, the Koni class of frigate was intended solely for export, only one unit being retained by the Russians as a crew training ship for the naval personnel from those countries whose navies bought the vessels. Algeria purchased three, named *Mourad Rais*, *Rais Kellik* and *Rais Korfou*. The Libyan Government was also interested in purchasing a number of ex-GDR Koni-class vessels, but the sale was rejected by the German Government. The Libyan vessels underwent minor modifications between 1992 and 1994; all were still active in 1999, the *Rais Korfou* being used for training cruises. There is little doubt that, although the former Soviet Union tried hard to meet the needs of smaller nations with the Koni class of frigate, sales of the class fell a long way short of expectations.

Country:	Soviet Union/Algeria
Type:	Frigate
Launch date:	1978 (Delfin completed)
Crew:	130
Displacement:	1930 tonnes (1900 tons)
Dimensions:	95m x 12.8m x 4.2m (311ft 8 in x 42ft x 13ft 8in)
Range:	4076km (2200nm)
Main armament:	Two twin 76mm (3in) and two twin 30mm (1.1in) guns; SAMs
Powerplant:	Three shafts, two gas turbines and one diesel
Performance:	27 knots

Murasame

Launched in August 1994 and commissioned in March 1996, *Murasame* is one of a planned class of nine ships, their construction being given added priority because of the Kongo class being reduced to four vessels due to the high cost of the Aegis system installed in them. In fact, *Murasame* somewhat resembles a mini-Kongo-class vessel, with a vertical-launch missile system and a much reduced complement, despite the fact that she is intended to be an enlarged version of the Asagari class. Stealth features are evident in sloping sides and a rounded superstructure. *Murasame*'s sister ships, completed to date, are the *Harusame*, *Yuudachi* and *Kirisame*. The latter was commissioned in March 1999. The other five, as yet unnamed, were scheduled to commission between March 2000 and March 2002 greatly enhancing Japan's maritime capability.

Country:	Japan
Type:	Destroyer
Launch date:	September 1994
Crew:	166
Displacement:	5182 tonnes (5100 tons)
Dimensions:	151m x 17.4m x 5.2m (495ft 5in x 57ft 1in x 17ft 1in)
Range:	15,195km (8200nm)
Main armament:	One 76mm (3in) gun; Harpoon SSM; Sea Sparrow SAM; six 324mm (12.75in) torpedo tubes
Powerplant:	Two shafts, four gas turbines
Performance:	30 knots

Nagato

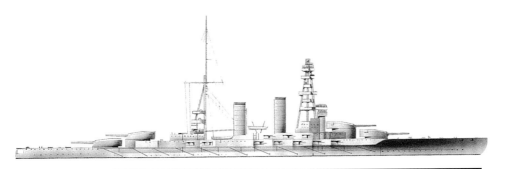

*N*agato and her sister *Mutsu* heralded a new era in battleship design with the adoption of the 406mm (16in) gun. Completed in 1920, it had a range of some 40,233m (44,000yds), combining great accuracy with greater destructive power. A massive tripod foremast rose above a large bridge structure, and in the mid-1920s the first funnel was angled back to clear the bridge and mast of smoke fumes. New machinery requiring only one funnel was installed between 1934 and 1936, and the first funnel was then removed. As flagship of the Combined Fleet she saw action at Midway and in the Battle of the Philippine Sea. In October 1944 she received bomb damage at Leyte Gulf and was out of action for the remainder of the war at Yokosuka. In July 1946 *Nagato* was a target ship for the US nuclear tests at Bikini; severely damaged in the second test, her wreck sank on 29 July.

Country:	Japan
Type:	Battleship
Launch date:	9 November 1919
Crew:	1333
Displacement:	39,116 tonnes (38,500 tons)
Dimensions:	215.8m x 29m x 9m (708ft x 95ft 1in x 29ft 10in)
Range:	9900km (5500nm) at 10 knots
Armament:	Eight 406mm (16in), 20 140mm (5.5in) guns
Powerplant:	Quadruple screw turbines
Performance:	23 knots

Nanuchka I class

Classed by the Russians as an MRK, or small rocket ship, the 17 units of the Nanuchka I class were built between 1969 and 1974 at Petrovsky, Leningrad with a modified variant, the Nanuchka II, following on. To Western observers, the vessels of the Nanuchka class were classed as coastal missile-corvettes, although the fact that they were often seen quite far from home waters tends to put them more in the light frigate category, especially when the firepower of the class is considered. Later classes of Nanuchkas were exported to several of the Soviet Union's regular customers, including India, Libya and Algeria. The Libyan vessels have occasionally been in confrontation with US naval units in the Mediterranean. On the night of 24/25 March 1986 one, the *Ean Mara,* was sunk by US carrier aircraft; a second was severely damaged in the action.

Country:	Soviet Union
Type:	Frigate
Launch date:	1969 (first unit completed)
Crew:	70
Displacement:	914 tonnes (900 tons)
Dimensions:	59.3m x 12.6m x 2.4m (194ft 7in x 41ft 3in x 7ft 11in)
Range:	2779km (1500nm)
Main armament:	Two triple launchers for SS-N-9 Siren anti-ship missiles; one twin 157mm (2.24in) AA or one 76mm (3in) DP gun
Powerplant:	Three shafts, three paired diesels
Performance:	32 knots

Nassau

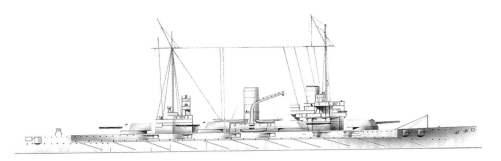

Nassau was laid down in 1906 as Germany's first dreadnought, though she was not commissioned until 1910. She was the first ship in the Nassau class, which also included *Westfalen*, *Posen* and *Rheinland*. Originally designed to carry only eight guns in her main armament, two extra double turrets were included in her construction which affected her performance, though she was still a steady gun platform. Present at the Battle of Jutland, during which she survived a collision with the British destroyer *Spitfire*, *Nassau* surrendered at the end of World War I and was scrapped in 1921. Of the other ships in her class, *Westfalen* survived being torpedoed by the British submarine *E23* in August 1916 and was broken up in 1924; *Posen* collided with the cruiser *Elbing* at Jutland and was stricken in 1919; and *Rheinland* went aground during landings in Finland in April 1918, and was stricken in 1919.

Country:	Germany
Type:	Battleship
Launch date:	7 March 1908
Crew:	966
Displacement:	20,533 tonnes (20,210 tons)
Dimensions:	146m x 27m x 8.5m (479ft 4in x 88ft 3in x 27ft 10in)
Range:	10,2609km (5700nm) at 10 knots
Armament:	12 150mm (5.9in), 12 279mm (11in) guns
Powerplant:	Triple screw, vertical triple expansion engines
Performance:	20 knots

Nautilus

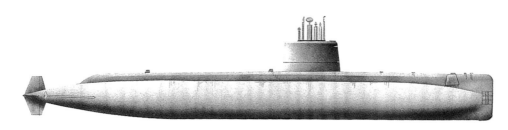

*N*autilus was the world's first nuclear-powered submarine. Apart from her revolutionary propulsion system, she was a conventional design. Early trials established new records, including nearly 2250km (1213nm) submerged in 90 hours at 20 knots, at that time the longest period spent underwater by an American submarine, as well as being the fastest speed submerged. There were two prototype nuclear attack submarines; the other, USS *Seawolf*, was launched in July 1955, the last US submarine to feature a traditional conning tower, as distinct from the fin of later nuclear submarines. *Nautilus* was the more successful; *Seawolf* was designed around the S2G reactor, intended as a backup to the S2W, but it had many operational problems and was replaced by an S2W in 1959. *Nautilus* was preserved as a museum exhibit at Groton, Connecticut, in 1982.

Country:	USA
Type:	Attack submarine
Launch date:	21 January 1954
Crew:	105
Displacement:	Surfaced: 4157 tonnes (4091 tons), submerged: 4104 tonnes (4040 tons)
Dimensions:	97m x 8.4m x 6.6m (323ft 7in x 27ft 8in x 21ft 9in)
Range:	Unlimited
Armament:	Six 533mm (21in) torpedo tubes
Powerplant:	Twin screws, one S2W reactor, turbines
Performance:	Surfaced: 20 knots, submerged: 23 knots

Navarin

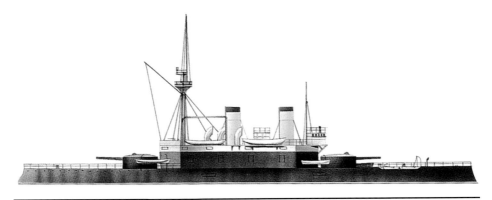

Navarin was based upon the successful British Nile class battleship. She was laid down in 1889 in St Petersburg. She had a rectangular central superstructure which held the 152mm (6in) guns in broadside, protected by 127mm (5in) armour. Her main 304mm (12in) guns were mounted in two twin armoured turrets, fore and aft of the superstructure. She was well-protected, with her main belt covering the centre section in two strakes. There was also a 76mm (3in) thick armoured deck which rested on top of the main belt. *Navarin* took part in the Battle of Tsushima in May 1905, where the Russian fleet was destroyed by superior Japanese gunnery and ship handling. The next day, on 28 May 1905, she made a run for Vladivostock, but was torpedoed by Japanese destroyers. She sank with heavy loss of life. She was named after the Battle of Navarino, in which an Allied fleet defeated Turkey in 1827.

Country:	Russia
Type:	Battleship
Launch date:	20 October 1891
Crew:	622
Displacement:	10,370 tonnes (10,206 tons)
Dimensions:	109m x 20.4m x 8.3m (357ft 7in x 67ft x 27ft 6in)
Range:	5652km (3050nm) at 10 knots
Armament:	Four 304mm (12in), eight 152mm (6in) guns
Powerplant:	Twin screw, vertical triple expansion engines
Performance:	15.5 knots

Navigatori class

Launched between 1928 and 1930, Italy's Navigatori-class destroyers were produced at a time when high speed was an obsession with the Italians. The veseels of this class were extremely lightly built and their seakeeping left something to be desired, though it was improved later by increasing their freeboard. Eleven of the 12 boats in the class were sunk during World War II. Six of these losses were as a result of direct action by the British and another by a mine; two were sunk in action against the Germans in September 1943; one was scuttled; and the last was sunk in error by an Italian submarine. The *Leone Pancaldo* was sunk twice, the first time by aircraft from HMS *Ark Royal* in July 1940. She was raised, repaired and recommissioned, only to be sunk again (and for good) by air attack off Cape Bon in April 1943.

Country:	Italy
Type:	Destroyer
Launch date:	12 August 1928 (Nicolo Zeno, first unit)
Crew:	225
Displacement:	2622 tonnes (2580 tons)
Dimensions:	107.75m x 10.2m x 3.5m (353ft 6in x 33ft 6in x 11ft 6in)
Range:	1816km (980nm)
Main armament:	Three twin 120mm (4.72in) and three single 37mm (1.4in) guns; two twin or triple 533mm (21in) torpedo tubes; up to 54 mines
Powerplant	Two sets of geared steam turbines, two shafts
Performance	38 knots

Nelson

*N*elson and her sister ship *Rodney* were the first battleships to be completed
within the limits of the Washington Treaty of 1922, which fixed the maximum
displacement for each class of vessel. They were also the first British warships to carry
406mm (16in) guns. Completed in 1927, *Nelson*'s main armament was concentrated
forward of the tower bridge in three triple turrets, saving on armour weight. More
weight was saved by adopting less powerful machinery. The secondary battery was
carried in twin turrets level with the main mast. The engine rooms were placed
forward of the boiler rooms to keep the bridge structure clear of funnel smoke. She
was out of action for nearly a year after being torpedoed by Italian aircraft while
escorting the Malta convoy 'Halberd' on 27 September 1941, and was damaged by a
German torpedo off Normandy in July 1944. Both ships were scrapped in 1948–49.

Country:	Great Britain
Type:	Battleship
Launch date:	3 September 1925
Crew:	1361 (as flagship)
Displacement :	38,608 tonnes (38,000 tons)
Dimensions:	216.8m x 32.4m x 9.6m (711ft x 106ft 4in x 31ft 6in)
Range:	30,574km (16,500nm) at 12 knots
Armament:	Nine 406mm (16in), 12 152mm (6in) guns
Powerplant:	Twin screw turbines
Performance:	23.5 knots

Neustrashimy

There were originally intended to be three frigates in the Neustrashimy class, but the third was launched in July 1993 with only the hull completed, and was scrapped in mid-1997 without any further work being done. *Neustrashimy* was launched in May 1988 and began her sea trials in the Baltic in December 1990, being commissioned in January 1993. The second unit, *Yaroslavl Mudry*, was scrapped unfinished in 1998. All three ships were built at Kaliningrad. The *Neustrashimy* is slightly larger than the Krivak class, and has a helicopter, following the pattern set by Western anti-submarine frigates. The ship has the same propulsion units as the Udaloy II class, and was assigned to the Baltic Fleet in 1999. Attempts have been made to incorporate stealth features into the vessel, though with what degree of success it is not known.

Country:	Soviet Union
Type:	Frigate
Launch date:	May 1988
Crew:	210
Displacement:	4318 tonnes (4250 tons)
Dimensions:	131.2m x 15.5m x 4.8m (430ft 5in x 50ft 10in x 15ft 9in)
Range:	7238km (3908nm)
Main armament:	Combined 30mm (1.1in) gun and SA-N-11 SAM system; fitted for SS-N-25 SSM; SA-N-9 SAM; six 533mm (21in) torpedo tubes; A/S mortars
Powerplant:	Two shafts, four gas turbines
Performance:	30 knots

Nevada

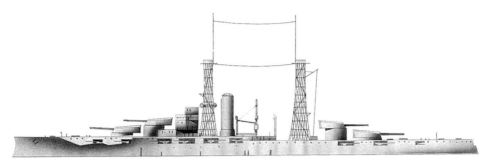

*N*evada was one of the first battleships to be built on the 'all-or-nothing' principle, adopted by other navies after World War I, in which the thickest possible armour was applied to vital areas, leaving the rest virtually unprotected. She and her sister *Oklahoma* were second-generation dreadnoughts, and were the first US battleships to burn only oil fuel. Launched in 1914, and seeing service off Ireland in World War I, *Nevada* was badly damaged at Pearl Harbor in December 1941. After repairs, she served as one of the bombardment force of warships at the Normandy landings of June 1944, and off southern France in August before returning to the Pacific, where she was damaged by a kamikaze and shore batteries. In July 1946 she was a target vessel at Bikini, an experience she survived. She was sunk as a target by aircraft and gunfire off Hawaii in July 1948.

Country:	USA
Type:	Battleship
Launch date:	11 July 1914
Crew:	1374 (during World War II)
Displacement:	29,362 tonnes (28,900 tons)
Dimensions:	177.7m x 29m x 9.5m (583ft x 95ft 3in x 31ft)
Range:	18,530km (10,000nm) at 10 knots
Armament:	21 127mm (5in), 10 355mm (14in) guns
Powerplant:	Twin screw turbines
Performance:	20.5 knots

New Ironsides

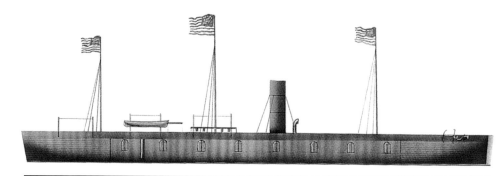

New Ironsides was one of three ironclads ordered in 1861. Launched in 1862 she was wooden-hulled, with iron plates covering her battery and located in a continuous belt below the waterline. Originally rigged as a barque, she served as the Union flagship, and although she saw constant action during the Civil War, her armour was never pierced. During that unhappy conflict she served successively with the South Atlantic and North Atlantic Blockading Squadrons. On 8 September 1863 she was hit 50 times during an attack on Fort Moultrie, and on 5 October she survived a spar torpedo attack by the Confederate topside boat *David* off Charleston without damage. Her crew became convinced that she was invulnerable, which she virtually was. She was destroyed by a fire in Philadelphia in 1865.

Country:	USA
Type:	Ironclad
Launch date:	10 May 1862
Crew:	449
Displacement:	4277 tonnes (4210 tons)
Dimensions:	70m x 17.5m x 4.8m (232ft x 57ft 6in x 15ft 8in)
Range:	2780km (1500nm) at 10 knots
Armament:	14 280mm (11in), two 150-pounder and two 50-pounder guns
Powerplant:	Single screw, horizontal direct acting engines
Performance:	6.5 knots

New York

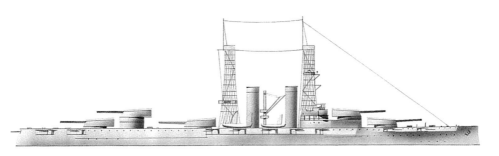

New York was laid down in September 1911 and completed in April 1914. Her engines developed 29,687hp and coal supply was 2964 tonnes (2917 tons), plus 406 tonnes (400 tons) of fuel oil. In 1916, she was the first American battleship to fit anti-aircraft guns. From 1914–19 she served with the US Atlantic Fleet, and for the last year of World War I she was assigned to the Royal Navy's Grand Fleet. After reconstruction work at Norfolk, during which her cage masts were replaced by tripods, she was again assigned to the Atlantic Fleet from 1936 to 1941, and in 1939 she was experimentally fitted with the first shipborne radar. Service in World War II took her to North Africa, Iwo Jima and Okinawa, where she was slightly damaged by a kamikaze. Having survived World War II, *New York* went on to survive the Bikini atomic bomb tests in 1946. She was sunk as a target off Pearl Harbor in 1948.

Country:	USA
Type:	Battleship
Launch date:	30 October 1912
Crew:	1042
Displacement:	28,854 tonnes (28,400 tons)
Dimensions:	174.6m x 29m x 9m (573ft x 95ft 2in x 29ft 6in)
Range:	12,708km (7060nm) at 12 knots
Armament:	10 356mm (14in), 21 127mm (5in) guns
Powerplant:	Twin screw, triple expansion engines
Performance:	21.4 knots

Nibbio

Launched in 1878, *Nibbio* was Italy's first torpedo boat. She was built by Thorneycroft, who had already constructed such small, high-speed vessels for Norway, France, Denmark, Sweden and Austria. Her engines developed 250hp, and steam was supplied by a single locomotive boiler. Two torpedoes were carried amidships, and she was also armed with a one-pounder gun. She carried a maximum of 10 crew members. *Nibbio* was commissioned in 1881, and in 1886 she was redesignated IT. She was discarded in 1904, but was later used as a steam boat for general harbour duties and was renumbered PE44. *Nibbio* was not an outstanding craft, but she provided a cadre of Italian Navy personnel with valuable experience in handling boats of her type. The first Italian-built torpedo boat was the *Clio* of 1882.

Country:	Italy
Type:	Torpedo boat
Launch date:	1878
Crew:	10
Displacement:	26 tonnes (25.5 tons)
Dimensions:	24.3m x 3m x 1m (80ft x 9ft 10in x 3ft 3in)
Range:	Not known
Main armament:	Two 355mm (14in) torpedo tubes
Powerplant:	Single screw, triple expansion reciprocating engine
Performance:	18 knots

Niels Juel

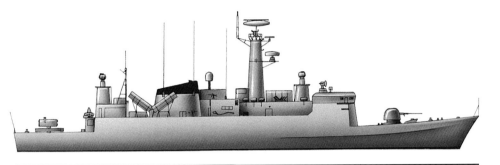

Designed in Britain by Yarrow of Glasgow and built at the Aalborg Vaerft in Denmark, the *Niels Juel* was commissioned in August 1980 and was followed by two other frigates, the *Olfert Fischer* and *Peter Tordenskiold*. The ships underwent a mid-life update between 1996 and 1999; this included the installation of a NATO Sea Sparrow vertical-launch system (VLS) and new communications equipment. The original Plessey air search radar was to be replaced by a modern TRS-3D. Other equipment includes a hull-mounted active search and attack sonar and an Ericsson combat data system; satellite communications equipment can also be fitted aft of the funnel. Like all of Denmark's ocean-going warships, *Niels Juel* is optimised for operations in Arctic waters. The ships are likely to be replaced in the twenty-first century by a new class of multi-role patrol vessel.

Country:	Denmark
Type:	Frigate
Launch date:	17 February 1978
Crew:	94
Displacement:	1341 tonnes (1320 tons)
Dimensions:	84m x 10.3m x 3.1m (275ft 6in x 33ft 9in x 10ft 2in)
Range:	4021km (2170nm)
Main armament:	One 76mm (3in) gun; Harpoon SSM; Sea Sparrow SAM; depth charges
Powerplant:	Two shafts, one gas turbine, one diesel
Performance:	28 knots

Nile

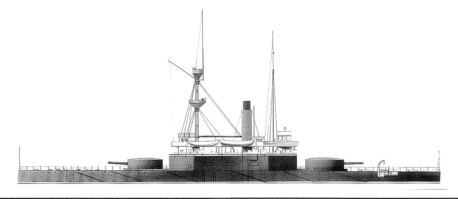

*N*ile and her sister *Trafalgar* were the heaviest battleships in the Royal Navy when construction. Launched in 1888, the *Nile*'s weaponry reflected the principle of combining the heaviest armament with maximum protection. The 343mm (13.5in) guns were mounted in twin, hydraulically operated, turrets on the centreline, some 4.2m (14ft) above the waterline. These were positioned fore and aft of the octagonal citadel. This held the 120mm (4.7in) guns, which were protected by bulkheads 127mm (5in) thick. Later the 120mm (4.7in) guns were replaced by more modern 152mm (6in) weapons. When she was completed in 1891, many naval officers felt that she would be one of the last capital ships to be built, because of the perceived threat of the torpedo boats then entering service. *Nile* spent most of her service in the Mediterranean before ending up as a training ship. She was scrapped in 1912.

Country:	Great Britain
Type:	Battleship
Launch date:	27 March 1888
Crew:	577
Displacement:	12,791 tonnes (12,590 tons)
Dimensions:	105m x 22m x 8.6m (345ft x 73ft x 28ft 6in)
Range:	12,044km (6500nm) at 10 knots
Armament:	Four 343mm (13.5in), six 120mm (4.7in) guns
Powerplant:	Twin screw, triple expansion engines
Performance:	17 knots

Niteroi

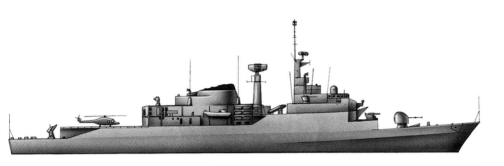

Of the six ships in the Niteroi class, four (*Niteroi, Defensora, Constituicao* and *Liberal*) were built in the UK by Vosper Thorneycroft Ltd. The other two, *Independencia* and *Uniao*, were built at the Arsenal de Marinha yards in Rio de Janeiro. The ships were based on Vosper's Mk10 frigate design which, fitted with a combined diesel or gas turbine propulsion plant, is considered to be exceptionally economical in terms of manpower when compared with previous warships of this size. The class was being upgraded in the late 1990s, modifications including the replacement of Seacat with the Aspide SAM system. The vessels carry the Westland Super Lynx helicopter, which is armed with the Sea Skua ASM. All are based at Niteroi and form the Brazilian Navy's First Frigate Squadron, which is the Brazilian Navy's premier surface attack unit.

Country:	Brazil
Type:	Frigate
Launch date:	8 February 1974
Crew:	217
Displacement:	3766 tonnes (3707 tons)
Dimensions:	129.2m x 13.5m x 5.5m (424ft x 44ft 2in x 18ft 2in)
Range:	8524km (4600nm)
Main armament:	One or two 115mm (4.5in) guns; Exocet SSM; Seacat SAM; Ikara ASW system
Powerplant:	Two shafts, two gas turbines, four diesels
Performance:	30 knots

North Carolina

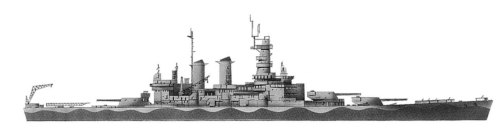

*N*orth Carolina and her sister *Washington* were the first US battleships built after the lifting of the 1922 Washington Naval Treaty. However, the original design followed the later London Treaty which allowed for 355mm (14in) guns, but as the Japanese refused to restrict their main armament, the USA decided to fit *North Carolina* with triple 400mm (16in) gun turrets after her launch in 1940. By 1945 her weaponry had been replaced by mainly anti-aircraft weapons, namely 96 x 40mm (1.6in), and 36 x 20mm (0.8in) guns. She fought in the Pacific, from Guadalcanal to the final strikes on Japan. On 15 September 1942 she was torpedoed by the Japanese submarine *I-19* near Espiritu Santu, together with the destroyer USS *O'Brien*, which was sunk, and on 6 April 1945 she was hit by friendly fire off Okinawa. She was stricken in 1960, and is now preserved at Wilmington, North Carolina.

Country:	USA
Type:	Battleship
Launch date:	13 June 1940
Crew:	1880
Displacement:	47,518 tonnes (46,770 tons)
Dimensions:	222m x 33m x 10m (728ft 9in x 108ft 3in x 32ft 10in)
Range:	32,334km (17,450nm) at 12 knots
Armament:	Nine 400mm (16in), 20 127mm (5in) guns
Powerplant:	Quadruple screw turbines
Performance:	28 knots

November class

B uilt as the Soviet Union's first nuclear submarine design from 1958 to 1963 at Severodvinsk, the November-class SSN was designed for the anti-ship rather than the anti-submarine role. They carried a full load of 24 nuclear torpedoes. They were provided with a targeting radar for use with the strategic-attack torpedo, presmably to confirm its position off an enemy coast. Thus armed, the task of these boats was to attack carrier battle groups. They were very noisy underwater and were prone to reactor leaks, which did not endear them to their crews. In April 1970 a November-class boat was lost south-west of the United Kingdom after an internal fire, the surviving crew being taken off before the boat sank, and there were numerous other incidents involving the boats during their operational career. All 14 boats were retired in the 1980s.

Country:	Soviet Union
Type:	Attack submarine
Launch date:	1958
Crew:	86
Displacement:	Surfaced: 4267 tonnes (4200 tons), submerged: 5080 tonnes (5000 tons)
Dimensions:	109.7m x 9.1m x 6.7m (359ft 11in x 29ft 10in x 22ft)
Range:	Unlimited
Armament:	Eight 533mm (21in) and two 406mm (16in) torpedo tubes
Powerplant:	Twin shafts, one nuclear PWR, two turbines
Performance:	Surfaced: 20 knots, submerged: 30 knots

Numancia

Numancia was an iron-hulled, broadside ironclad and was laid down at La Seyne in 1861. She was flagship during the war between Spain, Peru and Chile in 1865, and took part in the bombardment of Valparaiso on 27 March 1866. On 30 April she sustained 51 hits from shore batteries during an attack on Callao, but escaped undamaged. In 1867–68 she became the first armoured vessel to circumnavigate the world. In 1873 she was seized by insurgents during the Carlist civil war, and was damaged by gunfire and collision. Returned to the government, she operated against the Riffs in Spanish Morocco. She was completely rebuilt during 1897–98 when her armament was changed to include eight 254mm (10in), and seven 203mm (8in) rifled muzzle-loaders and two torpedo launchers. By 1914 she was a gunnery training ship. She sank while under tow to the breakers in 1916.

Country:	Spain
Type:	Ironclad
Launch date:	19 November 1863
Crew:	500
Displacement :	7304 tonnes (7189 tons)
Dimensions:	96m x 17.3m x 8.2m (315ft x 57ft x 27ft)
Range:	5559km (3000nm) at 10 knots
Armament:	40 68-pounder guns (as launched)
Powerplant:	Single screw, non-compound engines
Performance:	13 knots

Oberon

Built between 1959 and 1967 as a follow-on to the Porpoise class, the Oberon class was outwardly identical to its predecessor, although there were internal differences. These included the soundproofing of all equipment for silent running and the use of a high-grade steel for the hull to allow a greater maximum diving depth of up to 340m (1115ft). A total of 13 units was commissioned into the Royal Navy. *Oberon* was modified with a deeper casing to house equipment for the initial training of personnel for the nuclear submarine fleet but was paid off for disposal in 1986, together with HMS *Orpheus*. One of the class, *Onyx*, served in the South Atlantic during the Falklands war on periscope beach recon-naissance operations and for landing special forces. During these operations she rammed a rock, causing one of her torpedoes to become stuck in its tube.

Country:	Great Britain
Type:	Attack submarine
Launch date:	18 July 1959
Crew:	69
Displacement:	Surfaced: 2063 tonnes (2030 tons), submerged: 2449 tonnes (2410 tons)
Dimensions:	90m x 8.1m x 5.5m (295ft 3in x 26ft 6in x 18ft)
Surface range:	11,118km (6000nm) at 10 knots
Armament:	Eight 533mm (21in) torpedo tubes
Powerplant:	Two shafts, two diesel/electric motors
Performance:	Surfaced: 12 knots, submerged: 17.5 knots

Ohio

T he USS *Ohio* is the lead ship of a large class of nuclear-missile submarines
(SSBN) intended to form the third arm of America's nuclear triad. *Ohio* was
commissioned in November 1981. Boats of the class can remain submerged for
up to 70 days. Eighteen Ohio-class boats were in commission in the late 1990s.
These were the *Ohio* (SSBN 726), *Michigan* (SSBN 727), *Florida* (SSBN 728),
Georgia (SSBN 729), *Henry M. Jackson* (SSBN 730), *Alabama* (SSBN 731), *Alaska*
(SSBN 732), *Nevada* (SSBN 733), *Tennessee* (SSBN 734), *Pennsylvania* (SSBN 735),
West Virginia (SSBN 736), *Kentucky* (SSBN 737), *Maryland* (SSBN 738), *Nebraska*
(SSBN 739), *Rhode Island* (SSBN 740), *Maine* (SSBN 741), *Wyoming* (SSBN 742) and
Louisiana (SSBN 743). All USN SSBNs are under the control of USAF Strategic
Air Command. They are not due to begin retirement until 2023.

Country:	USA
Type:	Ballistic missile submarine
Launch date:	7 April 1979
Crew:	155
Displacement:	Surfaced: 16,360 tonnes (16,764 tons), submerged: 19,050 tonnes (18,750 tons)
Dimensions:	170.7m x 12.8m x 11m (560ft x 42ft x 36ft 5in)
Range:	Unlimited
Armament:	24 Trident C4 missiles, four 533mm (21in) torpedo tubes
Powerplant:	Single shaft, nuclear PWR
Performance:	Surfaced: 24 knots, submerged: 28 knots

Oliver Hazard Perry

The USS *Oliver Hazard Perry* was the first of a class of 51 general-purpose frigates designed to escort merchant convoys or amphibious squadrons. Their primary role was to provide area defence of surface forces against attacking aircraft and cruise missiles, with anti-surface warfare as a secondary role. Because of cost considerations, the first 26 ships were not retrofitted to carry two LAMPS III ASW helicopters, as originally planned, but retained the LAMPS I. LAMPS facilities include the Recovery Assistance, Security and Traversing (RAST) system which allows the launch and recovery of the Sikorsky SH-60 helicopters with the ship rolling through 28 degrees and pitching up to 5 degrees. Two ships of this class, the *Stark* and *Samuel B. Roberts*, were damaged in missile attacks while patrolling the Arabian Gulf during the Iraq–Iran war in 1987 and 1988.

Country:	USA
Type:	Frigate
Launch date:	25 September 1976
Crew:	215
Displacement:	3717 tonnes (3658 tons)
Dimensions:	135.6m x 13.7m x 4.5m (445ft x 45ft x 14ft 10in)
Range:	10,371km (5600nm)
Main armament:	One 76mm (3in) DP gun; two triple 324mm (12.75in) torpedo tubes; Harpoon SSMs and Standard ASMs
Powerplant:	Single shaft, two gas turbines
Performance:	29 knots

Oregon

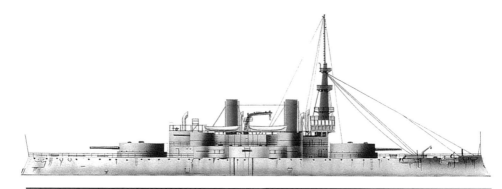

In 1889 the US Congress denied a request for 192 warships to be built over a 15-year period, and so the US Navy made do with three 'sea-going coastline battleships'. This designation was the only way the Navy could get the approval of Congress. The ships were the vessels of the Oregon class, and they carried heavy armament and protection on a small displacement which resulted in a low freeboard, limited endurance and low speed. In 1898 *Oregon* took part in the Battle of Santiago Bay during the war with Spain. After years as a floating monument, she was sold for scrap in 1942, but reprieved and in 1944 was used as an ammunition hulk in the Pacific. On 14 November 1948 she went adrift in a typhoon; she was not located until 8 December, when she was discovered 500 miles southeast of Guam and towed back. She was sold and broken up in Japan in 1956.

Country:	USA
Type:	Battleship
Launch date:	26 October 1893
Crew:	636
Displacement :	10,452 tonnes (10,288 tons)
Dimensions:	106.9m x 21m x 7.3m (351ft x 69ft 3in x 24ft)
Range:	8338km (4500nm) at 10 knots
Armament:	Four 330mm (13in), eight 203mm (8in), four 152mm (6in) guns
Powerplant:	Twin screw, vertical triple expansion engines
Performance:	15 knots

Orzel

*O*rzel was ordered in January 1935 and was funded by public subsciption. She was a large, ocean-going boat with excellent all-round qualities and was Dutch-built, together with her sister ship *Wilk* (Wolf). Diving depth was 80m (200ft) and submerged range was 190km (102nm) at five knots. *Orzel* was commissioned in February 1939. On 14 September 1939 the Polish submarines were ordered to break out from the Baltic and make for British ports; *Wilk* arrived on 20 September and *Orzel* (Lt-Cdr Grudzinski) on 14 October via Reval, after an adventurous voyage without charts. On 8 April 1940 *Orzel* sank two large troop transports at the start of the German invasion of Norway, but was lost in a mine barrage off the Norwegian coast on 8 June. Her sister, *Wilk*, attacked and sank a Dutch submarine in error on 20 June 1940.

Country:	Poland
Type:	Attack submarine
Launch date:	1938
Crew:	56
Displacement:	Surfaced: 1117 tonnes (1100 tons), submerged: 1496 tonnes (1473 tons)
Dimensions:	84m x 6.7m x 4m (275ft 7in x 22ft x 13ft 1in)
Surface range:	13,300km (7169nm) at 10 knots
Armament:	Twelve 550mm (21.7in) torpedo tubes, One 105mm (4in) gun
Powerplant:	Twin screws, diesel/electric motors
Performance:	Surfaced: 15 knots, submerged: 8 knots

Oscar class

The underwater equivalent of a Kirov-class battlecruiser, the first Oscar I-class cruise-missile submarine (SSGN) was laid down at Severodvinsk in 1978 and launched in the spring of 1980, starting sea trials later that year. The second was completed in 1982, and a third of the class – which became the first Oscar II – completed in 1985, followed by a fourth, fifth andf sixth at intervals of a year. The primary task of the Oscar class was to attack NATO carrier battle groups with a variety of submarine-launched cruise missiles, including the SS-N-19 Shipwreck; this has a range of 445km (240nm) at Mach 1.6. The SSM tubes are in banks of 12 either side and external to the pressure hull and are inclined at 40°, with one hatch covering each pair. Only the Oscar IIs remain in service. In 2000 118 men were lost aboard the *Kursk* when it sank after a torpedo's fuel exploded.

Country:	Soviet Union
Type:	Ballistic missile submarine
Launch date:	April 1980
Crew:	130
Displacement:	Surfaced: 11,685 tonnes (11,500t), submerged: 13,615 tonnes (13,400t)
Dimensions:	143m x 18.2m x 9m (469ft 2in x 59ft 8in x 29ft 6in)
Range:	Unlimited
Armament:	SS-N-15, SS-N-16 and SS-N-19 SSMs; four 533mm (21in) and four 650mm (25.6in) torpedo tubes
Powerplant:	Two shafts; two nuclear PWR; two turbines
Performance:	Surfaced: 22 knots, submerged: 30 knots

Oslo

The Royal Norwegian Navy's Oslo-class frigates are modifications of the Dealey class of escort destroyers which were built in the USA in the 1950s, with a higher freeboard forward (to suit the sea conditions off Norway) and many European-built sub-systems. The five ships in the class – *Oslo*, *Bergen*, *Trondheim*, *Stavanger* and *Narvik* – were built under the 1960 five-year naval plan, with half the cost borne by the USA. The class underwent modernization refits in the 1970s, including the fitting of Penguin Mk2 SSMs, a NATO Sea Sparrow launcher and Mk32 ASW self-defence torpedo tubes. During the height of the Cold War, the vessels of the Oslo class provided the only major ASW force in the North Norwegian Sea area. *Oslo* sank while under tow on 24 January 1994 after running aground following a complete engine failure. The class will be phased out of service from 2005.

Country:	Norway
Type:	Frigate
Launch date:	17 January 1964
Crew:	150
Displacement:	1880 tonnes (1850 tons)
Dimensions:	96.6m x 11.2m x 4.4m (316ft 11in x 36ft 8in x 14ft 5in)
Range:	8338km (4500nm)
Main armament:	Two twin 76mm (3in) DP guns; two triple 324mm (12.75in) torpedo tubes; Sea Sparrow SAM; ASW rocket launchers
Powerplant:	Single shaft, geared steam turbines
Performance:	25 knots

Oyashio

The first two boats in a new class of Japanese SSK, *Oyashio* and *Michishio*, were laid down in January 1994 and February 1995 respectively. Five boats are planned in all, the construction work shared between Mitsubishi and Kawasaki at the Kobe shipyards. Although some damage was caused to the latter by the Kobe earthquake in Kanuary 1995, production was not disrupted. The boats are fitted with large flank sonar arrays; there are anechoic tiles on the fin and double hull sections fore and aft. The class was developed from the earlier Harushio-class boats and the two classes strongly resemble one another, although the Oyashios have a greater displacement. The fifth boat is due to commission on March 2002. The Oyashios are thought to have a greater endurance than any previous Japanese submarines.

Country:	Japan
Type:	Attack submarine
Launch date:	15 October 1996
Crew:	69
Displacement:	Surfaced: 2743 tonnes (2700 tons), submerged: 3048 tonnes (3000 tons)
Dimensions:	81.7m x 8.9m x 7.9m (268ft x 29ft 2in x 25ft 11in)
Surface range:	Classified
Armament:	Six 533mm (21in) torpedo tubes; Sub Harpoon SSM
Powerplant:	Single shaft, diesel/electric motors
Performance:	Surfaced: 12 knots, submerged: 20 knots

PC Type

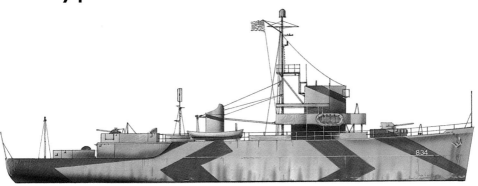

Given the immense length of the seaboards of the United States, together with major Caribbean routes and the Panama Canal, the US Navy had a big problem in protecting its coastal traffic. The vulnerability of shipping not in convoy on the eastern seaboard was ruthlessly exposed by the German U-boat campaign of 1942, but it had been anticipated, in that three prototype 53.26m (174ft 9in) Patrol Craft (PC Type) were completed before the USA's entry into the war. These were slim diesel craft which, although relatively well armed, were restricted by their size to inshore work. A massive building programme was instituted, and over 350 of these craft were built. Fifteen served with the Royal Navy as the Kil class (e.g. *Kilmarnock*). The latter participated in the destruction of the *U-731* off Tangier in May 1944 in the only U-boat sinking credited to the class.

Country:	USA
Type:	Escort
Launch date:	1938 (first unit)
Crew:	100
Displacement:	864 tonnes (850 tons)
Dimensions:	56.24m x 10.05m x 2.89m (184ft 6in x 33ft x 9ft 6in)
Range:	6485km (3500nm)
Main armament:	One 76mm (3in) gun; three 40mm (1.5in) and four 20mm (0.7in) AA; depth charges and Hedgehog
Powerplant:	Two shafts, two diesel engines
Performance:	16 knots

Papa

In 1970 the Soviet shipyard at Severodvinsk launched a single unit of what came to be known in NATO circles as the Papa class. The boat was considerably larger and had two more missile tubes than the contemporary Charlie-class SSGNs, and was for long a puzzle to Western intelligence services. The answer appeared in 1980 at the same shipyard with the even larger Oscar-class SSGN; the Papa-class unit had been the prototype for advanced SSGN concepts with a considerably changed powerplant and a revised screw arangement incorporating five or seven blades. The missile system's function had been to test the underwater-launched version of the SS-N-9 Siren for the subsequent Charlie II series of SSGN. The Oscar design produced yet further improvements, with two 12-round banks of submerged-launch long-range SS-N19 anti-ship missile tubes.

Country:	Soviet Union
Type:	Attack submarine
Launch date:	1970
Crew:	110
Displacement:	Surfaced: 6198 tonnes (6100 tons), submerged: 7112 tonnes (7000 tons)
Dimensions:	109m x 11.5m x 7.6m (357ft 7in x 37ft 9in x 24ft 11in)
Range:	Unlimited
Armament:	Six 533mm (21in) and two 406mm (16in) torpedo tubes
Powerplant:	Two shafts, one nuclear PWR, two turbines
Performance:	Surfaced: 20 knots, submerged: 39 knots

Pegaso

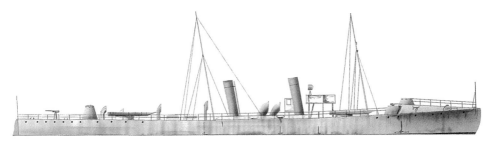

***P**egaso* was the lead ship of five vessels in a class that eventually increased to 27 units. Their design was very successful, proving strong and seaworthy. *Pegaso* was laid down at Pattison's yard in August 1904, launched a year later and completed in September 1905. Her engines developed 3200hp, and her range at maximum speed was nearly 646km (348nm). She was converted to oil fuel in 1908, and later served in World War I. *Pegaso* was discarded in March 1923; her name, however, was resurrected and given to an escort destroyer of the Orsa class in World War II. The latter vessel was launched in 1938 and scuttled in Pollensa Bay, Majorca, on 11 September 1943, following Italy's armistice with the Allies. The other vessels in the 1905 Pegaso class were *Perseo*, *Procione* and *Pallade*. They were classed as High Seas Torpedo Boats.

Country:	Italy
Type:	Torpedo boat
Launch date:	August 1905
Crew:	50
Displacement:	210 tonnes (207 tons)
Dimensions:	50.3m x 5.3m x 1.7m (165ft 2in x 17ft 5in x 5ft 8in)
Range:	2224km (1200nm)
Main armament:	Two 57mm (2.25in) guns; three 450mm (17.7in) torpedo tubes
Powerplant:	Twin screws, vertical triple expansion engines
Performance:	23 knots

Pelayo

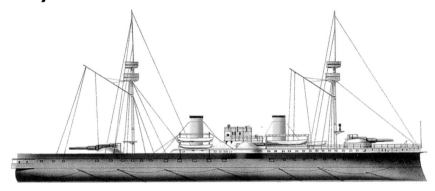

L aunched in 1887, *Pelayo* was Spain's most powerful warship for over 20 years.
She was built in France to designs by Lagane, one of the world's leading naval
architects. She was based on the French *Marceau*, with slightly increased length and
beam, and with reduced draught to allow her passage through the Suez Canal. *Pelayo*
was rebuilt in 1897, and was given new boilers and armour over the midship battery.
In 1898, at the time of the Spanish–American War, she set sail for the Philippines at the
head of a squadron of warships, but was held up at Port Said and recalled when the
conflict ended. The brief war with the USA cost Spain her entire Pacific Squadron,
destroyed in the Battle of Manila Bay, and a second squadron, despatched to the
Caribbean. It remained blockaded in Santiago harbour until it emerged and was
sunk by waiting US warships. *Pelayo* was removed from the effective list in 1925.

Country:	Spain
Type:	Battleship
Launch date:	5 February 1887
Crew:	520
Displacement :	9900 tonnes (9745 tons)
Dimensions:	102m x 20m x 7.5m (334ft 8in x 66ft 3in x 24ft 9in)
Range:	3204km (1780nm) at 10 knots
Armament:	Two 317mm (12.5in), two 279mm (11in), one 162mm (6.4in), 12 120mm (4.7in) guns
Powerplant:	Twin screw, vertical compound engines
Performance:	16.7 knots

Pellicano

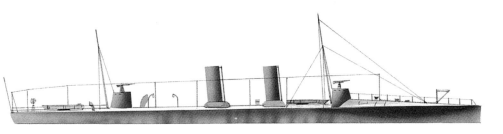

Launched in April 1899, *Pellicano* was commissioned in 1900 as a first-class torpedo boat with a design speed of 25.7 knots, but because of unreliable machinery, this speed was never achieved. Pellicano's vertical triple expansion engines were served by three Blechynden boilers, producing 2740hp. She was an excellent seaboat, however, and served as the prototype for a later group of ocean-going vessels launched between 1905 and 1906. She was discarded in 1920. *Pellicano* and others of her era laid the foundations for Italian torpedo-boat tactics, in which the Italian Navy excelled right up to World War II. Torpedo boats proved ideal vehicles for offensive operations in the Adriatic in World War I, where high speed and manoeuvrability were key factors in combat operations against the Austro–Hungarian fleet.

Country:	Italy
Type:	Torpedo boat
Launch date:	April 1899
Crew:	25
Displacement:	183 tonnes (181 tons)
Dimensions:	48.7m x 5.7m x 1.5m (159ft 10in x 18ft 10in x 5ft)
Range:	Not known
Main armament:	Two 37mm (1.5in) guns; two 355mm (14in) torpedo tubes
Powerplant:	Vertical triple expansion engines
Performance:	21 knots

Pennsylvania

***P*ennsylvania** was completed in 1916 and with her sister *Arizona* boasted a
main armament of 12 356mm (14in) guns triple-mounted in four turrets. The
triple mount later became a characteristic of American capital ships. *Pennsylvania*
was reconstructed between the wars to include a large anti-aircraft armament,
two aircraft catapults, two tripod masts and a strengthened submarine bulge and
bulkheads. She came through World War II, though *Arizona* did not, being destroyed
at Pearl Harbor in 1941. *Pennsylvania* herself was damaged by bombs while in dry
dock at Pearl Harbor, and after reconstruction she fought at Attu, the Gilbert
Islands, Kwajalein, Eniwetok, Saipan, Guam, Palau, Leyte Gulf, Surigao Strait and
Lingayen. On 12 August 1945 she was severely damaged by an aerial torpedo. After
the war she took part in two nuclear bomb tests, ending her days as a target ship.

Country:	USA
Type:	Battleship
Launch date:	16 March 1915
Crew:	915
Displacement :	33,088 tonnes (32,567 tons)
Dimensions:	182.9m x 185.4 x 29.6m x 8.8m (608ft x 97ft 1in x 28ft 10in)
Range:	14,400km (8000nm) at 12 knots
Armament:	12 356mm (14in), 22 127mm (5in) guns
Powerplant:	Four shaft,geared turbines
Performance:	21 knots

Perth

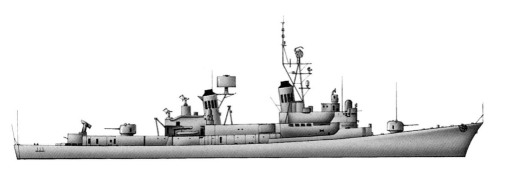

A ustralia's three Perth-class guided-missile destroyers (the others are the *Hobart* and *Brisbane*) were modified vessels of the American Charles F. Adams class, all commissioned in the mid-1960s. The ships underwent several updates; *Perth* was first modernised in 1974 in the USA, when Standard missiles, replacement gun mountings, a new combat data system, and modern radars were fitted. *Hobart* and *Brisbane* were brought up to the same standard in 1978 and 1979 at the Garden Island Dockyard in Sydney. A further upgrade was carried out between 1987 and 1991, all ships receiving the Phalanx CIWS, new search and fire control radars, decoy and ECM equipment, and the new Mk13 missile launcher for the Harpoon SSM. The earlier Ikara ASW system was removed at the same time as these updates were completed. All three were decommissioned by 2001.

Country:	USA/Australia
Type:	Destroyer
Launch date:	26 September 1963
Crew:	310
Displacement:	4692 tonnes (4618 tons)
Dimensions:	134.3m x 14.3m x 6.1m (440ft 9in x 47ft 1in x 20ft 1in)
Range:	9650km (5210nm)
Main armament:	Two 127mm (5in) guns; Phalanx CIWS; Harpoon SSM; Standard SAM; six 324mm (12.75in) torpedo tubes
Powerplant:	Two shafts, two geared steam turbines
Performance:	30+ knots

Petr Veliki

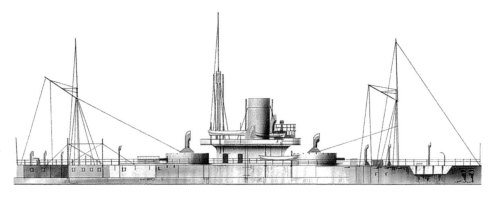

P etr Veliki was a large, breastwork turret ship with an iron hull and 2.4m (8ft) freeboard. Her armour belt was complete, but submerged at full load. Her side armour had 550mm (22in) of wood between two plates of 175mm (7in). Completed in 1872, she received new engines in a refit in 1881, and was reconstructed in 1905–06. Renamed *Barrikada* after the 1917 revolution, she served as a gunnery training ship with the Baltic fleet. She was scrapped in 1922. The Russian Revolution destroyed the effectiveness of the fleet, especially that of the larger ships, which were completely immobilised. Without their officers, who had either been killed or were with the White Russian forces, the ships were controlled by enlisted men, who had little idea of how to operate or maintain them. Many of the ships under White control sailed for Tunisia at the end of the civil war.

Country:	Russia
Type:	Battleship
Launch date:	27 August 1872
Crew:	432
Displacement:	10,572 tonnes (10,406 tons)
Dimensions:	103.5m x 18.9m x 8.2m (339ft 8in x 62ft 3in x 27ft)
Range:	3706km (2000nm) at 10 knots
Armament:	Four 305mm (12in), six 86mm (3.4in) guns
Powerplant:	Twin screw, horizontal return connecting rod engines
Performance:	10 knots

Petya class

The 18 units of the Petya I class were constructed at the Kaliningrad and Komsomolsk shipyards between 1961 and 1964. From the latter year until 1969 both shipyards switched to building a total of 27 Petya II class units, which differed from their predecessors in having an extra quintuple 606mm (16in) ASW torpedo tube mounting in place of the two aft ASW rocket launchers. From 1973 onwards, eight Petya I vessels were modified to give the 'Petya I (Mod)' sub-class. The conversion involved the addition of a medium-frequency variable-depth sonar in a new raised stern deckhouse. A further three units were converted as trials vessels. During the Cold War, the Petya-class boats were often used in the intelligence-gathering role, shadowing NATO warships during exercises in northern waters, particularly off North Cape and in the north Norwegian Sea.

Country:	Soviet Union
Type:	Frigate
Launch date:	31 December 1970 (first unit completed)
Crew:	98
Displacement:	1168 tonnes (1150 tons)
Dimensions:	81.8m x 9.1m x 2.9m (268ft 5in x 29ft 11in x 9ft 5in)
Range:	2779km (1500nm)
Main armament:	Twin 76mm (3in) DP guns; 533mm (21in) mounting for five or 10 AS torpedoes; ASW rocker launchers
Powerplant:	Three shafts, two gas turbines, two diesels
Performance:	33 knots

Pobieda

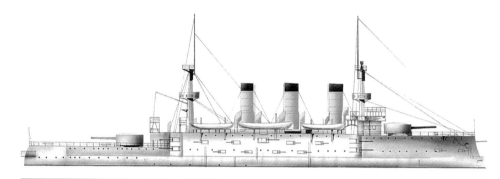

Completed in 1902, *Pobieda*'s engines developed 15,000hp, and coal supply was 2032 tonnes (2000 tons). *Pobieda*, *Peresviet* and *Osliabia*, all of the same class, were the first Russian warships to feature quick-firing guns. They had a high forecastle with their secondary armament mounted on two decks. *Pobieda* joined the Pacific squadron in 1903, in time for the war with Japan; in February 1904 she was slightly damaged by gunfire in action at Port Arthur, and further damaged by a mine in April, but survived thanks to the protection given by her coal bunker and internal armour. On 10 August she took 11 hits in the Battle of the Yellow Sea, and was again repeatedly hit by shore batteries in October–November. In December 1904 she was sunk by salvos of 279mm (11in) shells, but raised by the Japanese in 1905 and renamed *Suwo*. She was scrapped in 1922.

Country:	Russia
Type:	Battleship
Launch date:	May 1900
Crew:	757
Displacement:	12,872 tonnes (12,670 tons)
Dimensions:	133m x 21.7m x 8.3m (436ft 4in x 71ft 5in x 27ft 3in)
Range:	11,118km (6000nm) at 10 knots
Armament:	Four 254mm (10in), 11 152mm (6in), 20 75mm (3in), guns
Powerplant:	Triple screw, vertical triple expansion engines
Performance:	18.5 knots

Prat

The use of British warships is traditional in the Chilean Navy. The Chilean Navy's four ex-Royal Navy County-class destroyers, *Prat* (ex-*Norfolk*), *Cochrane* (ex-*Antrim*), *Latorre* (ex-*Glamorgan*) and *Blanco Encalada* (ex-*Fife*) were transferred from the UK between April 1982 and August 1987, extensive refits being carried out after transfer. All are named after senior officers, but the titles Almirante and Capitan are not used, a practice at variance with that of other Latin American navies. In 1988 *Blanco Encalada* was converted as a helicopter carrier for two Super Pumas, *Cochrane* being similarly converted in 1994. The two remaining vessels serve as flagships. All four ships are fitted with the Israeli Barak I short-range SAM system. The ships differ greatly in appearance, the helicopter carriers having a greatly enlarged flight deck continuing right aft.

Country:	Great Britain/Chile
Type:	Destroyer
Launch date:	16 November 1967
Crew:	470
Displacement:	6299 tonnes (6200 tons)
Dimensions:	158.7m x 16.5m x 6.3m (520ft 6in x 54 ft x 20ft 6in)
Range:	5620km (3038nm)
Main armament:	Two 115mm (4.5in) guns; Exocet SSM; Seaslug and Barak SAM; six 324mm (12.75in) torpedo tubes
Powerplant:	Two shafts, two geared steam turbines, four gas turbines
Performance:	30 knots

Prince Albert

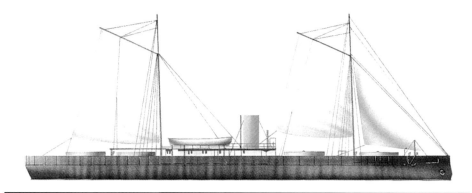

P*rince Albert* was Britain's first iron turret ship, and was built by Cowper Coles as a direct challenge to Admiralty policy. The turrets were all carried on the centreline, two forward of the midship superstructure and two aft. *Prince Albert* was originally designed with six turrets, but they were later reduced to four. Each turret weighed 112 tonnes (111 tons) and was hand-worked. The vessel was laid down in 1862, but construction was not completed until four years later, in 1866. Although *Prince Albert* enjoyed a fairly long military career, the warship had a singularly uneventful service life. She was on the reserve for most of her career and finished up in the Particular Service Squadron at Portsmouth in 1878. She was reboiled in the same year. *Prince Albert* was sold in 1899 and subsequently scrapped in 1904.

Country:	Great Britain
Type:	Battleship
Launch date:	23 May 1864
Crew:	201
Displacement:	3942 tonnes (3880 tons)
Dimensions:	73.1m x 14.6m x 6.2m (240ft x 48ft x 20ft 6in)
Range:	1500km (810nm) at 10 knots
Armament:	Four 229mm (9in) muzzle-loading guns
Powerplant:	Single screw, horizontal direct acting engines
Performance:	11.2 knots

Prince of Wales

*P**rince of Wales* was launched in 1939 and completed in 1941. Her main armament
was housed in two quadruple 356mm (14in) gun turrets fore and aft and a
double 356mm (14in) turret superfiring forward. She took part in the hunt for the
Bismark in May 1941 with her construction incomplete and workers still on her.
Whilst engaging the German battleship she took hits on her bridge and below her
waterline but survived. In August 1941 she took Winston Churchill to an historic
meeting with President Franklin D. Roosevelt in Newfoundland. Later in 1941 she was
sent to the Far East as a last-minute defence against the Japanese invasion of Malaya.
With the battlecruiser *Repulse* and four destroyers she sortied on 9 December. The
next day she and *Repulse* were attacked by Japanese aircraft and within two hours
both had been sunk. *Prince of Wales* had been operational for only seven months.

Country:	Great Britain
Type:	Battleship
Launch date:	3 May 1939
Crew:	1422
Displacement:	41,402 tonnes (42,076 tons)
Dimensions:	227.1m x 31.4m x 9.9m (745ft x 103ft x 32ft 7in)
Range:	25,942km (14,000nm) at 10 knots
Armament:	10 356mm (14in), 16 131mm (5.25in) guns
Powerplant:	Four shaft, geared turbines
Performance:	28 knots

Queen Elizabeth

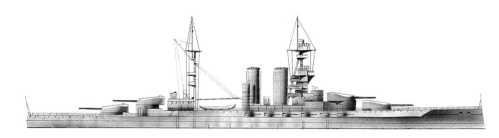

Completed in 1915, *Queen Elizabeth* was a major advance in battleship development, and was the first capital ship to be built with oil-burning boilers. She was fast, but her reliance upon oil fuel concerned critics, who foresaw disaster if oil supplies were ever interrupted. As a result, the following Revenge class carried both coal and oil fuel. She saw service in the Dardanelles in 1915, but missed the Battle of Jutland the following year due to a refit. Converted to a flagship, she was rebuilt between 1937–41. Assigned to the Mediterranean Fleet, she was in action off Crete in May 1941. In December that year she was severely damaged in a daring attack by Italian frogmen in Alexandria harbour. In 1943–44 she served with the Home Fleet, then sailed for the Indian Ocean, where she completed her war service. She was scrapped in 1948–49.

Country:	Great Britain
Type:	Battleship
Launch date:	16 October 1913
Crew:	951
Displacement:	33,548 tonnes (33,020 tons)
Dimensions:	196.8m x 27.6m x 10m (646ft x 90ft 6in x 30ft)
Range:	8100km (4500nm) at 10 knots
Armament:	Eight 380mm (15in), 16 152mm (6in) guns
Powerplant:	Quadruple screw turbines
Performance:	23 knots

Rattlesnake

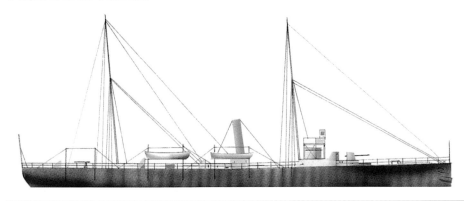

*R*attlesnake was one of the world's first torpedo gunboats, and was the first to be commissioned into the Royal Navy. She was the second ship to bear the name *Rattlesnake*; the first was a Jason-class wooden screw corvette, launched in 1861. She was built to counteract the expanding fleets of torpedo boats then being constructed by many countries – including Russia, with whom there was a threat of war over Afghanistan – and which constituted a serious threat to capital ships. Earlier vessels built for the same purpose, such as the British 1605-tonne (1580-ton) *Scout* and the French 1300-tonne (1280-ton) *Condor*, had proved too large and unwieldy, and so it was decided to build a smaller vessel able to maintain high speed. *Rattlesnake*'s engines developed 2700hp and she had a 19mm (0.75in) thick steel protective deck. She was sold in 1910.

Country:	Great Britain
Type:	Torpedo gunboat
Launch date:	11 September 1886
Crew:	66
Displacement:	558 tonnes (550 tons)
Dimensions:	60.9m x 7m x 3m (200ft x 23ft x 10ft 4in)
Range:	Not known
Main armament:	One 102mm (4in) gun; four 355mm (14in) torpedo tubes
Powerplant:	Twin screws, triple expansion engines
Performance:	19.2 knots

Redoutable

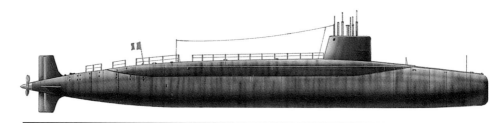

L aid down at Cherbourg Naval Dockyard on 30 March 1964, *Le Redoutable* was France's first ballistic-missile submarine, and the prototype of the seaborne element of the French Force de Dissuasion (Deterrent Force), which ultimately consisted of boats armed with the MSBS (Mer-Sol Ballistique Strategique) IRBM. The French term for SSBN is SNLE (Sous-marin Nucleaire Lance-Engins). The *Redoutable* reached IOC in December 1971; *Le Terrible* followed in 1973, *Le Foudroyant* in 1974, *Indomptable* in 1977 and *Le Tonnant* in 1979. Later, all units except *Le Redoutable* were armed with the Aerospatiale M4 three-stage solid fuel missile, which has a range of 5300km (2860nm) and carries six MIRV, each of 150kT. The M4 missiles can be discharged at twice the rate of the M20. The *Redoutable* was withdrawn in 1991.

Country:	France
Type:	Attack submarine
Launch date:	29 March 1967
Crew:	142
Displacement:	Surfaced: 7620 tonnes (7500 tons), submerged: 9144 tons (9000 tons)
Dimensions:	128m x 10.6m x 10m (420ft x 34ft 10in x 32ft 10in)
Range:	Unlimited
Armament:	16 submarine-launched MRBMs
Powerplant:	One nuclear PWR, turbines
Performance:	Surfaced: 20 knots, submerged: 28 knots

Renown

Constructed in just a year, *Renown* and her sister *Repulse* were the last British battlecruisers. Heavily armed, but sacrificing protective armour for high speed, within a month of her launch in October 1916 *Renown* was back in dock to be fitted with another 492 tonnes (500 tons) of steel plate. Even then she was thought to be too lightly built – even for the recoil of her 380mm (15in) guns – and was to receive extra armour during refits in 1918 and 1923. Converted into a fast carrier escort in 1936, she took part in operations against commerce raiders in the South Atlantic in 1939 and was damaged in action off Norway in April 1940. She subsequently took part in the hunt for *Bismarck*, escorted convoys to Malta, in the Atlantic and the Arctic, and formed part of the covering force during the Allied landings in North Africa. She served with the Eastern Fleet in 1944–45. She was broken up at Faslane in 1948.

Country:	Great Britain
Type:	Battlecruiser
Launch date:	4 March 1916
Crew:	1200
Displacement:	30,356 tonnes (30,850 tons)
Dimensions:	242.2m x 27.4m x 7.8m (794ft x 90ft x 25ft 6in)
Range:	6570km (3650nm) at 12 knots
Armament:	Six 380mm (15in), 17 102mm (4in) guns
Powerplant:	Four shaft, geared turbines
Performance:	30 knots

Resolution

In February 1963 the British Government stated its intention to order four or five Resolution-class nuclear-powered ballistic missile submarines, armed with the American Polaris SLBM, to take over the British nuclear deterrent role from the RAF from 1968. With characteristics very similar to the American Lafayettes, the lead ship HMS *Resolution* was commissioned in October 1967. HMS *Repulse* followed in September 1968, with the HMS *Renown* and HMS *Revenge* commissioning in November 1968 and December 1969 respectively. Early in 1968 *Resolution* undertook missile trials with Polaris off Florida, and four months later she made her first operational patrol. In the 1990s the Resolution-class boats were progressively replaced by the new Vanguard class SSBNs, armed with the Trident II missile. The first of these was commissioned in August 1993.

Country:	Britain
Type:	Ballistic missile submarine
Launch date:	September 1966
Crew:	154
Displacement:	Surfaced: 7620 tonnes (7500 tons), submerged: 8535 tonnes (8400 tons)
Dimensions:	129.5m x 10.1m x 9.1m (425ft x 33ft x 30ft)
Range:	Unlimited
Armament:	Sixteen Polaris A3TK IRBMs; six 533mm (21in) torpedo tubes
Powerplant:	Single shaft, one nuclear PWR, two steam turbines
Performance:	Surfaced: 20 knots, submerged: 25 knots

Retvisan

R *etvisan* was the only capital ship to be built for the Russians by a US yard, and her design was standard US type, with a flush-deck and central superstructure. During the Russo-Japanese war in 1904 she was torpedoed off Port Arthur. She survived, but was later hit by howitzers during the Battle of the Yellow Sea and sunk. When Port Arthur fell in 1905 she was raised by the Japanese. Renamed *Hizen*, she was used as a target and finally sunk in 1924. Numerically, the Russian Far Eastern and Japanese fleets were not dissimilar, but Japan commanded the approaches to Port Arthur and Vladivostok. The former was attacked without declaration of war by Japanese destroyers on the night of 8/9 February 1904, two battleships (one the *Retvisan*) and a cruiser being damaged. Weeks later a Japanese invasion force laid siege to the base, precipitating the war that resulted in the destruction of the Russian fleet at Tsushima.

Country:	Russia
Type:	Battleship
Launch date:	October 1900
Crew:	738
Displacement :	13,106 tonnes (12,900 tons)
Dimensions:	117.8m x 22m x 7.9m (386ft 8in x 72ft 2in x 26ft)
Range:	7412km (4000nm) at 10 knots
Armament:	Four 304mm (12in), 12 152mm (6in), 20 11-pounder guns
Powerplant:	Twin screw, vertical triple expansion engines
Performance:	18.8 knots

Richelieu

*R*ichelieu was first in a class of four battleships planned between 1935 and 1938, but she was the only one completed in time to see action during World War II. Launched in March 1940, *Richelieu* escaped the fall of France and joined the Allies in 1942, forming part of a powerful battle group that included battleships *Valiant*, *Howe* and *Queen Elizabeth*, battlecruiser *Renown* and carriers *Victorious*, *Illustrious* and *Indomitable*. She escorted many attack sorties by the carriers on Java, Sumatra and the various enemy-held island groups in the Indian Ocean. She underwent a substantial refit in the USA in 1943, when radar and an extra 100 anti-aircraft guns were added. Joining the British Eastern Fleet in 1944, she served until the end of the war. She later operated off Indo-China during France's war there. *Richelieu* was paid off and hulked in 1959, and was broken up in 1964.

Country:	France
Type:	Battleship
Launch date:	17 January 1939
Crew:	1670
Displacement :	47,084 tonnes (47,850 tons)
Dimensions:	247.85m x 33m x 9.63m (813ft 2in x 108ft 3in x 31ft 7in)
Range:	10,800km (6000nm) at 12 knots
Armament:	Eight 380mm (15in), nine 152mm (6in) guns
Powerplant:	Four shaft, geared turbines
Performance:	30 knots

Riga class

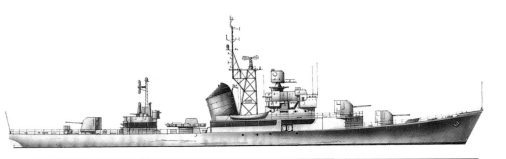

Built at the Kaliningrad, Nikolayev and Komsomolsk shipyards, the 64 units – including eight for export – of the Riga class were the design successors to the six slightly older Kola class destroyers. The class proved to be an excellent coastal defence design and followed the Soviet practice in the 1950s of building flush-decked hulls with a sharply raised forecastle. The Rigas were fitted with the Haymarket search radar.Over the years, the vessels of the Riga class constituted one of the larger Soviet warship classes, and numbers were exported. Two went to Bulgaria, five to the former German Deomocratic Republic (one of which was burnt out in an accident soon after being taken over), two went to Finland, and eight to Indonesia. These units have now been scrapped. All Riga-class units still on the Russian inventory, latterly used as training vessels, are now permanently laid up.

Country:	Soviet Union
Type:	Frigate
Launch date:	30 July 1952 (Gornostay, first unit)
Crew:	175
Displacement:	1534 tonnes (1510 tons)
Dimensions:	91.5m x 10.1m x 3.2m (300ft 2in x 33ft 1in x 10ft 6in)
Range:	4632km (2500nm)
Main armament:	Three single 100mm (3.9in) DP; two twin 37mm (1.4in) or 25mm (1in) AA guns; anti-ship torpedoes; ASW rockets
Powerplant:	Two shafts, geared steam turbines
Performance:	28 knots

River

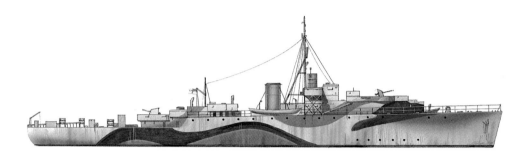

With the limitations of the Flower-class corvette readily apparent, the British Admiralty produced a design for a larger twin-screw corvette which became known as the River class (the term 'frigate' was not officially reintroduced into the Royal Navy until 1942). Overall they were about 28.3m (93ft) longer than the vessels of the later Flower class, and this made a very great difference in seakeeping, bunker capacity, installed power, and armament. Between 1941 and 1944, some 57 were launched in the UK, 70 in Canada and 11 in Australia. The River class was highly successful, but most of its survivors (seven were sunk in the war) had been scrapped by the mid-1950s. Further River-class vessels, to a slightly modified design, were built by the Americans as the PF type, 21 of which served in the Royal Navy as the Colony class.

Country:	Great Britain
Type:	Frigate
Launch date:	20 November 1941 (HMS Rother, first unit)
Crew:	107
Displacement:	1392 tonnes (1370 tons)
Dimensions:	91.9m x 11.12m x 3.91m (301ft 6in x 36ft 6in x 12ft 10in)
Range:	12,945km (6990nm)
Main armament:	Two 102mm (4in) guns; two two-pounders; depth charges
Powerplant:	Two shafts, triple expansion steam engines
Performance	20 knots

Roanoke

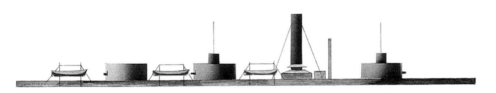

Roanoke was the only multi-turreted ironclad to see service in the American Civil War, and the first to be commissioned with more than two turrets. Originally she was a wooden-hulled, 40-gun steam frigate laid down in 1853. On March 9 1862 there was a celebrated action at Hampton Roads between the Union ironclad *Monitor* and the Confederate ironclad *Virginia*. The action was inconclusive, but it proved once and for all that the day of the turret ship had finally arrived. In May 1862 she was cut down to just above the waterline and the low freeboard was plated with iron armour. Three turrets were installed in January 1865 and she was rearmed, though the hull proved too weak for the weight of the turrets. When the war ended in 1865 she was taken out of service, and sold in 1883.

Country:	USA
Type:	Ironclad
Launch date:	April 1863
Crew:	350
Displacement:	4465 tonnes (4395 tons)
Dimensions:	80.7m x 16m x 7.4m (265ft x 52ft 6in x 24ft 3in)
Range:	Not known
Armament:	Two 380mm (15in), two 280mm (11in), two 150-pounder guns
Powerplant:	Single screw, horizontal direct acting engines
Performance:	6 knots

Romeo

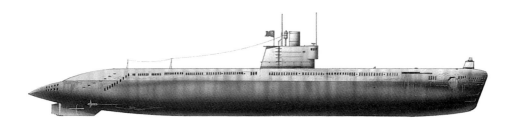

Although it was the Russians who built the first Romeo-class submarines in 1958 at Gorky, as an improvement on the Whiskey design, their construction coincided with the successful introduction of nuclear propulsion into Soviet submarines, so only 20 were completed out of the 560 boats originally planned. The design was passed to the Chinese and production began in China in 1962, at the Jiangnan (Shanghai) shipyard under the local designation Type 003. Three further shipyards then joined to give a maximum yearly production rate of nine units during the early 1970s. Production was completed in 1984 with a total of 98 built for the Chinese Navy; four more were exported to Egypt and seven to North Korea, with a further ten built locally with Chinese assistance. In February 1985 the North Koreans lost one of their Romeos with all hands in the Yellow Sea.

Country:	China
Type:	Attack submarine
Launch date:	1962
Crew:	60
Displacement:	Surfaced: 1351 tonnes (1330 tons), submerged: 1727 tonnes (1700 tons)
Dimensions:	77m x 6.7m x 4.9m (252ft 7in x 22ft x 16ft 1in)
Surface range:	29,632km (16,000nm) at 10 knots
Armament:	Eight 533mm (21in) torpedo tubes
Powerplant:	Twin screws, diesel/electric motors
Performance:	Surfaced: 16 knots, submerged: 13 knots

Royal Sovereign

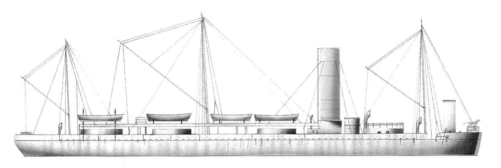

The battle of Hampton Roads between the turret ship *Monitor* and the broadside ship *Virginia* had a profound effect on British naval thinking. It was clear that the turret ship was far superior, so experimental ships, such as *Royal Sovereign,* were built. With the introduction of the ironclad, Britain was left with a large fleet of obsolete wooden battleships. In 1862, work began to convert one such vessel, the 121-gun three decker, *Royal Sovereign,* into Britain's first ironclad turret ship. The top two decks were cut off and five 266mm (10.5in) guns were mounted in four turrets, the fore turret housing two guns and the single turrets being placed on the centreline. The turrets weighed 153–165 tonnes (151–163 tons) and were manually operated. A light steadying rig was fitted. With the increased weight of her new armour, her speed fell from 12.2 to 11 knots. She was sold for scrap in 1885.

Country:	Great Britain
Type:	Battleship
Launch date:	25 April 1857
Crew:	300
Displacement :	5161 tonnes (5080 tons)
Dimensions:	73.3m x 18.9m x 7.6m (240ft 6in x 62ft x 25ft)
Range:	2779km (1500nm) at 10 knots
Armament:	Five 266mm (10.5in) guns
Powerplant:	Single screw, return connecting rod engine
Performance:	11 knots

Royal Sovereign

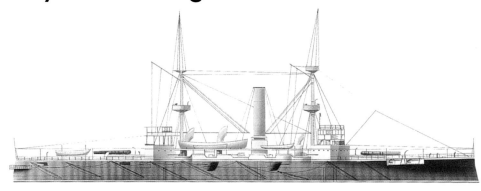

Designed by Sir William White, *Royal Sovereign* was laid down at Portsmouth Dockyard in September 1889 and was completed in 1892. She was one of 70 vessels ordered under the Naval Defence Act of 1889, and set the standard for most of the pre-dreadnought capital ships that followed. The idea of the new design was increased fighting efficiency, plus the maintenance of speed in a seaway. These requirements were only possible in a barbette ship carrying its guns high above the waterline, with a high freeboard for better seakeeping. *Royal Sovereign* was scrapped in 1919. Other ships in the Royal Sovereign class were *Empress of India*, *Ramillies*, *Repulse*, *Resolution*, *Revenge* and *Royal Oak*. Of these, only *Revenge* served in World War I, being returned to service as a bombarding ship in 1914. In August 1915 she was renamed *Redoubtable*. She was broken up in 1919.

Country:	Great Britain
Type:	Battleship
Launch date:	22 February 1891
Crew:	712
Displacement:	15,830 tonnes (15,580 tons)
Dimensions:	125m x 22.8m x 8.3m (410ft 6in x 75ft x 27ft 6in)
Range:	15,750km (4720nm) at 15 knots
Armament:	Four 343mm (13.5in), 10 152mm (6in) guns
Powerplant:	Twin screw, triple expansion engines
Performance:	16.5 knots

Rubis

The Saphir class of Fleet Nuclear-Attack Submarines (Sous-Marins Nucléaires d'Attaque, or SNA) comprises eight vessels, in two squadrons, one based at Lorient to cover the SSBN base and the other at Toulon. Eight boats are in service; *Rubis* (S601), *Saphir* (S602), *Casabianca* (S603), *Emeraude* (S604), *Améthyste* (S605), *Perle* (S606), *Turquoise* (S607) and *Diamant* (S608). The last five were built to a modified design, including a new bow form and silencing system, as well as new tactical and attack systems and improved electronics. The boats have a diving depth of 300m (984ft). Apart from the experimental 406-tonne (400-ton) *NR-1* of the US Navy, *Saphir* is the smallest nuclear-attack submarine ever built, reflecting France's advanced nuclear-reactor technology. *Rubis* became operational in February 1983, the last, *Diamant*, in 1999.

Country:	France
Type:	Attack submarine
Launch date:	7 July 1979
Crew:	67
Displacement:	Surfaced: 2423 tonnes (2385 tons), submerged: 2713 tonnes (2670 tons)
Dimensions:	72.1m x 7.6m x 6.4m (236ft 6in x 24ft 11in x 21ft)
Range:	Unlimited
Armament:	Four 533mm (21in) torpedo tubes; Exocet SSMs
Powerplant:	Single shaft, one nuclear PWR, auxiliary diesel/electric
Performance:	Surfaced: 25 knots, submerged: Classified

Ryujo

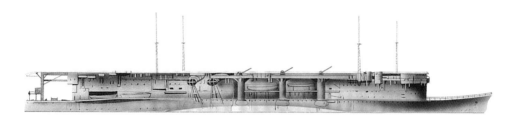

Launched in 1931, *Ryujo* was Japan's first major purpose-built aircraft carrier. She was designed with a cruiser hull, which restricted her width, and so a second hangar was built above the first. This resulted in increased top weight and instability, and almost immediately after her completion in May 1933 she was back in the dockyards for modification. Between 1934 and 1936 her hull was strengthened and her bulges widened. In December 1941 she was one of the ships covering the Japanese landings in the Philippines, followed by the Dutch East Indies in February 1942. The following April, she formed part of the Japanese carrier task force that made a major sortie into the Indian Ocean to strike at Ceylon. She subsequently moved back to the Pacific for operations against Midway Island, and was sunk by aircraft from USS *Saratoga* in August 1942 during the battle of the Eastern Solomons.

Country:	Japan
Type:	Aircraft carrier
Launch date:	2 April 1931
Crew:	924 (after 1936)
Displacement :	10,150 tonnes (9990 tons)
Dimensions:	175.3m x 23m x 5.5m (575ft 5in x 75ft 6in x 18ft 3in)
Range:	18,530km (10,000nm) at 14 knots
Armament:	12 127mm (5in) guns
Powerplant:	Twin screw, turbines
Performance:	29 knots

Sachsen

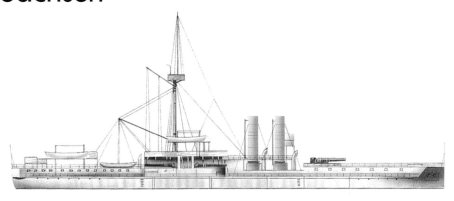

Completed in 1878, *Sachsen* was one of a class of four units which broke away from previous designs for German central battery and broadside ironclads. Two of the 260mm (10.25in) guns were carried in a pear-shaped redoubt on the forecastle, the rest being positioned in a rectangular barbette abaft the funnels. Armour covered the central citadel, and the armoured deck protected her ends. *Sachsen* did not have sails, but she carried a single military mast aft. In 1886 she was given three torpedo tubes, and in the late 1890s she was given new armour and engines. She was discarded in 1910. The other units in this class were *Baden*, *Bayern* and *Wurttemberg*. *Baden* was fleet flagship; she was used as a target hulk in 1920 and broken up at Kiel in 1938. *Bayern* suffered a similar fate, while *Wurttemberg* served as a torpedo school ship before being broken up at Wilhelmshaven in 1920.

Country:	Germany
Type:	Battleship
Launch date:	21 July 1877
Crew:	317
Displacement:	5767 tonnes (5677 tons)
Dimensions:	98.2m x 18.3m x 6.5m (322ft 2in x 60ft 4in x 21ft 5in)
Range:	9265km (5000nm) at 12 knots
Armament:	Six 260mm (10.25in), six 86mm (3.4in) guns
Powerplant:	Twin screw, horizontal single expansion engines
Performance:	13.5 knots

Salamander

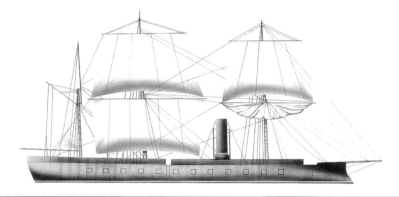

S *alamander* was Austria's first ironclad. She was laid down in 1861 and completed in 1862, one of the fastest building times for a new type of vessel. She was a wooden-hulled broadside, with a full-length waterline belt which rose at the foremast to protect the battery. She was refitted and rearmed between 1869–70 and given an increased sail area. Stricken in 1883, she then served as a mine store until she was scrapped in 1896. The other vessel in this class was *Drache* (Dragon), which was completed in November 1862. Like her sister ship, she took part in the Battle of Lissa in 1866, where she received some damage. She was refitted and rearmed in 1867–68, stricken in 1875 and broken up in 1883. Both vessels were designed as a response to Sardinia'a Formidabile class of iron hull armoured corvettes, which were originally designed as floating batteries.

Country:	Austria
Type:	Ironclad
Launch date:	22 August 1861
Crew:	346
Displacement:	3075 tonnes (3027 tons)
Dimensions:	62.8m x 13.9m x 6.3m (206ft x 45ft 7in x 20ft 8in)
Range:	2779km (1500nm) at 10 knots
Armament:	14 150mm (5.9in), 14 68-pounder guns
Powerplant:	Single screw, horizontal low pressure engines
Performance:	11.3 knots

Salisbury

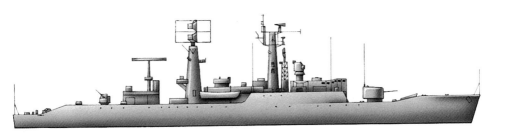

The Bangladesh Navy's sole ex-Salisbury-class (Type 61) frigate was formerly HMS *Llandaff*, now the *Umar Farooq*, completed in April 1958. The Salisbury class was designed primarily for the direction of carrier-borne and shore-based aircraft, but could also serve as a lighter type of destroyer on offensive operations. All ships of the class were named after cathedral cities. *Salisbury* underwent an extended refit in 1962, and *Llandaff* followed in 1966. Four ships of the class were completed; a fifth vessel was to have been named *Exeter*, and a sixth, to have been named *Coventry*, was originally ordered as *Panther* but was completed as the Leander-class frigate *Penelope*. In their fighter direction role, the Salisburys were integrated with the UK air defence system. In Royal Navy service, the obsolete Type 61s were replaced by the Type 21 Amazon-class general-purpose frigates.

Country:	Great Britain/Bangladesh
Type:	Frigate
Launch date:	25 June 1953
Crew:	207
Displacement:	2447 tonnes (2408 tons)
Dimensions:	103.6m x 12.2m x 4.7m (339ft 10in x 40ft x 15ft 6in)
Range:	12,056km (6510nm)
Main armament:	Two 115mm (4.5in) guns; two 40mm (1.5in) AA; A/S mortars
Powerplant:	Two shafts, eight diesel engines
Performance:	24 knots

San Francisco

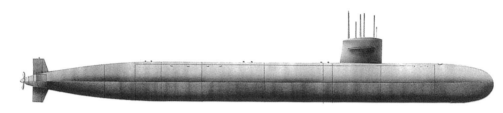

Originally designed as a counter to the Russian Victor-class SSN, this is one of a class of versatile vessels, fulfilling a variety of roles from land attack with their onboard GDC/Hughes Tomahawk TLAM-N missiles, to anti-ship with the Harpoon SSM, and anti-submarine with their Mk48 and ADCAP (Advanced Capability) torpedoes, the first of which was fired by the USS *Norfolk* on 23 July 1988 at the target destroyer *Jonas K Ingram*. Nine of the class were involved in the Gulf War of 1991, two firing Tomahawk missiles at targets in Iraq from stations in the eastern Mediterranean. By 1991 75 per cent of the attack-submarine force was equipped with the Tomahawk; from SN719 (USS *Providence)* onwards all are equipped with the vertical launch system, which places 12 launch tubes external to the pressure hull behind the BQQ5 spherical array forward.

Country:	USA
Type:	Attack submarine
Launch date:	27 October 1979
Crew:	133
Displacement:	Surfaced: 6180 tonnes (6082 tons), submerged: 7038 tonnes (6927t)
Dimensions:	110.3m x 10.1m x 9.9m (362ft x 33ft x 32ft 3in)
Range:	Unlimited
Armament:	Four 533mm (21in) torpedo tubes; Tomahawk Land Attack Cruise Missiles, Harpoon SSM
Powerplant:	Single shaft, nuclear PWR, turbines
Performance:	Surfaced: 20 knots, submerged: 32 knots

Saumarez

War emergency programmes produced 112 fleet destroyers for the Royal Navy, but only through a great degree of standardisation and reduction of minimum peacetime standards. The two so-called intermediate classes, the eight-gun O and P classes, came first; they were followed by the Q class, the first in a long line of standard groups, based on the very successful J-class design. All the Q class were well received, and eight R-class destroyers were almost identical. With the S class, also of eight, came a modification to the forward lines to reduce spray wetness, a longstanding cause for complaint. They were the first to have 40mm(1.5in) AA guns and a full complement of 20mm (0.7in) Oerlikons. HMS *Saumarez* was launched in November 1942; all the ships in her class survived the war. Damaged by a mine in the Corfu Channel in 1946, *Saumarez* was scrapped in 1950.

Country:	Great Britain
Type:	Destroyer
Launch date:	20 November 1942
Crew:	225
Displacement:	1758 tonnes (1730 tons)
Dimensions:	109.19m x 10.87m x 2.9m (358ft 3in x 35ft 7in x 9ft 6in)
Range:	8690km (4692nm)
Main armament:	Four 119mm (4.7in) guns; two 40mm (0.7in) AA; eight or 12 20mm (0.7in) AA; eight 533mm (21in) torpedo tubes
Powerplant:	Two-shaft geared turbines
Performance:	36 knots

Scharnhorst

Launched in 1936, *Scharnhorst* and her sister *Gneisenau* were designed as fast commerce raiders. Though outgunned by the 400mm (16in) weapons of British battleships, plans existed to improve the main armament to 380mm (15in). War intervened and proposed turrets for bigger guns went to the *Bismarck*. *Scharnhorst* took part in the invasion of Norway in April 1940 where she was damaged. Despite this, she sank the carrier *Glorious* the following month. Considered a deadly threat, she was attacked for the next two years by surface ships, aircraft and mini-submarines, but remained operational. In February 1942 she escaped from the French port of Brest, to make a famous dash through the English Channel. She was mined and damaged en route. *Scharnhorst* was finally sunk in December 1943 by *Duke of York* and three cruisers on her way to attack an Arctic convoy.

Country:	Germany
Type:	Battleship
Launch date:	30 June 1936
Crew:	1840
Displacement :	38,277 tonnes (38,900 tons)
Dimensions:	229.8m x 30m x 9.91m (753ft 11in x 98ft 5in x 32ft 6in)
Range:	16,306km (8800nm) at 19 knots
Armament:	Nine 279mm (11in), 12 150mm (5.8in) guns
Powerplant:	Three shaft, geared turbines
Performance:	32 knots

Sevastopol

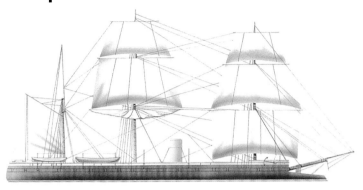

Sevastopol was Russia's first ocean-going ironclad. She was laid down in 1860 as a wooden-hulled, unarmoured frigate mounting 28 60-pounder guns. Conversion began in 1862, and she was completed as a battleship in 1865. Her armoured battery was 60m (195ft) long, and was positioned amidships. Two of the 203mm (8in) guns were placed outside the battery. Armoured bulkheads ran the length of the battery. *Sevastopol* was removed from the effective list during the 1880s. She was one of two wooden vessels converted to ironclads. They were followed by Russia's first armoured warship, *Pervenietz*, and more advanced ironclads such as the armoured frigates *Pozharski*, *Minin* and *General Admiral*. Some rather novel ships were designed by Russian naval constructors during this period, including a class of circular ironclads by A.A. Popov.

Country:	Russia
Type:	Ironclad
Launch date:	August 1864
Crew:	607
Displacement :	6228 tonnes (6130 tons)
Dimensions:	89.9m x 15.8m x 7.9m (295ft x 52ft x 26ft)
Range:	4632km (2500nm) at 10 knots
Armament:	16 203mm (8in), one 152mm (6in), eight 86mm (3.4in) guns
Powerplant:	Single screw, horizontal return engines
Performance:	12 knots

Shinano

At the time of her completion, *Shinano* was the world's largest aircraft carrier, but she was to have the shortest career of any major warship of her type when, on 29 November 1944, she was sunk by the US submarine *Archerfish*. *Shinano* was a Yamato class battleship, but after carrier losses at the Battle of Midway she was converted into an auxiliary carrier with massive internal capacity for transporting supplies of fuel and spares, plus aircraft, to the Japanese task forces. Her single storey hangar was 168m (550ft) long, and her own air group of 40–50 planes were housed forward, with the replacement aircraft for the task forces stowed aft. She was torpedoed and sunk while on her way to Kure for final fitting out. There is little doubt that the decisive Battle of Midway turned the tide of the Pacific war. The lack of strong carrier forces afterwards put an end to Japanese hopes of further conquest.

Country:	Japan
Type:	Aircraft carrier
Launch date:	8 October 1944
Crew:	2400
Displacement:	74,208 tonnes 973,040 tons)
Dimensions:	266m x 40m x 10.3m (872ft 9in x 131ft 3in x 33ft 9in)
Range:	13,340km (7200nm) at 16 knots
Armament:	16 127mm (5in), 145 25mm (1in) guns, 336 rocket launchers, 70 aircraft
Powerplant:	Quadruple screw turbines
Performance:	28 knots

Sierra class

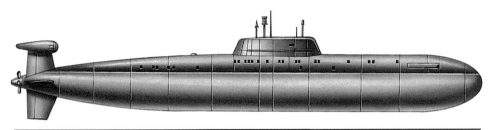

T wo SSNs of the Sierra I class were laid down at Gorky and Severodvinsk Shipyards in 1983, launched in July 1986 and commissioned in September 1987. The first boat, *Tula* (formerly *Karp*) was still operational in the late 1990s, but her sister vessel was deleted in 1997. *Tula* is based with the Northern Fleet at Ara Guba. *Sierra I*, known to the Russians as *Barracuda*, was augmented by two vessels of the Sierra II class, *Pskow* (formerly *Zubatka*) and *Nizhni-Novgorod* (formerly *Okun*). The former was launched in June 1988, the latter in July 1992. The Sierra II (Type 9456A Kondor class) boats have a diving depth of 750m (2460ft). One notable feature of the Sierras is the large space between the two hulls, which has obvious advantages for radiated noise reduction and damage resistance. It is thought that all the Sierra-class boats are now effectively in reserve.

Country:	Soviet Union
Type:	Ballistic missile submarine
Launch date:	July 1986 (Tula, Sierra I class)
Crew:	61
Displacement:	Surfaced: 7112 tonnes (7000 tons), submerged: 8230 tonnes (8100t)
Dimensions:	107m x 12.5m x 8.8m (351ft x 41ft x 28ft 11in)
Range:	Unlimited
Armament:	Four 650mm (25.6in) and four 533mm (21in) torpedo tubeses; SS-N-15 Starfish and SS-N-21 Samson SSMs
Powerplant:	Single shaft, one nuclear PWR, one turbine
Performance:	Surfaced: 10 knots Submerged: 32 knots

Siroco

The Spanish Navy ordered its first two Agosta-class boats (*Galerna* and *Siroco*) in May 1975, and a second pair (*Mistral* and *Tramontana*) in June 1977. Designed by the French Directorate of Naval Construction as very quiet but high-performance ocean-going diesel-electric boats (SSKs), the Agosta-class boats are each armed with four bow torpedo tubes which are equipped with a rapid-reload pneumatic ramming system that can launch weapons with a minimum of noise signature. The tubes were of a completely new design when the Agostas were authorized in the mid-1970s, allowing a submarine to fire its weapons at all speeds and at any depth down to its maximum operational limit, which in the case of the Agostas is 350m (1148ft). The Spanish Agostas were built with some French assistance, and upgraded in the mid-1990s.

Country:	Spain
Type:	Attack submarine
Launch date:	13 November 1982
Crew:	54
Displacement:	Surfaced: 1514 tonnes ((1490 tons), submerged: 1768 tonnes (1740 tons)
Dimensions:	67.6m x 6.8m x 5.4m (221ft 9in x 22ft 4 in x 17ft 9in)
Surface range:	Not known
Armament:	Four 550mm (21.7in) torpedo tubes; 40 mines
Powerplant:	Two diesels, one electric motor
Performance:	Surfaced: 12.5 knots, submerged:17.5 knots

Skate

Laid down in July 1955, the USS *Skate* was the world's first production-model nuclear submarine, followed by three more boats of her class, *Swordfish*, *Sargo* and *Seadragon*. *Skate* made the first completely submerged Atlantic crossing. In 1958 she established a (then) record of 31 days submerged with a sealed atmosphere; on 11 August 1958 she passed under the North Pole during an Arctic cruise; and on 17 March 1959 she became the first submarine to surface at the North Pole. Other boats of the class also achieved notable 'firsts'; in August 1960, *Seadragon* made a transit from the Atlantic to the Pacific via the Northwest Passage (Lancaster Sound, Barrow and McClure Straits). In August 1962 *Skate*, operating from New London, Connecticut, and *Seadragon*, based at Pearl Harbor, made rendezvous under the North Pole.

Country:	USA
Type:	Attack submarine
Launch date:	16 May 1967
Crew:	95
Displacement:	Surfaced: 2611 tonnes (2570 tons), submerged: 2907 tonnes (2861 tons)
Dimensions:	81.5m x 7.6m x 6.4m (267 ft 8in x 25ft x 21ft)
Range:	Unlimited
Armament:	Six 533mm (21in) torpedo tubes
Powerplant:	Two shafts, one nuclear PWR, turbines
Performance:	Surfaced: 20 knots, submerged: 25 knots

Skipjack

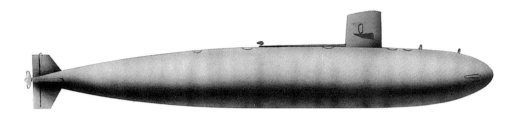

The USS *Skipjack* (SSN 585) was class leader of a group of six nuclear attack submarines built in the late 1950s. The other members of the class were *Scamp* (SSN 588), *Scorpion* (SSN 589), *Sculpin* (SSN 590), *Shark* (SSN 591) and *Snook* (SSN 592). In May 1968, *Scorpion* was lost with all 99 crew members on board some 740km (400nm) southwest of the Azores while en route from the Mediterranean to her base at Norfolk, Virginia. The original *Scorpion* was renumbered SSBN 598 and built as the nuclear ballistic-missile submarine *George Washington*. Until the advent of the Los Angeles class, the Skipjacks were the fastest submarines available to the US Navy, and had a crucial role to play in the detection, pursuit and destruction of missile submarines from an opposing fleet.

Country:	USA
Type:	Attack submarine
Launch date:	26 May 1958
Crew:	106-114
Displacement:	Surfaced: 3124 tonnes (3075 tons), submerged: 3556 tonnes (3500 tons)
Dimensions:	76.7m x 9.6m x 8.5m (251ft 9in x 31ft 6in x 27ft 10in)
Range:	Unlimited
Armament:	Six 533mm (21in) torpedo tubes
Powerplant:	Single shaft, one nuclear PWR, two steam turbines
Performance:	Surfaced: 18 knots, submerged: 30 knots

Sokol

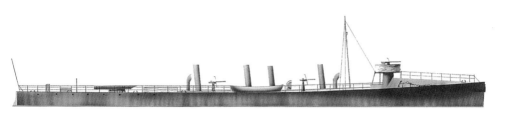

Designed by Yarrow, *Sokol* (Falcon) was Russia's first destroyer, laid down in 1894 and completed in 1895. Her 12-pounder gun was mounted on top of the conning tower, at the end of the turtleback foredeck. Two of the three-pounder guns were placed just aft of the first funnel, with the third gun mounted between the two aft funnels. Her armament was modified during her career, another 12-pounder being added, plus six torpedo tubes. To save weight, nickel steel was used in the construction of the hull and there was some use of aluminium in her fittings. Renamed *Prytki*, she served as a minesweeper in World War I and was scrapped in 1922. Although the Imperial Russian Navy had some excellent destroyers at its disposal during this period, its battle tactics left much to be desired and its crews were poorly trained.

Country:	Russia
Type:	Destroyer
Launch date:	1895
Crew:	54
Displacement:	224 tonnes (220 tons)
Dimensions:	57.9m x 5.6m x 2.2m (190ft x 18ft 6in x 7ft 6in)
Range:	1482km (800nm)
Main armament:	Three 3-pounder and one 12-pounder guns; two 380mm (15in) torpedo tubes
Powerplant:	Twin screws, vertical triple expansion engines
Performance:	29 knots

Soldati class

The extensive Soldati-class destroyers, all of which were named after types of soldier (e.g. *Lanciere* after lancer) was the ultimate development of a sequence that began with the four-ship Dardo class of 1930–32. They used deck space very effectively by successfully trunking all boiler uptakes into one substantial funnel casing. Four 120mm (4.72in) guns were carried, but unlike the disposition on British destroyers, they were sited in two twin mountings, one on the forecastle deck and one on the same level atop a house set well aft, saving both deck space and topweight. Slightly smaller than their British counterparts, the Italian ships were more highly powered, being deficient only in torpedoes, weapons the Italians never valued very highly. In fact, their destroyers were used more for minelaying than direct offensive action.

Country:	Italy
Type:	Destroyer
Launch date:	8 August 1937 (Camicia Nera, first unit)
Crew:	219
Displacement:	2499 tonnes (2460 tons)
Dimensions:	106.75m x 10.15m x 3.6m (350ft 2in x 33ft 4in x 11ft 10in)
Range:	7412km (4000nm)
Main armament:	Four or five 120mm (4.72in) and one 37mm (1.4in) AA guns; two triple 533mm (21in) torpedo tubes; up to 48 mines
Powerplant:	Twin screws, two sets of geared steam turbines
Performance:	39 knots

South Dakota

Commissioned into service in 1942, *South Dakota* was the first in a class of four battleships designed specifically to survive hits from 400mm (16in) shells while being able to perform at up to 27 knots. Launched in June 1941, *South Dakota* was fitted as a purposely designed force flagship. She saw service off Guadalcanal in 1942 where she was instrumental in defending the *Enterprise* task group, and later took part in the night action which saw the destruction of the Japanese battleship *Kirishima*. In 1944 she was in action during the Battle of the Philippine Sea, and was present at Tokyo Bay at the formal Japanese surrender in August 1945, when she flew the flag of the commander of the US Pacific Fleet, Admiral Halsey. She was damaged in action three times: at the Battle of Santa Cruz, at Guadalcanal, and off Saipan. *South Dakota* was withdrawn from service in 1946 and sold in 1962.

Country:	USA
Type:	Battleship
Launch date:	7 June 1941
Crew:	1793
Displacement:	43,806 tonnes (44,519 tons)
Dimensions:	207.3m x 34m x 10.7m (680ft x 108ft 2in x 35ft 1in)
Range:	27,000km (15,000nm) at 12 knots
Armament:	Nine 400mm (16in), 20 127mm (5in) guns
Powerplant:	Four shaft turbines
Performance:	27.5 knots

SP1 or Z40 class

Before World War II, the German Navy was concerned by the potential firepower of France's large destroyers and, perceiving a requirement for ships of their own capable of operating independently, initiated the *Spähkreuzer* (scout cruiser) or 'SP' concept. At the beginning of World War II, however, the planned number of destroyers was cut back in view of other priorities. Of the five stricken from the Type 36A programme, three – *Z40* to *Z42* – were reinstated early in 1941 as an enlarged trio, which were to be followed by another with an unspecified hull number. The design passed through several phases before losing favour and being recast into the so-called 'Zerstörer 1941', construction of which was suspended in 1942. The incomplete hulls were broken up at the Germaniawerft, Kiel, in 1943. There is no doubt that these vessels would have been very effective in combat.

Country:	Germany
Type:	Destroyer
Launch date:	not launched
Crew:	321
Displacement:	4613 tonnes (4540 tons)
Dimensions:	152m x 14.6m x 4.6m (498ft 8in x 47ft 11in x 15ft 1in)
Range:	22,250km (12,014nm)
Main armament:	Three twin 150mm (5.9in); one twin 88mm (3.46in) DP guns; two quintuple 533mm (21in) torpedo tubes; up to 140 mines
Powerplant:	Three shafts, two sets of geared steam turbines, one diesel
Performance:	36 knots on steam power

Sparviero

In 1936 it was suggested that the large liner *Augustus* could provide the possible basis for an aircraft carrier. Although the idea was initially rejected, it was revised in 1942, when it was decided to convert *Augustus* into an auxiliary carrier. She was renamed *Falco*, then *Sparviero*. Just as her upper works had been removed, she was seized by the Germans in 1944 for use as a blockship. She was scuttled in 1944. Although Italy, with four battleships, was the major power in the Mediterranean when she declared war in 1940, the battle fleet was always used in a defensive manner, especially after the strike on Taranto by British naval aircraft when three capital ships were put out of action. If Italy had had one or two aircraft carriers at the outset, armed with suitable aircraft, the war in the Mediterranean might have taken a different turn, as she could have then adopted an offensive posture.

Country:	Italy
Type:	Aircraft carrier
Launch date:	1927 (as *Augustus*)
Crew:	–
Displacement:	30,480 tonnes (30,000 tons)
Dimensions:	202.4m x 25.2m x 9.2m (664ft 2in x 82ft 10in x 30ft 2in)
Range:	–
Armament:	Six 152mm (6in), four 102mm (4in) guns (proposed)
Powerplant:	Quadruple screw, diesel engines
Performance:	18 knots (as liner)

Spica

Like its German counterpart, the Italian Navy favoured the construction of small destroyer-type escorts, usually referred to as 'torpedo boats'. Though a long series of related classes had been completed by the mid-1920s, the type had lapsed for a decade before being resumed with the 32-strong Spica class, laid down between 1934 and 1937. The design was influenced by that of the Maestrale-class destroyers then completing but, although superficially similar in overall profile, their single funnel lacked the massive trunking of that of the larger ships, serving as it did only one boiler room. Under the wartime construction programme a group of 42 improved Spica vessels was planned; known as the Ariete class, only 16 were laid down. Of the 32 Spica vessels, 23 became war casualties and two were sold to Sweden.

Country:	Italy
Type:	Destroyer escort
Launch date:	11 March 1934
Crew:	116
Displacement:	1036 tonnes (1020 tons)
Dimensions:	83.5m x 8.1m x 2.55m (273ft 11in x 26ft 6in x 8ft 4 in)
Range:	6670km (3600nm)
Main armament:	Three 100mm (3.9in) guns; four 450mm (17.7in) torpedo tubes
Powerplant:	Two shafts, geared steam turbines
Performance:	34 knots

Spruance

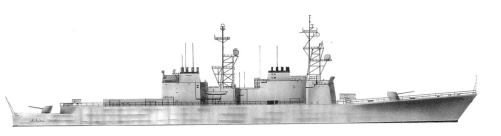

Built as replacements for the numerous Gearing-class destroyers, the 31 ships of the Spruance class are arguably the most capable anti-submarine warfare vessels ever built. Constructed by the modular assembly technique, whereby large sections of the hull are built in various parts of the shipyard and then welded together on the slipway, these were the first large US warships to employ all gas turbine propulsion. The successful hull design of the Spruance-class destroyers was used, with modifications, on two other classes of US warship, and has reduced rolling and pitching tendencies, thus providing a better weapons platform. All vessels in the Spruance class have undergone major weapons changes over the years. At least nine Spruance-class warships were operating in and around the Gulf in the war of 1991. They will all be phased out of service by 2007.

Country:	USA
Type:	Destroyer
Launch date:	10 November 1973
Crew:	15
Displacement:	31 tonnes (31 tons)
Dimensions:	29m x 3.5m x 0.9m (94ft x 11ft 6in x 3ft)
Range:	Not known
Main armament:	None when first completed
Powerplant:	Single screw, vertical compound engine
Performance:	18.2 knots

Stiletto

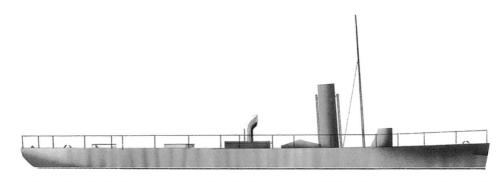

In 1881 the US Advisory Board recommended the construction of a number of torpedo boats of the Herreshoff type for harbour and inshore defence work. However, nothing was done until 1888 when the fast, wooden-hulled yacht *Stiletto* was purchased from the Herreshoff company for experimental trials. Originally she had been laid down as a private speculation at Herreshoff's yard, Bristol, Rhode Island, and had been commissioned in 1887. In 1898 *Stiletto* was given two Howell torpedo tubes, and for the next few years she was engaged in various tactical trials with new types of torpedo. Oil fuel trials in 1897 were unsatisfactory. She was removed from the US Navy List in early 1911, and was sold in July of the same year. There is no doubt that Stiletto played a considerable part in developing valuable tactical procedures for the US Navy.

Country:	USA
Type:	Torpedo boat
Launch date:	1886
Crew:	15
Displacement:	31 tonnes (31 tons)
Dimensions:	29m x 3.5m x 0.9m (95ft x 11ft 6in x 3ft)
Range:	Not known
Main armament:	None when first completed
Powerplant:	Single screw, vertical compound engine
Performance:	18.2 knots

Stonewall

Built in Bordeaux and commissioned in 1865, *Stonewall* was the last ironclad to serve in the Confederate Navy. The 229mm (9in) gun was housed in the bows above the ram, and could fire directly ahead or through a port on either side. Because of French neutrality, the vessel was delivered via Denmark, where she went under the names of *Staerkodder* and *Olinde*. Crossing the Atlantic, she arrived in Havana in May 1865 to find the Civil War over. *Stonewall* was handed over to Union forces. She was sold to Japan and renamed *Adzuma*. In 1888 she was removed from the effective list and used as an accommodation ship. In Confederate service, she was named in honour of General Thomas Jonathan 'Stonewall' Jackson (1824–1863), who was killed at the Battle of Chancellorsville. *Adzuma* saw brief action in Japanese service, against rebel forces at Hakodate.

Country:	Confederate States of America
Type:	Ironclad
Launch date:	21 June 1864
Crew:	130
Displacement:	1585 tonnes (1560 tons)
Dimensions:	60m x 32m x 16m (194ft x 31ft 6in x 15ft 8in)
Range:	3706km (2000nm) at 8 knots
Armament:	One 228mm (9in), two 70-pounder guns
Powerplant:	Twin screw, horizontal direct-acting engines
Performance:	10 knots

Sturgeon

An enlarged and improved Thresher/Permit design with additional quieting features and electronic systems, the Sturgeon-class SSNs built between 1965 and 1974 were the largest class of nuclear-powered warships until the advent of the Los Angeles class. The Sturgeons were frequently used in the intelligence-gathering role, carrying special equipment and National Security Agency personnel. In 1982 *Cavalla* was converted at Pearl Harbor to have a secondary amphibious assault role by carrying a swimmer delivery vehicle (SDV); *Archerfish, Silversides, Tunny* and *L. Mendel Rivers* were similarly equipped. *William H. Bates, Hawkbill, Pintado, Richard B. Russell* and others were modified to carry and support the Navy's Deep Submergence and Rescue vehicles. All Sturgeon-class boats but the modified special missions-dedicated *Parche* were scrapped in the late 1990s.

Country:	USA
Type:	Attack submarine
Launch date:	26 February 1966
Crew:	121-141
Displacement:	Surfaced: 4335 tonnes (4266 tons), submerged: 4854 tonnes (4777 tons)
Dimensions:	89m x 9.65m x 8.9m (292ft 3in x 31ft 8in x 29ft 3in)
Range:	Unlimited
Armament:	Four 533mm (21in) torpedo tubes; Tomahawk & Sub Harpoon SSMs
Powerplant:	Single shaft, one nuclear PWR, turbines
Performance:	Surfaced: 18 knots, submerged: 26 knots

Sultan

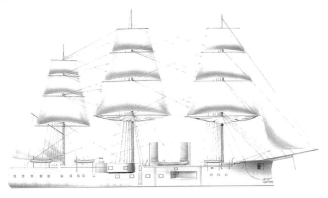

S ultan was laid down in 1868 and launched in 1870. All her 254mm (10in) rifled muzzle-loaders were in a 25.3m- (83ft-) long armoured battery, with the forward gun firing through an embrasured port to give ahead fire. She was ship-rigged, spreading 4589 square metres (49,395 sq ft) of canvas when carrying studding sails, but was a slow ship. *Sultan* was a very powerful vessel and one of the most heavily armed central battery ships ever built. In 1882 she took part in the bombardment of Alexandria, but hit a rock off Malta the same year. After salvage, she was reconstructed in 1893–96. In 1906 she saw inactive service as an artificers' training ship at Portsmouth, and was renamed *Fisgard IV*. She was used as a mechanical training ship for many years, reverting to her original name in 1932. Her final days were spent as a mine-sweeping depot ship and she was scrapped in 1945.

Country:	Great Britain
Type:	Battleship
Launch date:	31 May 1870
Crew:	633
Displacement :	9693 tonnes (9540 tons)
Dimensions:	99m x 18m x 8m (324ft 10in x 59ft x 26ft 3in)
Range:	3965km (2140nm) at 10knots
Armament:	Eight 254mm (10in), four 228mm (9in) guns
Powerplant:	Single screw, horizontal trunk engine
Performance:	14.13 knots

Swift

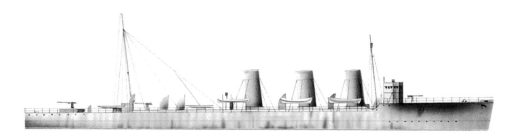

HMS *Swift* was the world's first purpose-built flotilla leader. The design, however, was very ambitious, and the vessel failed to make the contract speed of 36 knots. After many changes to the propeller, and with the funnels heightened, she finally made just over 35 knots, and was eventually accepted into the Royal Navy in 1910, after two years of trials. On 15 October 1914 she had a lucky escape when she was attacked by the German submarine *U9*, which had just sunk the destroyer HMS *Hawke* in the North Sea. Despite being narrowly missed by the submarine's torpedoes, *Swift*'s captain stayed in the area and picked up one officer and 20 men from the *Hawke*. *Swift* later joined the Dover patrol, and on 21 April 1917, she sank the German *TBD G42*, which was part of a force attempting to raid Dover. *Swift* was broken up in 1921.

Country:	Great Britain
Type:	Flotilla Leader
Launch date:	7 December 1907
Crew:	160
Displacement:	2428 tonnes (2390 tons)
Dimensions:	107.8m x 10.4m x 3.2m (353ft 8in x 34ft 2in x 10ft 6in)
Range:	4632km (2500nm)
Main armament:	Four 102mm (4in) guns; two 457mm (18in) torpedo tubes
Powerplant:	Quadruple screws, turbines
Performance:	35 knots

Swiftsure

There were six boats in this SSN class, completed between July 1974 and March 1981; *Swiftsure, Sovereign, Superb, Sceptre, Spartan* and *Splendid*. All had major refits in the late 1970s or early 1990s, with a full tactical weapons system upgrade. Each was fitted with a PWR 1 Core Z, providing a 12-year life cycle, although refits remain on an eight-year schedule. As a result of budget cuts *Swiftsure* paid off in 1992, but the others will remain in service until replaced by the *Astute* class from 2006. Two of the class are usually in refit or maintenance. *Splendid* was the first British submarine to carry Tomahawk cruise missiles, and used them in the 1999 NATO strikes on Serbia. The sonar fit is the Type 2074 (active/passive search and attack), Type 2007 (passive), Type 2046 (towed array), 2019 (intercept and ranging) and Type 2077 (short range classification).

Country:	Great Britain
Type:	Attack submarine
Launch date:	7 September 1971
Crew:	116
Displacement:	Surfaced: 4471 tonnes (4400 tons), submerged: 4979 tonnes (4900 tons)
Dimensions:	82.9m x 9.8m x 8.5m (272ft x 32ft 4in x 28ft)
Surface range:	Unlimited
Armament:	Five 533mm (21in) torpedo tubes; Tomahawk and Sub Harpoon SSMs
Powerplant:	Single shaft, nuclear PWR, turbines
Performance:	Surfaced: 20 knots, submerged: 30+ knots

Tachikaze

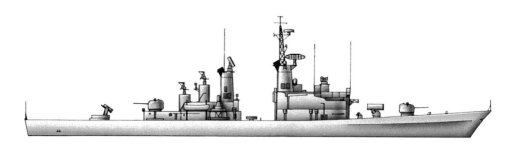

During the early 1970s the Japanese Maritime Self-Defence Force needed to improve its medium-range area-defence SAM capabilities, and thus laid down three Tachikaze-class ships at three-yearly intervals from 1973. The vessels are the *Tachikaze*, *Asakaze* and *Swakaze*, which were commissioned in 1976, 1979, and 1982 respectively. They each carry a single-rail Mk13 launcher for the Standard SM-1MR missile. No helicopter facilities were provided, and ASW armament was confined to ASROC missiles and Mk46 self-defence torpedoes. In order to save on production costs, the class adopted the propulsion plant and machinery of the Haruna class of helicopter-carrying ASW destroyers. In 1999, *Tachikaze* was the flagship of the JMSDF's Escort Force whose vessels provide an important component of the JMSDF's air defence capability.

Country:	Japan
Type:	Destroyer
Launch date:	12 December 1974
Crew:	250
Displacement:	3912 tonnes (3850 tons)
Dimensions:	142m x 14.3m x 4.6m (459ft 4in x 47ft x 15ft 1in)
Range:	9265km (5000nm)
Main armament:	Two 127mm (5in) guns; Harpoon SSM; Standard SAM; ASROC; six 324mm (12.75in) torpedo tubes
Powerplant:	Two shafts, two geared steam turbines
Performance:	32 knots

Taiho

Taiho (Giant Phoenix) was Japan's largest purpose-built aircraft carrier and the first to feature an armoured deck. She was laid down in July 1941 and went into service in March 1944. The two-tier hangars were 150m (500ft) long and unarmoured at the sides. The lower hangar was 124mm (4.9in) thick over the boiler and machinery spaces, which also had 150mm- (5.9in-) thick side armour; the flight deck had 75mm- (3in-) thick armour to withstand a 455kg (1,000lb) bomb. Total armour protection came to 8940 tonnes (8800 tons). *Taiho* was blown up within a few weeks of entering service by the US submarine *Albacore* on 19 June 1944 during the Battle of the Philippine Sea. Two more vessels of this class were planned (Nos 801 and 802) together with five more of a modified Taiho type (Nos 5021 to 5025) but none was ever laid down. *Taiho* was similar in design to the earlier *Shokaku*.

Country:	Japan
Type:	Aircraft carrier
Launch date:	7 April 1943
Crew:	1751
Displacement :	37,866 tonnes (37,270 tons)
Dimensions:	260.6m x 30m x 9.6m (855ft x 98ft 6in x 31ft 6in)
Range:	14,824km (8000nm) at 18 knots
Armament:	12 100mm (3.9in), 71 25mm (1in) guns
Powerplant:	Quadruple screw turbines
Performance:	33.3 knots

Tango

The Tango class of 18 diesel-electric attack submarines was built as an interim measure, filling the gap between the Foxtrot-class DE boats and the Victor nuclear-powered SSNs. The first unit was completed at Gorky in 1972, and over the next ten years 17 more units were built in two slightly different versions. The later type were several metres longer than the first in order to accommodate the fire-control systems associated with the tube-launched SS-N-15 anti-submarine missile, the equivalent of the US Navy's SUBROC. The bow sonar installations were the same as those fitted to later Soviet SSNs, while the powerplant was identical to that installed in the later units of the Foxtrot class. Production of the Tango class ceased after the 18th unit was built; all are now stricken or unserviceable in reserve, after being taken out of service in the 1990s.

Country:	Soviet Union
Type:	Attack submarine
Launch date:	1971
Crew:	60
Displacement:	Surfaced: 3251 tonnes (3200 tons), submerged: 3962 tonnes (3900 tons)
Dimensions:	92m x 9m x 7m (301ft 10in x 29ft 6in x 24ft)
Surface range:	22,236km (12,000nm) at 10 knots
Armament:	Six 533mm (21in) torpedo tubes
Powerplant:	Twin screws, diesel/electric motors
Performance:	Surfaced: 20 knots, submerged: 16 knots

Temeraire

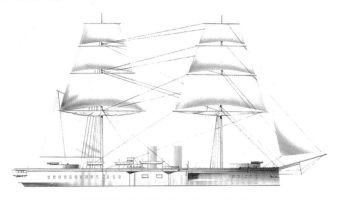

Commissioned in 1877, *Temeraire* was Britain's first barbette ship, with one 280mm (11in) gun mounted at each end of the upper deck in a pear-shaped barbette. The 254mm (10in) guns were in a central battery. The largest of her type, she was originally brig-rigged carrying 2322 square metres (25,000 sq ft) of canvas, though her rig was later reduced. She took part in the bombardment of Alexandria in 1882. In 1902 she became a depot ship and workshop. She was renamed *Indus II* in 1904 and later *Akbar*, and was sold in 1921. *Temeraire* saw her peak at a time when Europe was undergoing significant change. A new and mighty German state had forged a triple alliance with Austria and Italy. In 1892 a dual alliance was concluded between Russia and France; the power blocs that would be the catalyst of World War I were taking shape. Britain remained aloof; her fleet still ruled the oceans.

Country:	Great Britain
Type:	Battleship
Launch date:	9 May 1876
Crew:	580
Displacement :	8677 tonnes (8540 tons)
Dimensions:	86.9m x 18.9m x 8.2m (285ft x 62ft x 27ft)
Range:	5003km (2700nm) at 10 knots
Armament:	Four 280mm (11in), four 254mm (10in) guns
Powerplant:	Twin screw, vertical inverted compound engines
Performance:	14.7 knots

Tennessee

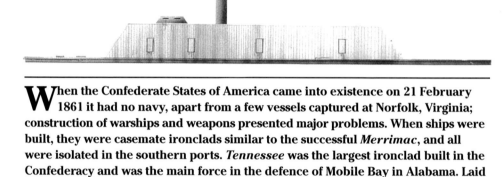

When the Confederate States of America came into existence on 21 February 1861 it had no navy, apart from a few vessels captured at Norfolk, Virginia; construction of warships and weapons presented major problems. When ships were built, they were casemate ironclads similar to the successful *Merrimac*, and all were isolated in the southern ports. *Tennessee* was the largest ironclad built in the Confederacy and was the main force in the defence of Mobile Bay in Alabama. Laid down in 1862, she was towed down to Mobile after launching by the ironclad *Baltic* for completion. The falling waters of the river made it almost impossible to get Tennessee over the bars and giant wooden pontoons were constructed and lashed to the vessel to lift her over. *Tennessee* was captured by Union forces on 5 August 1864 after a three-hour battle. She was later commissioned into the US Navy.

Country:	Confederate States of America
Type:	Ironclad
Launch date:	February 1863
Crew:	113
Displacement:	1293 tonnes (1273 tons)
Dimensions:	64m x 14.6m x 4.3m (209ft x 48ft x 14ft)
Range:	Not known
Armament:	Two 181mm (7.1in), four 152mm (6in) guns
Powerplant:	Single screw, non-condensing engines
Performance:	7 knots

Texas

Texas was the last major warship to be launched in the Confederacy. She was one of the most powerful ironclads, and the only twin-screw, to be built in the South. She was laid down at Rocketts, a suburb just outside Richmond, and was moved into the city after launching to be fitted out. Four of her guns were mounted on pivots, giving direct ahead and astern fire, as well as broadside firing through ports. The two remaining guns were positioned on each broadside. The guns were Brooke rifles – powerful, advanced weapons. When Richmond fell to the Union Army on 3 April 1865, the Confederates failed to blow up *Texas*, and she was seized by the Union and moved to the Norfolk Navy Yard. Throughout the Civil War, the Confederate Navy was never able to bring its forces together, and no attempt could be made to gain command of the seas. In the end, all its vessels were sunk, captured or scuttled.

Country:	Confederate States of America
Type:	Ironclad
Launch date:	1865
Crew:	50
Displacement:	Unknown
Dimensions:	66m x 15.3m x 3.9m (217ft x 50ft 4in x 13ft)
Range:	Not known
Armament:	Six 163mm (6.4in) guns
Powerplant:	Twin screw, horizontal direct-acting engines
Performance:	8 knots

Texas

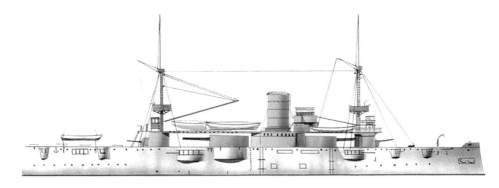

Texas was authorised in 1886, laid down in June 1889 and completed in 1895. She was designed in Britain and proved to be a good seaboat, but after initial trials the hull needed strengthening. By 1904, the funnel had been raised and more armour added to the turret hoists. She took part in the Battle of Santiago Bay in 1898 during the Spanish–American War. During this battle, which was fought on 3 July, the Spanish cruisers stood little chance against the American warships, which included the battleship *Iowa*, armed with four 12in and eight 8in guns. However, the battle underlined the need for improved naval gunnery; the victorious Americans expended 9500 shells and registered only 123 hits, a hit rate of 1.2 per cent. In 1911 *Texas* was renamed *San Marcos*, and was destroyed as a target in 1912.

Country:	USA
Type:	Battleship
Launch date:	28 June 1892
Crew:	508
Displacement:	6772 tonnes (6665 tons)
Dimensions:	91m x 19.5m x 6.8m (299ft x 64ft x 22ft 6in)
Range:	5373km (2900nm) at 10 knots
Armament:	Two 305mm (12in), two 152mm (6in) guns
Powerplant:	Twin screw, vertical triple expansion engines
Performance:	17 knots

Thetis

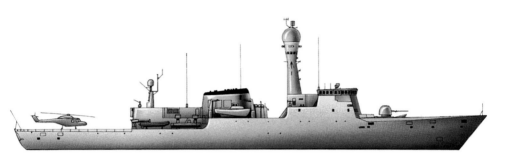

T he four frigates of the Thetis class (*Thetis, Triton, Vaedderen, Hvidbjornen*) were all commissioned between 1991 and 1992. Their primary role is fishery protection; *Thetis* is employed for several months every year in carrying out oceanographic and seismological surveys in the Greenland area, a very vital task, as the region is constantly threatened by volcanic activity. The hull is strengthened to enable the vessels to penetrate 1m (3ft 4in-) -thick ice, and efforts have been made to incorporate stealth technology by installing anchor equipment, bollards and winches below the upper deck. The flight deck has been strengthened to permit the operation of Sea King or Merlin helicopters. A rigid inflatable boarding craft is installed alongside the helicopter hangar. There are plans for the installation of a new air search radar and surface-to-air missiles of an unspecified type.

Country:	Denmark
Type:	Frigate
Launch date:	14 July 1989
Crew:	60
Displacement:	3556 tonnes (3500 tons)
Dimensions:	112.5m x 14.4m x 6m (369ft 1in x 47ft 2in x 19ft 8in)
Range:	13,672km (7378nm)
Main armament:	One 76mm (3in) gun; one 20mm (0.7in) gun; depth charges
Powerplant:	Single shaft, three diesel engines
Performance:	20.8 knots

Thresher/Permit class

The first of the SSNs in the US Navy with a deep-diving capability, advanced sonars mounted in the optimum bow position, amidships angled torpedo tubes with the SUBROC ASW missile, and a high degree of machinery-quieting, the Thresher class formed an important part of the US subsurface attack capability for 20 years. The lead boat, USS *Thresher*, was lost with all 129 crew on board, off New England on 10 April 1963, midway through the building period 1960–66. The class was then renamed after *Permit*, the second ship. As a result of the enquiry following the loss of Thresher, the last three of the class were modified during construction with SUBSAFE features. The names of the class were *Permit, Plunger, Barb, Pollack, Haddo, Guardfish, Flasher* and *Haddock* (Pacific Fleet); and *Jack, Tinosa, Dace, Greenling* and *Gato* (Atlantic Fleet).

Country:	USA
Type:	Attack submarine
Launch date:	9 July 1960 (Thresher)
Crew:	134–141
Displacement:	Surfaced: 3810 tonnes (3750 tons), submerged: 4380 tonnes (4311 tons)
Dimensions:	84.9m x 9.6m x 8.8m (278ft 6in x 31ft 8in x 28ft 10in)
Range:	Unlimited
Armament:	Four 533mm (21in) torpedo tubes
Powerplant:	Single shaft, one nuclear PWR, steam turbines
Performance:	Surfaced: 18 knots, submerged: 27 knots

Tiger

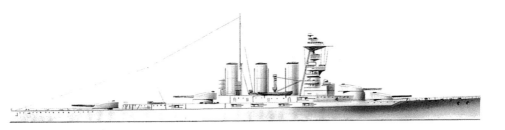

Completed in 1914, it had been intended to fit *Tiger* with small tube boilers and geared turbines, and had this suggestion been adopted her top speed may have been 32 knots. However, as it was, *Tiger* was still the fastest, as well as the largest, capital ship of her day. She was also the last coal-burning capital ship in the Royal Navy, and was the only British battlecruiser to carry 152mm (6in) guns. She took part in the battles of Dogger Bank in 1915 and Jutland in 1916, receiving 15 direct hits during the latter. Battlecruisers, such as *Tiger*, were vulnerable when unable to exploit their speed and firepower, but survival depended on where they were hit, not the number of times. *Tiger* took 15 hits and survived, but the three that were sunk were struck by just six 11in and 12in shells. After World War I *Tiger* served in the Atlantic Fleet until becoming a training ship in 1924. She was paid off in 1933.

Country:	Great Britain
Type:	Battlecruiser
Launch date:	15 December 1913
Crew:	1121
Displacement:	35,723 tonnes (35,160 tons)
Dimensions:	214.6m x 27.6m x 8.6m (704ft x 90ft 6in x 28ft 5in)
Range:	8370km (4650nm) at 12 knots
Armament:	Eight 343mm (13.5in), 12 152mm (6in) guns
Powerplant:	Quadruple screw turbines
Performance:	30 knots

Trafalgar

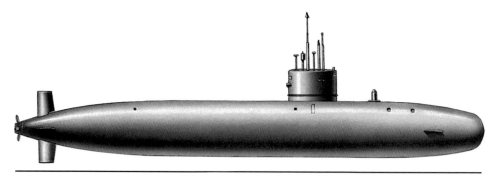

Essentially an improved *Swiftsure*, HMS *Trafalgar* and her sister ships consitute the third generation of British SSNs to be built by Vickers Shipbuilding and Engineering Ltd (VSEL) at Barrow-in-Furness. Improvements included a new reactor system and a pump-jet propulsion system in place of a conventional propeller. *Trafalgar* was the first boat to be fitted with the Type 2020 sonar, and was used as development test platform. The deployment of the Trafalgar class brought the Royal Navy's SSN fleet to 12 boats by the mid-1990s, a lean but highly effective force. The end of the Cold War and increasing global instability has led to the widespread dispersal of the Royal Navy's SSNs; for example, in 1995 HMS *Trenchant*'s operational programme took her to Guam, Singapore, Hong Kong, Diego Garcia and South Korea.

Country:	Great Britain
Type:	Attack submarine
Launch date:	1 July 1981
Crew:	130
Displacement:	Surfaced: 4877 tonnes (4800 tons), submerged: 5384 tonnes (5300t)
Dimensions:	85.4m x 10m x 8.2m (280ft 2in x 33ft 2in x 27ft)
Range:	Unlimited
Armament:	Five 533mm (21in) torpedo tubes; Tomahawk and Sub Harpoon SSMs
Powerplant:	Pump jet, one PWR, turbines
Performance:	Surfaced: 20 knots, submerged: 32 knots

Tribal class

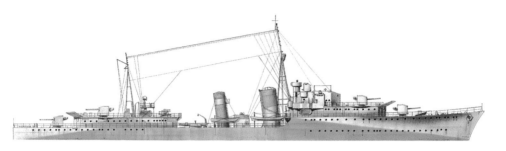

A mong the finest destroyers ever built for the Royal Navy, the 16 Tribal-class vessels nevertheless seem to have been produced to counter to those being built by potential enemies, rather than to fill any clearly-identifiable role within the fleet. They were regarded as gun-armed super-destroyers, and there was much disagreement over their correct classification. By any standards, they were magnificent-looking ships, their nicely balanced profile in harmony with the high-freeboard hull that was introduced to improve their fighting qualities in poor weather. The class was launched in 1937, but only four of the 16 were still afloat at the end of 1942. All saw a great deal of action, and one, HMS *Cossack*, became famous for rescuing British merchant seamen from the supply ship *Altmark* inside Norwegian territorial waters.

Country:	Great Britain
Type:	Destroyer
Launch date:	8 June 1937 (HMS *Afridi*. first unit)
Crew:	190
Displacement:	2007 tonnes (1975 tons)
Dimensions:	115.1m x 11.13m x 2.74m (377ft 6in x 36ft 4in x 9ft)
Range:	10,523km (5682nm)
Main armament:	Four twin 119mm (4.7in) guns; one quadruple 533mm (21in) torpedo tube mounting
Powerplant:	Two sets of geared steam turbines
Performance:	36 knots

Le Triomphant

Le Triomphant is leader of the latest class of French nuclear-powered ballistic-missile submarines, all built by DCN Cherbourg. She was ordered on 10 March 1986 and floated in dock in November 1993. The second, *Le Téméraire,* was ordered on 18 October 1989 and launched on 8 August 1997, while the third, *Le Vigilant,* ordered on 27 May 1993, is scheduled to be launched in 2004. A fourth vessel, *Le Terrible,* ordered in 2000, is due to be launched in 2010. All four will have Brest as their homeport. *Le Triomphant* began sea trials in April 1994, and her first sea cruise took place from 16 July to 22 August 1995. The first submerged launch of an M45 SLBM (range 8000km/4300nm, 6 MRVs) was made on 14 February 1995. The vessels will replace *L'Inflexible* class in French naval service.

Country:	France
Type:	Ballistic missile submarine
Launch date:	13 July 1993
Crew:	111
Displacement:	Surfaced: 12,842 tonnes (12640 tons), submerged: 14,335 tonnes (14,565 tons)
Dimensions:	138m x 17m x 12.5m (453ft x 77ft 9in x 41ft)
Range:	Unlimited
Armament:	Sixteen M45/TN75 SLBM; four 533mm (21in) torpedo tubes
Powerplant:	Pump jet, one nuclear PWR, two diesels
Performance:	Surfaced: 20 knots, submerged: 25 knots

Tromp

The *Tromp* and her sister ship *Jacob van Heemskerck* were interesting in being more 'pocket cruisers' than destroyers. They demonstrated how, at the top of the size scale, the distinction between the two could be blurred. The pair had true destroyer ancestry, however, being classed as leaders. Their design was enlarged, and welding and aluminium were extensively used in order to save weight. An interesting reflection on *Tromp*'s use in the vast Dutch East Indies was the incorporation of a Fokker seaplane. The *Tromp* was completed in August 1938 and deployed to the Far East at the outbreak of war, being extensively damaged during the Japanese invasion of Bali. She survived the war, and took part in the reoccupation of the East Indies in September 1945. The *Heemskerck* served alongside British naval forces in the Indian Ocean and Mediterranean.

Country:	Netherlands
Type:	Destroyer
Launch date:	24 May 1937
Crew:	Not known
Displacement:	4979 tonnes (4900 tons)
Dimensions:	131.9m x 12.41m x 5.41m (432ft 9in x 40ft 9in x 17ft 9in)
Range:	Not known
Main armament:	Three twin 150mm (5.9in) and four single 75mm (2.95in) guns.
Powerplant:	Twin shafts, two sets of geared steam turbines
Performance:	32.5 knots

Tsessarevitch

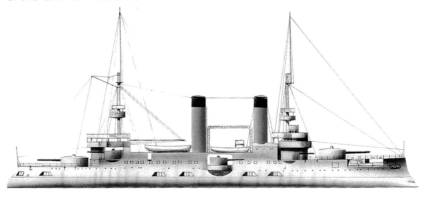

*T*sessarevitch was part of the Russian naval expansion programme of 1898. She was laid down at La Seyne in June 1899, and was completed in 1903. Her design followed the French practice of the period, having a pronounced tumble-home and high forecastle. Assigned to the Pacific Fleet, where she flew the flag of Rear‹Admiral Vitgeft, commanding the First Pacific Squadron, she was damaged in the surprise Japanese attack on Port Arthur on 9 February 1904. On 7 August that year she was hit by siege batteries at Port Arthur, and three days later she was damaged by 15 hits in the Battle of the Yellow Sea, Rear-Admiral Vitgeft being killed in the action. She was afterwards interned at Kiauchau, China. While serving in the Baltic in World War I, during which time she engaged the German dreadnought *Kronprinz*, she was renamed *Grazhdanin*. She was scrapped in 1922.

Country:	Russia
Type:	Battleship
Launch date:	23 February 1901
Crew:	782
Displacement :	13,122 tonnes (12,915 tons)
Dimensions:	118.5m x 23.2m x 7.9m (388ft 9in x 76ft x 26ft)
Range:	10,192km (5500nm) at 10 knots
Armament:	Four 304mm (12in), 12 152mm (6in), 20 3-pounder guns
Powerplant:	Twin screw, vertical triple expansion engines
Performance:	18.5 knots

Tsukuba

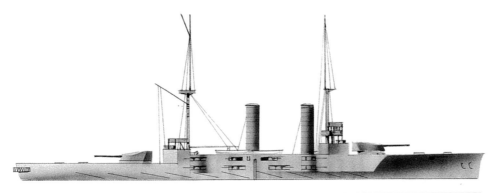

Tsukuba was ordered in 1904 as a replacement for one of two powerful
battleships lost during the war with Russia. She was laid down at Kure Naval
Dockyard in 1905, and originally classified as an armoured cruiser. By the time she
was completed in 1907, much more powerful battlecruisers were being built for the
Japanese Navy, and in 1921 her sister *Ikoma* was rerated as a first-class cruiser. In
January 1917 her magazine caught fire and she blew up in Yokosuka Bay killing 305
crew. She was later raised and broken up. In 1914, as part of the Imperial Japanese
Navy's 1st South Seas Squadron, *Tsukuba* took part in the search for the German
Admiral von Spee's battle squadron, which had been sighted east of the Marshall
Islands. Admiral von Spee eluded his pursuers and won the Battle of Coronel in
November 1914, but was defeated and killed off the Falklands on 8 December.

Country:	Japan
Type:	Battleship
Launch date:	26 December 1905
Crew:	879
Displacement :	15,646 tonnes (15,400 tons)
Dimensions:	137m x 23m x 8m (449ft 10in x 75ft 6in x 26ft 3in)
Range:	7412km (4000nm) at 14 knots
Armament:	Four 304mm (12in), 12 152mm (6in) guns
Powerplant:	Twin screw, vertical triple expansion engines
Performance:	20.5 knots

Turbine

Dating from between 1927 and 1928, the eight Turbine-class destroyers were nearly identical with the quartet of Sauro-class boats that preceded them. The major difference was an increase in length of 3m (9.84ft) in the Turbine-class vessels to accommodate more powerful machinery. A feature of both types was a massive armoured 'pillbox' of a conning tower that topped off the enclosed bridge. The four Sauro-class ships were destroyed as part of the hopelessly isolated Red Sea Squadron, and no less than six of the Turbine class were sunk in 1940. The first casualty was the *Espero*, sunk by the Australian cruiser HMAS *Sydney* on 28 June 1940. *Turbine* herself was taken over by the Germans and was destroyed by American aircraft off Salamis in 1944. She was probably the fastest of the class, reaching 39 knots during her trials.

Country:	Italy
Type:	Destroyer
Launch date:	21 April 1927
Crew:	180
Displacement:	1727 tonnes (1700 tons)
Dimensions:	92.65m x 9.2m x 2.9m (304ft x 30ft 2in x 9ft 6in)
Range:	3890km (2100nm)
Main armament:	Two twin 120mm (4.7in) guns; six 533mm (21in) torpedo tubes
Powerplant:	Two sets of geared steam turbines
Performance:	36 knots

Type 36A

The Type 36A destroyers were war-built and launched between 1940 and 1942. The initial order for the Type 36As comprised *Z23* to *Z30*; seven more, *Z31* to *Z34* and *Z37* to *Z39* (to a slightly modified design) were later added. These ships, though unnamed, were popularly known as the Narvik class, and spent most of their careers operating in Arctic waters in support of the German battle squadrons stationed in the harbours of northern Norway. Perhaps surprisingly, only six of the 15 Type 36As were lost during the war. Two of the survivors gave the French Navy over a decade of post-war service while another, the *Z38*, was commissioned into the Royal Navy as HMS *Nonsuch* and used for a variety of special trials. *Z37* had a very active war, finally being scuttled at Bordeaux in August 1944 to avoid capture by the advancing Allies.

Country:	Germany
Type:	Destroyer
Launch date:	14 December 1939 (Z23, first unit)
Crew:	321
Displacement:	3658 tonnes (3600 tons)
Dimensions:	127m x 12m x 3.9m (416ft 7in x 39ft 5in x 12ft 9in)
Range:	10,935km (5904nm)
Main armament:	Three single and one twin 150mm (5.9in) guns; two quadruple 533mm (21in) torpedo tube mountings; up to 60 mines
Powerplant:	Twin shafts, two sets of geared steam turbines
Performance:	36 knots

Type 82 and Type 42

U sed during the Falklands War, the Type 82-class destroyer HMS *Bristol* was originally to have been the lead ship of four vessels designed to act as area defence escorts for the new CVA-01-class of British aircraft carriers. These and the other three Type 82s were cancelled. With the cancellation of the planned aircraft carriers in the mid-1960s, a Naval Staff Requirement was issued for a small fleet escort to provide area defence. This resulted in the Type 42-class design, which suffered considerably during gestation from constraints placed on the dimensions as a result of Treasury cost-cutting. The ships lacked any close-range air defence system, had reduced endurance, and a short forecastle which resulted in a very wet forward section. The main armament included the Sea Dart SAM system, which proved to be a very effective area defence in the Falklands and the Gulf.

(Specification refers to Type 42)	
Country:	Great Britain
Type:	Destroyer
Launch date:	30 June 1969
Crew:	300–312
Displacement:	4851 tonnes (4775 tons)
Dimensions:	141m x 14.9m x 508m (463ft x 48ft x 19ft)
Range:	5188km (2800nm)
Main armament:	One 114mm (4.5in) gun; helicopter-launched Mk44 torpedoes; two triple mounts for Mk46 AS torpedoes; one Sea Dart SAM launcher
Powerplant:	Twin screw, gas turbines
Performance:	30 knots

Type F2000

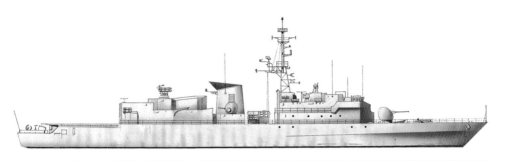

Although optimized for anti-submarine warfare in the world's leading navies, frigates tend to be used as general purpose 'workhorse' vessels in smaller navies. Only those that serve wealthier countries have the benefit of custom-built ships. A good example of this is Saudi Arabia, which purchased four Type F2000-class frigates (known locally as the Al Madinah class) from France in the 1980s. In terms of capability and equipment, these vessels (*Al Madinah*, *Hofouf*, *Abha* and *Taif*) at the time of their delivery, could out-perform many of the frigates in service with NATO and the Warsaw Pact, with particular regard to their state-of-the-art electronic equipment. The weapon systems are predominantly French in origin, although the SSMs are the Franco–Italian Otomat rather than the Exocet. A Dauphin helicopter is carried for ASW work.

Country:	France/Saudi Arabia
Type:	Frigate
Launch date:	23 April 1983
Crew:	179
Displacement:	2652 tonnes (2610 tons)
Dimensions:	115m x 12.5m x 4.7m (377ft 4in x 41ft x 15ft 5in)
Range:	9265km (5000nm)
Main armament:	One 100mm (3.9in) DP and two 40mm (1.5in) AA guns; Otomat SSMs; Crotale SAMs; four 533mm (21in) and two 324mm (12.75in) torpedo tubes
Powerplant:	Twin shafts, four diesel engines
Performance:	30 knots

Typhoon

Capable of hitting strategic targets anywhere in the world with its Makayev
SS-N-20 Sturgeon three-stage solid fuel missiles, each of which has 10 200kT
nuclear warheads and a range of 8300km (4500nm), Typhoon is the largest class of
submarine ever built. The launch tubes are positioned forward in the bow section,
leaving space abaft the fin for two nuclear reactors. The fin can break through ice
up to 3m (9ft 10in) thick, and diving depth is in the order of 300m (1000ft). Six
Typhoons were commissioned between 1980 and 1989; their designations, in order,
are *TK208, TK202, TK12, TK13, TK17* and *TK20*. Two were laid up in reserve in
1996; two more are awaiting refit and unlikely to go to sea again. *TK17* was
damaged by fire in a missile loading accident in 1992 but was subsequently
repaired. The Typhoons are based in the Northern Fleet at Nerpich'ya.

Country:	Russia
Type:	Ballistic missile submarine
Launch date:	23 September 1980
Crew:	175
Displacement:	Surfaced: 18,797 tonnes (18,500t), submerged: 26,925 tonnes (26,500t)
Dimensions:	171.5m x 24.6m x 13m (562ft 7in x 80ft 7in x 42ft 6in)
Range:	Unlimited
Armament:	Twenty SLBMs; four 630mm (25in) and two 533mm (21in) torpedo tubes
Powerplant:	Two shafts, two nuclear PWR, turbines
Performance:	Surfaced: 12 knots, submerged: 25 knots

U1

Strangely enough, the German Naval Staff at the turn of the century failed to appreciate the potential of the submarine, and the first submarines built in Germany were three Karp-class vessels ordered by the Imperial Russian Navy in 1904. Germany's first practical submarine, *U1*, was not completed until 1906. She was, however, one of the most successful and reliable of the period. Her two kerosene engines developed 400hp, as did her electric motors. She had an underwater range of 80km (43nm). Commissioned in December 1906, she was used for experimental and training purposes. In February 1919 she was stricken, sold, and refitted as a museum exhibit by her builders, Germaniawerft of Kiel. She was damaged by bombing in World War II, but subsequently restored. Double hulls and twin screws were used from the first in German U-boats.

Country:	Germany
Type:	Attack submarine
Launch date:	4 August 1906
Crew:	22
Displacement:	Surfaced: 241 tonnes (238 tons), submerged: 287 tonnes (283 tons)
Dimensions:	42.4m x 3.8m x 3.2m (139ft x 12ft 6in x 10ft 6in)
Surface range:	2850km (1536nm) at 10 knots
Armament:	One 450mm (17.7in) torpedo tube
Powerplant:	Twin screws, heavy oil (kerosene)/electric motors
Performance:	Surfaced: 10.8 knots, submerged: 8.7 knots

U12

U12 was the last of the German Federal Republic's Type 205 coastal submarines, the fourth such class to become operational since the FDR rearmed as part of NATO in the 1950s. The first was the *Hai* (Shark) class, comprising that boat and the *Hecht* (Pike), both of which were reconstructed World War II Type XXIII U-boats. These were followed by the Types 201 and 202. With the exception of two boats all were to have been of the Type 201 model, but there were severe hull corrosion problems, the non-magnetic material used proving quite unsatisfactory. As an interim measure the hulls of *U4* to *U8* were covered in tin, suffering severe operational limitations as a consequence, and construction of *U9* to *U12* was suspended until a special non-magnetic steel could be developed.

Country:	Germany
Type:	Attack submarine
Launch date:	10 September 1968
Crew:	21
Displacement:	Surfaced: 425 tonnes (419 tons), submerged: 457 tonnes (450 tons)
Dimensions:	43.9m x 4.6m x 4.3m (144ft x 15ft x 14ft)
Surface range:	7041km (3800nm) at 10 knots
Armament:	Eight 533mm (21in) torpedo tubes
Powerplant:	Single screw, diesel/electric motors
Performance:	Surfaced: 10 knots, submerged: 17.5 knots

U21

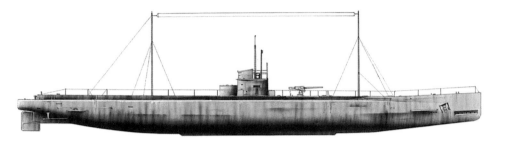

The *U21* was one of a class of four U-boats, built at Danzig and completed in 1913. Although the Germans got away to a slow start in their submarine construction programme before World War I, the vessels were well engineered and used double hulls and twin screws from the start. German engineers refused to employ petrol engines in the early boats, preferring to use smellier but safer kerosene fuel. In 1908 suitable diesel engines were designed, and these were installed in the *U19* class (to which *U21* belonged) and used exclusively thereafter. Of the four boats in the class, *U19* and *U22* surrendered in November 1918 and were scrapped at Blyth, Northumberland; *U20* was scuttled after being stranded on the Danish coast in 1916, and broken up in 1925; and *U21* foundered in the North Sea on 22 February 1919 as she was sailing to surrender.

Country:	Germany
Type:	Attack submarine
Launch date:	8 February 1913
Crew:	35
Displacement:	Surfaced: 660 tonnes (650 tons), submerged: 850 tonnes (837 tons)
Dimensions:	64.2m x 6.1m x 3.5m (210ft 6in x 20ft x 11ft 9in)
Surface range:	9265km (5500nm) at 10 knots
Armament:	Four 508mm (20in) torpedo tubes; one 86mm (3.4in) gun
Powerplant:	Two shafts, diesel/electric motors
Performance:	Surfaced: 15.4 knots, submerged: 9.5 knots

U28

Studies for a replacement submarine to follow the Type 205 class were initiated in 1962. The result was the new Type 206 class which, built of high-tensile non-magnetic steel, was to be used for coastal operations and had to conform with treaty limitations on the maximum tonnage allowed to West Germany. New safety devices for the crew were fitted, and the armament fit permitted the carriage of wire-guided torpedoes. After final design approval had been given, construction planning took place in 1966-68, and the first orders (for an eventual total of 18 units) were placed in the following year. By 1975 all the vessels (*U13* to *U30*) were in service. The submarines were later fitted with two external containers for the carriage of up to 24 ground mines in addition to their torpedo armament.

Country:	Germany
Type:	Attack submarine
Launch date:	22 January 1974
Crew:	21
Displacement:	Surfaced: 457 tonnes (450 tons), submerged: 508 tonnes (500 tons)
Dimensions:	48.6m x 4.6m x 4.5m (159 ft 5in x 15ft 2in x 14ft 10in)
Surface range:	7041km (3800nm) at 10 knots
Armament:	Eight 533mm (21in) torpedo tubes
Powerplant:	Single shaft, diesel/electric motors
Performance:	Surfaced: 10 knots, submerged: 17 knots

U32

In September 1939 the German Navy had only 56 submarines in commission, and of these only 22 were ocean-going craft, suitable for service in the Atlantic. They were Type VIIs, the class to which *U32* belonged. With a conning tower only 5.2m (17ft) above the waterline they were hard to detect even in daylight, and under night conditions they were practically invisible. They could dive in less than half a minute; they could go to a depth of 100m (328ft) without strain and 200m (656ft) if hard pressed. They could maintain a submerged speed of 7.6 knots for two hours, or two knots for 130 hours. In fact, their depth and endurance performance at high speed was twice as good as that of any other submarine. *U32* was sunk in the North Atlantic on 30 October 1940 by the RN destroyers *Harvester* and *Highlander.*

Country:	Germany
Type:	Attack submarine
Launch date:	1937
Crew:	44
Displacement:	Surfaced: 636 tonnes (626 tons), submerged: 757 tonnes (745 tons)
Dimensions:	64.5m x 5.8m x 4.4m (211ft 6in x 19ft 3in x 14ft 6in)
Surface range:	6916km (3732nm) at 12 knots
Armament:	Five 533mm (21in) torpedo tubes; one 88mm (3.5in) gun; one 20mm AA gun
Powerplant:	Two screws, diesel/electric motors
Performance:	Surfaced: 16 knots, submerged: 8 knots

U47

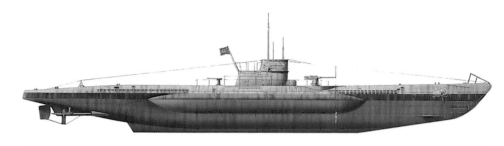

The Type VIIB U-boat was a slightly enlarged version of the Type VIIA, with a greater range and slightly higher surface speed. The most famous boat of this class was undoubtedly the *U47*, commanded by Lt Cdr Gunther Prien, who on the night of 13-14 October 1939 penetrated the defences of Scapa Flow and sank the 27,940-tonne (27,500-ton) battleship *Royal Oak,* a veteran of World War I, with three torpedo hits. The attack, in which 833 lives were lost, was carried out with great coolness, skill and daring, and came as a great shock to Britain. Prien returned home to a hero's welcome. He had already sunk three small merchant ships on the first day of the war, and went on to sink 27 more before *U47* was sunk in the North Atlantic on 7 March 1941 by the RN corvettes *Arbutus* and *Carmellia.*

Country:	Germany
Type:	Attack submarine
Launch date:	1938
Crew:	44
Displacement:	Surfaced: 765 tonnes (753 tons), submerged: 871 tonnes (857 tons)
Dimensions:	66.5m x 6.2m x 4.7m (218ft x 20ft 3in x 15ft 6in)
Surface range:	10,454km (5642nm) at 12 knots
Armament:	Five 533mm (21in) torpedo tubes; one 88mm (3.5in) gun; one 20mm AA gun
Powerplant:	Two-shaft diesel/electric motors
Performance:	Surfaced: 17.2 knots , submerged: 8 knots

U106

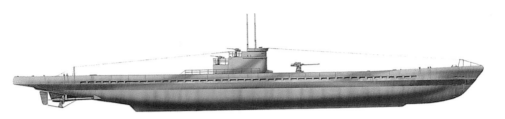

The Type IXB U-boats, of which *U106* was one, were improvements of the ocean-going Type IXAs with increased radius. Some Type IXBs were modified for service in the Far East, their range being increased to 16,100km (8700nm) at 12 knots. Their hunting ground was the Indian Ocean, using bases in Japanese-occupied Malaya and Singapore for replenishment. In March 1941 the *U106* (Lt Cdr Oesten), having already sunk several merchant ships on her Atlantic patrols, torpedoed the British battleship *Malaya*, which was escorting a convoy. The battleship was repaired in New York, but was effectively out of the war. Under Capt Rasch, *U106* went on to sink many more merchantmen in the Atlantic before being destroyed by air attack off Cape Ortegal, Biscay, on 2 August 1943. Their high surface speed made the Type IXs very effective in surface night attacks.

Country:	Germany
Type:	Attack submarine
Launch date:	1939
Crew:	48
Displacement:	Surfaced: 1068 tonnes (1051 tons), submerged: 2183 tonnes (1178t)
Dimensions:	76.5m x 6.8m x 4.6m (251ft x 22ft 3in x 15ft)
Surface range:	13,993km (7552nm) at 10 knots
Armament:	Six 533mm (21in) torpedo tubes; one 102mm (4.1in) gun, one 20mm AA gun
Powerplant:	Twin shafts, diesel/electric motors
Performance:	Surfaced: 18.2 knots, submerged: 7.2 knots

U160

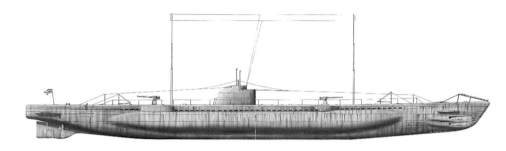

The *U160* was leader of a class of 13 fast U-boats laid down in the last months of the war. She was built by Bremer Vulcan at Kiel. Five of these boats, *U168* to *U172*, were scrapped before they were completed. Of the remainder, *U160* was surrendered to France and scrapped at Cherbourg in 1922; *U161* was stranded en route to the breakers; *U162* was also surrendered to the French, serving as the *Pierre Marast* before being scrapped in 1937; *U163* was handed over to Italy and scrapped in 1919; U164 was scrapped at Swansea in 1922; *U165* was sunk by accident in the Weser; *U166* was completed after the Armistice and handed over to France, serving as the *Jean Roulier* before going to the breaker's yard in 1935; and *U167* was scrapped in 1921. Because of their high speed, boats of this class usually attacked on the surface.

Country:	Germany
Type:	Attack submarine
Launch date:	27 February 1918
Crew:	39
Displacement:	Surfaced: 834 tonnes (821 tons), submerged: 1016 tonnes (1000 tons)
Dimensions:	71.8m x 6.2m x 4.1m (235ft 6in x 20ft 6in x 13ft 6in)
Surface range:	15,372km (8300nm) at 8 knots
Armament:	Six 509mm (20in) torpedo tubes; two 104mm (4.1in) guns
Powerplant:	Two shafts, diesel/electric motors
Performance:	Surfaced: 16.2 knots, submerged: 8.2 knots

U1081

The *U1081* was leader of a planned class of ten Type XVIIG coastal U-boats powered by the revolutionary Walter geared turbine, but still fitted with diesel/electric drive to extend their radius of action. The Type XVIIG class were generally similar to the Type XVIIB, although about 1.5m (5ft) shorter. A further class of experimental boats, the Type XVIIK, was planned for the purpose of testing the closed-cycle diesel engine as an alternative to the Walter turbine, but like the XVIIG it never advanced beyond project status. Three XVIIBs were built, all being scuttled in May 1945; one of them, the *U1407*, was salvaged, repaired and allocated to the Royal Navy under the name *Meteorite*. She was used to make exhaustive tests of the Walter propulsion system and was scrapped in 1950. Had they become available in World War II, the Type XV11s would have been formidable opponents.

Country:	Germany
Type:	Attack submarine
Launch date:	Project cancelled (1945)
Crew:	19
Displacement:	Surfaced: 319 tonnes (314 tons), submerged: 363 tonnes (357 tons)
Dimensions:	40.5m x 3.3m x 4.3m (129ft 6in x 11ft x 14ft)
Surface range:	Not known
Armament:	Two 533mm (21in) torpedo tubes
Powerplant:	Single-shaft geared turbine; diesel/electric motors
Performance:	Surfaced: 23 knots (estimated), submerged: 8.5 knots

U2326

In the latter months of the war Germany launched a massive submarine construction programme, the aim of which was to get two types of submarine – the Type XXI and Type XXIII - into service as quickly as possible. Both were fitted with diesel/electric motors plus electric 'creeping' motors that made them extremely hard to detect. The *U2326* was a Type XXIII U-boat, one of 57 that were either at sea, in various stages of construction or projected at the end of the war in Europe. The building programme was severely disrupted by Allied bombing, and only a few Type XXIIIs were operational in the final weeks of the war. After the surrender the *U2326* went to Britain, where she was used for experimental work as the N25. She was handed over to France in 1946, and lost in an accident off Toulon in December that year.

Country:	Germany
Type:	Attack submarine
Launch date:	Not known
Crew:	14
Displacement:	Surfaced: 236 tonnes (232 tons), submerged: 260 tonnes (256 tons)
Dimensions:	34m x 2.9m x 3.7m (112ft x 9ft 9in x 12ft 3in)
Surface range:	2171km (1172nm) at 7 knots
Armament:	Two 533mm (21in) torpedo tubes
Powerplant:	Single-shaft diesel/electric motors; silent creeping electric motor
Performance:	Surfaced: 9.75 knots, submerged: 12.5 knots

U2501

U2501, the first of the Type XXI ocean-going U-boats, was a milestone in the development of the submarine, a stop on the evolutionary road that led to the nuclear-powered vessels of today. She was a double-hulled vessel, with high submerged speed plus the ability to run silently at 3.5 knots on her 'creeper' electric motors. The outer hull was built of light plating to aid streamlining; the inner hull was 28-37mm (1.1-1.5in) thick carbon steel plating. She had new, super-light batteries, and could maintain a submerged speed of 16 knots for one hour; at four knots, she could remain submerged for three days on a single charge. Some 55 Type XXIs were in service when Germany surrendered in 1945, but a great many were destroyed by bombing during construction – fortunately for the Allies, for they were very dangerous war machines.

Country:	Germany
Type:	Attack submarine
Launch date:	1944
Crew:	57
Displacement:	Surfaced: 1647 tonnes (1621 tons), submerged: 2100 tonnes (2067 tons)
Dimensions:	77m x 8m x 6.2m (251ft 8in x 26ft 3in x 20ft 4in)
Surface range:	17934km (9678nm) at 10 knots
Armament:	Six 533mm (21in) torpedo tubes; four 30mm (1.2in) AA guns
Powerplant:	Twin screws, diesel/electric motors, silent creeping motors
Performance:	Surfaced: 15.5 knots, submerged: 16 knots

Udaloy

The Udaloy class of large anti-submarine-warfare destroyers was originally designated BalCom 3 (Baltic Combatant No 3) by NATO. The original seven ships, all operational by 1987, were *Udaloy, Vitse Admiral Kulakov, Marshal Vasilievsky, Admiral Zakorov, Admiral Spiridinov, Admiral Tributs* and *Marshal Shaposhnikov. Udaloy* herself achieved Initial Operational Capability (IOC) in 1981. The vessels of the Udaloy class are similar to the US Spruance-class destroyers. Each Udaloy can carry two Ka-27 Helix helicopters, and they were the first Soviet destroyers to have this capability. All Udaloy units were built at either the Yantar shipyard in Kaliningrad or the Zhdanov shipyard in Leningrad (St Petersburg). Five have been scrapped or are unserviceable, and only seven remain usable. A single example of an improved Udaloy II class was built in 1993.

Country:	Soviet Union
Type:	Destroyer
Launch date:	5 February 1980
Crew:	300
Displacement:	8332 tonnes (8200 tons)
Dimensions:	162m x 19.3m x 6.2m (531ft 6in x 63ft 4in x 20ft 4in)
Range:	23,162km (12,500nm)
Main armament:	Two 100mm (3.9in) guns; SS-N-14 ASW missiles; SA-N-9 SAMs; eight 533mm (21in) torpedo tubes
Powerplant:	Two shafts, four gas turbines
Performance:	34 knots

Ugolini Vivaldi

The *Ugolini Vivaldi* was one of a group of powerful destroyers authorised in 1926 and laid down between 1927 and 1928. Slightly smaller than their French counterparts, the Chacal class, the Italian vessels carried the same armament and were several knots faster. Some vessels in the class achieved considerable speeds; *Alvise da Mosto*, for example, developed 70,000hp and reached 45 knots. *Ugolini Vivaldi* served throughout the war until the Italian armistice of September 1943, when she set out from Castellamare with the destroyer *Da Noli* to surrender. As the two vessels passed through the Straits of Bonifacio, they came under fire from German shore batteries. *Da Noli* was sunk by mines and *Ugolini Vivaldi*, heavily damaged by shellfire, sank a few hours later after being targeted by German air attack.

Country:	Italy
Type:	Destroyer
Launch date:	9 January 1929
Crew:	225
Displacement:	2621 tonnes (2580 tons)
Dimensions:	107.3m x 10.2m x 3.4m (352ft x 33ft 6in x 11ft 2in)
Range:	6485km (3500nm)
Main armament:	Six 120mm (4.7in) guns
Powerplant:	Twin screws, turbines
Performance:	38 knots

Ulsan

The nine Ulsan-class frigates of the Republic of Korea Navy were commissioned between 1981 and 1993, the last being the *Chung Ju*. Together with the *Che Ju*, this vessel conducted the South Korean Navy's first ever deployment to European waters during a four-month tour from September 1991 to January 1992. The last four vessels of the class feature a built-up gun platform aft and have a different combination of search, target indication and navigation radars from the others. Three of the class have a shore datalink and act as local area command ships to control attack craft engaged in coastal protection duties. The last five vessels are equipped with a Ferranti combat data system; others have been fitted with the Litton Systems Link 11. These warships monitor North Korean naval movements as tension remains high between the two countries.

Country:	Republic of Korea
Type:	Frigate
Launch date:	8 April 1980
Crew:	150
Displacement:	2215 tonnes (2180 tons)
Dimensions:	102m x 11.5m x 3.5m (334ft 7in x 37ft 8in x 11ft 6in)
Range:	6434km (3474nm)
Main armament:	Two 76mm (3in) guns; Harpoon SSM; six 324mm (12.75in) torpedo tubes; depth charges
Powerplant:	Two shafts, two gas turbines, two diesels
Performance:	34 knots

Unicorn

Launched in 1941, *Unicorn* was built as part of the 1938 Naval Expansion Programme, and was intended to be a depot/maintenance support ship. She was modified during construction so that she could operate her own aircraft, as well as maintain aircraft from other carriers. Her engines developed 40,000hp, and range at 13 knots was 20,900km (11,000 miles). After completion in 1943 she served in the Mediterranean, then on Atlantic patrols, before moving to the Pacific. She later became a depot ship in Hong Kong, and was scrapped in 1959–60. In Royal Navy circles, *Unicorn* is well remembered for her role in the Korean War, ferrying aircraft, spare parts and personnel to the theatre. The British Commonwealth air commitment in Korea comprised a squadron of Gloster Meteor fighters (RAAF) and thirteen naval air squadrons on five light fleet carriers.

Country:	Great Britain
Type:	Aircraft carrier
Launch date:	20 November 1941
Crew:	1200
Displacement :	20,624 tonnes (20,300 tons)
Dimensions:	186m x 27.4m x 7.3m (610ft x 90ft x 24ft)
Range:	20,900km (11,000nm) at 13 knots
Armament:	Eight 102mm (4in) guns
Powerplant:	Twin screw turbines
Performance:	24 knots

Upholder

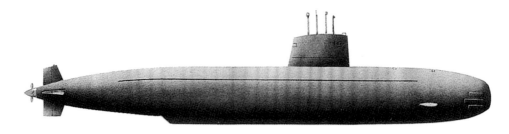

The Upholder class of four SSKs was ordered in response to an Admiralty requirement, identified in the 1970s, for a new class of diesel-electric attack submarine. The result was the Type 2400, revealed in 1979. The first boat, HMS *Upholder*, was ordered from Vickers SEL on 2 November 1983 and orders were placed for three more, named *Unseen*, *Ursula* and *Unicorn*. Plans for more of the class were dropped as part of an economic exercise. The structure comprises a single-skinned NQ1 high tensile steel hull, with a five-man lockout chamber in the fin. The boats have an endurance of 49 days, and can remain submerged for 90 hours at 3 knots. All were based at Devonport as part of the 2nd Submarine Squadron, but by the mid-1990s all had been placed in reserve. In 1998 they were leased for eight years (with the option to buy) to the Canadian Navy.

Country:	Great Britain
Type:	Attack submarine
Launch date:	December 1986
Crew:	47
Displacement:	Surfaced: 2203 tonnes (2168 tons), submerged: 2494 tonnes (2455 tons)
Dimensions:	70.3m x 7.6m x 5.5m (230ft 7in x 25ft x 17ft 7in)
Surface range:	14,816km (8000nm) at 8 knots
Armament:	Six 533mm (21in) torpedoes; Sub Harpoon SSMs
Powerplant:	Single shaft, diesel/electric motors
Performance:	Surfaced: 12 knots, submerged: 20 knots

Uragan

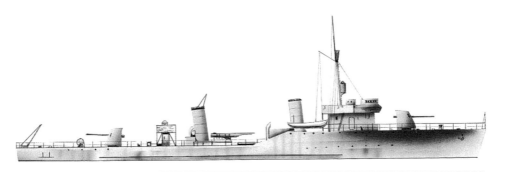

Uragan ('Hurricane') was laid down in 1927, the lead ship in the Soviet Navy's first new major construction programme. Eighteen ships were ordered but only 12 were laid down, with the remaining six being held over for five years. Their engines developed 6300hp, and design speed, which was never attained, was 29 knots. Additional anti-aircraft armament was added before World War II, and complement was increased from 70 to 108 to service and man the extra weaponry. All ships of the class served during the war, mainly in the Baltic and Black sea theatres, where they were used as troop and supply transports. Both the Black Sea and the Baltic saw bitter naval skirmishing during the war. Many survived the conflict, including *Uragan*; she served as a training ship for many years after the war, being discarded in 1959.

Country of origin:	Soviet Union
Type:	Torpedo boat
Launch date:	1929
Crew:	70
Displacement:	629 tonnes 619 tons
Dimensions:	71.5m x 7.4m x 2.6m (234ft 7in x 24ft 9in x 8ft 6in)
Range:	1524km (1500nm)
Main armament:	Three 102mm (4in) guns
Powerplant:	Twin screws, turbines
Performance:	24 knots

Van Speijk

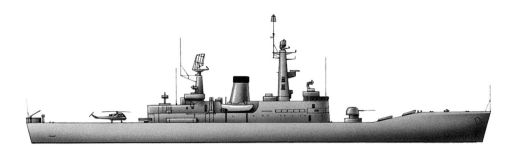

L aid down in June 1964, the Van Speijk was one of five frigates built for the Royal Netherlands Navy in the mid-1960s, the others being the *Tjerk Hiddes, Van Galen, Van Nes, Evertsen* and *Isaac Sweers*. Although in general the ships were based on the design of the British Improved Type 12 Leander class, a number of modifications were carried out in order to meet the requirements of the Netherlands Naval Staff, and equipment of Dutch manufacture was installed wherever possible. This resulted in a number of changes in the ships' superstructure when compared with the Leanders. To avoid delaying their entry into service, in some cases the ships were fitted with equipment that was already available but rather less than modern, being retrofitted with new gear at a later date. The ships replaced the frigates of the Van Amstel class (former US DEs).

Country:	Netherlands
Type:	Frigate
Launch date:	5 March 1965
Crew:	251
Displacement:	2896 tonnes (2850 tons)
Dimensions:	113.46m x 12.5m x 5.5m (372ft x 41ft x 18ft)
Range:	8042km (4340nm)
Main armament:	Two 114mm (4.5in) guns; Seacat SAMs; Limbo AS mortar
Powerplant:	Twin screws, geared turbines
Performance:	28.5 knots

Vanguard

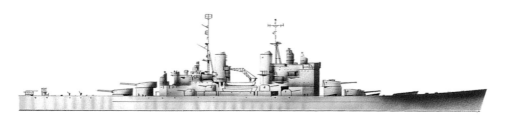

Vanguard was the last battleship built for the Royal Navy. She was ordered in 1941 under the Emergency War Plan of 1940, but did not enter service until 1946. *Vanguard* was basically a lengthened *King George V*, and could accommodate four twin turrets on the centreline. In 1947 she took members of the British Royal Family on tour to South Africa, and after a refit she served in the Mediterranean in 1949–51, primarily as a training ship. In the 1950s she became part of the NATO reserve. The decision to complete the building of *Vanguard* was prompted both by the desire to have at least one modern capital ship embracing war experience (which in the event she did not have) and the availability of the twin 15in guns removed from *Courageous* and *Glorious* when the latter ships were converted to aircraft carriers. She was sold for scrap in 1960.

Country:	Great Britain
Type:	Battleship
Launch date:	30 November 1944
Crew:	1893
Displacement :	52,243 tonnes (51,420 tons)
Dimensions:	248m x 32.9m x 10.9m (813ft 8in x 108ft x 36ft)
Range:	16,677km (9000nm) at 20 knots
Armament:	Eight 380mm (15in), 16 140mm (5.5in) guns
Powerplant:	Quadruple screw turbines
Performance:	30 knots

Vanguard

The decision to buy the US Trident I (C4) submarine-launched ballistic-missile system was announced by the UK Government on 15 July 1980. A little under two years later, the government announced that it had opted for the improved Trident II system, with the more advanced D5 missile, to be deployed in four SSBNs: these would be named *Vanguard, Victorious, Vigilant* and *Vengeance*. The four British Vanguard-class Trident submarines incorporate a missile compartment based on that of the Ohio-class boats, but with 16 rather than 24 launch tubes. Trident II D5 is able to carry up to 14 warheads of 100–120kT per missile, each having sufficient accuracy to hit underground missile silos and command bunkers, but low-yield sub-strategic warheads are also carried. The Vanguards undergo a refit and refuelling every eight or nine years.

Country:	Great Britain
Type:	Ballistic missile submarine
Launch date:	4 March 1992
Crew:	135
Displacement:	Surfaced: not available, submerged: 16,155 tonnes (15,900 tons)
Dimensions:	149.9m x 12.8m x 12m (491ft 10in x 42ft x 39ft 5in)
Range:	Unlimited
Armament:	Sixteen Lockheed Trident D5 missiles; four 533mm (21in) torpedoes
Powerplant:	One nuclear PWR; two turbines
Performance:	Surfaced: not available, submerged: 25 knots

Vauban

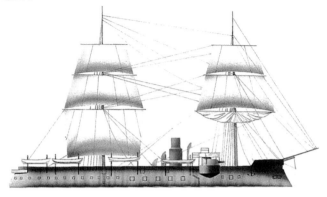

The French battleship *Vauban* was the epitome of the French ironclad cruising ship. She was based on the preceding Bayard class, but instead of having a wooden hull, she had a steel hull, sheathed with wood and coppered. As completed in 1885, *Vauban* was brig-rigged and carried 2155 square metres (23,200 sq ft) of canvas, but this was later removed and she was given two military masts instead. She was discarded in 1905. *Vauban* was built at a time when the French Navy was going through a period of crisis; in 1884 Admiral Aube, a significant naval reformer, had suspended battleship construction, turning French naval policy on its head. A few years earlier, France had captured the technological maritime lead with the launching of *Gloire*, the world's first ironclad, which development started a naval race with Britain.

Country:	France
Type:	Ironclad
Launch date:	July 1882
Crew:	440
Displacement :	6210 tonnes (6112 tons)
Dimensions:	81m x 17.5m x 7.7m (265ft 9in x 57ft 3in x 25ft 3in)
Range:	4632km (2500nm) at 12 knots
Armament:	Four 238mm (9.4in), one 190mm (7.5in), six 150mm (5.9in) guns
Powerplant:	Twin screw, vertical compound engines
Performance:	14.5 knots

Viborg

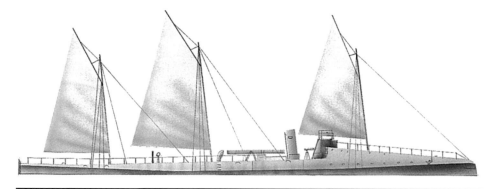

Viborg was the largest torpedo boat of her period. She was built at Thompson's Yard, Clydebank, Scotland, the company being specialists in the construction of this type of vessel. Two 37mm (1.5in) revolving Hotchkiss cannon were placed forward, abreast of the funnels. The third torpedo tube was on a trainable mount abaft the twin funnels, which were mounted side by side. The forward part of the boat's turtle deck was thickly plated in front of the conning tower. After *Viborg*, which was discarded in 1910, the Imperial Russian Navy turned increasingly to German and French shipyards for its gunboats; the next two classes, Abo and Yalta (nine boats in all) were built at the German yard of Schichau, while the following Izmail class was built by Normand. After the revolution, the Russians sought help from the Italians.

Country:	Russia
Type:	Torpedo boat
Launch date:	1886
Crew:	21
Displacement:	169 tonnes (166 tons)
Dimensions:	43.4m x 5m x 2m (142ft 6in x 17ft x 7ft)
Range:	Not known
Main armament:	Three 381mm (15in) torpedo tubes
Powerplant:	Twin screws, vertical compound engines
Performance:	20 knots

Victor III

An improvement on the Victor II, the first Victor III class SSN was completed at Komsomolsk in 1978, and production proceeded at a rapid rate at both this yard and Leningrad up to the end of 1984, after which it began to tail off. The Victor III incorporated major advances in acoustic quietening, so that the vessel's radiated noise level is about the same as that of the American Los Angeles class. Apart from anti-ship and ASW submarines and torpedoes, the Victor IIIs are armed with the SS-N-21 Samson submarine-launched cruise missile, which has a range of 3000km (1620nm) at about 0.7M and carries a 200kT nuclear warhead. A total of 25 Victor III class boats was produced, with only eight still operational, although they are likely to be retired in the near future. Its design successor was the Akula class, the first of which was launched in 1984.

Country:	Soviet Union
Type:	Attack submarine
Launch date:	1978
Crew:	100
Displacement:	Surfaced: not available, submerged: 6400 tonnes (6300 tons)
Dimensions:	104m x 10m x 7m (347ft 9in x 32ft 10in x 23ft)
Range:	Unlimited
Armament:	Six 533mm (21in) torpedo tubes; SS-N-15/16/21 SSMs
Powerplant:	Single screw, nuclear PWR, turbines
Performance:	Surfaced: 24 knots, submerged: 30 knots

Victoria

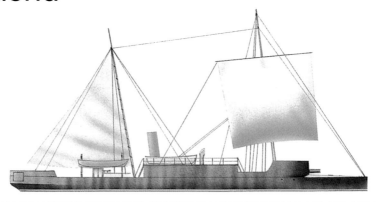

During the 1880s, Britain's Australian colony began to build up a sizeable navy for local defence. As Australia had no suitable construction facilities, the new additions were built in Britain. *Victoria* was a steel-hulled vessel armed with a single 254mm (10in) gun mounted forward behind a raised bulwark. The entire vessel had to be turned in order to train the gun on its target. Engines developed 800hp and coal supply was 91 tonnes (90 tons). Although relatively small, vessels such as *Victoria* proved a useful deterrent against raiding cruisers, which could not afford to run the risk of being damaged so far from their home ports, and whose activities were hampered by a lack of coaling facilities. Setting these up was a major drain on the resources of the European naval powers. *Victoria* was sold in 1896.

Country:	Australia
Type:	Gunboat
Launch date:	1884
Crew:	20
Displacement:	538 tonnes (530 tons)
Dimensions:	42.6m x 8.2m x 3.3m (140ft x 27ft x 11ft)
Range:	Not known
Main armament:	One 254mm (10in) gun
Powerplant:	Twin screws, compound engines
Performance:	12 knots

Vincenzo Gioberti

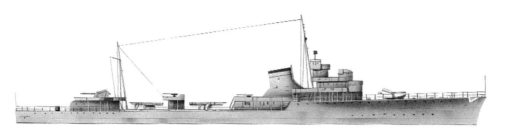

Launched in September 1936, *Vincenzo Gioberti* was one unit in a class of four vessels that were repeats of the Maestrale class, but which had increased power. The 120mm (4.7in) guns were in twin mounts, one forward and one aft on the raised superstructure. Six 533mm (21in) torpedo tubes were mounted on triple carriages down the centreline. The class also had eight 13.2mm (5.2in) weapons, later replaced by 20mm (0.8in) anti-aircraft guns. *Vincenzo Gioberti* was laid down by Odero Terni-Orlando of Livorno (Leghorn) in January 1936, and was completed in October 1937. She was torpedoed and sunk by the British submarine *Simoon* on 9 August 1943. The other vessels in the class were the *Vittorio Alfieri*, *Giosue Carducci* and *Alfredo Oriani*; the latter served in the French Navy after the war as the *d'Estaing*, and was retired in 1954.

Country:	Italy
Type:	Destroyer
Launch date:	19 September 1936
Crew:	207
Displacement:	2326 tonnes (2290 tons)
Dimensions:	106.7m x 10m x 3.4m (350ft x 33ft 4in x 11ft 3in)
Range:	4074km (2200nm)
Main armament:	Four 120mm (4.7in) guns; six 533mm (21in) torpedo tubes
Powerplant:	Twin-shaft geared turbines
Performance:	39 knots

Vincenzo Giordano Orsini

*V**incenzo Giordano Orsini*** was one of a quartet of fast destroyers of the Sirtori class, which were improved versions of the Pilo class. A higher-calibre gun armament was now carried, plus twin torpedo mountings. The engines developed 15,000hp, and endurance at 14 knots was 3800km (2051nm) or 760km (410nm) at 29 knots. All vessels in the class were reclassified as torpedo boats in 1929. On 8 April 1941 *Orsini* was scuttled at Massawa, Eritrea, together with other torpedo boats and many merchant vessels, shortly before British forces entered the port. Another vessel in the class, *Giovanni Acerbi*, was destroyed by RAF bombing at Massawa on 4 April 1941. Of the two remaining vessels, *Giuseppe Sirtori* was damaged by German bombs and scuttled in September 1943, while *Francesco Stocco* was sunk by German bombs at the same time.

Country:	Italy
Type:	Destroyer
Launch date:	23 April 1917
Crew:	98
Displacement:	864 tonnes (850 tons)
Dimensions:	73.5m x 7.3m x 2.8m (241ft x 24ft x 9ft)
Range:	3800km (20451nm)
Main armament:	Six 102mm (4in) guns; four 500mm (17.7in) torpedo tubes
Powerplant:	Twin screws, turbines
Performance:	33.6 knots

Viper

L aunched in September 1899, *Viper* was the world's first turbine driven warship. The principle of the turbine had been known for centuries, but it was not until the 1880s that Charles Parsons succeeded in making practical use of a steam turbine. In fact, he proved the concept in dramatic style by sailing his steam turbine-powered prototype, *Turbinia*, at full speed between the rows of warships anchored for Queen Victoria's Diamond Naval Review at Spithead in 1897. None of the picket boats or duty torpedo boats that set off in pursuit were able to catch her. *Viper* had eight screws on four shafts, and on a three-hour trial she developed 1041hp and achieved 33.9 knots. She had not been in service long when she ran aground in a thick mist off the Channel Islands in August 1901. A similar vessel, *Cobra*, built by Armstrong, was also lost in 1901.

Country:	Great Britain
Type:	Destroyer
Launch date:	6 September 1899
Crew:	65
Displacement:	350 tonnes (344 tons)
Dimensions:	64m x 6.4m x 3.8m (210ft 3in x 21ft x 12ft 6in)
Range:	Not known
Main armament:	One 12-pounder gun; two 457mm (18in) torpedo tubes
Powerplant:	Eight screws, turbines
Performance:	37 knots

Vitoria

Upon her completion in 1867, *Vitoria* helped to push Spain into fifth place among the world's naval powers behind Britain, France, Italy and Austria. She was an iron-hulled, broadside frigate with a ram bow. All her guns were mounted on the main deck. *Vitoria* had a chequered career; in 1873 she was seized by insurgents at Cartagena, and afterwards she surrendered to the British battleship *Swiftsure* and the German *Friedrich Carl* after her crew went ashore at Escombera. She was returned to the Spanish government, and in October 1973 she saw action against insurgent warships off Cartagena. In January 1874 she was involved in a collision with the British steamer *Ellen Constant*, which sank. She was rebuilt in France in 1897–98 and was given quick-firing guns. She was used as a training ship after 1900 and stricken in 1912.

Country:	Spain
Type:	Frigate
Launch date:	4 November 1865
Crew:	500
Displacement :	7250 tonnes (7135 tons)
Dimensions:	96.3m x 17.3m x 8m (316ft 2in x 57ft x 26ft 3in)
Range:	4447km (2400nm) at 10 knots
Armament:	30 68-pounder guns
Powerplant:	Single screw, single compound engine
Performance:	12.5 knots

Vittorio Veneto

Vittorio Veneto was badly damaged several times during World War II. She was hit by a torpedo during the Battle of Matapan in March 1941. During this attack, which was carried out by Swordfish aircraft from the carrier HMS *Formidable*, *Veneto* narrowly escaped destruction; out of three torpedoes dropped at close range to port and two to starboard, one struck her just above her port outer propeller, quickly flooding her with thousands of tons of water. She managed to get away, but the Italians lost three cruisers, two destroyers and 2400 men. Having been repaired she was torpedoed again, this time by the submarine *Urge*. As a finale she was bombed in 1943 on her way to Malta to surrender. After Italy joined the Allies, she was laid up in the Suez Canal. She was broken up between 1948 and 1950.

Country:	Italy
Type:	Battleship
Launch date:	22 July 1937
Crew:	1950
Displacement :	46,484 tonnes (45,752 tons)
Dimensions:	237.8m x 32.9m x 9.6m (780ft 2in x 108ft x 31ft 6in)
Range:	8487km (4580nm) at 16 knots
Armament:	Nine 381mm (15in), 12 152mm (6in), four 120mm (4.7in), 12 89mm (3.5in) guns
Powerplant:	Quadruple screw turbines
Performance:	31.4 knots

Vittorio Veneto

Vittorio Veneto was a purpose-built helicopter cruiser that followed on from the smaller Andrea Doria class of the 1950s. The addition of a second deck aft gave her greater hangar capacity. A large central lift is set immediately aft of the super-structure, and two sets of fin stabilisers make her a steady helicopter platform. Laid down in 1965 and completed in 1969, she underwent a major refit between 1981 and 1984 which upgraded her missiles and radar. Her normal air group comprises six anti-submarine Sea King or nine AB212 helicopters. She is fitted with an Aster SAM/ASW launcher system with three rotary drums loaded with 40 surface-to-air missiles and 20 ASROC anti-submarine missiles; her operations centre can elect the missile type to be fired according to the nature of the threat detected. Her role as the Italian Navy's flagship was handed over to carrier *Giuseppe Garibaldi* in 1995.

Country:	Italy
Type:	Helicopter cruiser
Launch date:	5 February 1967
Crew:	550
Displacement :	8991 tonnes (8850 tons)
Dimensions:	179.5m x 19.4m x 6m (589ft x 63ft 8in x 19ft 8in)
Range:	9000km (5000nm) at 10 knots
Armament:	12 40mm (1.6in), eight 76mm (3in) guns, four Teseo SAM launchers, one ASROC launcher
Powerplant:	Twin screw turbines
Performance:	32 knots

Von der Tann

Completed in 1911, *Von der Tann* was Germany's first battlecruiser, and the first major German warship to have turbines. On 16 December 1914, following an earlier attack on Yarmouth, *Von der Tann* and other warships shelled Hartlepool, Whitby and Scarborough on the northeast coast of England, killing 127 civilians and wounding 567. The fact that 38 women and 39 children were among the dead caused a great anti-German outcry in Britain. *Von der Tann's* protection was good, and though she was hit by four shells at the Battle of Jutland in 1916, which caused severe fire damage and put all her main guns out of action, she reached home without difficulty. She was surrendered at the end of World War I, and scuttled at Scapa Flow in June 1919. She was raised in December 1930, and was broken up at Rosyth between 1931 and 1934.

Country:	Germany
Type:	Battlecruiser
Launch date:	20 March 1909
Crew:	1174 (at Jutland)
Displacement :	22,150 tonnes (21,802 tons)
Dimensions :	172m x 26.6m x 8m (563ft 4in x 87ft 3in x 26ft 7in)
Range:	7920km (4400nm) at 10 knots
Armament:	Eight 280mm (11in), 10 150mm (5.9in) guns
Powerplant:	Quadruple screw turbines
Performance:	27.7 knots

Vulcan

Vulcan was the world's first purpose-built torpedo depot ship. She was designed to accompany the main fleet and launch her squadron of six second-class torpedo boats at the first suitable opportunity. Her boats were normally stowed on cross-trees on the upper deck, aft of the two funnels. They were launched and retrieved by two large goose-necked cranes in the centre of the hull. She could also act as a depot and resupply ship to other torpedo boats as the situation required. She had a full-length armoured deck, 64mm (2.5in) thick on the flat, and 128mm (5in) thick on the slopes and engine hatches. Her engines developed 12,000hp from four double-ended boilers, and a further boiler provided steam to power machinery in the vessel's repair shop. *Vulcan* became a training hulk, renamed *Defiance III*, in 1931, and was eventually broken up in 1955.

Country:	Great Britain
Type:	Torpedo depot ship
Launch date:	13 June 1889
Crew:	432
Displacement:	6705 tonnes (6000 tons)
Dimensions:	113.6m x 17.6m x 6.7m (373ft x 58ft x 22ft)
Range:	Not known
Main armament:	Eight 120mm (4.7in) guns
Powerplant:	Twin screws, triple expansion engines
Performance:	20 knots

Walker

Instantly recognisable through their two thick and thin funnels, the V-class and W class-destroyers served the Royal Navy well for over a century. Stemming from five new half-leaders ordered in 1916 to counter rumoured German construction, the class introduced superfiring guns both forward and aft, and featured extra length and freeboard for improved seaworthiness. Once proved, the design was extended by 25 V class and then 25 W class. Most were cancelled with the Armistice, but the survivors formed the backbone of the fleet destroyer strength between the wars, and entered their second war in 1939. HMS *Walker* was one of the most successful of all U-boat hunters. She sank the *U99* (Lt Cdr Kretschmer) on 17 March 1941 and participated in the destruction of *U100* (Lt Cdr Schepke), after its ramming by HMS *Vanoc*. *Walker* was scrapped at Troon, Scotland, in March 1946.

Country:	Great Britain
Type:	Destroyer
Launch date:	29 November 1917
Crew:	134
Displacement:	1529 tonnes (1505 tons)
Dimensions:	95.1m x 8.99m x 3.28m (312ft x 29ft 6in x 10ft 9in)
Range:	6426km (3470nm)
Main armament:	Four 119mm (4.7in) and one 76mm (3in) guns; six 533mm (21in) torpedo tubes
Powerplant:	Two shafts, two sets of geared steam turbines
Performance:	34 knots

Walrus

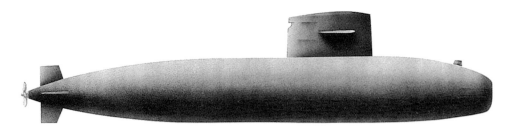

In 1972 the Royal Netherlands Navy identified a need for a new class of submarine to replace the elderly Dolfijn and Potvis classes. The new design evolved as the Walrus class, and was based on the *Zwaardvis* hull form with similar dimensions and silhouette, but with more automation, a smaller crew, more modern electronics, X-configuration control surfaces and the French MAREI high–tensile steel hull material that permits a 50 per cent increase in maximum diving depth to 300m (985ft). The first unit, *Walrus,* was laid down in 1979 for commissioning in 1986, but in August that year she suffered a serious fire (enough to make her hull glow white-hot) while in the final stage of completion, so she was not completed until 1991. Despite the intensity of the blaze, her hull had luckily escaped serious damage.

Country:	Netherlands
Type:	Attack submarine
Launch date:	October 1985
Crew:	49
Displacement:	Surfaced: 2490 tonnes (2450 tons), submerged: 2800 tonnes (2755 tons)
Dimensions:	67.5m x 8.4m x 6.6m (222ft x 27ft 7in x 21ft 8in)
Surface range:	18,520km (10,000nm) at 9 knots
Armament:	Four 533mm (21in) torpedo tubes
Powerplant:	Single screw, diesel/electric motors
Performance:	Surfaced: 13 knots, submerged: 20 knots

Warrior

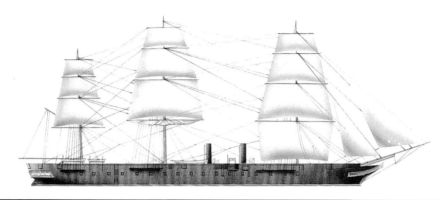

Warrior was the world's first iron-hulled capital ship. Designed by Isaac Watts, she was laid down in May 1859 and on completion was the most powerful warship in the world, faster and more heavily armed than even the French *Gloire*. High speed was achieved by the 'V' formation of the forward part of the hull. Originally designated as a frigate because she only had one deck, *Warrior* and her sister *Black Prince* were reclassified as armoured cruisers in 1880. *Warrior* became a depot ship in 1902 and was hulked in 1923 after which she was used a pipeline pier. Her hulk was rediscovered and restored during the 1980s, and she is now stationed at Portsmouth, England. As a depot ship she was briefly renamed *Vernon III* before reverting to her original name. Her sister, *Black Prince*, became a boys' training ship at Queenstown and was renamed *Emerald* then *Impregnable III*.

Country:	Great Britain
Type:	Ironclad
Launch date:	29 December 1860
Crew:	707
Displacement:	9357 tonnes (9137 tons)
Dimensions:	115.8m x 17.8m x 8m (420ft x 58ft 4in x 26ft)
Range:	3780km (2100nm) at 12 knots
Armament:	10 110-pounder, four 70-pounder, 26 68-pounder guns
Powerplant:	Single screw, single expansion trunk engine
Performance:	17 knots with combined steam and sail

Warspite

Completed in 1916, *Warspite* belonged to the Queen Elizabeth class, developed from the Iron Duke class, but her displacement was increased by 2540 tonnes (2500 tons), and 6m (20ft) were added to the length. The 380mm (15in) guns fired an 871kg (1916lb) shell to a range of 32,000m (35,000yd) with extreme accuracy. She was badly damaged at Jutland taking 15 hits from 279mm (11in) 304mm (12in) shells. *Warspite* was extensively modernised between 1934 and 1937. During operations in World War II she was severely damaged by German bombs off Crete, and later by German radio-controlled bombs off Salerno, Italy, when covering the Allied landings. She was partially repaired, and used as part of the bombardment force covering the D-Day landings in Normandy. She was further damaged by a mine off Harwich on 13 June 1944. She was paid off in 1945 and scrapped in 1948.

Country:	Great Britain
Type:	Battleship
Launch date:	26 November 1913
Crew:	951
Displacement :	33,548 tonnes (33,020 tons)
Dimensions:	197m x 28m x 9m (646ft x 90ft 6in x 29ft 10in)
Range:	8100km (4500nm) at 10 knots
Armament:	Eight 380mm (15in), 16 152mm (6in) guns
Powerplant:	Quadruple screw turbines
Performance:	23 knots

Washington

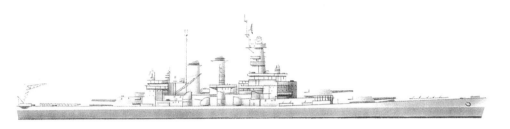

***W**ashington* and her sister *North Carolina* were the first US battleships built
after the lifting of the 1922 Washington Naval Treaty. Original designs complied
with the 356mm (14in) gun limitations of the later London Treaty, but when Japan
refused to ratify the agreement the design was recast to carry three triple 400mm
(16in) gun turrets. The additional weight of the larger weapons caused a two-knot
reduction in top speed. *Washington* began her World War II service escorting Arctic
convoys to Russia, then transferring to the Pacific Theatre, where she fought at
Guadalcanal, Leyte, Okinawa and Iwo Jima and took part in many raids on Japanese-
held territory. She suffered damage in a collision with the battleship *Indiana* in
February 1944. *Washington*, along with *South Dakota*, sank the Japanese battlecruiser *Kirishima* at Guadalcanal in November 1942. She was scrapped in 1960–61.

Country:	USA
Type:	Battleship
Launch date:	1 June 1940
Crew:	1880
Displacement :	47,518 tonnes (46,770 tons)
Dimensions:	222m x 33m x 10m (728ft 9in x 108ft 4in x 33ft)
Range:	31,410km (17,450nm) at 12 knots
Armament:	Nine 400mm (16in), 20 127mm (5in) guns
Powerplant:	Quadruple screw turbines
Performance:	28 knots

Weapon class

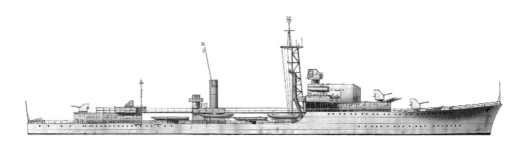

Hard wartime experience had exposed the limitations of fleet destroyers as anti-submarine platforms. Nevertheless, the fleet still required a fast anti-submarine screen of ships that could not only protect themselves but also contribute to the AA defences of a task group, allowing the carrier's aircraft complement to be devoted to offensive, rather than defensive operations. It was for these reasons that the Weapon-class destroyers came into being. The choice of the high-angle 102mm (4in) gun for the main battery was logical, its 14kg (31lb) projectile enabling fast hand-working even up to the maximum elevation of 80 degrees. Only two twin mountings ould be shipped, however, as the hull length was limited by available building berths. Close-in AA protection was provided by two twin stablised 40mm (1.5in) mountings aft, with single guns flanking the bridge structure.

Country:	Great Britain
Type:	Destroyer
Launch date:	12 June 1945 (HMS *Battleaxe*, first unit)
Crew:	255
Displacement:	2870 tonnes (2825 tons)
Dimensions:	111.2m x 11.58m x 3.2m (365ft x 38ft x 10ft 6in)
Range:	4447km (2400nm)
Main armament:	Two 102mm (4in) DP guns; two quintuple 533mm (21in) torpedo tube mountings
Powerplant:	Two shafts, two sets of geared steam turbines
Performance:	35 knots

Whiskey

The Soviet Union's first post-war submarine, and essentially a modified version of the German Type XXI design, the Russians mass-produced 236 Whiskey class diesel-electric submarines between 1949 and 1957, using prefabricated sections. All the early variants (Whiskey I–IV) were eventually converted to the Whiskey-V configuration, with no gun armament and a streamlined sail. Some were configured for special duties operations, fitted with a deck-mounted lockout diving chamber for use by Special Forces' combat swimmers. A submarine of this class (No137) went aground inside Swedish territorial waters on 27 October 1981, near Karlskrona naval base, providing evidence that the Whiskey boats were routinely engaged in clandestine activities. Some 45 Whiskey boats were transferred to countries friendly to the Soviet Union.

Country:	Soviet Union
Type:	Attack submarine
Launch date:	1949 (first unit)
Crew:	50
Displacement:	Surfaced: 1066 tonnes (1050 tons), submerged: 1371 tonnes (1350 tons)
Dimensions:	76m x 6.5m x 5m (249ft 4in x 21ft 4in x 16ft)
Surface range:	15,890km (8580nm) at 10 knots
Armament:	Four 533mm (21in) and two 406mm (16in) torpedo tubes
Powerplant:	Twin screws, diesel/electric motors
Performance:	Surfaced: 18 knots, submerged: 14 knots

Wielingen

The Belgian Navy has three Wielingen-class frigates (*Wielingen*, *Westdiep* and *Wandelaar*), all commissioned in the late 1970s. Designed by the Belgian Navy and built in Belgian yards, the ships are compact and well-armed. Plans to install a CIWS were abandoned in 1993, but the Sea Sparrow SAM system has been updated. In addition, the vessels' WM25 surface search/fire control radar is being updated to improve electronic counter-countermeasures (ECCM). New sonars have been installed from 1998. The ships are likely to remain in service well into the twenty-first century; two are operational at any one time, a third being laid up on a rotational basis. The Belgian Navy's principal area of operations within the NATO framework is the English Channel and the North Sea, and the Wielingens are capable of operating in the aircraft direction role.

Country:	Belgium
Type:	Frigate
Launch date:	30 March 1976
Crew:	159
Displacement:	2469 tonnes (2430 tons)
Dimensions:	106.4m x 12.3m x 5.6m (349ft x 40ft 4in x 18ft 5in)
Range:	9650km (5186nm)
Main armament:	One 100mm (3.9in) gun; Exocet SSM; Sea Sparrow SAM; two 533mm (21in) torpedo tubes
Powerplant:	Two shafts, one gas turbine, two diesels
Performance:	26 knots

Wilmington

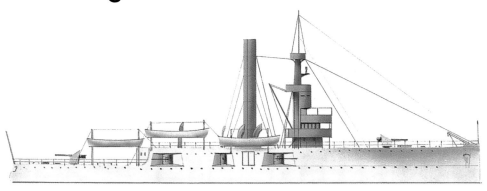

*W*ilmington** was laid down in 1894 and completed in May 1897. She and her sister *Helena* were patrol gunboats for use in the waters around Florida. They had one tall funnel and the hull cut down to form a long poop. Two of the 102mm (4in) guns were mounted on the foredeck, with two more mounted aft and two on each broadside behind 38mm (1.5in) armour. The ships had a shallower draught than other US gunboats, making them ideal for river work. *Wilmington*'s engines developed 1900hp. She saw service in the 1898 war with Spain, later serving as a training ship, but she was retained on the Navy List along with other former combatant vessels that were unclassified but were kept as relics, for use as training ships or adapted for other duties. *Wilmington* was renamed *Dover* and she was allocated the number IX.30. She was scuttled in 1947.

Country:	USA
Type:	Gunboat
Launch date:	19 October 1895
Crew:	80
Displacement:	1716 tonnes (1689 tons)
Dimensions:	76.4m x 12.4m x 2.7m (250ft 9in x 41ft x 9ft)
Range:	Not known
Main armament:	Eight 102mm (4in) guns
Powerplant:	Twin screws, triple expansion engines
Performance:	12 knots

Xia class

The first type of nuclear ballistic-missile submarine built by the People's Republic of China, *Xia* is roughly similar to the Russian Yankee II missile boat. The first launch of a JL-1 SLBM took place on 30 April 1982 from a submerged position near Hulodao in the Yellow Sea. The second was launched on 12 October 1982 from a specially-modified Golf-class trials submarine, and the first launch from *Xia* herself was made in 1985 and was unsuccessful, delaying the submarine's entry into service while modifications were carried out. A satisfactory launch was finally made on 27 September 1988. The JL-1 missile had a range of 972nm (1800km) and carries a single 350kT warhead. A second Xia-class boat was launched in 1982, and there are unconfirmed reports that one of the pair was lost in an accident. The survivor has been refitted to launch the upgraded JL-2 SLBM.

Country:	China
Type:	Ballistic missile submarine
Launch date:	30 April 1981
Crew:	140
Displacement:	Surfaced: Not known, submerged: 6604 tonnes (6500 tons)
Dimensions:	120m x 10m x 8m (393ft 7in x 33ft x 26ft 2in)
Range:	Unlimited
Armament:	Six 533mm (21in) torpedo tubes; 12 JL1 SLBMs
Powerplant:	Single shaft, nuclear PWR, turbo-electric drive
Performance:	Surfaced: Not known, submerged: 22 knots

Yamato

Yamato, together with her sister *Musashi*, were the world's largest and most powerful battleships ever built when they were launched. No fewer than 23 designs were prepared for *Yamato* between 1934 and 1937 when she was laid down. When she was launched, her displacement was only surpassed by that of the British liner *Queen Mary*. Her main turrets each weighed 2818 tonnes (2774 tons), and each 460mm (18.1in) gun could fire two 1473kg (3240lb) shells per minute over a distance of 41,148m (45,000yds). As flagship of the Combined Fleet she saw action in the battles of Midway, the Philippine Sea and Leyte Gulf. On 25 December 1943 she was torpedoed by the US submarine *Skate* south of Truk, and in October 1944 she was damaged by two bomb hits at Leyte Gulf. On 7 April 1945 she was sunk by US carrier aircraft 130 miles southwest of Kagoshima with the loss of 2498 lives.

Country:	Japan
Type:	Battleship
Launch date:	8 August 1940
Crew:	2500
Displacement :	71,110 tonnes (71,659 tons)
Dimensions:	263m x 36.9m x 10.3m (862ft 10in x 121ft x 34ft)
Range:	13,340km (7200nm) at 16 knots
Armament:	Nine 460mm (18.1in), 12 155mm (6.1in), 12 127mm (5in) guns
Powerplant:	Quadruple screw turbines
Performance:	27 knots

Yankee class

During the Cold War period three or four Yankee boats were on station at any one time off the eastern seaboard of the USA, with a further unit either on transit to or from a patrol area. The forward-deployed Yankees were assigned the wartime role of destroying targets such as SAC bomber alert bases and carriers/SSBNs in port, and of disrupting the American higher command echelons to ease the task of follow up ICBM strikes. As they progressively retired from their SSBN role, some Yankees were converted to carry cruise or anti-ship missiles as SSNs. Despite the removal of the ballistic missile section the overall length of the Yankee's hull has increased by 12m (39.4ft) with the insertion of a 'notch waisted' central section, housing three tubes amidships on either side, and the magazine holds up to 35 SS-N-21s or additional torpedoes and mines.

Country:	Soviet Union
Type:	Ballistic missile submarine
Launch date:	1967
Crew:	120
Displacement:	Surfaced: 7925 tonnes (7800 tons), submerged: 9450 tonnes (9300 tons)
Dimensions:	129.5m x 11.6m x 7.8m (424ft 10in x 38ft x 25ft 7in)
Range:	Unlimited
Armament:	Six 533mm (21in) torpedo tubes; 16 SS-N-6 missiles
Powerplant:	Twin screws, two nuclear PWRs, turbines
Performance:	Surfaced: 20 knots, submerged: 30 knots

Yubari

The Yubari class of frigate is basically an improved and enlarged variant of the Ishikari design, authorized between 1977 and 1978. The greater length and beam improved the seaworthiness and reduced the internal space constrictions of the earlier design. The original number of units to be built was three, but this was reduced to two (*Yubari* and *Yubetsu*) when the Japanese Government deleted funds from the naval budget in the early 1980s. Although not heavily armed and having no helicopter facilities, the vessels of the Yurabi class are ideal for use in the waters around Japan, where they are able to operate under shore-based air cover. Most of their weapons, sensors and machinery have been built under licence from foreign manufacturers. It was originally planned to fit Phalanx, but this has not occurred and seems unlikely to happen.

Country:	Japan
Type:	Frigate
Launch date:	22 February 1982
Crew:	95
Displacement:	1717 tonnes (1690 tons)
Dimensions:	91m x 10.8m x 3.6m (298ft 6in x 35ft 5in x 11ft 10in)
Range:	7412km (4002nm)
Main armament:	One 76mm (3in) gun; Harpoon SSM; six 324mm (12.75in) torpedo tubes; A/S mortars
Powerplant:	Two shafts, one gas turbine, one diesel
Performance:	25 knots

Yukikaze

Completed in 1956, *Yukikaze* (Snow Wind) and her sister ship *Harukaze* (Spring Wind) were authorized under the 1953 fiscal year programme and were the first destroyer-hulled vessels to be built in Japan since World War II. Electric welding was extensively used in their hull construction; another novelty was the development and usage of high tension steel in the main hull and of light alloy in the superstructure. Nearly all the armament was supplied by the USA and was modified in March 1959, when homing torpedo tubes were mounted and depth charge equipment correspondingly reduced. *Harukaze* was built at Nagasaki and *Yukizake* at Kobe, both by the Mitsubishi company. The other Japanese destroyer classes in service at this time were named Cloud, Moon, Rain, River, Thunder, Twilight and Rain.

Country:	Japan
Type:	Destroyer
Launch date:	20 August 1955
Crew:	240
Displacement:	2378 tonnes (2340 tons)
Dimensions:	106m x 10.5m x 3.7m (347ft 8in x 34ft 6in x 12ft)
Range:	9636km (5203nm)
Main armament:	Three 127mm (5in) DP guns; eight 40mm (1.5in) AA; A/S mortars
Powerplant:	Two shafts, geared steam turbines
Performance:	30 knots

Yuushio class

Essentially a development of the earlier Uzushio class with an increased diving depth capability, the first of the Yuushio diesel-electric submarines was laid down in December 1976 and completed in 1980. Of double-hull construction, the boats follow the US Navy practice of having a bow sonar array with the torpedo tubes moved to an amidships position and angled outwards. The names of the class after *Yuushio* are *Mochishio, Setoshio, Okishio, Nadashio, Hamashio, Akishio, Takeshio, Yukishio* and *Sachishio*. The class is equipped to fire the Sub Harpoon SSM and is fitted with indigenously-designed ASW and anti-ship torpedoes. All but the first three boats of the class are still operational, although they will be retired over the next ten years. The Japanese Maritime Self-Defence Force maintains some 18 patrol submarines on operational status at any one time.

Country:	Japan
Type:	Attack submarine
Launch date:	29 March 1979
Crew:	75
Displacement:	Surfaced: 2235 tonnes (2200 tons), submerged: 2774 tonnes (2730 tons)
Dimensions:	76m x 9.9m x 7.5m (249ft 3in x 32ft 6in x 24ft 7in)
Surface range:	17,603km (9500nm) at 10 knots
Armament:	Six 533mm (21in) torpedo tubes
Powerplant:	Single shaft, diesel/electric motors
Performance:	Surfaced: 12 knots, submerged: 20 knots

Z37

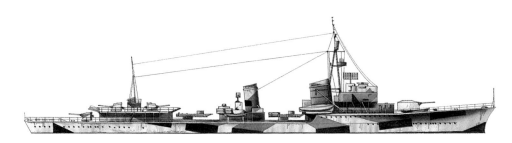

The German destroyer *Z37* was one of seven modified Type 36A boats, popularly known as Narviks because they spent most of their operational careers in Arctic waters. The Z-class destroyers were formidable fighting ships, but between 1943 and 1944, were no match for the weight of Allied air power directed against them, even though their AA armament was constantly increased. Three were sunk by air attack, and several severely damaged. Like most German equipment, their quality was of limited value against overwhelming odds. Attacking them was a risky business; on 28 March 1943, four Z-class boats, including *Z37*, were escorting the Italian blockade runner *Pietro Orseleo* on her voyage from the Gironde to Japan when they beat off an attack by a strike wing of RAF Beaufighter torpedo-bombers and shot down five aircraft. *Z37* was scuttled at Bordeaux in August 1944.

Country:	Germany
Type:	Destroyer
Launch date:	24 February 1941
Crew:	321
Displacement:	3658 tonnes (3600 tons)
Dimensions:	127m x 12m x 3.9m (416ft 7in x 39ft 5in x 12ft 10in)
Range:	10,935km (5904nm)
Main armament:	Four 150mm (5.9in) guns; two quadruple 533mm (21in) torpedo tubes
Powerplant:	Two shafts, geared steam turbines
Performance:	36 knots

Zaragosa

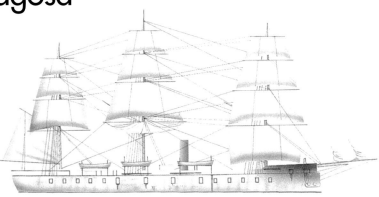

Zaragosa was a wooden-hulled broadside battleship. She was originally armed with 68-pounder guns, but in 1885 she was given four 228mm (9in) guns on the main deck, one 180mm (7.1in) gun under the forecastle and two more 180mm (7.1in) weapons on sponsons. She formed part of the Spanish force sent to Cuba in 1873. She was recalled to Spain upon the outbreak of the civil war, and became a torpedo training ship in 1895. She was stricken in 1899. Mainly because of corruption in the Spanish colonial government, there was continual unrest in Cuba at this time, and various attempts at independence – often influenced by external enouragement, not least from the USA – were met with ruthless military repression, supported by the Spanish Navy. The result was a bitter and bloodthirsty civil war in the closing years of the 19th century.

Country:	Spain
Type:	Ironclad
Launch date:	1867
Crew:	500
Displacement :	5618 tonnes (5530 tons)
Dimensions:	85.3m x 16.6m x 8m (280ft x 54ft 7in x 26ft 6in)
Range:	3335km (1800nm) at 6 knots
Armament:	21 68-pounder guns
Powerplant:	Single screw, horizontal single expansion engines
Performance:	8 knots

Zeeleeuw

The *Zeeleeuw* (Sealion) is a Walrus-class SSK, a design based on the *Zwaardvis* hull form with similar dimensions and silhouette, but with more automation, a smaller crew, more modern electronics, X-configuration control surfaces and the French MAREI high-tensile steel hull material that permits a 50 per cent increase in maximum diving depth to 300m (985ft). The first unit, *Walrus,* was laid down in 1979 for commissioning in 1986, but in August that year she suffered a serious fire that destroyed her wiring and computers while in the final stage of completion, so she was not commissioned until March 1992, two years after *Zeeleeuw.* The other two vessels in the class are *Dolfijn* and *Bruinvis.* Two submarines of this class are in service with the Taiwanese Navy; they were the first to be exported by the Netherlands.

Country:	Netherlands
Type:	Attack submarine
Launch date:	20 June 1987
Crew:	49
Displacement:	Surfaced: 2490 tonnes (2450 tons), submerged: 2800 tonnes (2755 tons)
Dimensions:	67.5m x 8.4m x 6.6m (222ft x 27ft 7in x 21ft 8in)
Surface range:	18,520km (10,000nm) at 9 knots
Armament:	Four 533mm (21in) torpedo tubes
Powerplant:	Single screw, diesel/electric motors
Performance:	Surfaced: 13 knots, submerged: 20 knots

Zieten

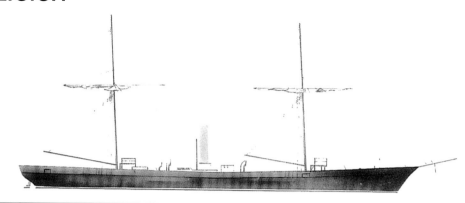

Designed and built by the Thames Ironworks, London, *Zieten* was Germany's first major torpedo vessel. An elegant ship with a clipper bow, she had a very good speed for her day. Thanks to her good qualities as a seaboat, and the number of torpedo reloads she was able to carry (10 rounds), she would probably have given a good account of herself in action, despite her lack of guns. She was initially armed with one submerged torpedo tube at bow and stern. Later, six 50mm (1.95in) guns were added, making her an effective torpedo gunboat. From 1899 she served as a fishery protection vessel, and in 1914 she became a coastal patrol ship, a duty which she shared with the old torpedo boats *D3*, *T61*, *T62* and the sloop *Schwalbe*. She was scrapped in 1921. Nearly all subsequent classes of German torpedo boats were built by Schichau.

Country:	Germany
Type:	Torpedo gunboat
Launch date:	9 March 1876
Crew:	94
Displacement:	1170 tonnes (1152 tons)
Dimensions:	79.4m x 8.5m x 4.6m (260ft 6in x 28ft x 15ft 2in)
Range:	Not known
Main armament:	Two 380mm (15in) torpedo tubes
Powerplant:	Twin screws, horizontal compound engines
Performance:	16 knots

Zuikaku

Zuikaku and her sister *Shokaku* were the most successful carriers operated by the Japanese Navy. They were considerably larger than previous purpose-built carriers, and were better armed, better protected and carried more aircraft. The wooden flight deck was 240m (787ft) long and 29m (95ft) wide, and was serviced by three lifts. She formed part of the carrier task force whose aircraft attacked the US Pacific Fleet base at Pearl Harbor in December 1941, and subsequently participated in every notable fleet action of the Pacific war – Java, Ceylon, the Coral Sea, the Eastern Solomons, Santa Cruz, the Philippine Sea and Leyte Gulf. Her name means Lucky Crane and her sister ship was *Shokaku* (Happy Crane), sunk in June 1944 by the US submarine *Cavalla*. *Zuikaku* was sunk in action by American forces on 25 October 1944, during the Battle of Cape Engano in Leyte Gulf.

Country:	Japan
Type:	Aircraft carrier
Launch date:	27 November 1939
Crew:	1660
Displacement:	32,618 tonnes (32,105 tons)
Dimensions:	257m x 29m x 8.8m (843ft 2in x 95ft x 29ft)
Range:	17,974km (9700nm) at 18 knots
Armament:	16 127mm (5in) guns
Powerplant:	Quadruple screw turbines
Performance:	34.2 knots

Index

Index

Index

Index

Index

Index

Index

Index

Index

Index

Index